Regional Community Building in East Asia

This volume is a collection of papers written by nationals or former nationals of their respective countries in ASEAN and Northeast Asia. Unlike other works written by scholars outside ASEAN or East Asia, it offers an insider's point of view of the 10 ASEAN states, China, Japan and South Korea on regional community building. While a nationalist perspective may permeate throughout the study, it is also clear that pursuing regional cooperation is considered to be important by the chapter authors, denoting the non-exclusivity between nationalism and regionalism and the mutual reinforcement of the two.

Each author of this volume has made a deliberate effort to introduce and survey the developmental challenges and experiences of his or her country from a historical perspective. All authors, without exception, have emphasized the importance and advantages in staying with ASEAN or the linking of ASEAN with China, Japan and South Korea in political-security, economic and socio-cultural terms. Their papers also reveal that the self-help and self-strengthening mechanism emphasized by the ASEAN Plus Three process will take time to bear fruit. In the meantime, it seems that bilateral interactions and cooperation between ASEAN and Northeast Asian states remain very dominant as shown in this study. One can argue that bilateral interactions are the building blocks of multilateral interactions. To be sure, there is a deliberate effort in this study to highlight 'unity in diversity' in East Asia in general and ASEAN in particular.

Lee Lai To is Founding President and Advisor of the Political Science Association (Singapore), and former Head of the Department of Political Science, National University of Singapore.

Zarina Othman is Associate Professor and former Head of the Program of Strategic Studies and International Relations, Universiti Kebangsaan Malaysia (UKM/National University of Malaysia), Bangi, Malaysia.

Politics in Asia

Democracy in Eastern Asia
Issues, problems and challenges in a region of diversity
Edited by Edmund S. K. Fung and Steven Drakeley

The US Versus the North Korean Nuclear Threat
Mitigating the nuclear security dilemma
Er-Win Tan

Democratization in China, Korea and Southeast Asia?
Local and national perspectives
Edited by Kate Xiao Zhou, Shelley Rigger, and Lynn T. White III

Japan's Civil-Military Diplomacy
The banks of the Rubicon
Dennis T. Yasutomo

Constructing a Security Community in Southeast Asia
ASEAN and the problem of regional order
Third edition
Amitav Acharya

China's Rise and Regional Integration in East Asia
Hegemony or community?
Edited by Yong Wook Lee and Key-young Son

New Dynamics in US–China Relations
Contending for the Asia Pacific
Edited by Mingjiang Li and Kalyan M. Kemburi

Illiberal Democracy in Indonesia
The ideology of the family-state
David Bourchier

China's Power and Asian Security
Edited by Mingjiang Li and Kalyan M. Kemburi

Sino–U.S. Energy Triangles
Resource diplomacy under hegemony
Edited by David Zweig and Yufan Hao

Advancing the Regional Commons in the New East Asia
Edited by Siriporn Wajjwalku, Kong Chong Ho and Osamu Yoshida

Institutionalizing East Asia
Mapping and reconfiguring regional cooperation
Edited by Alice D. Ba, Cheng Chwee Kuik and Sueo Sudo

Singapore
Negotiating state and society, 1965–2015
Edited by Jason Lim and Terence Lee

Regional Community Building in East Asia
Countries in focus
Edited by Lee Lai To and Zarina Othman

Regional Community Building in East Asia

Countries in focus

Edited by
Lee Lai To and Zarina Othman

Routledge
Taylor & Francis Group

LONDON AND NEW YORK

First published 2017
by Routledge
2 Park Square, Milton Park, Abingdon, Oxon OX14 4RN

and by Routledge
711 Third Avenue, New York, NY 10017

First issued in paperback 2018

Routledge is an imprint of the Taylor & Francis Group, an informa business

British Library Cataloguing in Publication Data
A catalogue record for this book is available from the British Library

Library of Congress Cataloging in Publication Data
Names: Lee, Lai To, editor. | Zarina Othman, editor.
Title: Regional community building in East Asia : countries in focus / edited
by Lee Lai To and Zarina Othman.
Description: New York, NY : Routledge, 2016. | Series: Politics in Asia
series | Includes bibliographical references and index.
Identifiers: LCCN 2016010200| ISBN 9781138640436 (hardback) | ISBN
9781315636610 (ebook)
Subjects: LCSH: East Asian cooperation. | ASEAN.
Classification: LCC JZ1720 .R43 2016 | DDC 303.48/25–dc23
LC record available at https://lccn.loc.gov/2016010200

ISBN 13: 978-1-138-60464-3 (pbk)
ISBN 13: 978-1-138-64043-6 (hbk)

Typeset in Times New Roman
by Taylor & Francis Books

Contents

List of illustrations

Figures

Tables

Contributors

Sengchanh Chanthsasene is Associate Professor and Vice Dean of the Faculty of Economics and Business Management, National University of Laos. She obtained her Bachelor's degree in Mechanic Engineering at High Technical Institut in Germany and a Bachelor's degree in Economics at the University of Chemnitz-Zwickau in Germany. She obtained a masters degree in Commerce at the University of Chemnitz-Zwickau in Germany.

Jose Rhommel B. Hernandez is currently an Associate Professor and the Graduate Program Coordinator of the Department of History, College of Liberal Arts, De La Salle University, Manila, Philippines. He holds a Master's degree and a Ph.D. in History from the University of the Philippines, Diliman, Quezon City. Dr. Hernandez has published several articles dealing with various topics on the history of the Philippines and Southeast Asia including colonialism, religion and culture. He has also translated and annotated Spanish manuscripts on the Philippine Revolution into Filipino and is now researching the relationship of religion and development in the Philippines.

Sachiko Hirakawa is Assistant Professor at the School of International Liberal Studies, Waseda University. She specializes in international politics of East Asia, Asian regional integration, and Sino-Japan relations. She received her B.A. in Economics from Waseda University, MALD from Fletcher School of Law and Diplomacy, Tufts University, USA, and Ph.D. in International Studies from Waseda University. Her recent publications include: *Two-China Dilemma and Japanese Formula* (in Japanese, Keiso Shobo, 2012), *Historicizing Asian Regional Integration* (co-ed, in Japanese, Keiso Shobo, 2012), 'Southeast Asia in the Post-war Period', in S. Amako et al. *Regional Integration in East Asia* (United Nations University Press, 2013).

Kong Chong Ho is Associate Professor of Sociology at the Faculty of Arts and Social Sciences, National University of Singapore. Dr Ho's research interests are in the political economy of cities, urban communities, and higher education. He is an editorial board member of *Pacific Affairs* and the

International Journal of Comparative Sociology. Kong Chong is co-author of *City-States in the Global Economy: Industrial Restructuring in Hong Kong and Singapore* (Westview, 1997) and co-editor of *Service Industries, Cities and Development Trajectories in the Asia-Pacific* (Routledge, 2005), *The City and Civil Society in Pacific Asian Cities* (Routledge, 2008), *New Economic Spaces in Asian Cities* (Routledge, 2012), and 'Globalising Higher Education and Cities in Asia and the Pacific' (*Asia Pacific Viewpoint*, 55[2], 2014).

Nor Azizan Idris (Ph.D., University of Wales, Aberystwyth), is an Associate Professor in the International and Strategic Studies Programme and Head of Postgraduate Studies, School of History, Politics and Strategic Studies, Universiti Kebangsaan Malaysia/UKM. His research interests are in the area of security and foreign policy studies, international organization and politics of development. His recent publications include: Zarina Othman and Nor Azizan Idris (eds), *Migration and Security* (in Malay) (Dewan Bahasa dan Pustaka, 2015).

Azaharaini Hj. Mohd Jamil is a retired government servant. Prior to his retirement he was the Director of the Institute of Civil Service, a national institution providing training services to government employees. Immediately after his retirement, on 1 July, 2006, he was appointed as the Executive Director of the Centre for Strategic and Policy Studies (CSPS), a corporate body dedicated to research and policy analysis in Brunei Darussalam. He is currently a Senior Lecturer at the Institute of Policy Studies, *Universiti Brunei Darussalam*, a position he has held since October 2008.

Pan Suk Kim is Professor of Public Administration in the College of Government and Business at Yonsei University, Wonju Campus, South Korea. He was the Dean of the College of Government and Business at Yonsei University, the President of the International Institute of Administrative Sciences (IIAS) in Brussels, and a Vice Chairperson of the UN Committee of Experts on Public Administration (UNCEPA) in New York. He is currently the President of the Asian Association for Public Administration (AAPA). He can be reached at pankim@gmail.com.

Phouphet Kyophilavong is Associate Professor, and Vice Dean of the Faculty of Economics and Business Management, National University of Laos. He received his Ph.D. in economics from Kobe University in 2003. He also been selected as a Fulbright U.S.-ASEAN Visiting Scholar to the Department of Economics at Harvard University. He has several articles in journals such as *International Review of Economics and Finance*, and *Economic Modelling*.

Lee Lai To was Head of the Department of Political Science, National University of Singapore (NUS). He was also active in international/regional academic and track two organizations. He left NUS in 2010 and joined the School of Humanities and Social Sciences as Senior Teaching Fellow/Senior Lecturer and subsequently S. Rajaratnam School of International Studies as Adjunct Senior Fellow at Nanyang Technological University. Lee Lai To's major publications include three single-authored books, nine edited or co-edited books and a vast number of articles in regional and international journals. His major research interest is regional security in the Asia-Pacific. He is the founding President and Advisor of the Political Science Association (Singapore).

Hong Son Nguyen (Assoc. Prof. Dr.) received his Ph.D. in Political Economy at the Moscow State University named Lomonoxop, Russia. As an expert on public policy and national development, he has presided over many research projects on economic integration of Vietnam and Asia; development of the services sector in Vietnam (education and training, science and technology, finance and banking services); and the international financial and monetary system. He has been the author of many books and papers published locally and internationally. Currently, he is the Rector of the University of Economics and Business, Vietnam National University, Hanoi.

Zarina Othman earned her Ph.D. in International Studies from the University of Denver, Colorado (USA). Associate Professor Othman is currently teaching at the Program of Strategic Studies and International Relations, Universiti Kebangsaan Malaysia (UKM/ National University of Malaysia), Bangi, Malaysia. Her research interests focus mainly on human security issues in Southeast Asia, non-traditional threats, East Asian community, regional security, and human and drug trafficking. Her recent publications include: Sity Daud, Zarina Othman and Rashila Ramli, *Human Security and Peace in Archipelagic Southeast Asia* (UKM Publishers, 2015).

Sorpong Peou (MA and Ph.D., York University, Canada) is Chair of the Department of Politics and Public Administration, Ryerson University, Toronto and was Chair of the Department of Political Science, University of Winnipeg. Prior to these appointments, he was Professor of International Security at Sophia University (Tokyo), Canada-ASEAN Fellow and Fellow at the Institute of Southeast Asian Studies (Singapore). He has written extensively on Cambodian politics and regional security. He is Distinguished Senior Fellow at the Cambodian Institute for Peace and Cooperation, Distinguished Visiting Scholar at the Cambodian Development Research Institute, a member of International Experts Network on UN Peacekeeping and on various editorial boards.

Pinn Siraprapasiri previously taught at the Faculty of Political Science, Thammasat University, Thailand. She earned her Master's Degree from the University of Oxford and is now pursuing a Ph.D. at the University of

California, Santa Barbara. Her research interests include international negotiation, the Mekong subregion, Asia-Pacific security landscape, and ASEAN
regionalization. She recently concluded a research project and co-authored
a book with Chanintira na Thalang on ASEAN regional identity.

Mangadar Situmorang is a senior lecturer at the Department of International
Relations, Parahyangan Catholic University, Bandung, Indonesia. An
awardee of the Australian Development Scholarship, Chevening Awards,
and Endeavour Awards, he has interest in Indonesian politics, conflict
resolutions, and international humanitarian intervention. He is the author
of *International Humanitarian Intervention in Intrastate Conflicts: Indonesian
Case Study* (Johannes Herrmann Verlag, 2009).

Maung Maung Soe is a retired professor from the Yangon Institute of Economics (YIE). He began his study of economics at YIE. He received B.
Econ (PD) in 1973; he earned Master's and Doctoral degrees from the
International Institute of Social Sciences (The Hague) and Christian
International School of Theology (Manila). Today he is a lecturer in mac-
roeconomics in the Robinson Business School, Yangon Campus and the
Business School of Management, Yangon Campus. Dr Soe is also an
author of economic articles for journals and magazines. He was the first
prize winner of the National Level Manuscript Competition, Ministry of
Information, Myanmar in 2000 and Token Awarded Excellence in teaching
Economics for 2008 conferred by ABBEY DLD, London.

Somchith Souksavath is Associate Professor and Dean of Faculty of Economics and Business Management, National University of Laos. He
obtained a Bachelor's degree in Political Science at Vietnam and obtained
his Master's degree in Economics at Kasetsart University, Thailand.

Min Wei is Associate Professor at School of International Studies, Peking
University, China. His research interests are Southeast Asian Studies, East
Asian Studies and the studies of small states in international relations. He
teaches Political Economy in East Asia, Southeast Asian Studies, Globalization and East Asia, and Psychology in International Relations for
undergraduate and graduate students. He is the author of *New Perspective
on ASEAN: The Interaction between Nationalism and Regionalism*, and *Small
State and International Relations*, and also the translator and co-translator
of several books.

Foreword

In Southeast Asia today, spaces of economic and political activity are seen to be the predominant and determinative sites of regional integration. Less heralded is the role of pedagogical materials, scholars and academic institutions in creating the knowledge and understanding required for effective and informed regionally oriented actors. Bringing together scholars from Brunei, Cambodia, China, Indonesia, Japan, Laos, Philippines, Malaysia, Myanmar, Singapore, South Korea, Thailand, and Vietnam (the 'Association of South East Asian Nations Plus Three' or APT countries), the Community of East Asian Scholars project focuses on the potential of academic practice to promote an emergent and responsible regional consciousness.

Supported initially by Thammasat University in Bangkok and later by the first higher education grant awarded to an ASEAN-based project by the ASEAN Plus Three Fund, CEAS's aim was twofold. The first goal was to commission papers by leading scholars from the ASEAN and APT community. They were asked to analyze, from their viewpoints of being in their respective countries and in the region, the key promises, issues and challenges faced by ASEAN and APT. The results of their work will appear in three edited volumes. This book, *Regional Community Building in East Asia: Countries in Focus*, was preceded by two other volumes, *Advancing the Regional Commons in the New East Asia* and *Institutionalizing East Asia: Mapping and Reconfiguring Regional Cooperation*. In providing rigorous and expert perspectives on the history, politics and institutional processes of Southeast and East Asia, CEAS hopes to encourage mutual understanding among and of APT countries.

The second aim of the project was to stimulate collaboration, as well as longstanding connections among scholars and academic institutions in APT countries. Indeed, one of the highlights of the project has been the process through which the three volumes were developed. In biannual workshops over the past three years, CEAS authors have shared, debated and modified chapter outlines and drafts. All three volumes reflect the collegial spirit of these workshops.

As our efforts become realized in print, CEAS would like to thank the ASEAN Plus Three Fund for its generous support. Special thanks also go to the Ministry of Foreign Affairs of Thailand, particularly the ASEAN Department and the Permanent Mission of Thailand to ASEAN, for its continuous efforts and coordination, without which the project would not have successfully achieved its goals. The editors recognize the invaluable assistance of Miyo Hanazawa and Malavika Reddy who kept the project on track with their efficient management of tasks and timely reminders. Finally, this volume, as well as the two preceding volumes, is the product of a long-term commitment by participant authors and editors for which CEAS would like to express its deep gratitude.

Community of East Asian Scholars
Thammasat University
Bangkok, Thailand
November 2015

Preface

ASEAN came into being as a rule-based organization, a grouping founded on and interacting with each others on the basic of clear rules and regulations. The challenge was to construct the administrative infrastructure and institutions required to bring to life a *community* through the *organization*'s rules. This was a particular challenge because, as the present volume, *Regional Community Building in East Asia: Countries in Focus*, attests, the diversity of governance among member states is great. Allying the varied values, norms, perceptions, and understandings of rule-based cooperation among such a historically, politically and culturally diverse set of countries takes patient and flexible calibration. Some member countries are, in Susilo Bambang Yudhoyono's words, "noisy democracies." Bringing these countries into the process in sync with others was complicated. Other countries are more centralized. They may be prompt in their willingness to join the community, but find it more difficult to agree on rules and regulations pertaining to the soft issues of governance, like minority and human rights. Cultivating a sense of community – of a collective perspective – among the noisy, the centralized and those that fall between the two can take time. And ASEAN seems to move at the speed of its slowest member.

What is remarkable, however, is that ASEAN *has* thrived, acquiring recognition from important actors on the world stage precisely *because* ASEAN has a demonstrated ability to work with a varied group of dissimilar member countries. ASEAN's instrumental role in helping the victims of Cylcone Nargis or its Chiang Mai Initiative are exemplary of its potential. These successes established ASEAN's 'convening power'. They proved that we were able to attract not only tremendous capital investment in our region, as the world long knew, but also that we possessed the diplomatic and political clout to bring the region into alignment.

As ASEAN grew to ASEAN Plus Three, the particular quality of its 'convening power' – its demonstrated track record of enabling countries with entrenched differences to work together – has become more significant. For we have shown that we can contain the problems among ourselves in the service of shared objectives. We have demonstrated that, while we may not forget the past, we can manage it to work for the future. As the community has grown to include China, Japan and South Korea, three members for whom the stakes of difference and disagreement, conflict and contestation are high, the future-oriented, flexible convening power of ASEAN suggests a way forward. This convening power works on different scales, as, for example, in the cooperation over higher education that is envisioned by the Community of East Asian Scholars. Funded by the ASEAN Plus Three's Fund for Education, CEAS is a product of different voices nonetheless speaking to one another. The CEAS community, this volume, and the two that preceded it are emblematic of ASEAN Plus Three's potential to work with and across substantial difference.

Surin Pitsuwan
Former Secretary-General of ASEAN (2008–2012)

List of abbreviations

AAPA	Asian Association for Public Administration
ABIM	Angkatan Belia Islam Malaysia
ABMI	Asian Bond Markets Initiative
ACIA	ASEAN Comprehensive Investment Agreement
ACSC	AAN Civil Society Conference
ACWC	ASEAN Commission for the Promotion and Protection of the Rights of Women and Children
ADB	Asian Development Bank
ADMM	ASEAN Defence Ministers' Meeting
ADMM+8	ASEAN Defense Ministerial Meeting Plus 8
AEC	ASEAN Economic Community
AEEAP	ASEAN Environmental Education Plan
AEGCD	ASEAN Expert Group on Communicable Diseases
AEGE	ASEAN Expert Group on the Environment
AEM	ASEAN Economic Ministers
AERR	ASEAN Emergency Rice Reserve
AEY	ASEAN Environment Year
AFAFGIT	ASEAN Framework Agreement on the Facilitation of Goods in Transit
AFAMT	ASEAN Framework Agreement on Multimodal Transport
AFAS	ASEAN Framework Agreement on Services
AFMM	ASEAN Foreign Ministers Meeting
AFP	Armed Forces of the Philippines
AFSIS	ASEAN Food Security Information System
AFTA	ASEAN Free Trade Area
AGPA	Asian Group for Public Administration
AHA	ASEAN Coordinating Center for Humanitarian Assistance
AIA	ASEAN Investment Area
AICHR	ASEAN Intergovernmental Commission on Human Rights
AIDS	Acquired Immune Deficiency Syndrome

AIF	ASEAN Infrastructure Fund
AIPR	ASEAN Institute for Peace and Reconciliation
AKFTA	ASEAN-Korea Free Trade Area
AMAF	ASEAN Ministerial Meeting on Agricultural and Forestry
AMEM	ASEAN Ministers on Energy Meeting
AMF	Asian Monetary Fund
AMMTC+3	APT Ministerial Meeting on Transnational Crime
AMMY+3	ASEAN+3 Ministerial Meeting on Youth
AMRO	ASEAN Plus Three Macroeconomic Research Office
APEC	Asia-Pacific Economic Cooperation
APL	ASEAN Plus Three Partnership Laboratories
APSC	ASEAN Political Security Community
APT	ASEAN Plus Three
APTA	Asia-Pacific Trade Agreement
APTCF	ASEAN Plus Three Cooperation Fund
APT-EMM	ASEAN Plus Three Education Ministers Meeting
APTERR	ASEAN Plus Three Emergency Rice Reserve
ARF	ASEAN Regional Forum
ASA	Association of Southeast Asia
ASAS	Association of Southeast Asian States
ASCC	ASEAN Socio-Cultural Community
ASEAN	Association of Southeast Asian Nations
ASEAN COCI	ASEAN Committee on Culture and Information
ASEAN-6	Brunei, Indonesia, Malaysia, Philippines, Singapore and Thailand
ASEAN-EPG	ASEAN Eminent Persons Group
ASEAN-Japan EPA	ASEAN-Japan Economic Partnership Agreement
ASEM	Asia-Europe Meeting
ASEON	ASEAN Senior Officials on the Environment
ASF	ASEAN Social Forum
AsiaDHRRA	Asian Partnership for the Development of Human Resources in Rural Asia
ASW	ASEAN Single Window
ATIGA	ASEAN Trade in Good Agreement
AUN	ASEAN University Network
AWARE	Association of Women for Action and Research
AWGPPR	ASEAN Working Group on Pandemic Preparedness and Responses
BCG	Bacille Calmette Guerin (an effective immunization against tuberculosis)
BDEB	Brunei Darussalam Economic Board
BDKI	Brunei Darussalam Key Indicators
BIA	Brunei Investment Agency
BIC	Brunei Islamic Council

BIMP-EAGA	Brunei, Indonesia, Malaysia and the Philippines – East ASEAN Growth Area
BND	Brunei Dollar
CAFTA	China-ASEAN Free Trade Area
CCP	Chinese Communist Party
CEAS	Community of East Asian Scholars
CEO	Chief Executive Officer
CEPT	Common Effective Preferential Tariff
CGDK	Coalition Government of Democratic Kampuchea
CLMV	Cambodia, Laos, Myanmar and Vietnam
CLOB	Central Limit Order Book
CMI	Chiang Mai Initiative
CMI	Commission for Migrants and Itinerant People
CMI	Crisis Management Initiative
CMIM	Chiang Mai Initiative Multilateralization
CNP	Chinese Nationalist Party
CNRP	Cambodian National Rescue Party
COCI	Committee on Culture and Information
CPM	Communist Party of Malaya
DAC	Development Assistance Committee
DBP	Defined Benefit Plan
DepEd	Department of Education
DK	Democratic Kampuchea
DOC	Declaration on the Conduct of Parties in the South China Sea
DOD	Department of Defense
DPR	Dewan Perwakilan Rakyat (People Representative Council – Parliament)
DSWD	Department of Social Welfare and Development
EABC	East Asia Business Council
EAC	East Asian Community
EAEC	East Asia Economic Caucus
EAEG	East Asian Economic Group
EAS	East Asia Summit
EASG	East Asian Study Group
EAVG	East Asia Vision Group
EAVG II	East Asia Vision Group II
EC	European Commission
EC	European Community
EDB	Economic Development Board
EEZ	Exclusive Economic Zone
EPF	Employees' Provident Fund
EROPA	Eastern Regional Organization of Public Administration
ERPD	Economic Review and Policy Dialogue

EU	European Union
FDI	Foreign Direct Investment
FOCPF	Future Oriented Cooperation Fund
FTA	Free Trade Area
FTAs	Free Trade Agreements
FUNCINPEC	United National Front for an Independent, Neutral, Peaceful, and Cooperative Cambodia
GATT	General Agreement on Tariffs and Trade
GDP	Gross Domestic Product
GMS	Greater Mekong Subregion
GNI	Gross National Income
GNP	Gross National Product
Golkar	Golongan Karya
GSO	General Statistical Office
HADR & MM Ex	Humanitarian Assistance and Disaster Relief and Military Medicine Exercise
HCI	Heavy and Chemical Industry
HDI	Human Development Index
HIV	Human Immunodeficiency Virus
HoB	Heart of Borneo
HOME	Humanitarian Organization for Migration Economics
HSN	Human Security Network
IAI	Initiative for ASEAN Integration
IB	Implementation Blueprint
ICAO	International Civil Aviation Organization
ICT	Information and Communication Technology
ICW	Indonesian Corruption Watch
IMF	International Monetary Fund
IMT-GT	Indonesia-Malaysia-Thailand Growth Triangle
INSEAD	Institut européen d'administration des affaires
IPR	Intellectual Property Rights
ISIS	Institute of Strategic and International Studies
IT-BPO	Information Technology and Business Process Outsourcing
ITE	Institute of Technical Education
JAGEF	Japan-ASEAN General Exchange Fund
JAIF	Japan ASEAN Integration Fund
JENESYS	Japan-East Asia Network of Exchange for Students and Youths
JI	Jemaah Islamiyah
JICA	Japan International Cooperation Agency
JTC	Joint Trade Commission
K12 PROGRAM	Kinder Plus 12 Years Program
KDI	Korea Development Institute

KKN	Kolusi, Korupsi, Nepotisme (Corruption, Collusion, and Nepotism)
KOICA	Korea International Cooperation Agency
KPNLF	Khmer People's National Liberation Front
KTO	Korean Tourism Organization
LDRRMC	Local Disaster Risk Reduction Management Councils
LECS	Lao Expenditure and Consumption Surveys
LEP	Look East Policy
LFS	Labor Force Survey
LNTA	Lao National Tourism Administration
LPP	Laos Pilot Program
MAFLPAS	ASEAN Multilateral Agreement on the Full Liberalization of Passenger Air Services
MAPHILINDO	Malaysia, Philippines, Indonesia
MCA	Malaysian Chinese Association
MDGs	Millennium Development Goals
MENGO	Peace Malaysia and the Malaysian Environmental NGOs
MIB	Melayu Islam Beraja (Malay Islamic Monarchy)
MIC	Malaysian Indian Congress
MIPR	Ministry of Industry and Primary Resources
MM	Ministers Meetings
MOD	Ministry of Development
MOE	Ministry of Education
MOFA	Ministry of Foreign Affairs
MOFAT	Ministry of Foreign Affairs and Trade
MOGEF	Ministry of Gender Equality and Family
MOM	Ministry of Manpower
MOU	Memorandum of Understanding
MRC	Mekong River Commission
MSDF	Maritime Self-Defense Force
NAFTA	North American Free Trade Area
NAM	Non-Aligned Movement
NCDs	Non-Communicable Diseases
NDRRMC	National Disaster and Risk Reduction Management Council
NEDA	National Economic Development Authority
Nekolim	Neo Colonialism and Imperialism
NEM	New Economic Mechanism
NEP	New Economic Policy
NGO	Non-Governmental Organization
NHK	Japan Broadcasting Corporation (Nippon Hōsō Kyōkai)
NIC	Newly Industrialized Country
NIEs	Newly Industrialized Economies

NOC	National Operations Council
NSO	National Statistics Office
NUS	National University of Singapore
ODA	Official Development Assistance
OECD	Organization for Economic Cooperation and Development
OFW	Overseas Filipino Workers
OTCA	Overseas Technical Cooperation Agency
PAFTAD	Pacific Trade and Development
PAP	People's Action Party
PBEC	Pacific Basin Economic Council
PECC	Pacific Economic Cooperation Conference
PIS	Priority Integration Services
PKO	Peacekeeping Operation
PMC	Post Ministerial Conferences
PMO	Prime Minister's Office
POA	Plan of Action
PONREPP	Post-Nargis Recovery and Preparedness Plan
PPP	Purchasing Power Parity
PRC	People's Republic of China
PRK	People's Republic of Kampuchea
PSA	Philippine Statistics Authority
PTA	Preferential Trade Area
RCEP	Regional Comprehensive Economic Partnership
ROC	Republic of China
ROK	Republic of Korea
ROP	Rules of Procedures
RTA	Regional Trade Agreements
SAARC	South Asian Association for Regional Cooperation
SARS	Severe Acute Respiratory Syndrome
SCAP	Supreme Commander for the Allied Powers
SCF	Special Cooperation Fund
SCI	Sub-Committee on Information
SCO	Shanghai Cooperation Organization
SCP	Supplementary Contribution Pension
SCWO	Singapore Council of Women's Organizations
SDF	Self-Defense Force
SEACA	Southeast Asian Committee for Advocacy
SEAFET	Southeast Asia Friendship and Economic Treaty
SEANWFZ	Treaty on the Southeast Asian Nuclear Weapon Free Zone
SEATO	Southeast Asia Treaty Organization
SEOM	Senior Economic Officials' Meeting
SII	Structural Impediments Initiative
SLD	Shangri-La Dialogue

SMEs	Small and Medium Enterprises
SOC	State of Cambodia
SOEs	State-Owned Enterprises
SOM	Senior Officials Meeting
SOMHD	Senior Officials Meeting on Health Development
SOMTC	Senior Officials Meeting on Transnational Crime
SSME	Sulu-Sulawesi Marine Eco-region
STB	Singapore Tourism Board
TAC	Treaty of Amity and Cooperation in Southeast Asia
TCG	Tripartite Core Group
TPP	Trans-Pacific Partnership
TPPA	Trans-Pacific Partnership Agreement
TWC2	Transient Workers Count Too
TWN	Third World Network
UBD	Universiti Brunei Darussalam
UGM	Gadjah Mada University
UiTM	University Teknologi MARA
UMNO	United Malays National Organization
UN	United Nations
UNCLOS	United Nations Convention of the Law of the Sea
UNDP	United Nations Development Programme
UNGA	United Nations General Assembly
UNHCR	United Nations High Commissioner for Refugees
UNPKO	United Nations Peacekeeping Operation
UNSC	United Nations Security Council
UNTAC	United Nations Transitional Authority in Cambodia
US	United States
USA	United States of America
VAP	Vientiane Action Programme
VCP	Vietnamese Communist Party
VJEPA	Vietnam Japan Economic Partnership Agreement
VNSW	Vietnam's National Single Window
WB	World Bank
WHO	World Health Organisation
YADIM	Yayasan Dakwah Islamiah Malaysia
ZOPFAN	Zone of Peace, Freedom and Neutrality

Introduction

Lee Lai To

EDITOR-IN-CHIEF

With the help of globalization and regionalization, ASEAN, or for that matter, East Asia and the Asia-Pacific, is more inter-linked and integrated and a regional community is evolving, albeit slowly and incrementally.

While all states, including those discussed in this volume, are naturally concerned with their own domestic challenges, there is a general recognition that it is important to plug into the regional and global circuits to regionalize or globalize their national interests for the sake of developmental advancement. Within the larger Asia-Pacific region, there have been many calls for the establishment of an Asia-Pacific framework to further cooperation. A notable effort was the inauguration of the Asia-Pacific Economic Cooperation (APEC) meeting in 1989. Another one is the convening of the ASEAN Regional Forum (ARF) starting from 1994. In both set-ups, particularly in the ARF, the centrality of ASEAN is obvious. As a regional body for mostly developing Southeast Asian countries, ASEAN is not seen to be a threat to anyone. Although there were some false starts in creating a regional Southeast Asian organization as noted in some of the chapters, ASEAN, established in 1967, has been able to pull it off and thrive. While it was not so successful in dealing with economic cooperation in the early periods, ASEAN was seen to be rather successful in handling security issues, ostensibly the Cambodia conflict. It has also been able to engage major powers as dialogue partners. Its experiences in multilateralism would suggest that ASEAN is a suitable and strong candidate to host dialogues on security for the region, the major function of the ARF. On top of these, the ASEAN Way, that is decision-making by consensus and non-interference into other's domestic affairs, seems to be agreeable to most, if not all, of the states in the Asia-Pacific region. Thus ASEAN took the initiative in starting the ARF, hoping that small and medium states would also have some say in structuring the Asia-Pacific security architecture in the post-Cold War era.

To be sure, ASEAN has to put its own house in order if it wants to play a leading role in multilateral cooperation. In spite of years of interactions among themselves, there are still problems in regional integration. These include, *inter alia*, unresolved territorial disputes, economic nationalism hampering cooperation, lack of connectivity, developmental gaps between the developed and developing member states, and last but not least, insufficient trust in each other. Within each state, there are also various developmental challenges. In this regard, each author of this volume has made a deliberate effort to introduce and survey the developmental challenges and experiences of his or her country from a historical perspective. At the same time, all authors, without any exception, have emphasized the importance and advantages in staying with ASEAN. In fact, plans and agreements were drawn up to promote ASEAN cooperation even though the compliance rate by member states may not be ideal. More importantly, there is a deliberate effort to enhance 'unity in diversity', especially in external and inter-regional relations as aptly highlighted in the chapters of this volume. Thus, Nguyen Hong Son would like to suggest in his paper that Vietnam has benefited from regional cooperation in ASEAN, or for that matter, the ASEAN Plus Three (APT) process through the expansion of trade, investment and finance with the member states. Such cooperation has promoted Vietnam's domestic institutional reforms, improved the competitiveness of its enterprises, and strengthened its position in the region. Nguyen Hong Son would add that Vietnam has contributed its share to regional economic integration and closer political and security cooperation and that Vietnam would continue its efforts to maintain peace and stability and create the sense of trust in nurturing the spirit of community in East Asia. Likewise, the other newer members of ASEAN, namely, Laos, Cambodia and Myanmar would find it beneficial to join ASEAN from the political-security, economic and socio-cultural perspectives and they have done their part in contributing to the building of an ASEAN and East Asian community as presented by Phouphet Kyohilavong, Somchith Souksavath and Sengchanh Chanthasene, Sorpong Peou, and Maung Maung Soe in the respective chapters. For these relatively new ASEAN members who joined the regional organization in the 1990s, they have done their part in contributing to the community spirit, notably by hosting some ASEAN meetings, in spite of their limited resources. In the mean time, efforts are made, especially in capacity building and human resources, by more developed ASEAN member states, dialogue partners, and some external partners to help narrow the developmental gaps between Cambodia, Laos, Myanmar, and Vietnam (CLMV) and other ASEAN states to promote deeper regional integration.

For the more developed or 'older' members of ASEAN, namely, Brunei, Indonesia, Malaysia, the Philippines, Singapore and Thailand, they have done their share in contributing to regional community building as documented by the respective chapters. All, except Brunei, are founding members of ASEAN. Thus, Indonesia, the largest country in Southeast Asia with the world's fourth largest population and the potential to be a regional power, has been emphasizing the importance of the consensual principle in decision making in ASEAN, or for that matter in the APT process as highlighted by Mangadar Situmorang. He suggested that this is a reflection of how Indonesia runs its own domestic politics. He added by emphasizing that the diversity of ASEAN member states in economic, cultural and political terms has obviously fortified the centrality of dialogues, negotiations, and deliberation mechanisms before they come up with an agreement collectively. Thailand, the second largest economy in ASEAN, also plays an important role, especially in mainland Southeast Asia. It took pride in the fact that ASEAN was inaugurated in Bangkok. However, because of its concern with domestic affairs and the communist threat, Thailand was not really active in ASEAN affairs until the end of the Cold War as noted by Pinn Siraprapasiri. Having explored and detailed Thailand's role and contributions toward ASEAN and APT, it is interesting to note that the author has cautioned that Thailand could be preoccupied with unstable domestic politics rather than regional and international cooperation. As such, the author has recommended that Thailand should place more importance on the education of ASEAN and APT structures and activities. In the case of Malaysia, Nor Azizan Idris and Zarina Othman would like to emphasize that 'Malaysian leaders have put a priority on ASEAN as a vehicle for the internationalization of its national aspirations'. Notably, its prime ministers have been playing significant roles in pushing for regional cooperation through ASEAN. They have come up with ideas like Zone of Peace, Freedom and Neutrality (ZOPFAN), East Asia Economic Grouping (EAEG), and others to promote regional community building. For Malaysia, ASEAN is the conduit for engaging major powers and the instrument for bringing about a new regional order. With reference to the Philippines, Jose Rhommel Hernandez suggests in his analysis that it may have the weakness of a fragile state. In this regard, he analyzed some of the major challenges in the nation-building process of the Philippines. These include natural disasters, poverty, budgetary constraints for the educational and health sectors, migrant labour rights, and others. In economic terms, Jose Rhommel Hernandez indicates that the Philippines is not much involved with intra-ASEAN trade. Nonetheless, he still believes that the Philippines always has the enthusiasm of exploring things which are for the common good and that Filipinos have shown their resilience in spite of disasters and setbacks. Finally, for the two small member states, namely, Singapore and Brunei, it would be useful to note some of the common characteristics of small states in its foreign policy orientations. These could include their interests in participating in regional groupings to pool together their resources in exerting a stronger voice or bargaining position in international affairs, the predisposition in institutionalizing rules and norms, such as international law, the emphasis on creating niches in trade and others as highlighted in Ho Kong Chong's chapter on Singapore. To be sure, these orientations are applicable to Singapore. In this regard, Ho Kong Chong noted that Singapore has benefited from ASEAN in terms of regional security and economic cooperation. He adds that Singapore has contributed in human resources, the promotion of migrant worker rights, and other developmental experiences in regional cooperation. Likewise, Brunei would play its part in ASEAN and APT and support the idea of 'family' or community life at the regional level primarily because of its limited resources and its small economic market as pointed out by Azaharaini Haji Jamil in his chapter. Specifically, by plunging into regional activities, Brunei has been able to maintain its sovereignty and gain administrative experiences to provide better services at home. Economically, Azaharaini Haji Jamil suggests Brunei has yet to tap the potential of the bigger market in the ASEAN region and beyond.

It should be noted that in terms of developmental strategies, there are differences in areas like the centralization of the economy, use of market forces, opening up to the outside world, and other issues among the member states. However, at least in economic terms, there is gradually an ASEAN move towards the regionalization and globalization of the economies even among the most conservative and relatively closed economies in the group. For example, as shown in the chapter on Vietnam, *Doi Moi* (Renovation) has been reforming, if not changing, the centralized Vietnamese economy by introducing the use of market forces and opening up the economy to the region and the world since the 1980s. Likewise, the chapter on Laos shows that the country has loosened up its control of the economy and turned it into a market-oriented one under its 'New Economic Mechanism'. Just like Vietnam, Laos is also trying to bank on the regionalization and globalization of its economy. Cambodia, the last Southeast Asian state to join ASEAN, is trying to catch up in its transition to a market economy and hitch a ride from the regional and international system as briefly noted in the Cambodia chapter. Last but not least, Myanmar, one of the most isolated economies and polities in ASEAN, is opening up under the new civilian government. Greater emphasis seems to be placed on attracting foreign investments and increasing trade. Thus, the overall trend in the developmental strategy of the whole ASEAN region would be helpful to economic cooperation, be it within the region or with extra-regional actors. In various degrees, and especially in economic terms, a more liberal approach seems to be acceptable or agreeable to member states.

In the treatise on nation and community building in this study, most, if not all chapters do reflect the nationalist sentiments of the authors. This is only natural in the light of rising nationalism in the region. Unlike other works written by scholars outside ASEAN, or for that matter the East Asian region, the analysis by nationals or former nationals of the respective countries offers us an insider's point of view. While a nationalist perspective may permeate throughout the study, it is clear that pursuing regional cooperation is also considered to be important, denoting the non-exclusivity between nationalism and regionalism and the mutual reinforcement of the two, at least to a certain extent. This is precisely one of the rather unique features of the ASEAN Way, or East Asian regionalism. On top of that, such regionalism may allow member states, notably China, Indonesia, Japan, South Korea, Malaysia, Thailand and others to exert their leadership in the region, if they want to, as revealed by selected chapters in this volume. It should be emphasized that the views in the chapters reflect the authors' ideas/perspectives, but not the editors'.

It remains to be noted that ASEAN, or for that matter the other states in East Asia, have learned from hard experiences that opening up too soon and too fast to promote regionalism could be a disaster. The lessons of the Asian Financial Crisis in 1997 and 1998 certainly have revealed vividly to them the problem of opening up and liberalizing the economy without strengthening one's domestic institutions and infrastructure in the processes of regionalization and globalization. It is useful to recall that while most of the Asian states suffered in the Crisis, the hardest hit in ASEAN were Thailand and Indonesia as examined in the respective chapters in this volume. The neglect of the voices for help by the West and the hard terms laid down by the International Monetary Fund rescue packages had signalled to Asia, particularly ASEAN, that they would have to do something to help themselves. They noted that China, the rising power in the Asia-Pacific region, was helpful, notably by its move of not devaluing the Yuan. Japan has also been an important economic partner of ASEAN and an early proponent of working closely with ASEAN, or for that matter, with the rest of the Asia-Pacific. On top of these, South Korea, which has its own ideas on promoting East Asian cooperation, was keen to plug into the ASEAN circuit in earnest starting from the 1980s, if not earlier. As such, a self-help and self-strengthening mechanism, namely, the APT process for ASEAN plus China, Japan, and South Korea was established. Certain quarters, especially in China, may hail this as a long overdue mechanism that would allow Asians to deal with their challenges in the 'Oriental' way without the interference of Westerners (particularly the Americans). Thus, Wei Min's chapter denotes that the neighbouring region is the focus of China's diplomacy. Close ties in political-security, economic and cultural affairs between China and its neighbouring states, especially those in the APT, are essential to serve the needs of Chinese national interests. He argues that China is peaceful and its peaceful development is inseparable from the promotion of regional community building. Likewise, Sachiko Hirakawa highlights Japan's identity with the Asia-Pacific in her chapter. She emphasizes that Japan, as a pacifist trading nation, essentially needs a peaceful and open international and regional space, especially in Asia, for its own security and prosperity. In this light, multilateral ASEAN forums and APT meetings give Japan institutional opportunities or arrangements to improve the living conditions at home and abroad in a safe, amicable, and stable environment. South Korea also does not want to be left behind in these regional community-building efforts. As documented by Pan Suk Kim in his chapter, South Korea became more interested in Asian regionalism as it became fully democratic. In this regard, it was instrumental in creating ideas like the East Asian Study Group and East Asian Vision Group. In concrete terms, Pan Suk Kim examines the cooperation between ASEAN and Korea in political-security, economic and socio-cultural terms and comes to the conclusion that there have been expanded collaborations between the two sides over the decades in spite of the temporary slowdown as a result of the Asian Financial Crisis. While predicting that the relationship between

ASEAN and South Korea will grow significantly, Pan Suk Kim would like to point out that the relationship is as yet to reach its full potential and that South Korea could play a crucial role in the regional cooperation efforts.

However, it is appropriate to add that the APT was a process designed at the top, or a rather elitist strategy in regional community building. It is still very much a work in progress, especially at the people-to-people level. While the initial purpose of the APT was to deal with economic issues in the aftermath of the Asian financial crisis, it is obvious that selected security issues will also have to be looked into by the APT to provide a safe framework or backdrop for economic and regional cooperation. As usual, gradualism and incrementalism is the way forward for APT if and when it inches into the security arena. As a multilateral process, it will take time for the APT to bear fruits. In the meantime, it seems that bilateral interactions and cooperation remain more dominant. This is reflected by the fact that some of the ASEAN chapters, if and when they deal with Northeast Asia, have placed more emphasis on bilateral relations with China, Japan or Korea respectively but not so much on the APT process *per se*. One can argue that bilateral interactions are the building block of multilateral interactions and that bilateralism and multilateralism are not mutually exclusive.

Finally, it is important to bear in mind that there are always others arguing for inclusivity and not exclusivity in membership to promote regional community building, and that if there is a move toward regionalism, they prefer open regionalism. Thus East Asianization, or for that matter, Asianization, could be or should be complemented or supplemented by regionalization and globalization. As it turns out, while the APT process has worked out some concrete measures like the Chiang Mai Initiative to help member states, it was also instrumental in paving the way for the setting up of the much larger East Asia Summit starting from 2005. Quite obviously, the East Asia Summit has a very flexible interpretation of the term 'East Asia'. This is demonstrated by the fact that the initial membership of 16 countries (APT countries plus Australia, New Zealand, and India) was later expanded to 18 countries by including Russia, and last but not least, the US in 2011. And it seems that the US, in its push to be the pivot to Asia and the Pacific under President Obama, will be active not only in the East Asia Summit but also in the Trans-Pacific Partnership (TPP), a proposed trade agreement under negotiation by Australia, Brunei, Chile, Canada, Japan, Malaysia, Mexico, New Zealand, Peru, Singapore, the US and Vietnam as of August 2013. All indications show that the TPP would be President Obama's signature initiative as the centrepiece of keeping the US engaged in the Asia-Pacific region in its 'rebalancing' strategy. In the meantime, it is also worth noting that another relatively new process mooted and initiated by the ASEAN Summit in 2011 and 2012, namely, the Regional Comprehensive Economic Partnership is working on a free trade agreement scheme involving ASEAN and its free trade agreement partners (Australia, China, India, Japan, Korea and New Zealand). Last but not least, there is the Free Trade Area of the Asia-Pacific (FTAAP), first mooted in 2004 but lifted out of limbo by China at the APEC meeting in Beijing in November 2014. Making the FTAAP the centre-piece of the APEC meeting, China, under Xi Jinping, seems to be taking the initiative to persuade the 21 APEC leaders to launch another trade arrangement. In fact, China has also been promoting its own frameworks/meetings like the 'one belt, one road' (Maritime Silk Road and Silk Road Economic Belt) and Asian Infrastructure Investment Bank for regional cooperation.

With the proliferation of ideas and multilateral bodies trying to promote cooperation in the Asia-Pacific, one critical question that may be asked is: will ASEAN lose its centrality in East Asian regionalism? It can be argued that ASEAN is probably the most active in regional diplomacy. It is the most enthusiastic and important contributory grouping in promoting regional community building. While cynics or critics may disparage ASEAN or ASEAN-led processes as talk shops and that ASEAN agreements are based on the lowest common denominator, no one could deny the fact that ASEAN has been proactive in initiating processes such as the ARF, APT and East Asia Summit, for regional community building in East Asia and the Asia-Pacific. Whereas major states like China, US and Japan may have problems in initiating regional meetings, especially in the security arena, because of mutual suspicions, history and power ambitions, ASEAN is probably more suitable to serve as the coordinator or facilitator for regional cooperation as it is not a threat to anyone as noted earlier. In fact, China has openly suggested that ASEAN should be in the 'driver's seat' in regional cooperation, at least for the time being. Most importantly of all, ASEAN has taken concrete steps to strengthen itself and beef up its own community building in Southeast Asia. Ostensibly, it has adopted the rule-based ASEAN Charter. In terms of economic cooperation, there are sub-regional processes such as the growth triangles, East ASEAN Growth Area, and ASEAN Mekong Basin Development Cooperation as well as the phasing in of the agreed upon ASEAN Free Trade Area. Most important of all, roadmaps have been drawn for the establishment of the ASEAN Community comprising the ASEAN Political-Security Community, ASEAN Economic Community and ASEAN Socio-Cultural Community as analyzed by the chapters in this volume. A major concrete step in this direction is the proposed establishment of the ASEAN Economic Community, or for that matter, the ASEAN Community in 2015. Readers of this volume will not fail to see the support from ASEAN members for such a momentous endeavour as part and parcel of regional community building. And as of early 2015, ASEAN members have already implemented 92 per cent to 93 per cent of the measures under the ASEAN Community blueprint. Of course, ASEAN will have to bridge many gaps, notably economic and what are called trust gaps, before it can be successfully integrated. When compared with the European Union (EU), arguably the only regional body that has done well, ASEAN may be seen to be less cohesive as it has no common currency, foreign and defense policies. However, it should be noted that even though the ASEAN region is more diverse than mono-civilizational

Europe, it has been successful in preventing war among its members. In fact, the region, which used to be dubbed as the Balkans of Asia, has been by and large at peace, in spite of conflicts like the territorial disputes in the South China Sea. Level-headed leaders in the region will continue to look at the big picture, making ASEAN more resilient and coherent and promoting interactions not only among member states but also with major powers and other regional and international bodies. This is quite remarkable, at least in political-security terms, when compared with other parts of Asia. As a whole, one could remain cautiously optimistic that while most if not all ASEAN countries may focus on state and nation building at home, they would also promote the ultimate goal of forming an ASEAN community, out of enlightened self-interest. This is especially true for ASEAN officials, bureaucrats, and selected NGOs, academics, think tanks and journalists. The hope is that the ASEAN mindset will flourish among the people of ASEAN, given more time. To be sure, economic integration and cooperation has been enhanced over the years and will be further strengthened. This has been and will be helpful in attracting foreign direct investments, trade and technology. As a diplomatic community, ASEAN has the expertise and ability to make itself relevant not only to Southeast Asian, but also East Asian and Asia-Pacific cooperation and regionalism.

1 Brunei Darussalam

Participation in ASEAN and ASEAN Plus Three[1]

Azaharaini Hj. Mohd Jamil

1 National perspectives

Brunei is believed to be an old established Malay State situated in the Southeast Asian region which had a trading connection with countries in the Asian continent as early as the sixth or seventh century A.D. Traders and missionaries from Arabia, India and China sailed via the country's port because of its strategic geographic location as well as good security. Archaeological work in Brunei and in neighbouring Sarawak (East Malaysian State) supports such a claim (Broadcasting & Information Department 1985).

The Islamic tradition in Brunei is believed to have been established as early as the sixth or seventh century because of the frequent visits of Muslim traders and missionaries. But many Bruneian academics argue that the coming of Islam to Brunei was associated with Sultan Muhammad Shah in A.D. 1368, who embraced Islam and became the first Islamic ruler of the country. During his reign, Islam was made the official religion, a practice that has continued to this day.

Europeans came to know about the prosperity and success of the Kingdom of Brunei through the writings of an Italian historian, Antonio Pigafetta. He was a crew member of Magellan's ship in 1521, which sailed round the world and passed through Brunei.[2] As European influence in the region began to grow, the power of the Brunei Kingdom began to decline. It lost much of its territories to western powers such as the Spanish, Dutch and British. To stop further encroachment to the Kingdom, Sultan Hashim (the 26th ruler of Brunei) entered into agreement with the British in 1888 (known as the 'Treaty of Protection'). The treaty, however, did not save the last piece of Brunei territory, Limbang, from being taken away in 1890, resulting in the present size of the country, consisting of two unconnected pieces of land (ibid.).

1.1 Political-security perspective

Brunei believes that for socio-economic development to take place, the co-existence of peace and stability is an important requirement. For this reason, security has always been Brunei's highest priority to be pursued and maintained. The

Sultan of Brunei in 1847, for example, entered into a treaty with Britain for the purpose of strengthening commercial relations and mutual suppression of piracy. In 1888, another treaty was signed between the two countries, which placed Brunei under British protection. This treaty strengthened the British rule in Brunei.

In 1906 Brunei again signed a treaty under which it agreed to be directly ruled by Britain through the introduction of a Residential System of Government where a British representative or the first British Resident was required to be based in Brunei. The British Resident was to advise the ruler (Sultan) in all matters except those pertaining to the local customs and religion (Umar 1990, 18).

When the Second World War broke out in 1941, the Japanese army occupied Brunei for three and a half years. The Japanese army system of governance was enforced until 1945 when the army was driven out. The Residential System of Government was restored and the social-economic development of Brunei slowly returned to normal.

When the father of the present Sultan, Sultan Omar Ali Saifuddien ascended the throne as the 28th ruler of Brunei in June 1950 Brunei continued to be modernised. During his reign (1950–1967), national security continued to be pursued. In fact, he laid down the political and structural foundation of modern Brunei when he signed the Anglo-Brunei Treaty with Britain in 1959 (also known as the 1959 Brunei Constitution). The Treaty terminated the enforcement of the previous treaties and provided for the establishment of Brunei's internal political structure. Under this new arrangement, Brunei took over the administration of all internal affairs while the external affairs and defence were still under the responsibility of the British Government (Umar 1990, 18). Brunei gained full internal autonomy and was no longer a protected state under the new agreement signed with Britain in November 1971. Brunei's foreign relations and defence, however, were still under the responsibility of the British.

In 1979 both countries signed a Treaty of Friendship and Cooperation, which terminated the 1971 agreement and paved the way for full political independence from Britain in 1984. When Brunei gained its independence in January 1984, its first initiatives as a means of achieving recognition of its sovereignty and full independence from the world community was to become members of regional and international organisations. The country became the 49th member of the Commonwealth immediately on the day of its independence on 1 January 1984 facilitating its close traditional ties with the United Kingdom. It became the sixth member of ASEAN on 7 January 1984 and a full member of the United Nations on 21 September 1984. Brunei's main purpose to secure membership of international organisations has been to build friendship and work collaboratively with member nations for socio-economic and political developments.

While initiatives continued to be taken to build a more diplomatic relationship with other regional and international organisations (bilateral/multilateral), the internal political system of the country was also readjusted to better maintain order and provide support through the development of administrative infrastructures. Features of the current political system are partly based on the English Common Law because of the British influence, and partly on the 1959 written Constitution and on the conception of the traditional Malay Islamic Monarchy (*Melayu Islam Beraja* abbreviated as MIB). The MIB ideology has been shaping the life of Bruneians for generations. The current political system is thus a blend of traditional and reformed policies within the ministerial structure.

Based on the 1959 constitution, His Majesty Paduka Seri Baginda Sultan Haji Hassanal Bolkiah Mu'izzaddin Waddaulah is the 29th ruler of Brunei. The Sultan's role in the ruling of the country is enshrined in the MIB national ideology. The three elements of the national ideology are the 'Malay culture', 'Islamic religion' and 'the Monarchical system of government'. The three elements combined together to form an ideology, which describes the nature of the country's administration, that is, the country is ruled by a monarchy system of government, which upholds Islamic values and laws and preserves Malay culture and traditions. The system of government and the political culture of the country are thus shaped by the MIB ideology.

The Prime Minister's Office is the central policymaking agency of government. It coordinates the activities of Government Ministries and Agencies in relation to the formulation and implementation of national policies. It is also the central agency in the management and administration of the Government and the Civil Service. At a lower administrative level, a District Officer who acts as an intermediary person between villagers and the government manages each of the country's four districts. They are responsible for the welfare of villagers and ensure proper provision and maintenance of public utilities.

1.2 Economic perspective

Brunei is the fourth largest oil producer in Southeast Asia with average production of 135,000 barrels per day in 2013. Brunei is also currently the ninth largest exporter of liquefied natural gas in the world (Department of Economic Planning and Development 2011). The oil and gas sector account for 50 per cent of the Gross Domestic Product (GDP), around 80–90 per cent of total exports, and 77–90 per cent of government revenues.[3] Other sources of income come from rents, royalties, corporate tax and from investment activities made by the Brunei Investment Agency (BIA).

Brunei has been described as 'one of the richest countries in the world' based on per capita GDP, which is mainly contributed by oil, and gas revenues supplemented by revenues from overseas investments. The country's small population explains the reason for its high per capita income, which is less than half a million people. Based on its per capita GDP which is about BND $49,625 in 2013 and Brunei's oil and gas exports earning of more than $14 billion (in 2013), Bruneians have been able to enjoy one of the highest standards of living in Asia (Borneo Bulletin Brunei Yearbook 1997). However, the presence of abundant hydrocarbons does not guarantee the country's economic stability and sustainability in the long run. As shown in Table 1.1, in 2013, GDP at constant prices decreased by 2.1 per cent, compared to an increase of 0.9 per cent recorded in 2012 and 3.7 per cent in 2011. It is seen, therefore, that the country's revenue fluctuates depending on the price of oil and gas. Heavy dependence on oil and gas as the main source of income can result in unstable economic growth and development. The non-renewable nature of these resources also makes it difficult to anticipate long-term sustainability.

Recognising the need to develop a more stable economy, the Government of Brunei has started 'diversification initiatives' with emphasis on the development of such sectors as Islamic Banking, tourism, IT, *Halal* Branding, oil and gas upstream and downstream developments; enhancing the private sector growth, reducing the size of the public sector through corporatisation and privatisation of public sector enterprises and attracting foreign direct investments into the country. The nation's ability to diversify, however, has been limited. Nevertheless, the oil and gas revenues up to this point have provided the nation with the socio-economic development and political stability needed for the country to continue to plan and implement policies, which would bring Brunei towards a more sustainable and well balanced economic structure. The country's resources have been used to improve the overall welfare, economic development and political stability of the nation through the provision of free education, free healthcare, free social security, zero income tax, and subsidies for housing, some food stuff and utilities. The substantial hydrocarbon reserves and the country's exports have made the balance of payments possible. For example, Brunei Darussalam recorded continuous surpluses in 2012 and 2013 with BND 11,765.5 million and BND 9,788.4 million respectively.[4] Such surpluses help to improve the current socio-economic development and build up financial reserves for the future generation.

1.3 Social-cultural perspective

The close relationship between the ruled (citizen) and the ruler (King) can be taken as an informal 'social contract' which revolves around the understanding that the '*Ruler could do no harm to his Subjects whilst his Subjects could not disobey the Ruler*' (Salleh 2012). The relationship in such a social contract was stated by His Majesty the Sultan and Yang Di-Pertuan of Brunei Darussalam in his *Titah* (speech) at the 1st Bali Democracy Forum in 2008.[5] He said that like all contracts in any system:

> .... *if it is maintained, we all succeed. If it lapses, we all suffer*... [and as a government, its prime responsibility is to look after the welfare of the people by practicing good governance which] ... *means providing*

Table 1.1 Gross domestic product per capita and population (2010–2014)

Year	2010	2011	2012	2013	2014
GDP at current prices (BND million)	18,689.8	23,302.6	23,802.3	22,638.8	21,671.7
Oil & gas sector	12,199.8	16,432.9	16,436.9	14,957.4	13,930.2
Non-oil & gas sector	6,843.1	7,243.1	7,744.1	8,123.5	8,076.9
Government sector	2,759.3	2,890.2	2,930.4	2,993.3	3,107.0
Private	4,083.8	4,352.8	4,813.7	5,130.2	4,969.9
GDP growth rate (percentage)	–	24.7	2.1	−4.9	−4.3
GDP per capita	48,319.0	59,238.1	59,535.5	55,733.1	52,614.0
GDP per capita growth rate (percentage)	–	22.6	0.5	(6.4)	(5.6)
GDP at constant prices	18,689.8	19,389.6	19,566.7	19,150.9	18,702.1
Oil & gas sector	12,199.8	12,510.3	12,199.7	11,426.9	10,999.4
Non-oil & gas sector	6,843.1	7,245.7	7,736.8	8,086.0	8,056.1
Government sector	2,759.3	2,887.3	2,925.1	2,989.6	3,097.0
Private	4,083.8	4,358.4	4,811.7	5,106.3	4,959.2
GDP growth rate (percentage)	–	3.7	0.9	(2.1)	(2.3)
Gross domestic product per capita	48,319.0	49,290.7	48,941.2	47,146.5	45,404.5
GDP per capita growth rate (percentage)	–	2.0	(0.7)	(3.7)	(3.7)
Population (thousand)	386.8	393.4	399.8	406.2	411.9
Population growth rate (percentage)	–	1.7	1.6	1.6	1.4

Source: Department of Economic Planning and Development, Prime Minister's Office.

> *maximum health care to all; good education from early childhood onwards;*
> *easy personal access to government and its departments and agencies; the*
> *rule of law applying equally to everyone and respect for each individual, each*
> *family and each community, whatever their background, culture or faith.*
>
> 'Sultan Addresses Bali Democracy Forum', *Borneo Bulletin*,
> 11th December 2008

Understanding the historical and cultural context of the country is important if the current country's political system is to be appreciated. Brunei Darussalam is an old Malay State, which historically can be traced back to more than a thousand years ago. Likewise, the current system of ruling (absolute monarchy) also can be traced back to the fifteenth century when Islam was established as the official religion of the country (Umar 1990, 18). The societal life during those days revolved around Islamic faith and Malay culture. The extended family system and close-knit community played a dominant role in everyday life of the people, which constituted the foundation of the Bruneian society. Brunei's social fabric, though it may be referred by some people as 'conservative', is still seen with some elements of modernisation until the present day.

Under this environment of 'informal' social contract, the government is obligated to look after the well being of its people, and in keeping with such obligation, the government ensures that the lifelong basic needs of all citizens and residents of Brunei Darussalam are adequately met. Through formal governmental structures, the government fulfils its obligation to its people by providing them with pensions, healthcare, education, housing, and various allowances and subsidies as well as means of livelihood to the entire population.

Although oil and gas resources have contributed much to the nation's prosperity, the growth of the economy has not been able to keep pace with the growing population. The number of young people wishing to enter the workforce, for example, is growing each year but the employment opportunities being created are limited; the local business community is not growing fast enough to generate employment opportunities, and the expectations and capabilities of the youth are limited in comparison to the knowledge and skills required by the industry. In such a situation, social protection becomes even more important than if the economy is growing at pace with the growth of the population. In the context of Brunei Darussalam, the public sector is largely responsible for the social protection of the people. First, the government has various legislations/acts in place to safeguard the welfare of all, especially women and children and enforces the promotion and protection of human rights in the country ranging from *Children and Young Persons Order 2006* and *Women and Girls Protection Act (Cap 120)* to *Workmen's Compensation Act (Cap 74)*.

Second, a new scheme, *Provident Fund Scheme* (TAP), has been established for new entrants to the public sector since 1993 to ensure that they have income during their retirement age. Prior to 1993, government employees and all Army and Police personnel are eligible for the Defined Benefit Plan (DBP) which is about 75 per cent of final pre-retirement income during retirement. In addition, there is also a universal pension (Old Age Pension) payable to citizens at the age of 60 which is set at BND$250 per month. Both benefits provide them with lifetime income. Currently, the government spends more than BND$4 million per month on old age pension. This figure is increasing each year as Bruneians enjoy a healthier and more secure old age life because of modern technology and developments in the field of medicine (Saim 2013, 24).

In 2009, the government introduced an additional contributory scheme called Supplementary Contribution Pension (SCP), the aim of which is to raise the retirement income to about 50 per cent of average pre-retirement levels because the TAP scheme introduced in 1993 does not provide adequate income level to meet living expenses when they retire in the future. The SCP scheme requires an additional contribution of 3.5 per cent from the employee in which the employers are obliged to match the contribution. The SCP scheme is also open to self-employed persons whose contribution (3.5 per cent) will be matched by the government contribution (3.5 per cent). Under the SCP scheme, a retiree will benefit a minimum of BND$400 per month upon reaching the age of 60 depending on the total amount contributed. Higher income earners can accumulate the desired amount in much shorter time (ibid., 25).

The provision of education to the people has always been regarded by the government as an important strategy in social protection and national development. Education in Brunei Darussalam is provided free at the primary level, available to all children at the secondary level, and full scholarships offered to children at the highest level of attainment. Brunei Darussalam has achieved universal primary education and universal secondary education is the next target to be achieved which will prepare Bruneians for a high technology environment.

Housing for the people is also among the social needs that the government is obligated to provide. Under its long-term national goal, the government is providing low interest housing loans for its employees and soft loans through the Development Bank of Brunei for housing estates. In addition, two housing schemes have been made available to its citizens, namely, landless citizen's scheme and the resettlement scheme. The landless scheme is affordable to low-income residents as the housing units are provided at subsidised prices to be paid over a period of 20–30 years. The government also provides government housing for its employees at subsidised rents for those who do not have their own houses (ibid., 18).

In the area of healthcare, Brunei Darussalam has well-developed health facilities. The provision of universal health services to the population is seen as a priority by the government for human development. The quality of health and medical services is reflected in the life expectancy at birth of 78.1 and the death rate of 3.0 per 1,000 populations in 2012. The virtually free immunisation programmes have resulted in positive health outcomes. Children are also given the basic WHO immunisations such as BCG, Rubella and

Polio. Health and medical services are provided for all citizens and permanent residents at a highly subsidised minimal rate of BND$1 registration fee and BND$5 for foreigners. Vaccination against the H1N1 influenza is currently provided free to citizens and residents of Brunei Darussalam (ibid., 19).

Being referred to as one of the richest countries in the world, it is hard to believe that there are 'poor' people living in the country particularly given the fact that the government is providing subsidies to basic needs. Nevertheless, there are people who can be described as the 'poor' but the term 'relative poverty' would be more appropriate to use in describing the state of hardship and deprivation in the country as opposed to 'absolute' or extreme poverty as used in third world countries. The government has officially recognised that 'relative poverty' needs to be addressed. In fact, one of the measures directed towards alleviating poverty to a zero level under the social security strategy of the '2035 Vision', is to provide an economically sustainable social security system for the people such as providing an educational support scheme for students from poor families (hostel, transportation, school uniforms); a self-sustaining system of unemployment benefits; and a comprehensive system of welfare support for their children (Hambali 2013).

The charity system is also playing its role in providing social protection to the people. *Zakat* (tithe) monies are in this category, which is managed by the Brunei Islamic Council (BIC) under the Ministry of Religious Affairs. According to the teachings of Islam, every Muslim is required to pay two kinds of taxation; first, *zakat fitrah* or tithe of about BND$3 annually during the month of Ramadan and, second, *zakat harta* or property tax of 2.5 per cent on their savings, goods or property kept untouched for a year (Sapar 2011). The collected *zakat* monies are distributed to eligible individuals as prescribed by Islamic teaching. They include the destitute, the poor, tithe collector, new converts, a person who is in debt, and a traveller who travels for lawful purposes and is in need of financial assistance (ibid.).

Another protection system available in Brunei Darussalam is the informal family extended system. The informal family extended system refers to the pooled resources of the extended families, which may be made available for the family members in need of assistance. Parents and family members still support their grown-up or married children/family members who are unemployed. In exchange, unemployed family members normally assist the family by doing housework or taking care of children or aged family members. This system of extended family assistance has been the Bruneian culture for generations (Saim 2013, 15).

2 Brunei's participation in the ASEAN region

2.1 Political-security perspective

ASEAN was established in 1967 by five original member countries – Indonesia, Malaysia, Philippines, Thailand, and Singapore. These countries (except Thailand) had just acquired political independence from centuries of colonisation and foreign domination. Brunei's motivation to be part of ASEAN is driven by the belief that the region's common interest can be achieved through regional cooperation and observance of fundamental principles on which the relationship (ASEAN) was built, namely, 'mutual respect for the territorial integrity, sovereignty, independence and national identity of all nations; recognition of the equality of all nations large and small; non-interference in internal affairs; peaceful settlement of disputes and cooperation for mutual benefit'.[6] Being a small country with small local market and unbalanced economic development, Brunei Darussalam believes that the country can achieve much more by being a member of ASEAN, especially in achieving national peace, stability and socio-economic development through collaborative regional efforts. In other words, ASEAN is seen as providing a framework for effective cooperation in the political, economic, social, cultural and security aspects, which would benefit member states.

The proclamation of His Majesty the Sultan and Yang Di-Pertuan of Brunei Darussalam at the United Nation's assembly in 1984 expresses the country's political stand governing its relationship with other countries. According to this proclamation, Brunei upholds the UN Charter and its own right to maintain its sovereignty, independence and territorial integrity. Brunei pledges to carry out its duty to enhance the economic and social well being of all its peoples, along with their political, cultural and religious identity. His Majesty's *Titah* (keynote speech) (Government of Brunei 1988, 18) to the United Nations on the country's admission in 1984 was as follows:

> *We will uphold the principle that each country has the inalienable right to establish its own form of government, without any form of outside interference and always having regard to the prevailing circumstances in each country and the aspirations of its own people for a better standard of livelihood and well being.*

This means that Brunei Darussalam has its own policies and way of existence designed to be appropriate for the nation and its people without any interferences from outside forces. Brunei Darussalam will always maintain good relations with foreign nations by adopting the principles of strengthening cooperation, understanding and mutual assistance without intervening in the internal affairs of other countries regardless of their ideology and belief system.

Brunei will continue to give importance to the maintenance of regional peace and stability in order for the country and the region as a whole to continue to enjoy economic development and prosperity. It will continue to be committed to and contribute to regional security through the collective efforts of member nations. It has contributed in the form of its commitment to regional processes by hosting a series of important ASEAN meetings such as the ASEAN Summits, the annual ASEAN Foreign Ministers Meetings (AFMM) and the Post Ministerial Conferences (PMC). So far it has chaired

ASEAN four times – in 1989, 1995, 2001 and 2013. These events serve to reinforce the country's commitment to building better understanding, friendship and trust in the region. It makes contributions to countries in need of assistance by sharing some of its resources as part of its commitment to peace and security.

Many people have referred to Brunei Darussalam as 'truly ASEAN' as it joined the Association immediately after independence in 1984. The country wishes to be small, positive and moderate in international affairs.[7] It avoids any forms of direct confrontation and in fact, it has never stirred up any controversy throughout the decades of membership. This is contributing indirectly to the achievement of ASEAN goals. It will continue to choose diplomacy or peaceful means of resolving any differences through negotiation. The country will continue to protect such an image so that a high level of trust is placed in the country and other countries give it recognition for respecting their sovereignty.

2.2 Economic perspective

ASEAN Free Trade Area (AFTA) was launched on 28 January 1992 in Singapore. The primary mechanism for achieving the goals of AFTA is the Common Effective Preferential Tariff (CEPT) scheme. The scheme involves a programme of gradual tariff reduction schedule for implementation starting in 1993 for 15 years to increase the *'region's competitive advantage as a production base geared for the world market'*. The target deadline was subsequently moved forward to 2010.[8] This AFTA process is aimed at facilitating ASEAN countries to liberalise their economy, strengthen the countries' competitiveness, and enhance regional economic integration through collaboration to gain advantage in investments and infrastructure development.

Brunei Darussalam contributes to ASEAN economic integration by agreeing to grant duty free treatment on some products produced by ASEAN countries. This will benefit the business potential of the grouping. Along with the other five original ASEAN member countries, it agreed to set time for reduction of tariffs to the beginning of 2002. In fact, ASEAN-6 (Brunei, Indonesia, Malaysia, Philippines, Singapore and Thailand) had already complied with the CEPT scheme by 2003. Up to the present time, tariffs on 99 per cent of products in the CEPT Inclusion List of the ASEAN-6 countries have been reduced to 0 to 5 per cent.[9]

Brunei Darussalam is also strengthening its trade and economic links with other countries through Free Trade Agreements (FTAs). This will not only help bridge ASEAN with other regional economic groupings but also indirectly advances the objectives of APEC and WTO. At the same time it ensures wider markets access for its people, goods, services and investments rather than depending on the small Bruneian local market. Considering that Brunei Darussalam has unbalanced economic development, being dependent too heavily on the oil and gas revenues (see Table 1.2) and a small population but highly educated workforce, the government strongly believes that active engagement in FTAs with a number of key strategic partners will open up markets for Brunei's exports and services. This will also help facilitate the flow of foreign direct investment into Brunei Darussalam because FTAs provides greater predictability and transparency to business transactions.

In the interest of its future economic sustainability, Brunei Darussalam is actively promoting a climate of open and non-discriminatory trade in order to build its global partnerships. It is strengthening its commitment to enhance good governance and is pursuing a policy of rapid economic diversification by focusing on the development of Small and Medium Enterprises (SMEs) and integrating them effectively into the ASEAN market (Cleary and Wong 1994). SMEs constitute nearly 98 per cent of the business sector of Brunei Darussalam (Ministry of Industry and Primary Resources 1994). While policymakers have taken steps to liberalise and link the Brunei economy to the ASEAN region, the success of this policy depends, to a great extent, on the positive response of SMEs to take advantage of what has been made available to them.

In an effort to integrate the country into the global economy, Brunei Darussalam is continuing its efforts in strengthening its international relationships through free trade agreements at the bilateral and multilateral levels. Through its membership of ASEAN, Brunei Darussalam has been able to actively engage in FTAs. To date it has entered into agreements with Australia, New Zealand, China, India, Japan and South Korea and also with Chile, New

Table 1.2 Total Percentage of Brunei Darussalam Export by Commodity Section (2009–2014)

Commodity Section	2009	2010	2011	2012	2013	2014
Food and Live Animals	0.0	0.0	0.0	0.0	0.1	0.3
Beverages and Tobacco	0.0	0.0	0.0	0.0	0.0	0.1
Crude Materials Inedible	0.1	0.2	0.1	0.1	0.1	0.1
Mineral Fuels	96.1	95.2	95.4	95.7	96.5	92.5
Vegetables Oils and Animals Fats	0.0	0.0	0.0	0.0	0.0	0.0
Chemicals	0.1	1.1	1.6	1.9	0.8	4.5
Manufactured Goods	0.4	0.4	0.4	0.4	0.7	0.5
Machinery and Transport Equipment	2.1	1.8	2.0	1.2	1.1	1.4
Miscellaneous Manufactured Articles	1.1	1.2	0.4	0.4	0.4	0.4
Miscellaneous Transaction and Commodities Not Elsewhere Classified	0.1	0.2	0.1	0.1	0.2	0.1
Total	**100**	**100**	**100**	**100**	**100**	**100**

Source: Department of Economic Planning and Development, Prime Minister's Office.

Note: Total figures may not tally due to rounding.

Zealand and Singapore for the Trans Pacific Strategic Economic Partnership. Brunei signed the Trans Pacific Strategic Economic Partnership in August 2005 and this will not only benefit the four signing partners through sharing of expertise, ideas, technology and resources to improve their competitiveness in the global market but also will result in bridging Latin America with the Asia-Pacific region and advancing the APEC and WTO objectives. The Trans Pacific Strategic Economic Partnership also has side agreements, namely, the Environment Cooperation Agreement and Labour Cooperation Memorandum of Understanding, to reflect a shared desire to encourage and promote sound labour and environmental practices. These agreements establish mechanisms for on-going cooperation and dialogues on labour and environmental issues.[10]

Brunei has a close relationship with the Philippines in particular and other nations in general such as Singapore. In April 2009, Brunei and the Philippines signed a Memorandum of Understanding (MOU) that seeks to strengthen the bilateral cooperation of the two countries in the fields of agriculture and farm-related trade and investments.[11] Brunei Darussalam has also been playing a leading role in the promotion of economic cooperation and integration at the sub-regional level through the mechanism of East ASEAN Growth Area (EAGA) involving Indonesia, Malaysia, Brunei Darussalam and the Philippines (BIMP-EAGA). It has invested heavily in this project to take advantage of the ASEAN network for the development of its SMEs. BIMP-EAGA covers the entire state of Brunei; the provinces of Kalimantan, Sulawesi, Maluku and West Papua of Indonesia; the states of Sabah and Sarawak and federal territory of Labuan in Malaysia; and Mindanao region and the province of Palawan in the Philippines. It covers a land area of 1.6 million square kilometres with an estimated population of more than 69 million.[12]

BIMP-EAGA cooperation aims to increase trade, tourism and investments by facilitating the free movement of people, goods, and services making the best use of common infrastructure and natural resources and taking the fullest advantage of economic complementation. Its goal is to accelerate economic development in focus areas, which are in strategic proximity to each other, in one of the world's most resource-rich regions, namely, Heart of Borneo (HoB), and Sulu-Sulawesi Marine Eco-region (SSME). The principal mechanism for consultation between the participating countries is the Senior Officials Meeting (SOM) and the Ministers Meetings (MM) that meet at pre-agreed dates and venues. A national secretariat for each member country coordinates in-country and sub-regional activities.

The 8th BIMP-EAGA Summit was held on 4 April 2012 in Phnom Penh, Cambodia. Organised on the sidelines of the 20th ASEAN Summit and chaired by Brunei Darussalam, the event endorsed the programme's Implementation Blueprint (IB) 2012–2016. The Blueprint serves as guide for timely and effective achievement of the strategic focus areas. To ensure the successful implementation of the activities identified in the Implementation Blueprint, stakeholders at the local and national levels, particularly the private sector, have been called to expedite the implementation of the projects as well as strengthening of the operational and institutional mechanism.[13]

2.3 Social-cultural perspective

ASEAN has a commitment to promote the well being, the livelihood and welfare of its people through various collaborative activities in areas ranging from poverty alleviation, social welfare and protection to provision of adequate and affordable healthcare, medical services and medicine. One initiative taken by ASEAN to uphold its commitment is to develop its Socio-Cultural Community (ASCC) Blueprint (2009–2015) which was decided by ASEAN leaders at the 13th ASEAN Summit Meeting held in Singapore in 2007. The proposed ASCC Blueprint was then adopted by the ASEAN leaders at the 14th ASEAN Summit in 2009 in Thailand. The ASCC aims to contribute to 'realising an ASEAN Community that is people-oriented and socially responsible with a view to achieving enduring solidarity and unity among the peoples and Member States of ASEAN'.[14]

Brunei Darussalam, through its membership with the ASEAN, has been able to participate in its socio-cultural community initiatives while engaging with the ASEAN market in the development of its economy. It has chaired the Senior Officials Meeting (SOM) in January 2013 to handle the mid-term review of the ASCC Blueprint to determine the progress of implementation for submission to the 23rd ASEAN Summit Meeting, which was held in Bandar Seri Begawan in October 2013. Brunei continues to improve its collaborative relationships in various fields to contribute to the long-term goal of ASEAN socio-culture in defending the sustainability of the unity and solidarity of the region.

ASEAN recognises that despite its economic achievements, socio-economic disparities still exist, particularly the quality of life of the socially vulnerable groups in the region. It also realises that this concern has similarities with the United Nation's Millennium Development Goals (MDGs). Therefore, at the 14th ASEAN Summit held in Thailand in March 2009, the ASEAN Leaders, in the Joint Declaration on the Attainment of the MDGs in ASEAN, called for the development of a Roadmap on the MDGs. The Roadmap would serve as a framework for collective action among ASEAN Member States to achieve the MDGs.[15] In this respect Brunei Darussalam continues its commitment in support of the UN's Millennium Declaration and ASEAN's Joint Declaration on the attainment of the MDGs in ASEAN. Brunei Darussalam has already achieved almost all of the targets of the United Nations' Millennium Development Goals (MDGs). For example, extreme poverty has been eradicated and universal primary education has been achieved and now the country's target is to achieve universal secondary education.

Brunei Darussalam has been listed 37th out of 169 countries in the Human Development Index (HDI) having attained a value of 0.805, which is above the average of 0.650 for countries in East Asia and the Pacific.[16] Brunei

Darussalam's HDI value increased from 0.773 in 1990 to 0.805 in 2010, an increase of 4 per cent or an average annual increase of about 0.2 per cent. Brunei Darussalam has made substantial achievements in improving and upgrading the health status and services. For example, infectious diseases have been eliminated; life expectancy at birth increased by almost four years since 1990 and now life expectancy has stabilised to 76.3 years for males and 79.9 for females; infant mortality has declined from above 20.01 per thousand before the 1970s to about 9.3 per thousand in 1912 and maternal mortality has been reduced to about 0/1000 live births since 1988.[17]

Brunei Darussalam is now focusing on improving income distribution among the population, promoting investment, increasing food self-sufficiency, encouraging greater opportunities for women, and maintaining high standards of governance in public and private sectors. These are reflected in Brunei's Wawasan 2035 (Department of Economic Planning and Development 2008). Brunei Darussalam also acknowledges that there is a need to raise the level of environmental awareness at all levels of society inclusive of government and non-governmental organisations and school children. Environmental components have been integrated in the primary and secondary curricula and are part of extra curricular activities. Brunei Darussalam actively supports regional efforts in promoting environmental awareness. One such effort was the ASEAN Environment Year (AEY) 1995 with the theme on 'Green and Clean'. The main objective of AEY 1995 was to promote ASEAN's efforts and achievements in protecting the environment to the international community. ASEAN agrees to have such celebration once every 3 years to be hosted by member nations. Brunei Darussalam hosted AEY in 2000 with the theme on *Our Heritage, Our Future.*[18]

ASEAN seeks to promote ASEAN awareness and a sense of community, preserve and promote ASEAN cultural heritage, promote cultural creativity and industry, and engage with the community. One of the main bodies in ASEAN cooperation in culture is the ASEAN Committee on Culture and Information (COCI). This body was established in 1978 and its mission is to promote effective cooperation in the fields of culture through its various projects and activities. The COCI comprises representatives of various government ministries in ASEAN as well as radio and television broadcasters, museums, libraries and national archives. They meet once a year to formulate and agree on projects to fulfil their mission. Brunei Darussalam chaired the 48th meeting of COCI in 2013.[19] Brunei also hosted the 14th meeting of the Committee on Culture and Information (COCI) Sub-Committee on Information (SCI) (ASEAN-COCI SCI) in which Brunei stressed the need for ASEAN to play a 'bigger role in promoting ASEAN awareness in order to accelerate the building process of the ASEAN community'.[20] Brunei is actively implementing and coordinating various projects under the ASEAN-COCI SCI, such as the ASEAN Media Exchange Programme with its dialogue partners and a radio programme known as ASEAN in Action.

3 Brunei's participation in the ASEAN Plus Three (APT)

ASEAN Plus Three (APT) is made up of ASEAN countries plus China, Japan and Republic of Korea. This grouping was conceptualised in 1997 but it was only in 1999 that a formal process was initialised where various mechanisms were established to further the goals of APT.[21] Today APT has widened its cooperation to include many fields ranging from political and security areas, trade and investment, transnational crime to food, agriculture, and the development of small and medium enterprises. Brunei has been participating in all these mechanisms and it has been contributing to the goals of APT directly or indirectly commensurate with its size and available resources. In the political and security area, Brunei Darussalam chaired the APT and the ARF Ministerial Meeting in July 2002. It also chaired the 23rd ASEAN and related Summits including APT Summit on 9–10 October 2013. Brunei Darussalam supports regional processes as they provide avenues for officials to interact with one another, promoting mutual trust and understanding among member nations contributing to regional peace and stability.

Among the contributions made by Brunei in the political security area is the hosting of the 7th ASEAN Defence Ministers' Meeting (ADMM) in May 2013. Two major deliverables (military exercises) were carried out during the Brunei Darussalam's Chairmanship of ADMM and ADMM-Plus in 2013. One is the 1st ASEAN Defence Ministers' Meeting Plus (ADMM-Plus) Humanitarian Assistance and Disaster Relief and Military Medicine Exercise (HADR & MM Ex) in June 2013, which brought together more than 2,500 military personnel from the 10 ASEAN countries and other countries, which include Australia, China, India, Japan, New Zealand, Russia, South Korea and the United States. The other exercise is the 2nd ASEAN Militaries' Humanitarian and Disaster Relief Exercise, which was (co-hosted with Singapore) held back-to-back with the 1st ADMM-Plus HADR & MM Exercise.[22] Both exercises were designed to enhance military-to-military interoperability, coordination and cooperation amongst participating countries. Such exercises promote people-to-people interactions and provide avenues for confidence building measures through development of common understanding, camaraderie and mutual respect.

Brunei shares with the other member countries in believing that APT cooperation plays an important role in realising the goals of the East Asia community with ASEAN as the driving force. Brunei reaffirms the central role of ASEAN in the evolving regional architecture and recognises the mutually reinforcing and complementary roles of the APT and other regional processes such as the ASEAN Plus Ones, East Asia Summit (EAS), and ARF in the East Asia community building process. The APT Cooperation Work Plan (2007–2017) adopted at the 11th APT Summit in November 2007 in Singapore is instrumental in providing guidance for the future direction of APT co-operation and avenues for officials of member countries to interact and foster closer relationship between them, thus encouraging the 'give and take' culture or 'ASEAN Way' in the maintenance of peace, stability and security in the region. Since funding for the Work Plan has also been established in which Brunei Darussalam and other member countries are contributing based on an agreed index, the programmes and activities/projects planned during the Plan period should be feasible to further the goals of APT. Brunei Darussalam hosted the 14th ASEAN Plus Three Foreign Ministers' Meeting in June 2013 and one of the outcomes of the meeting was an endorsement for a mid-term review of the APT Work Plan (2013–2017) to be conducted. The idea was to identify gaps and propose recommendations to revise the remaining years of the planned period (2013–2017) of the Work Plan for subsequent adoption by the 16th ASEAN Plus Three Summit 2013.[23] The recommendations, contained in the East Asia Vision Group II (EAVG II) Report which was submitted to the ASEAN Plus Three Commemorative Summit in Phnom Penh, Cambodia, in November 2012, would be further considered by the ASEAN Plus Three Ministers for the future direction of the APT process, regional cooperation and community building.

In the area of counter-terrorism and other non-traditional security issues, the leading agency in Brunei Darussalam has been the Prime Minister's Office (PMO) through its Security and Enforcement Division. The Division recently attended the 6th APT Ministerial Meeting on Transnational Crime (AMMTC+3), which was held on 18 September 2013 in Vientiane, Lao PDR. The meeting reaffirmed APT commitment to strengthen efforts to prevent and combat transnational crimes in order to ensure peace and stability in the region. Brunei Darussalam condemns any acts of terrorism as it has an impact on peace and stability of the region. Brunei Darussalam agrees that the war against terrorism ought to be fought comprehensively. It therefore, continues to work with its neighbours either bilaterally or multilaterally in order to strengthen its capacity to fight against terrorism.

In the area of economic development, ASEAN has signed a Comprehensive Economic Partnership Agreement with Japan (ASEAN-Japan EPA) in April 2008 to cover comprehensive areas of cooperation ranging from trading goods, trading services, investment and economic cooperation. Such agreement would strengthen not only the economic ties between ASEAN and Japan but also create a larger and more efficient market to be exploited positively by the member countries.[24] Brunei Darussalam has been implementing this Agreement since 1 January 2009. Brunei also has a bilateral Economic Partnership Agreement with Japan (Brunei-Japan EPA) initiated in 2007. The scope of the agreement includes improvement of market access through the reduction of import duties and services and the inclusion of new areas such as energy, improvement of business environment and cooperation. ASEAN has also signed FTAs with the other two Plus Three countries, i.e. Republic of Korea and China.

In terms of trading with ASEAN Plus Three countries (see Table 1.3), Brunei's total exports increased from BND 12,143.7 million in 2011 to BND 12,528.9 million in 2012, registering a rise of 3.1 per cent. On the contrary,

Table 1.3 Export by country of destination (2009–2014)

Country/Year	2009	2010	2011	2012	2013	2014
ASEAN:	**1,788.85**	**1,505.43**	**2,176.52**	**2,380.92**	**3,315.96**	**2,646.91**
Cambodia	0.08	0.08	0.05	0.01	0.00	0.05
Indonesia	1,123.13	859.94	1,068.53	573.77	671.59	812.22
Lao PDR	0.05	0.01	0.12	0.00	0.00	0.03
Malaysia	**163.69**	**180.08**	**464.00**	**111.30**	**560.19**	**472.25**
Peninsular	75.96	156.91	443.60	75.88	500.33	384.11
Sabah	0.45	1.92	0.80	2.75	17.80	45.29
Sarawak	87.28	21.24	19.60	32.67	42.07	42.85
Myanmar	0.11	0.05	0.05	0.03	0.04	0.08
Philippines	33.21	8.31	11.42	75.65	103.33	97.38
Singapore	267.89	341.69	275.09	290.96	626.40	436.74
Thailand	200.42	106.28	120.91	590.18	601.53	698.15
Vietnam	0.25	8.99	236.35	739.02	752.88	130.01
Plus 3 Countries	**6,437.16**	**8,087.43**	**9,967.17**	**10,147.98**	**8,223.20**	**6,932.57**
China	421.60	798.32	665.73	435.37	197.64	121.61
Japan	4,809.74	5,267.07	6,797.14	7,158.92	5,691.73	5,342.13
Republic of Korea	1,205.82	2,022.05	2,504.30	2,553.68	2,333.84	1,468.83

Source: Department of Economic Planning and Development, Prime Minister's Office.

Note: Total figures may not tally due to rounding.

Brunei exports to these countries declined by 8.6 per cent from BND 12,528.9 million in 2012 to BND 11,539.2 million in 2013. The total exports to the region also decreased from BND 11,539.2 million in 2013 to BND 9,579.5 million in 2014, registering a decline of 20.5 per cent.

One of the notable achievements under the APT framework is its cooperation in finance. This is pursued through the implementation of the Asian Bond Market Initiative (ABMI), and the Chiang Mai Initiative Multilateralisation (CMIM), which was doubled, to US$240 billion in 2012 for managing regional short-term liquidity. The CMIM is supported by the APT Macroeconomic Research Office (AMRO) in Singapore, which commenced its operations in May 2011. Brunei Darussalam is represented by officials from the Ministry of Finance in this area of work. The 16th Meeting of the ASEAN Plus Three Finance Ministers, held on 3 May 2013 in Delhi, India, announced the finalisation of the amendment of the CMIM Agreement and the agreement to transform AMRO to an international organisation.

Brunei's import of goods from these countries declined from BND 3,428.2 million in 2011 to BND 3,340.2 million in 2012, registering a decline of 2.6 per cent (see Table 1.4). The total Brunei imports in 2013 stood at BND

Table 1.4 Import by country of origin (2009–2014)

Country/Year	2009	2010	2011	2012	2013	2014
ASEAN:	**1,808.45**	**1,768.76**	**2,025.98**	**2,328.21**	**2,301.52**	**2,235.61**
Cambodia	0.13	0.01	0.01	0.05	0.06	3.49
Indonesia	84.23	88.28	90.69	101.83	191.93	132.20
Lao PDR	0.00	0.06	–	0.00	0.00	0.00
Malaysia	**677.05**	**816.45**	**839.28**	**887.00**	**991.17**	**938.07**
Peninsular	572.17	683.01	687.97	734.33	814.17	792.25
Sabah	32.20	56.33	64.54	61.76	66.08	61.23
Sarawak	72.67	77.11	86.77	90.91	110.92	84.59
Myanmar	0.09	0.14	0.43	0.19	1.07	0.86
Philippines	9.04	9.14	11.66	13.49	15.44	11.87
Singapore	894.06	660.44	882.81	1,051.25	863.05	931.47
Thailand	138.05	185.86	191.27	260.38	225.84	204.90
Vietnam	5.79	8.40	9.83	14.01	12.96	12.76
Plus 3 Countries	**603.40**	**691.47**	**1,402.24**	**1,012.04**	**925.62**	**1,032.63**
China	204.14	271.21	414.34	508.06	508.44	453.01
Japan	312.03	343.88	262.01	334.77	261.52	183.55
Republic of Korea	87.23	76.38	725.89	169.21	155.65	396.07

Source: Department of Economic Planning and Development, Prime Minister's Office.

Note: Total figures may not tally due to rounding.

3,227.1 million, a decrease of 3.5 per cent from BND 3,340.2 million in 2012. Total Brunei trade with the ASEAN Plus Three Countries reached BND 14,766.3 million in 2013, a decline by 7.5 per cent compared to BND 15,869.2 million reported in 2012. In addition, Plus Three Countries trading constituted 62 per cent of the total ASEAN Plus Three share.

The foreign direct investments (FDIs) from the Plus Three countries declined from BND 69.4 million in 2012 to BND 19.8 million in 2013 (see Table 1.5). Cumulative FDIs from the Plus Three countries during the period 2009–2013 were valued at BND 188.9 million comprising 70.6 per cent of total FDI inflows from ASEAN Plus Three countries in the same period. Total trade with Plus Three countries (BND 9,148.8 million) accounted for a 61.9 per cent share of ASEAN Plus Three's total trade (BND 5,617.5 + BND 9,148.8 million) in 2013.

FDI inflows from the Plus Three countries (BND 19.8 million) accounted for 212.9 per cent of the total share of FDI inflows from ASEAN Plus Three countries (BND 19.8 + BND −10.5 million) in 2013.

In the area of energy security, Brunei Darussalam is in agreement with APT member countries on the need to strengthen cooperation to secure a

Table 1.5 Foreign Direct Investment (FDI) by country of origin (2008–2014)

Year	2008	2009	2010	2011	2012	2013	2014[P]
ASEAN:	**4.0**	**0.8**	**42.9**	**7.0**	**39.3**	**(10.5)**	**178.8**
Indonesia	–	–	0.4	–	–	–	–
Malaysia	(3.3)	3.2	10.8	4.4	6.5	4.3	116.8
Philippines	–	–	0.0	–	–	–	–
Singapore	7.3	(2.4)	31.7	2.6	32.8	(14.8)	62.0
Thailand	–	–	–	–	–	–	–
+ 3 Countries	**36.8**	**(7.1)**	**30.0**	**69.7**	**69.4**	**19.8**	**33.7**
China	–	–	–	–	–	–	–
Japan	36.8	(7.1)	30.0	69.7	69.4	19.8	33.7
Republic of Korea	–	–	–	–	–	–	–

Source: Department of Economic Planning and Development, Prime Minister's Office.

Note: P – Provisional data.

sustainable energy future in response to the challenges faced by the region. Among the APT activities and projects, which have been agreed by the APT member countries, are 'regular APT forum on oil market, APT forum on energy security, as well as APT forum on new and renewable energy and energy efficiency and conservation'.[25] Brunei Darussalam has been involved in these activities and it chaired the 29th ASEAN Ministers on Energy Meeting (AMEM) on 20 September 2011. The 8th Meeting of Energy Ministers of the ASEAN Plus Three countries (ASEAN, China, Japan and the Republic of Korea), the 5th East Asian Summit Energy Ministers Meeting, and a consultation with the International Energy Agency were also held on this occasion.[26]

Many APT countries, particularly Brunei Darussalam, see food security as a key factor in the regional socio-economic development sustainability. Brunei imports most of its food consumption from the ASEAN region, and as such, it supports the idea of strengthening food security under the APT cooperation. The Ministry of Industry and Primary Resources is the main agency involved in the coordination of agricultural and forestry regional activities. It signed the APT Emergency Rice Reserve (APTERR) Agreement on 7 October 2011 during the 11th AMAF Plus Three Meeting in Jakarta, Indonesia in support of the implementation of the scheme for meeting emergency requirements and achieving humanitarian purposes.[27]

In the socio-cultural areas, a new mechanism for cooperation at the ministerial level was established on education, namely, the ASEAN Plus Three Education Ministers Meeting (APT-EMM). In one of their meetings, the Ministers agreed to endorse the APT Plan of Action on Education (2010–2017), which details wide-ranging areas of cooperation, concrete plans, proposals and future directions in the education sector (ASEAN Secretariat, 2014). The Brunei Ministry of Education (MOE) through its Special Education Unit, coordinates the programmes associated with APT gifted children. From 10th to 17th June 2012 the Special Education Unit of the MOE with the cooperation of Ministry of Development (MOD) and the Universiti Brunei Darussalam (UBD) hosted the ASEAN Plus Three Junior Science Odyssey involving science competition for students of ages 13 to 15 involving APT member nations. The Brunei Takaful Brunei Am Bhd. was the main sponsor of the event.

In the area of environment, Brunei Darussalam has shown its strong commitment in the implementation of the ASEAN Environmental Education Plan (AEEAP) 2008–2012. It organised the ASEAN Environment Youth Forum on 'Creating a Climate for Change' on 22–25 April 2010. The forum brought together a larger number of ASEAN youth participants as well as from the Plus Three Countries. The forum was sponsored by the Brunei government together with Japan ASEAN Integration Fund (JAIF). The Forum aimed at generating interest and awareness among youth from ASEAN and Plus Three countries on climate change issues. Brunei also hosted the ASEAN Plus Three Youth Environment Forum, which was held from 2nd to 4th December 2013. The forum provided a consultative platform for youth in the region to share experiences, gain knowledge and ideas, and to learn the value of collaboration and cooperation for collective action in the protection of the global environment.

Other areas in which Brunei Darussalam has been involved with the activities of APT include health development, culture and arts, information, social welfare and development, youth, and civil service matters. The nature of involvement in various cooperative areas varies from attending and hosting of the APT and related meetings, and participating in the relevant workshops/ training programmes to financial contributions based on an agreed index and implementation of agreed actions at national level, and sharing of data/ information on related issues. In the area of Health Development, for example, Brunei funded and hosted the Senior Official Meeting (SOM) in January 2013 to handle the mid-term review of ASCC Blueprint (2009–2015) to determine the progress of implementation. The ASCC Blueprint has many health action lines/elements, which are now grouped into four categories and have evolved to become the ASEAN Strategic Framework on Health Development (2010–2015). This framework serves as a guide to the development of implementation Work Plans (2011–2015) of the relevant technical working groups/health subsidiary bodies/task forces endorsed by SOMHD. One of these bodies, the ASEAN Expert Group on Communicable Diseases (AEGCD) has finalised the ASEAN Medium Term Plan on Emerging Infectious Diseases (2011–2015). Another one is the ASEAN Working Group on Pandemic Preparedness and Responses (AWGPPR), which has updated its Work Plan and is endorsed by SOMHD. Brunei hosted the Planning Workshop on ASEAN Plus Three Partnership Laboratories (APL) in February 2010. As chair of ASEAN Working Group on Pandemic Preparedness and Response (AWGPPR), Brunei Darussalam hosted the 4th AWGPPR Work Plan in 2012. Brunei is also involved in working together with Malaysia and Singapore on a Dengue Case and Virus Database (United Dengue). Brunei Darussalam is also involved in the formulation and subsequent signing of Bandar Seri Begawan Declaration on Non-Communicable Diseases (NCDs) in October 2013 (Hajar 2013). In the area of culture and arts, Brunei participates by sending officials for human resource development and policy sharing in the implementation of arts and culture policies. In Civil Service matters, Brunei Darussalam has agreed to be the coordinating state for Information Technology in terms of training of trainers on IT security awareness. Likewise, in the youth areas, Brunei's contribution involves the hosting of regular APT youth forums and hosting of the 4th AMMY+3 on 23 May 2013 to exchange views on effective and practical ways of enhancing youth relationships.

4 Conclusions

Being a small country with vulnerable economic and security situations, a logical option for Brunei Darussalam is to 'invest' in a good multilateral relationship with the neighbouring countries particularly ASEAN and APT as well as bilateral relationships with countries such as Great Britain and the USA. Such relationships and its participation in regional processes particularly in the form of hosting of significant meetings and international forums have given the Bruneian officials a wealth of experience and knowledge needed in serving its people and in maintaining its culturally based customs through mutual collaborations and commitments in the preservation of one another's culture. Such knowledge and experience have enabled the national needs to be integrated with the needs of the international community for the continued peace, stability and economic prosperity of the region. Treating member nations like a 'family' rather than merely a 'political or economic' entity is seen by Bruneians as contributing indirectly to peace and stability in the region. Trust and respect in such a situation are important elements in the maintenance of such a relationship.

Notes

1 The opinions and viewpoints expressed in this report are not necessarily those of the Brunei Government or Universiti Brunei Darussalam.
2 See Umar (1990). The full title of the author is Yang Dimuliakan Pehin Orang Kaya Amar Diraja Dato Seri Utama (Dr.) Haji Awang Mohd. Jamil Al-Sufri bin Begawan Pehin Udana Khatib Dato Seri Paduka Awang Haji Umar.
3 'Brunei Darussalam', Extractive Industries Watch website, accessed 22 August 2015, www.eiwatch.org/country-profile/brunei-darussalam.
4 U.S Department of State, "Investment Climate Statements 2014 – Brunei", Posted June, 2014, www.state.gov/e/eb/rls/othr/ics/2014/index.htm.
5 'Sultan Addresses Bali Democracy Forum', *Borneo Bulletin*, 11 December 2008, www.sultanate.com/news_server/2008/11_dec_2.html.
6 'Overview: Fundamental Principles', Association of Southeast Asian Nations Official Website, Posted 2014, www.asean.org/asean/about-asean/overview.
7 See Bolkiah (2000, 147). The full name of the author is Duli Yang Teramat Mulia Paduka Seri Pengiran Perdana Wazir Sahibul Himmah Wal-Waqar Pengiran Muda Mohamed Bolkiah.

8 'ASEAN: AFTA and other Free Trade Agreements – Development and Impact on the International Automotive Industry', GRIN.com, accessed 22 August 2015, www.grin. com/en/e-book/51626/asean-afta-and-other-free-trade-agreements-development-an d-impact-on.

9 Agusnuramin, 'ASEAN Free Trade Area (AFTA Council)'. Wordpress.com, 2 June 2013, http://agusnuramin.wordpress.com/2013/06/02/asean-free-trade-area-afta-council.

10 'Overview of Brunei FTAs', Ministry of Foreign Affairs and Trade website, 2015, www.mofat.gov.bn/SitePages/Brunei%20Darussalam%27s%20FTA%20Policy.aspx.

11 'Embassy History', Philippines Embassy in Brunei Darussalam website. Posted 22 August 2015, http://philippine-embassybrunei.org/the-embassy/embassy-history.

12 'Brunei Darussalam-Indonesia-Malaysia-The Philippines East ASEAN Growth Area (BIMP-EAGA)', ADB website, www.adb.org/countries/subregional-program s/bimp-eaga.

13 Debbie Too, 'Private sector key to EAGA growth', *The Brunei Times*, 5 April 2012, www.bt.com.bn/news-asia/2012/04/05/private-sector-key-eaga-growth.

14 The ASEAN Secretariat, ASEAN Socio-Cultural Community Blueprint, June 2009, 1. Also available at www.asean.org/archive/5187-19.pdf.

15 'Asean Roadmap for the Attainment of the Millennium Development Goals', Association of Southeast Asian Nation website, 5 August 2011, www.asean.org/a rchive/documents/19th%20summit/MDG-Roadmap.pdf.

16 'Brunei Climbs up HDI', The Brunei Resources Blog, 23 March 2013, http://bru neiresources.blogspot.com/2013/03/brunei-climbs-up-hdi.html.

17 'Social Aspects of Sustainable Development in Brunei Darussalam', UN Website, 2014, www.un.org/esa/agenda21/natlinfo/countr/brunei/social.htm.

18 ASEAN Ministerial Meeting on the Environment (AMME), Joint Press State-ment, 5th Information ASEAN Ministerial Meeting on the Environment, Bandar Seri Begawan, 4 April, 2000.

19 'ASEAN – Association of South-East Asian Nations: ASEAN Committee on Cul-ture and Information pushes for stronger regional identity', 4-traders.com, posted 22 November 2013, www.4-traders.com/news/ASEAN-Association-of-South-East-Asia n-Nations–ASEAN-Committee-on-Culture-and-Information-pushes–17488516.

20 Rabiatul Kamit, '14th meeting of ASEAN-COCI SCI Bandar Seri Begawan', *The Brunei Times*, 11 June 2013. Also available at http://asean-summit-2013.tumblr. com/post/52874670621/call-to-raise-asean-awareness.

21 Hadi Soesastro, 'Whither ASEAN Plus Three?' Paper presented at the REGIONAL TRADING ARRANGEMENTS: Stocktake and Next Steps Trade Policy Forum, Bangkok, June 12–13, 2001. Also available at www.hkcpec.org/files/r37.pdf.

22 Ubaidillah Masli, 'Multi-national disaster drill kicks off," *The Brunei Times*, 18 June 2013. Also available at www.bt.com.bn/2013/06/18/multi-national-disaster-drill-kicks.

23 'Overview: ASEAN Plus Three Cooperation', Asean.org, accessed 22 August 2015, www.asean.org/news/item/asean-plus-three-cooperation.

24 'ASEAN Plus Three Cooperation', Embassy of the People's Republic of China in Malaysia. Posted 22 November 2010, http://my.china-embassy.org/eng/zt/eastasia/ jzjk/t771053.htm.

25 'Overview: ASEAN Plus Three Cooperation', Asean.org, accessed 22 August 2015, www.asean.org/news/item/asean-plus-three-cooperation.

26 'Joint Ministerial Statement of the 29th ASEAN Ministers on Energy Meeting (AMEM), Jerudong, Brunei Darussalam', Asean.org, posted 22 September 2011, www.asean.org/news/asean-statement-communiques/item/joint-ministerialstatem ent-of-the-29th-asean-ministers-on-energy-meeting-amem-jerudong-bruneidarussalam-20-september-2011.

27 Adam Radhi and Syazwan Sadikin, 'ASEAN Plus Three to ink rice reserve agreement', *Brunei Times*, 7 October 2011. Also available at www.bt.com.bn/ news-national/2011/10/07/asean-plus-three-ink-rice-reserve-agreement.

References

Agusnuramin (2013) 'ASEAN Free Trade Area (AFTA Council)'. *Wordpress.com*, 2 June. Available from: http://agusnuramin.wordpress.com/2013/06/02/asean-free-trade-area-afta-council.

ASEAN (2013) 'ASEAN – Association of South-East Asian Nations: ASEAN Committee on Culture and Information Pushes for Stronger Regional Identity'. *4-traders.com*, 22 November. Available from: www.4-traders.com/news/ASEAN-Association-of-South-East-Asian-Nations–ASEAN-Committee-on-Culture-and-Information-pushes–17488516.

ASEAN (2010) 'ASEAN Plus Three Cooperation'. Embassy of the People's Republic of China in Malaysia, 22 November. Available from: http://my.china-embassy.org/eng/zt/eastasia/jzjk/t771053.htm.

ASEAN (2011) 'Asean Roadmap for the Attainment of the Millennium Development Goals'. Association of Southeast Asian Nation website, 5 August. Available from: www.asean.org/archive/documents/19th%20summit/MDG-Roadmap.pdf.

ASEAN (2011) 'Joint Ministerial Statement of the 29th ASEAN Ministers on Energy Meeting (AMEM), Jerudong, Brunei Darussalam'. *Asean.org*, 22 September. Available from: www.asean.org/news/asean-statement-communiques/item/joint-ministerialstatement-of-the-29th-asean-ministers-on-energy-meeting-amem-jerudong-bruneidarussalam-20-september-2011.

ASEAN (2000) Ministerial Meeting on the Environment (AMME). *Joint Press Statement, 5th Information ASEAN Ministerial Meeting on the Environment*. Bandar Seri Begawan, 4 April.

ASEAN (n.d.) 'Overview: ASEAN Plus Three Cooperation'. *Asean.org*. Available from: www.asean.org/news/item/asean-plus-three-cooperation (accessed 22 August 2015).

ASEAN (2014) 'Overview: Fundamental Principles'. Association of Southeast Asian Nations Official Website. Available from: www.asean.org/asean/about-asean/overview.

ASEAN Secretariat (2009) *ASEAN Socio-Cultural Community Blueprint*, June, 1.

Asian Development Bank (2015) 'Brunei Darussalam-Indonesia-Malaysia-The Philippines East ASEAN Growth Area (BIMP-EAGA)'. ADB website. Available from: www.adb.org/countries/subregional-programs/bimp-eaga.

Bolkiah, Mohamed (2000) *Time and The River: Brunei Darussalam 1947–2000 a Memoir*. Bandar Seri Begawan: Brunei Press, p. 147.

Borneo Bulletin (2008) 'Sultan Addresses Bali Democracy Forum'. *Borneo Bulletin*, 11 December.

Borneo Bulletin Brunei Yearbook (1997) Brunei Darussalam, Key Information on Brunei.

Broadcasting & Information Department, Prime Minister's Office (1985) *Brunei Darussalam Selamat Datang (Welcome)*, p. 18.

Brunei Ministry of Foreign Affairs and Trade (2015) 'Overview of Brunei FTAs'. Ministry of Foreign Affairs and Trade website. Available from: www.mofat.gov.bn/SitePages/Brunei%20Darussalam%27s%20FTA%20Policy.aspx.

Brunei Resources (2013) 'Brunei Climbs up HDI'. *The Brunei Resources Blog*, 23 March. Available from: http://bruneiresources.blogspot.com/2013/03/brunei-climbs-up-hdi.html.

Cleary, Mark and Wong, S. Yann (1994) *Oil, Economic Development and Diversification in Brunei Darussalam*. London: Macmillan, New York: St. Martin's Press.

Department of Economic Planning and Development, Prime Minister's Office (2008) *Brunei Darussalam Long-Term Development Plan: Wawasan Brunei 2035 Outline of*

Strategies and Policies for Development (OSPD) 2007–2017 and National Development Plan (RKN) 2007–2012.

Department of Statistics, Department of Economic Planning and Development, Prime Minister's Office (2011) *Brunei Darussalam Key Indicators.*

Extract Industries Watch (n.d.) 'Brunei Darussalam'. Extractive Industries Watch website. Available from: www.eiwatch.org/country-profile/brunei-darussalam (accessed 22 August 2015).

Government of Brunei (1988) *Brunei Darussalam in Profile*, London: Shandwick, p. 18.

GRIN (n.d.) 'ASEAN: AFTA and other Free Trade Agreements – Development and Impact on the International Automotive Industry'. *GRIN.com.* Available from: www.grin.com/en/e-book/51626/asean-afta-and-other-free-trade-agreements-development-and-impact-on (accessed 22 August 2015).

Hajar, Siti (2013) 'Reducing Risks of Non-Communicable Diseases'. *The Brunei Times*, 10 October.

Hambali, Norezan (2013) *Case Study on Zero-Poverty Policy of Brunei Darussalam.* IPA, Unpublished report.

Kamit, Rabiatul (2013) '14th meeting of ASEAN-COCI SCI Bandar Seri Begawan'. *The Brunei Times*, 11 June.

Masli, Ubaidillah (2013) 'Multi-national Disaster Drill Kicks Off'. *The Brunei Times*, 18 June.

Ministry of Industry and Primary Resources (MIPR) (1994) *SMEs in Brunei Darussalam*, Bandar Seri Begawan, Brunei Darussalam.

Philippines Embassy (2015) 'Embassy History'. Philippines Embassy in Brunei Darussalam website, 22 August. Available from: http://philippine-embassybrunei.org/the-embassy/embassy-history.

Radhi, Adam and Sadikin, Syazwan (2011) 'ASEAN Plus Three to Ink Rice Reserve Agreement'. *The Brunei Times*, 7 October.

Saim, Sainah (2013) *Social Protection Arrangements in Brunei Darussalam.* Universiti Brunei Darussalam. Unpublished report, p. 24.

Salleh, Yusra (2012) *Towards Enhancing the Promotion and Protection of Human Rights: A Preliminary Study on the Perspective of Human Rights and the Possibility of Establishing a National Human Rights Institution.* Unpublished individual project, Executive Development Programme for Senior Government Officers.

Sapar, Wahab (2011) *Cabaran-cabaran Dalam Pengagihan Zakat Kepada Fakir Miskin Di Negara Brunei Darussalam.* Unpublished individual project, Executive Development Programme for Senior Government Officers, 10 May.

Soesastro, Hadi (2001) 'Whither ASEAN Plus Three?' Paper presented at the REGIONAL TRADING ARRANGEMENTS: Stocktake and Next Steps Trade Policy Forum, Bangkok, 12–13 June.

Too, Debbie. 'Private Sector Key to EAGA Growth'. *The Brunei Times*, 5 April 2012.

Umar, Jamil (1990) *Latar Belakang Sejarah Brunei*, Publication of Jabatan Pusat Sejarah Kementerian Kebudayaan, Belia dan Sukan, Negara Brunei Darussalam.

United Nations (2014) 'Social Aspects of Sustainable Development in Brunei Darussalam'. UN Website. Available from: www.un.org/esa/agenda21/natlinfo/countr/brunei/social.htm.

U.S. Department of State (2014) 'Investment Climate Statements 2014 – Brunei'. Posted June. Available from: www.state.gov/e/eb/rls/othr/ics/2014/index.htm.

2 Cambodia

From isolation to involvement in regional community building

Sorpong Peou

1 Introduction

This chapter contends that Cambodia has since the early 1990s gradually become a positive force for the process of regional integration and community building in Southeast Asia and East Asia. Cambodia overcame its international isolation in the 1980s and, as a member of ASEAN and ASEAN-Plus-Three, has since played a helpful role in the process of regional community building. The Cambodians as a national community have a long history and their history helps shed light on how fast and how far the regional process can be achieved. Their experience further shows that foes can become friends, but any collective vision for a community is not built on an imagined collective identity alone. Friendly states can build a community when their individual identities are protected and when their individual interests are also served. Based on Cambodian experience, the process of regional community building in East Asia is likely to evolve more slowly than expected and any community that emerges in this region is likely to be pluralistic, rather than highly centralised as evident in the European Union.

2 National perspectives

2.1 National identity formation

Cambodia is one of the oldest nations in Southeast Asia, but its long history shows its rise as a kingdom and an empire, its fall accompanied by a series of tragedies, and its recovery. Cambodia did not emerge as a united kingdom; it remained a collection of small states or principalities that traded among themselves and invaded each other for spoils, such as slaves. The kingdom was referred to as Funan. This lasted until the sixth century, but Funan gave way to a new powerful state known as Chenla. According to David Chandler (1993, 15), 'pre-Angkorean Cambodia was not an integrated despotic state … [but] a collection and a sequence of principalities sharing a despotic language of politics and control'. In the tenth century, Cambodia emerged as a unified kingdom under a new name, "Kambuja" – the term first popularised abroad by the Portuguese. The ancient kingdom reached the peak of its glory during the Angkor era (802–1431). King Jayavarman II (r. 802–850) started to build a unified kingdom. He and his twelve Angkorean successors built numerous temple-mountains. King Suryavarman II (r. 1113–c. 1150) built the most famous of these, known today as Angkor Wat. He ruled over a unified kingdom and was the first Angkorean king to establish diplomatic relations with China.

During his visit to Cambodia from 1296 to 1297, a young Chinese envoy by the name of Zhou Daguan (1270–1350) wrote a detailed account of Angkor's everyday life. He found a mighty ecclesiastic capital called Angkor Thom in the centre of Bayon, a great gold tower, and Bapuon, an even taller bronze tower. According to one translation (Zhou 2007, 19), 'In the centre of the kingdom is a golden tower … On the east side is a golden bridge; two gold lions are placed to the left and right of the bridge. Eight gold Buddhas are arranged at the base of stone chambers … To the north of the golden tower is a bronze tower, higher still than the golden tower and really impressive to see …' Observing one marvel after another during his stay in the kingdom, Zhou put down these words: 'I suppose all this explains why from the start there have been merchant seamen who speak glowingly about "rich, noble Cambodia"' (2007, 48).

Still the largest religious temple on our planet and regarded as the supreme masterpiece of Khmer architecture, the temple remains one of the architectural wonders of the world and the pinnacle of a great ancient civilisation – often compared to the architecture of ancient Greece and Rome. In the fifteenth century, some European missionaries even mistakenly referred to 'the ruins of an ancient city … built by the Romans or Alexander the Great'. According to Henri Mouhot, Angkor (with its more than 100 temples and remarkable carvings) was 'grander than anything left by Greece or Rome'. One Portuguese traveller, who passed through Angkor between 1585 and 1588, wrote: 'The temple … is such a strange construction that it cannot be described with the pen, nor can one compare it to any other building in the world … the roof of their vaults is lavishly decorated and terminates in a very high pointed dome, built on innumerable columns with all the refinement that human genius can conceive' (Finot 2001, 141–142). Western visitors even questioned whether the Khmer could build such a temple. Cambodians also used to wonder if angels or a vanished race of giants built it.

Angkor's political glory did not last, however. The empire failed to build effective institutions, including an army, to maintain its power and status. Zhou Daguan (2007, 99), for instance, observed, 'The troops go both barefoot and unclothed … They have neither bows nor arrows, neither ballista nor shot, neither breastplates nor helmets … Generally speaking, these people have neither tactics nor strategy.' Wars between Cambodia and Siam (Thailand) broke out frequently in the fourteenth and fifteen centuries. The most important of the Siamese invasions occurred in 1431. Cambodia's first capital, Yasodharapura, fell when the Siamese army razed it. The Khmer migrated southward to the vicinity of a place known as Phnom Penh, which has remained the capital until today. Conflict among Khmer rulers developed, often leading them to seek protection and support from their two neighbours, Siam and Vietnam.

The Khmer empire continued to decline and often lost its independence to its neighbours. Angkor lay in ruins for centuries, and the ruins did not come to light until the French naturalist Henri Mouhot discovered them when he arrived at Angkor in 1860. Then in 1863, the kingdom became a protectorate of France, and the French called it 'Cambodge'. A new colonial era began in Cambodia that extended until 1953. French hegemony over the kingdom lasted about 90 years. During the latter period of French colonial rule, the colony experienced domestic revolts and rebellions against its rulers. The French then tightened their control over the country and began to regard the latter as part of French administration in Indochina. They also institutionalised communes, whose officials responded directly to the French authorities and later to handpicked Cambodian kings. According to historian David Chandler (1993, 148), 'Until 1953, except for a few months in the summer of 1945, Cambodian officials of high rank played a subordinate, ceremonial role, and those at lower levels of the administration are underpaid servants of a colonial power. At no point in the chain of command was initiative rewarded.' French colonial rule thus left the kingdom politically and institutionally fragmented.

Political and institutional fragmentation also resulted from anti-colonial resistance and inter-colonial competition between France and Japan, but a sense of national identity resurged. Anti-French nationalism began to grow in intensity in the early 1940s, after World War II had broken out. As Japanese forces advanced on Southeast Asia and occupied most countries in the region, and as the French began to lose control after the Japanese jailed French officials and ruled through local leaders, Cambodian nationalism grew. Cambodian intellectuals did not fail to observe the realities of French military weakness then and may have drawn strength from Japanese sympathy for their anti-French sentiments. During this period, the hand-picked king of Cambodia, Norodom Sihanouk, responded to a formal request from the Japanese and declared Cambodian independence on 13 March 1945. Sihanouk then changed the French name for Cambodia, from 'Cambodge', to 'Kampuchea', issued a decree that invalidated Franco-Cambodian agreements, and pledged his country's cooperation with the Japanese. But Cambodia did not gain its independence from France then; the colonial power made a comeback following Japan's defeat and resumed its colonial rule in the summer of 1945. The French soon loosened its hold on the colony, but still maintained control over key areas of government, most notably finance, foreign affairs and national defence. Cambodia eventually gained its independence in 1953.

In short, the Cambodians developed a collective identity over a long period of time, and it was during the Angkor period that they saw themselves as a unified nation. Although not known for their philosophical sophistication, these people identify themselves as one whose ancestors built many magnificent temples, most notably Angkor Wat – their cultural home. Foreign attacks, domination and interferences helped reinforce their sense of national identity and victimhood, but their collective identity did not prevent domestic turmoil, violence and war.

2.2 Political-security development

Cambodia's democratic act, introduced in 1946 and allowing Cambodians to establish political parties and compete in elections, gave way to Prince Sihanouk's paternalistic authoritarianism. After independence, Cambodia enjoyed more than a decade of political stability before the country plunged into the abyss of war and violent repression. The initial stability resulted from the authoritarian politics of Sihanouk, who abdicated the throne in March 1955 and founded a national political movement known as the *Sangkum Reastr Niyum* (People's Socialist Community). As the father of independence, the Prince regarded himself as the 'natural ruler' of his country. Although his regime first brought about stability, it faced growing opposition from the left and right, subsequently ran into trouble, and eventually collapsed when his Minister of Defence, General Lon Nol, ousted him in a bloodless coup in 1970 (Peou 2000a).

The Khmer Republic under the leadership of President Lon Nol emerged as an electoral democracy but the system was subsequently afflicted by traditional authoritarianism. Soon afterwards, the new regime faced growing challenges, most notably a civil war launched by a leftist movement known as the Khmer Rouge (Red Khmer or Communist Khmer) led by Pol Pot and other Cambodian intellectuals. The war spread across the country in a short period of time and came to an end in April 1975, when the Khmer Rouge army defeated the republican forces (Peou 2000a).

The end of the civil war did not usher in a new era of freedom, peace and security for Cambodians, however. The new Khmer Rouge regime under the radical leadership of Prime Minister Pol Pot quickly began its reign of terror, turning the country into 'killing fields'. The murderous totalitarian regime proved far more ruthless than any other regimes the country had ever known; in just a few years, between one and two million Cambodians perished. In view of its responsibility for the deaths of its own people and the destruction of its political enemies and the nation as a whole, the Pol Pot regime did not last long. Late in December 1978, Vietnam intervened militarily in Cambodia, putting an end to the nightmare (Peou 1997, 2000a).

The Vietnamese military intervention did not bring peace to Cambodia, however. In fact, the war – known as the Third Indochina War – became further internationalised and continued through the 1980s. A new regime – the People's Republic of Kampuchea (PRK) – was set up in Phnom Penh, led by a group of former Khmer Rouge officials who enjoyed the support of their

Vietnamese and other allies in the Soviet bloc. The new socialist regime offered Cambodians more freedom and security, but could not put an end to the war. Three major armed resistance factions were the United National Front for an Independent, Neutral, Peaceful, and Co-operative Cambodia (FUNCINPEC) founded by Prince Sihanouk, the Khmer People's National Liberation Front (KPNLF) led by former Prime Minister Son Sann, and the Democratic Kampuchea (DK) led by Khmer Rouge remnants. Together they formed a collation government-in-exile known as the Coalition Government of Democratic Kampuchea (CGDK).

On 23 October 1991, the armed factions – the PRK (later changed to State of Cambodia or SOC) and the three CGDK partners – signed a peace deal, known as the Paris Peace Agreements, which offered Cambodia a new lease of life by enabling the United Nations Transitional Authority in Cambodia (UNTACT) to undertake a massive UN peace-keeping operation in Cambodia and later supervise general elections in 1993 (Peou 1997). (The fighting did not end until 1998, however. The Khmer Rouge turned its back on the Agreements, defying the international community and continuing its rebellion until its final disintegration, after internal fighting within the movement and especially after Pol Pot's death in 1998.)

After the national election in 1993, in which FUNCINPEC won but was forced to share power with the Cambodian People's Party of the SOC, Cambodia re-emerged as a kingdom, whose motto 'Nation, Religion, and King' appears in the Constitution, and established itself as a constitutional monarchy. Following King Sihanouk's abdication, his son Norodom Sihamoni took over the throne from his father on 14 October 2004. The monarch serves as Head of State. Cambodia now has a large number of political parties, but the extent to which Cambodia has become democratic remains a matter of debate. The ruling party, the CPP, regards the country as a democracy based on free and fair elections, but the opposition parties continue to challenge this label. The truth lies somewhere in between. On the positive side, Cambodians have witnessed the regular holding of national and communal elections. National elections took place in 1993, 1998, 2003, and 2013. Three commune elections were held in 2001, 2007 and 2012. On the negative side, however, the CPP has always dominated the political arena. It lost in the 1993 election, but Hun Sen managed to be elected Second Prime Minister. The end of the co-prime minister system, devised after the 1993 elections, followed disagreements between the two political leaders, Prince Norodom Ranariddh and Hun Sen, resulting in the ouster of Prince Ranariddh. After the 1998 parliamentary election, Hun Sen emerged as the sole leader of the country and has managed to stay in power since 1985, when he emerged as the world's youngest prime minister at the age of 33. The CPP has won the subsequent elections (Peou 2014).

Democracy became more liberal as evident in the 2013 election in that the CPP government allowed elections to take place but still sought to prevent the opposition from winning them (Peou 2014). Hun Sen's grip on political power weakened when two opposition parties (Sam Rainsy Party and Human Rights Party) formed the Cambodian National Rescue Party (CNRP) in 2012 prior to the election in July 2013. The election results came as a shock to the CPP, when it lost 22 seats as the CNRP captured 55 out of 123 seats. The CNRP, however, claimed that it won 63 seats. The government subsequently deployed troops and armed vehicles to crack down on any anti-government protests, but the opposition continued to lead demonstrations. Although armed politics began to disappear in the early 2000s, the government continued to rely on force as a way to maintain power and regime security. Thus, peace and security have improved but are far from ideal.

2.3 Socioeconomic development

The immediate post-French colonial period saw Cambodia enjoy a period of economic development, thanks in part to French colonial rule, which contributed to the urbanisation of the country, the development of infrastructure and public works, and the construction of rubber plantations and the introduction of cotton and corn crops. Political stability under Prince Sihanouk's authoritarian rule was a major factor for economic development. The Cambodian economy, however, began to suffer badly from many years of instability, war and poor policies (especially during the Khmer Rouge period when the Pol Pot regime dismantled the existing economic system, including the abolishment of money and transformation into a socialist system based on the policy of autarky). The Cambodian forces that toppled the Pol Pot regime in 1979 were backed by Vietnam and established a socialist command economy.

Late in the 1980s, the new regime moved away from the centrally planned to a market-based economy and '[t]he principal goal of the Cambodia's foreign economic policy is to expand and strengthen economic ties [with other states] … through the integration of the Cambodian economy into the regional and world economy' (Hang 2012, 275).

The post-Cold War capitalist-oriented economy has resulted in commendable growth rates with gross domestic product or GDP growing at an average rate of about 6 or 7 per cent (4 per cent in 2000, 4 per cent in 2001, 5.3 per cent in 2002, 5.2 per cent in 2003, 5 per cent in 2004, 5.4 per cent in 2005, 13.4 per cent in 2006, 7.2 per cent in 2007, 10.1 per cent in 2008, 5 per cent in 2009, −1.5 per cent in 2010, 6.9 per cent in 2011, and 7.3 per cent in 2012). According to the Asian Development Bank (2013), the economy was expected to grow by 7.2 per cent and to pick up to 7.5 per cent in 2014. As per Senior Country Economist Aldaz Caroll, 'Cambodia has joined the Olympians of growth. With an annual average of 7.7 percent for two decades, it is now the sixth-fastest in the world from 1993 to 2013' (Cited in World Bank 2014).

Several factors have fuelled economic growth, including agricultural production, the expansion of domestic consumption, construction, garment exports, tourism, foreign investment, and foreign aid which amounted to approximately $9 billion from 1992 to 2010 (Asian Development Bank 2014; Pou 2012, 339, 341). Foreign direct investment continues to grow; from only $2.65 billion in 2007 to $10.8 billion in subsequent years. Commercial banks have fuelled consumerism by providing loans recently worth about $9.5 billion (Prak 2014). The average inflation rate from 1995 to 2014 was 5.39 per cent (Trading Economics, Undated).

Various recent indicators also show progress on the socioeconomic front. The human development index (HDI) for Cambodia from 1980 to 2012 shows a sign of slow but gradual improvement. The HDI scores increased to 0.543 in 2012 (placing Cambodia in 138th place among 187 countries), from 0.411 in 1980. When the 2012 HDI was inequality-adjusted, the score was lower: only 0.402. Life expectancy at birth also increased: by 24.9 years between 1980 and 2012 and by 8 years between 1990 and 2012. Another source indicates that life expectation increased from only 19.50 years (1977) to 41.93 (1982), 54.75 (1990), 61.89 (2000), 70.64 (2010), and 71.41 (2012) (Countyeconoy.com). Expected years of schooling rose to 10.5 in 2012 from 6.5 in 1990 (UNDP 2013). Poverty declined to below 20 per cent (Asian Development Bank 2014, 219), compared to nearly 50 per cent in the early 1990s and 35 per cent in 2004 (Pou 2012, 341). Recent research findings are encouraging when pointing to an increase in overall inequality between 1993–1994 and 2007 but a decrease after that. According to one report, 'The trend since 2007–08 [0.42] is that of a decline in overall inequality, with a sharper reduction in the period 2010–13 and with "sustained and dramatic decline in Gini Index" [0.34 in 2010 and 0.32 in 2013]' (Kumar & Ny, Undated). The employment rate is high. Over 97 per cent of the population (14.9 million) was employed in 2012 (NIS and ILO 2013), although the quality of jobs remains poor. This shows economic growth has created jobs – a positive sign that the socioeconomic conditions have improved – but unskilled or semi-skilled labour remains a problem.

These positive indicators should not, however, be translated to mean most Cambodians remain content with the status quo and that the regime now enjoys unconditional legitimacy. Public demonstrations after the 2013 election, for instance, were not directed only at the election results but also against corruption, illegal land-grabbing and low wages. Garment workers received an average wage of $80 per month and pushed for a monthly minimum wage of $160; but the government was prepared to increase the wage to only $100 (Diplomat 2014). Political and social discontent is likely to continue unless or until most Cambodians enjoy a much higher standard of living. Due to economic growth, the country's tax revenue has increased in recent years but it is not large enough to cover all expenditures. Cambodia's reliance on import taxes would make it difficult for the country to comply with AEC tariff requirements. As will be seen later, Cambodian trade has experienced deficits, as the country has imported far more than it has exported.

2.4 Socio-Cultural development

Since the early 1980s, there has been a revival of socio-cultural identity. Cambodia now has a fast-growing population made up of different ethnic groups: Khmer, Chinese, Cham, Vietnamese, Thai, and various tribes. However, the country remains largely homogeneous in that the Khmer make up the largest ethnic group, with its own language and cultural traditions.

The Cambodian people use their common language to describe themselves as 'Khmer', identify themselves as a collective group ('*Khmer Yoeung*'), and refer to their country as '*Srok Khmer*'. The Khmer have their own unique cultural history in terms of language. History reveals the Khmer as a distinct cultural identity amongst the inhabitants of Cambodia. Before the Angkor period, they spoke languages related to that spoken by contemporary Cambodians – known as Khmer. These languages belonged to the Mon-Khmer family, found scattered widely over mainland Southeast Asia and even some parts of India.

The Cambodians remain proud of their cultural tradition and are generally conservative. Their proverbs provide some clues to their conservative mentality. One proverb, for instance, admonishes them: 'Don't reject the crooked road and don't take the straight one; instead, take the road travelled by the ancestors.' Another says: 'Don't brag about yourself; you may be shamed by traditional wisdom.' According to one scholar, these Khmer proverbs provide a theme highlighting 'the importance of tradition, including respect for the ways things have always been done. Trying something new is not encouraged' (Fisher-Nguyen 1994, 97).

Cambodians also consider themselves bound by a common form of fine arts. Three Western scholars have pointed out that, 'the arts...are often taken as the hallmarks of Khmer culture'. Khmer traditional culture includes masked dance, shadow play, *basăk* and *yike* theatres, and alternate singing called '*ayai*'. According to one Cambodian scholar, Sam-Ang Sam (1994, 41–42), 'present-day Khmer musical forms are the living continuation of the musical tradition of the ancient Khmer ... Before 1975 the arts reached audiences of every class in society; the University of Fine Arts ... had organized several performing tours each year, taking artistic productions to villages throughout the country, even to remote areas'. The Khmer Rouge regime destroyed much of the fine arts, killing most Cambodian artists and musicians, both performers and teachers (approximately 90 per cent of them), who fell victim to its 'cultural revolution' between 1975 and 1978. According to Sam (1994, 47), 'We have lost our most able musicians, artists who have devoted their entire lives to gaining knowledge and ability'. During the 1980s, however, Cambodians tried to revive their art and music. Those living overseas have contributed greatly to the restoration of their traditions. They hold traditional wedding ceremonies and participate in major cultural events (e.g., the New Year in April), often accompanied by traditional dances, theatre performances and traditional Khmer music.

One cannot fully understand Cambodian culture and identity without an understanding of religious influence, however. Cambodians are now allowed to practise different religions and religious tolerance is a norm. Christian churches enjoy freedom of worship. At the end of the 1990s, there were 376 churches (with 49,026 followers) and 85 Christian schools. Christians freely exercise their faith. A few churches have antagonised angry villagers, but this type of threat has been isolated and died down quickly. Muslims also enjoy the same religious freedom. By the end of the 1990s, they had built at least 202 mosques and 150 Muslim schools. In 2003, about 500,000 Cham Muslims lived in Cambodia. Other religions permitted to operate include Baha'i, Kao Dai, Khong Moeng, Kong Si Im, Mahayana Buddhism, and Miloeuk. Buddhism, however, remains Cambodia's most dominant religion. At the end of the 1990s, Cambodia had approximately 3,685 pagodas (of which 3,588 belonged to the Mahanikay). Today, some 95 per cent of Cambodians practise Theravada Buddhism, which was promoted by Cambodian kings and has existed at least since the fifth century. For Cambodian Buddhists, 'to be Khmer is to be Buddhist'.

In short, Cambodia as a nation has a long history and a rich cultural tradition, but these factors alone have not prevented its people from engaging in violence and armed conflict. Political instability and social unrest rooted in political and socioeconomic injustices have stood in the way of Cambodia becoming a mature national community. All this helps shed further light on the process of regional community building in Southeast and East Asia.

3 Cambodia's role in ASEAN

3.1 Political-security relations: From enmity to amity

Cambodia–ASEAN relations improved noticeably after the country became a member of the regional group in 1999. Prior to obtaining ASEAN membership, as will be discussed, Cambodia was regarded by ASEAN as a security challenge to regional peace and stability.

Throughout the 1980s, members of ASEAN considered the Vietnamese military intervention in Cambodia as a form of invasion against a sovereign state. As a result, ASEAN extended its diplomatic support to the Coalition Government of Democratic Kampuchea (CGDK). The 10-year struggle to find a peaceful solution to the Cambodian problem included ASEAN and Indonesia-led efforts, notably at the two Jakarta Informal meetings during the second half of the 1980s, to find a political settlement to the situation (Acharya et al. 1991). The Indonesian efforts to resolve the Cambodia conflict did not bear much fruit, however, because of the competing interests between external great powers, namely China, the Soviet Union and the United States. Overall, however, the Cambodia conflict helped ASEAN, according to Rodolfo C. Severino and Mark Hong (2012, 46), 'solidify ASEAN as a cohesive regional association'.

It was not until the Vietnamese troop withdrawal from Cambodia in 1989 and the collapse of the Berlin Wall in November 1989 as the result of the Soviet Union's decision to loosen its grip on its East European allies, that the Cambodian peace process took a promising turn. Moscow, Beijing and Washington were then ready to work on a resolution to the Cambodia conflict. Under growing pressure from members of the international community, especially from the permanent members of the UN Security Council (namely, China, France, Russia, the United Kingdom, and the United States), the PRK (later renamed the State of Cambodia or SOC) signed the Paris Peace Agreements on 23 October 1991 with the three resistance forces.

The Peace Agreements ended Cambodia's international isolation. Until the early 1990s, it maintained diplomatic ties with states within the socialist bloc led by the former Soviet Union. Vietnam remained Cambodia's most important regional military ally. After the 1993 election, however, the new government restored its diplomatic relations with non-socialist states. The Peace Agreements paved the way for the UN to intervene in Cambodia. The United Nations Transitional Authority in Cambodia began the deployment of its civilian and military personnel in 1992 and then prepared the 1993 election. ASEAN supported the Paris Peace Agreements. The six ASEAN members – Brunei, Indonesia, Malaysia, Singapore, Thailand, and the Philippines – were also signatories of the Peace Agreements. Although ASEAN proved ineffective in terms of its ability to end the Cambodia conflict, its support for the peace process and UNTAC proved to be very useful in terms of ending Cambodian isolation.

Cambodia's contributions to the process of regional peace and community building became even more positive after the country joined ASEAN in 1999. The country would have entered ASEAN together with Laos and Myanmar in July 1997, but a political turmoil led to the postponement of Cambodia's membership. As a new member of ASEAN, Cambodia initially raised alarms when it was perceived as a force that was part of an alliance within ASEAN. In October 1999, for example, Cambodia and the other two most recent entrants to ASEAN (Laos and Vietnam) held an unofficial Indochina summit meeting, where Hun Sen and his Laotian and Vietnamese counterparts expressed their joint opposition to outside intervention in the newly independent territory of East Timor (now Timor-Leste), previously part of Indonesia. The initial concern that Cambodia may have undermined ASEAN unity turned out to be less serious than it appeared. At the ASEAN Summit in November 2012, Hun Sen urged the ASEAN leaders to prioritise the 2015 deadline for ASEAN community building, viewing this development as a way to ensure regional peace and security. He called for more action to strengthen and complete a legal regional framework in line with the ASEAN Charter. In spite of his earlier reservation about settling competing claims over the South China Sea, to be discussed later, he also contended that the culture of compliance with ASEAN could be strengthened if the protocol on the Charter's Dispute Settlement Mechanisms could be ratified (Hun 2012).

The call for the ratification of dispute settlement mechanisms sheds some light on Cambodia's frustrations with ASEAN's inability to resolve its territorial disputes with Thailand, as the two countries had exchanged fire across their borders over an ancient temple known as Preah Vihear. It is questionable whether ASEAN will be able to establish such mechanisms and make them work effectively in the foreseeable future. Even if the group could establish such mechanisms, the question remains: Would they have enough teeth to enforce judicial decisions? Thailand, for instance, has refused to accept the recent ruling in favour of Cambodia by the International Court of Justice. As long as ASEAN remains unable to resolve disputes among its members, the group is unlikely to become a mature politico-security community.

On the positive side of things, the ongoing territorial disputes between Cambodia and Thailand may encourage ASEAN to think more seriously about the need to establish dispute settlement mechanisms, especially if the 2015 timeframe is not met. The group cannot keep coming up with new timeframes based on wishful thinking. Somewhere down the road, they must take concrete steps away from the so-called 'ASEAN Way' that basically allows member states to have their way subject to no higher body of authority. Scant evidence suggests that ASEAN has moved in a positive direction, however. When Indonesia was ASEAN Chair in 2011, President Susilo Bambang Yudhoyono did something unprecedented when he put pressure on Bangkok and Phnom Penh to sit down for talks over their disputes (Moss 2011).

Overall, Cambodia has made a positive contribution to ASEAN's politico-security community project, particularly after it joined the group in 1999. As one of the small states in Southeast Asia, the country tends to rely on both major powers and international institutions for its survival and security. The fact that Cambodia took its case against Thailand to the International Court of Justice over their territorial disputes means that Phnom Penh had some faith in the institution, although it did not have faith in ASEAN's ability to decide on the matter. It came as no surprise then that the government in Phnom Penh has favoured the idea of establishing dispute settlement mechanisms in ASEAN, as it realised that it could not deal with more powerful states like Thailand from the position of strength, military or otherwise. Furthermore, the CPP government has a strong interest in ensuring its hold on political power through the ASEAN norm of non-interference in members' domestic affairs. This does not mean that Cambodia's role in the process of security community building is ideal because much of what has been achieved so far remains almost exclusively elite-driven.

3.2 Economic relations: From cooperation to integration

The government of Cambodia has been formally supportive of regional economic integration and community building. As a matter of policy, the

Cambodian government has been a strong advocate of an ASEAN Economic Community. According to a top-ranking Cambodian official, his government 'has strengthened its efforts to meet the demands of ASEAN membership. Domestic laws are being changed to conform to ASEAN standards in trade, finance, commerce and investment' (Hang 2012, 277). At the ASEAN Summit in April 2012, Prime Minister Hun Sen further made the case for the economic community: 'We should place priority on the establishment of the ASEAN Economic Community by 2015, to transform ASEAN as a single market and production base, with free flow of goods services, investment and skilled labor' (Hun 2012, 4).

The Cambodian support of a regional economic community rests on several conditions, one of which is that Phnom Penh would like to see the wide gaps between rich and poor ASEAN members narrow. In November 2002, Cambodia hosted the eighth ASEAN Summit meeting and Prime Minister Hun Sen reaffirmed his support for ASEAN's commitment to the 'Initiative for ASEAN Integration', which aims to close the development gap between the older and newer members of ASEAN. In fact, GDP per capita (2009) shows that Cambodia ($692) remained the second poorest country in Southeast Asia, poorer than Laos ($910), Vietnam ($1,119), the Philippines ($1,749), Indonesia ($2,363), Thailand ($3,950), Malaysia ($6,822), Brunei ($26,486), and Singapore ($36,631) (Furuoka, Lim, Mahmud, and Hanim Pazim, 2012, p.70). During a speech at the ASEAN Summit in April 2012, Prime Minister Hun Sen again emphasised the need for ASEAN to further narrow development gaps among the member states. His words are quite telling: 'Although the development gap among ASEAN members has been noticeably narrowed, it is still huge....Indeed, narrowing such development gaps is not only a precondition for ensuring ASEAN competitiveness and reducing poverty of our people but also for helping ASEAN achieve real regional integration' (Hun 2012, 3).

Cambodian officials have expressed hesitation about joining the ASEAN Economic Community in 2015. The hesitation is understandable, given that its economy is among the least competitive and dependent on import taxes (Hruby 2014). The ASEAN Economic Community requires that its members open their doors to foreign workers and reduce important taxes to zero. Cambodia would not be in a position to attract skilled labour, since it would not be able to pay them enough in the foreseeable future and would experience a brain drain as skilled and professional Cambodians would seek employment in wealthier ASEAN countries.

Even if the overall level of economic growth has been positive, most Cambodian products have been exported to the West, especially the European Union and the United States. Moreover, trade balances between Cambodia and other ASEAN states tend to be negative. Cambodia continues to import more ASEAN products than it exports. In 2013, for instance, Cambodia's exports to ASEAN countries were worth $482 million, but its imports amounted to $3.68 billion. While the overall trade volume was up by 12 per cent – to \$4.16 billion in 2013 from \$3.71 billion in 2012, Cambodia's trade deficit remained substantial (Xinhua 2014). Trade deficit persists and remains a concern for the Cambodians. As one Cambodian scholar, Chhean Vannarith, puts it, 'Cambodia does not have many goods for exporting to other ASEAN countries while imports keep increasing. Hence, its trade deficit is anticipated to significantly enlarge in terms of trade in the ASEAN region' (cited in *Economics Today* 2012). Another long-term challenge for Cambodia is that the country mainly exports raw materials and imports manufactured and high-tech products and, as a result, the country will continue to experience negative terms of trade, namely, selling cheap products in order to buy expensive products.

Confronted by trade deficits with countries in Southeast Asia, weak bureaucratic structures and limited national revenue, Cambodia remains unprepared for entry into an ASEAN economic community. The AEC requires all members to reduce tariff rates to zero and have a one-step shop to expedite custom clearance. Scepticism about Cambodia's preparedness continues, however, despite the fact that its government has approved a draft law to simplify customs procedures in line with other ASEAN members and that it 'would implement a simplified, automated Certificate of Origin service by March 2015' (Morton 2014).

As long as Cambodia is still behind other ASEAN members in socio-economic terms, the prospects for success in the process of economic regional community building still look far from complete. Because of poor socio-economic conditions at home, many Cambodians have sought work in other ASEAN countries, but their working conditions in the host countries are far from ideal. From the Cambodian government's perspective, regional economic integration requires that the other ASEAN states that host Cambodian workers improve their working conditions, which are poor. The rights of Cambodian workers in Malaysia and Thailand, for instance, have been subject to abuse and violence. After the military coup in May 2014 that ousted the civilian government in Thailand, approximately 250,000 Cambodian migrant workers crossed the border back to Cambodia. The ASEAN community project still excludes the free movement of workers and offers no effective measures for migrant worker rights (Furuoka et al. 2012). These shortcomings make it difficult for the ASEAN members, especially the poorer ones, to develop a stronger sense of community.

3.3 Socio-cultural relations: Unity in cultural diversity

Cambodia's socio-cultural values also have the potential to contribute to the process of socio-cultural community building. This does not mean to suggest that the Cambodians and other peoples in Southeast Asia completely share what has come to be known as 'Asian values'.

As noted earlier, Buddhism plays a central role in Cambodian society and is a national religion that three other countries in the region also share: Laos,

Myanmar and Thailand. The other ASEAN countries have embraced other religions: Catholicism (the Philippines), Islam (Brunei, Indonesia, and Malaysia). Confucianism has influenced Singapore (although it prides itself on being a secular state) and Vietnam (still a socialist state). In other words, ASEAN may never become as highly centralised as the EU with some form of a top-down government structure. Unlike the European Union where the member states share similar Christian traditions and modern secularism, the ASEAN members remain diverse in religious and cultural terms. What such diversity suggests is that ASEAN has the potential to develop a sense of cultural community that is pluralistic in the form of unity in cultural diversity.

The Declaration on ASEAN Unity in Cultural Diversity adopted in 2011 came as no surprise to observers of the region. Any attempts to unify by force the cultural values in Southeast Asia under one umbrella are likely to fail. At the same time, the notion of community in cultural diversity is a challenging task indeed. It is through this lens of regional cultural diversity that a loose or decentralised community can be built. Cambodia provides a lesson on how such community can be built. Cambodia embraces the idea (Hun 2012), but it needs to be emphasised that cultural similarities do not necessarily help bind states as a community. Throughout their history, Cambodia and Thailand as well as Myanmar and Thailand shared similar Buddhist traditions, but they were often at war with each other. The recent territorial disputes and armed clashes between Cambodia and Thailand provide testimony to the fact that the two neighbouring Buddhist countries could not avoid using force to settle their disputes, despite the shared Buddhist doctrine of pacifism. In July 2008, for instance, UNESCO registered the temple as a world cultural heritage, but Thailand contested. A series of armed clashes between the two ASEAN members broke out and bilateral tensions remain.

Overall, the recognition of distinct cultural traditions embraced by ASEAN may provide important glue that helps bind them together. Since the Cambodians are proud of their cultural traditions and heritage, the ASEAN project to build a socio-cultural community based on the recognition of each member's cultural achievements has been a positive step. Although cultural exchanges and appreciation grow, ASEAN members cannot expect socio-cultural integration to deepen automatically. More needs to be done to ensure that cultural pride does not become a source of competition and hostility, as the territorial disputes over Preah Vihear Temple between Cambodia and Thailand show. Academic institutions and students may need to be mobilised for further action on intellectual and cultural learning that will give rise to a socio-cultural identity within ASEAN (Koh 2014). Prime Minister Hun Sen (2012) suggested that ASEAN 'push for the establishment of the ASEAN Socio-Cultural Fund in order to carry out social-cultural activities aimed at promoting people-to-people connectivity in ASEAN Countries, as well as other activities under the framework of the ASEAN Socio-Cultural Council'.

Overall, Cambodia has contributed to the process of ASEAN community building, but it remains difficult to see how Cambodia would effectively meet the 2015 AEC deadline. It is reasonable to assume that the country would do its best to adapt under any challenging circumstances but that the AEC would not get off to a smooth start. Regional integration is after all a process, not an outcome, and thus bound to evolve by fits and starts. With political and cultural diversity, ASEAN as a whole is likely to develop into a pluralistic regional community different from the EU or North America (Peou 2002). This regional character helps explain why ASEAN has emerged more as an open-regional community as opposed to closed regionalism in Europe and further explains a broader but similar regional community development in the form of ASEAN+3, which includes China, Japan, and South Korea, to be discussed next.

4 Cambodia and ASEAN Plus Three (ASEAN+3)

Cambodia has adopted a formal policy that supports an East Asian (ASEAN+3) community. At the third international conference on Asian political parties in 2004 held in Beijing, Prime Minister Hun Sen confirmed that, 'East Asia cooperation has been growing through the ASEAN+3 mechanism, moving step by step towards an East Asian community' (Hun 2004). Cambodia's rich cultural traditions have also attracted regional attention, recognition and support, and deepening sociocultural relations have contributed to the process of regional integration. The country's contributions to the process of East Asian community building have been especially in the realm of its bilateral partnership with Japan and China.

4.1 Cambodia–South Korean relations

Since normalisation of diplomatic ties between Cambodia and South Korea in 1996 (after their ties were severed in 1975), relations between the two countries have deepened. Cambodia saw South Korea as a role model for economic development. Korean investment in Cambodia has grown. Cambodia has considered South Korea an important development partner.

On the economic front, Cambodia and South Korea have deepened their relations. In 2008, the two countries signed six agreements to strengthen their bilateral cooperation. In 2012, South Korea became one of the largest investors in Cambodia when it invested $287 million (Ser 2009). South Koreans have invested in building projects, like skyscrapers in Phnom Penh, such as Golden Tower 42, Camko City, and the billion-dollar International Finance Complex. Bilateral trade rose dramatically in recent years, reaching nearly $1 billion in 2012 (compared to $540 million in 2011, $376.442 in 2010, $26.431 in 2009; $308.76 in 2008; $290.12 in 2007) (Ser 2009; Kun 2011, 2010, 2009). However, Cambodia continued to experience trade deficits. In 2012, South Korean exports to Cambodia were worth more than $900 million, whereas Cambodian exports to South Korea were worth only $70 million (Chheang 2013).

As its business interests in Cambodia grew, South Korea also began to deepen its political-military relations with the Hun Sen government. One of Hun Sen's foreign economic advisors, Lee Myung Bak (appointed in 2000), was elected South Korea's president in 2008. In October 2009, President Lee visited Cambodia, where the two countries signed additional economic cooperation agreements. South Korea was the first democracy to congratulate the CPP on its victory in the 2013 election. According to one source (Cain 2014), 'Over the past decade, the South Korean military has dispatched a handful of retired military officers to advise the Royal Cambodian Armed Forces'. South Korea is also known as 'a patron' of Hun Sen's bodyguard unit, Brigade 70 and helped fund the brigade's $28 million tank storage facility. Critics even accused Seoul of pulling the strings behind the violent crackdowns on protests by angry factory workers late in 2013 (Cain 2014). However, it is reasonable to conclude that the Cambodian government simply sought to help protect Korean business interests.

In short, Cambodian–South Korean relations have grown in various forms – from the severance to the restoration of diplomatic ties and subsequently to the deepening of investment, trade, and political-military relations. Personal relations between political elites in the two countries and their economic interests have made a difference in terms of enhancing bilateral cooperation between the two countries – a positive development for the multilateral framework of an East Asian community.

4.2 Cambodian–Japanese partnership

Although Japan did not initially play a major role in the Cambodian process, its contributions to peace and security in Cambodia have been significant. From early on after the Vietnamese military intervention, Japan did make an effort to help put pressure on Vietnam to end its military presence in Cambodia. Japan was involved in the Paris International Conference on Cambodia in 1989. In 1990, Japan also sought to establish direct contact with the government in Phnom Penh as part of the peace efforts, seeing the regime as a party to reconcile with because of its control over 90 per cent of the country, and held a conference in Tokyo. Japan continued this diplomatic effort in 1991. However, the Japanese role was more supportive of the UN P-5 peace plan than impactful. With the expectation that Japan would make financial contributions to the work of UNTAC, in January 1992 the United Nations appointed a Japanese citizen and a senior UN bureaucrat as Special Representative of the UN Secretary General and head of the UN mission. In June 1992, Japan also contributed troops to the mission, after having passed a controversial peace-keeping law. Seventy-five police officers, 1,200 troops from its Self-Defense Forces and 50 election observers were dispatched to Cambodia (Pou and Imagawa 2012, 128). Japan also played a key role in brokering a peace deal between rival Cambodian factions after the coup that ousted the first Prime Minister Norodom Ranariddh in July 1997 (Lam 2012, 110).

After the UN mission ended in 1993, Japan continued to play a major role as a donor in Cambodia and trade relations between the two countries have increased. On average, Tokyo has provided Cambodia with more than $100 million in aid per year. Between 1992 and 2010, Japan gave Cambodia about $1.76 billion (Pou and Imagawa 2012, 122). In December 2013, Japan pledged to give Cambodia $134 million in new loans for three infrastructure projects. According to official data, Cambodia has also enjoyed a trade surplus with Japan. Cambodia's exports to Japan totaled $209 in 2010, $309 million in 2011 and $404 million in 2012. Japanese exports to Cambodia were less: $158 million in 2010, $205 million in 2011 and $244 million in 2012 (Phnom Penh Post 23 December 2013). Overall, their bilateral relations have favoured Cambodia, and this suggests that economic integration between the two countries has deepened.

Overall, Japan's role in Cambodia has given rise to a positive development in their bilateral relationship and thus contributed to the process of East-Asian community building. Cambodia has benefited from Japanese aid, which seems to pay off when the Cambodian government decided in December 2013 to upgrade its relations with Japan – from the existing form of 'new partnership' to 'strategic partnership'. What this meant was that Cambodia and Japan finally concluded a memorandum on military cooperation (Phorn 2013). Cambodia's dependence on Japanese investment has deepened. Japanese investment in Cambodia has increased from just $35 million in 2010 to $328 million in 2012. During this period, the number of Japanese business registrations increased from 19 to 195.

4.3 Sino–Cambodian partnership

Economic and diplomatic relations between Cambodia and China have grown. According to Xinhua (2013), China's loans and grants given to Cambodia since 1992 amounted to $2.7 billion, making China Cambodia's largest bilateral donor. In November 2014, Chinese President Xi Jinping pledged to provide Cambodia with annual aid of $500 to $700 million. China has also become Cambodia's largest military donor. From 1994 to 2012 China's total investment in Cambodia totaled $9.17 billion. Bilateral trade has also grown, reaching $2.9 billion in 2012 and is expected to reach $5 billion by 2017.

The rise of China, close Sino–Cambodian relations and ongoing Sino–Japanese territorial disputes, however, present some of the key challenges to regional community building in East Asia in the form of ASEAN+3. At the ASEAN Foreign Ministers Meeting in July 2012, Cambodia was viewed as undermining ASEAN unity on the territorial disputes in the South China Sea and was blamed for it. At the 2012 ASEAN Summit, Cambodia failed to put the territorial disputes on the agenda, and this failure raised controversy among some ASEAN officials and observers who accused Phnom Penh of bowing to Chinese pressure (Thayer 2012).

But one could argue that close relations between Cambodia and China may be a positive development in that Cambodia can play a role in keeping China engaged in the region and that Cambodia is not subservient to China's interests. It is worth recalling that Cambodia as ASEAN Chair in 2002 succeeded in getting the ASEAN members and China to adopt a legally non-binding Declaration on the Conduct of Parties in the South China Sea (DOC). Although it has proved to be far from successful in terms of its impact on the territorial disputes in the South China Sea, the DOC emphasises dispute settlement through peaceful means, meaning that the ASEAN members and China will refrain from using military means to settle their competing maritime claims. Further progress was made when ASEAN and China adopted another document in 2011 known as *The Guidelines for the Implementation of the Declaration of Conduct*.

The common perception that Cambodia was to blame for the ASEAN leaders' failure to issue a joint communique for the first time in its 45-year history is understandable, but the failure should also be treated as a potentially positive lesson for regional community building. It is far from clear that putting the disputes over maritime territories on the 2012 ASEAN agenda would have yielded more positive results for ASEAN+3, especially when China was opposed to it. Putting controversial issues on the back burner as part of ASEAN's culture of conflict avoidance may have served a good purpose for the incremental process of regional integration.

Moreover, blaming Cambodia would do ASEAN+3 little good. Disagreement within ASEAN is not uncommon and the group also needs to put its act together to strengthen their unity. As long as ASEAN remains loosely institutionalised (in fact, ASEAN remains largely an intergovernmental organisation that has the potential to become a pluralistic regional community), ASEAN is unlikely to succeed in taking a common stand on maritime territorial disputes with China. And as long as Cambodia remains economically poor, social unrest and political opposition are likely to threaten the Hun Sen regime. As long as Cambodia remains domestically unstable and the political regime in Phnom Penh remains insecure, the Hun Sen government may have no choice but to rely on a powerful state like China, as it did during the 1980s when it depended on the Soviet Union and its allies, including Vietnam. Progress in the ASEAN+3 community-building thus rests also on member states' domestic stability.

The counter-argument made by Phnom Penh that Cambodia was a sovereign state and did not submit to Chinese influence also has some truth. The Hun Sen government has been effective in maintaining a degree of autonomy from the influence of major powers because of its ability to balance against their interests. Until 2013, Sino–Cambodian relations had grown quite tight, as shown by the fact that the Chinese presidents visited Cambodia twice (in 2000 and 2012). The last visit by President Hun Jintao was widely perceived by observers as an attempt by China to prevent Cambodia from putting territorial claims over the South China Sea on the 2012 ASEAN summit agenda. In 2013, however, Cambodia must have done something that irritated Beijing so much that China's official news agency *Xinhua* published an article in December 2012 blasting the Hun Sen government for the lack of political reform. According to some observers (Hiebert and Nguyen 2014), 'Neither [China's] President Xi Jinping nor Premier Li Keqiang made a stop in Myanmar during their diplomatic blitz across Southeast Asia in 2013. Interestingly, Cambodia was not included in that itinerary either, despite being a staunch ally and a popular investment destination for Chinese businesses.' They also noted that 'relations between Vietnam and Cambodia have blossomed during the past few months'. What all this suggests is that the Hun Sen government can maintain a degree of autonomy, driven by the need to ensure its survival and security. Cambodia's new strategic partnership with Japan may also have made China more cautious about how it treats other states. Beijing cannot completely count on Phnom Penh to play any divide-and-conquer game in the region. Cambodia has stressed the importance of the ASEAN-China Comprehensive Strategic Partnership and the need to implement the Declaration on the Conduct of Parties in the South China Sea toward a Code of Conduct.

Overall, Cambodia's bilateral relations with both China and Japan are a positive contribution to multilateral efforts at regional community building in East Asia. The criticism that Cambodia's pro-China policy undermined ASEAN or ASEAN+3 unity overlooks the fact that Cambodian relations with other states, especially Japan, have also become strong. As a small state, Cambodia has adopted a balance-of-interest policy, which may prove to be useful to multilateral efforts at East Asian community building not driven by any dominant power.

4.4 East Asian unity in cultural diversity

Cambodia has done its part to promote cultural relations within the context of ASEAN+3. During the 2012 summit, the leaders welcomed the selection of Siem Reap City of Cambodia as the 'Cultural City of East Asia 2012 within the framework of the ASEAN Plus Three'. The cultural event called 'APT Joint Cultural Performance: Unity in Diversity' was held on 2–3 November 2012, in Siem Reap Province. Cambodian leaders viewed this cultural theme as positive in that it would help attract tourists from other countries. According to the minister of tourism (Thong 2012), more than half of the tourists have visited Angkor Wat:

> In 2011, Cambodia received 2.8 million international tourists with an increase of 15%; particularly Siem Reap-Angkor received 1.6 million international tourists increased 21.7% with million domestic tourists. For the 9-month of 2012, Cambodia received 2.5 million international tourists, an increase of 23.6%, in which Siem Reap-Angkor received 1.4 million international tourists, an increase of 27.4% compared to the same period in 2011. According to the projection, Siem Reap-Angkor is estimated to receive approximately 3 million international tourists by 2015 and 4 million by 2020 while the whole country will receive approximately 4.5 million and 7 million respectively.

With its recognition as a world cultural heritage, Angkor Wat has served as a world and regional tourist attraction that has also offered a major economic benefit. The number of Chinese tourists in Cambodia, second only to Vietnamese tourists (854,104), increased to 460,000 in 2013 from 333,900 in 2012 (Xinhua 2014). In 2013, 435,009 South Korean tourists visited Cambodia, making them the third largest tourist group. Japanese tourists numbered 20,932, placing them in sixth place. During this year, 871,646 Cambodians also travelled abroad (Bangkok Post 2014).

These figures show that Cambodia is no longer internationally isolated as it was during the 1980s and that the growing flow of people through tourism across national borders appears to help people appreciate each other's cultural achievements, contribute to mutual understanding, recognition and respect, as well as help facilitate the process of regional integration.

These positive trends, however, are unlikely to deepen Cambodian integration into East Asia. One of the challenges, as alluded to earlier, is that Cambodia's socioeconomic conditions remain poor. For instance, Cambodia's 2012 HDI was still below the average of 0.683 for countries in East Asia and the Pacific (UNDP 2013). It is important that major powers in the region do what they can to help narrow the gaps between Cambodia and other states.

In short, Cambodia has played a positive role in the process of East Asian (ASEAN+3) community building by striking a delicate balance of interest between China and Japan and helping to promote regional unity in cultural diversity. The recent Cambodian shift in policy – away from China and closer to Japan – may prove to be useful in terms of keeping the two major Asian powers mutually in check and engaged in the region. Even mature regional security communities are not set free from regional leadership and balance-of-power politics (Peou 2002; 2002–2003), which helps prevent any particular power from becoming too dominant and thus threatening to other states. However, the East Asian community is unlikely to consolidate until the two major powers in Northeast Asia succeed in resolving their territorial disputes and can provide joint leadership within the region. Because of East Asia's cultural diversity, however, the East Asian community will most likely become and remain pluralistic.

5 Conclusions

Cambodia offers a lesson of hope for regional community building in East Asia. The country has made a positive contribution to this process. Following the withdrawal of Vietnamese troops from Cambodia in 1989 and the end of the Cold War in 1991, foes in Southeast Asia became friends. They have sought to enhance their regional cooperation, and Cambodia has been part of this cooperative process. The country has become a member of numerous international organisations and groups, most notably ASEAN and ASEAN+3. As a member of ASEAN, the country has assumed the role of Chair twice (2002 and 2012) and its government took pride in playing this role. Cambodia's positive bilateral relations with China and Japan have further enhanced multilateral cooperation in the context of ASEAN+3, despite tensions between the two Northeast Asian powers. All this positive development has resulted from the efforts by the political elites who developed a collective vision for their region, but it still raises the question of whether a genuine ASEAN community is achievable (Moorthy and Benny 2012).

Institutional membership and elite-driven efforts alone appear to be insufficient for regional community building. A sense of community identity has been basically built through the process of socialisation among elite members within ASEAN, but this level of socialisation alone is not going to help strengthen and sustain a genuine sense of collective identity. The majority of Cambodians, for instance, consider themselves Khmer and this identity has made it possible for them to imagine themselves as a national community. But the historical and cultural sense of identity is not enough to prevent the country from experiencing violence, war, decline, and disintegration. The country remains politically unstable, despite the fact that the same ruling party has been in power for 35 years. There is growing discontent with the ongoing socioeconomic gaps between the rich and poor. Although the level of poverty has been reduced, the majority of Cambodians remain poor. Unless Cambodia becomes politically stable, democratically mature and economically beneficial to all citizens, its contribution to regional community building remains limited. If still afflicted by political instability, the country is unlikely to play a more active role within East Asia and any excessive repressive violence is likely to invite political opposition at home and criticism from abroad. Cambodia's political instability and social unrest may thus limit the process of regional integration and regional community building.

Overall, Cambodia provides a good lesson for East Asia: For a community to thrive and mature, all states in the region must also develop a collective identity based on democratic values and the type of economic development that helps narrow the gaps among themselves. Powerful states must also be on good terms with each other and provide joint leadership in ensuring that less powerful and poorer states benefit from multilateral arrangements. The good news is that countries like Japan and China have done this, despite the fact that they have not offered joint leadership that could strengthen regionalism in East Asia because of their ongoing territorial disputes and rivalry (Peou 2015). Because of cultural diversity and different levels of socioeconomic development among their members, ASEAN and ASEAN+3 should also be realistic about forging a collective future. A pluralistic regional community may thus be the best the member states should aspire to become.

References

Acharya, Amitav, Lizée, Pierre and Peou, Sorpong (1991) *Cambodia – The 1989 Paris Peace Conference.* New York: Kraus International Publishers.

Asian Development Bank (2014) *Asian Development Bank Outlook 2014: Fiscal Policy for Inclusive Growth*, April. Available from: http://adb.org/sites/default/files/pub/2014/ado-2014.pdf.

Bangkok Post (2014) '4.2 Million Tourists Visited Cambodia Last Year'. 14 February. Available from: http://khmerization.blogspot.ca/2014/02/42-million-tourists-visited-cambodia.html.

Cain, Geoffrey (2014) 'South Korea pulled strings as Cambodia's military cracked down on protesters.' *GlobalPost*, 19 January. Available from: www.globalpost.com/dispatch/news/regions/asia-pacific/south-korea/140107/globalpost-exclusive-south-korea-boasts-role-c.

Chandler, David (1993) *A History of Cambodia*. Boulder, CO: Westview Press.

ChheangSokha (2013) 'Korea trade nears \$1 billion.' *Phnom Penh Post*, 11 July. Available from: www.phnompenhpost.com/business/korea-trade-nears-1-billion.

Countryeconomy.com. 'Cambodia-life expectancy at birth'. Available from: http://countryeconomy.com/demography/life-expectancy/cambodia.

Diplomat (2014) 'Protests, Strikes Continue in Cambodia', 19 February.

Ebihara, May M., Mortland, Carol A. and Ledgerwood, Judy (eds) (1994) *Cambodian Culture Since 1975: Homeland and Exile*. Ithaca, NY: Cornell University Press.

Economics Today (2012) 'Cambodia and ASEAN Economic Community.' Available from: https://vannarithchheang.wordpress.com/2012/02/15/cambodia-and-asean-economic-community (accessed 3 August 2014).

Finot, Louis (2001) 'The Temple of Angkor Wat' in Zhou Daguan, in *The Customs of Cambodia*, edited and translated by Michael Smithies. Bangkok: The Siam Society under Royal Patronage.

Fisher-Nguyen, Karen (1994) 'Khmer Proverbs: Images and Rules',' in *Cambodian Culture since 1975*, edited by May M. Ebihara, Carol A. Mortland and Judy Ledgerwood. Ithaca, NY and London: Cornell University Press.

Furuoka, Fumitaka, Lim, Beatrice, Mahmud, Roslinah and Hanim Pazim, Khairul (2012) 'Making of the ASEAN Community: Economic Integration and its Impact on Workers in Southeast Asia',' *Journal of Arts, Science and Commerce* 3: 68–74.

Hang, Chuon Naron (2012) 'The Cambodian Economy: Charting the Course of a Brighter Future',' in *Cambodia: Progress and Challenges Since 1991*, edited by Pou Sothirak, Geoff Wade and Mark Hong. Singapore: Institute of Southeast Asian Studies.

Hiebert, Murray and Nguyen, Phuon (2014) 'Challenged at Home Cambodia Realigned its Foreign Relations." *Yale Global*, 6 February. Available from: http://yaleglobal.yale.edu/content/challenged-home-cambodian-regime-realigns-its-foreign-relations.

Hruby, Denise (2014) 'Official Says Cambodia Not Ready for ASEAN Free Trade'. *The Cambodia*, 29 March.

Hun, Sen (2012) 'Statement.' Delivered at the Opening Ceremony of the 20th ASEAN Summit and the Celebration of the 45th Anniversary of ASEAN, 4 April, Phnom Penh.

Hun, Sen (2004) 'Speech at the 3rd International Conference of Asian Political Party'. Beijing. Available from: www.idcpc.org.cn/icapp3/more/speeches_new5.htm.

Hun, Sen (2002) 'Opening Statement at the Opening Ceremony of the ASEAN Summit and the Celebration of the Anniversary of ASEAN, 3 April 2012'. Available from: www.eria.org/Opening%20Statement%20by%20H.E.%20Samdech%20Techo%20Hun%20Sen%20at%2020th%20ASEAN%20Summit.pdf (accessed 29 July 2014).

Koh, Kheng-Lian (2014) 'ASEAN Cultural Heritage – Forging an Identity for Realization of an ASEAN Community in 2015?' *Environmental Policy and Law* 44(1–2): 237–247.

Kumar, Suraj and Ny, Boret (n.d.) *Inequality and Regional Disparity in Cambodia: Status, Trends and Inequality: Background Paper for Cambodian Human Development Report 2014*. Available from: academia.edu/5861145/InequalityandRegionalDisparityinCambodia.

Kun, Makara (2011) 'Cambodian-Korean Trade on the increase'. *Phnom Penh Post*, 25 March. Available from: google.ca/webhp?source=search_app&gfe_rd=cr&ei=B0zXVfGtCKyC8QehjKvYDg&gws_rd=ssl#q=+Kun%2C+Makara.+2011+Cambodian-Korean+on+the+increase.

Kun, Makara (2010) 'Korean Trade Surges'. *Phnom Penh Post*, 28 November. Available from: www.phnompenhpost.com/business/south-korean-trade-surges.

Kun, Makara (2009) 'Trade with Korea Fell More than 11pc in First 10 Months.' *Phnom Penh Post*, 3 December. Available from: www.phnompenhpost.com/business/trade-korea-fell-more-11pc-first-10-months.

Lam, Peng Er, 2012) 'Japan's Roles in Cambodia',' in *Cambodia: Progress and Challenges Since 1991*, edited by Pou Sothirak, Geoff Wade and Mark Hong. Singapore: Institute of Southeast Asian Studies.

Lewis, Simon (2012) 'At Asean Summit, Hun Sen Pushes for More Unity'. *The Cambodia Daily*, 3 April.

Moorthy, Ravichandran and Benny, Guido (2012) 'Is an ASEAN Community Achievable?' *Asian Survey* 52(6): 1043–1066.

Morton, Eddie (2014) 'Cambodia May Miss AEC Date'. *Phnom Penh Post*, 30 September.

Moss, Trefor (2011) 'ASEAN: Losing Its Way?' *The Diplomat*, 22 May. Available from: http://thediplomat.com/2011/05/asean-losing-its-way.

NIS and ILO (National Institute of Statistics and International Labor Organization) (2013) *Cambodia Labor Force and Child Labor Survey 2012: Labour Force Report*. Phnom Penh: ILO. Available from: www.ilo.org/wcmsp5/groups/public/–asia/– ro-ba ngkok/– sro-bangkok/documents/publication/wcms_230721.pdf.

Peou, Sorpong (2015) 'Building an Asian-Pacific Security Community from a Human Security Perspective'. Keynote address delivered at the 2015 Asian and Political International Association Convention, 11–12 September.

Peou, Sorpong (2014) 'The Limits and Potential of Liberal Peacebuilding'. *Asian Journal of Peacebuilding* 2(1): 37–60

Peou, Sorpong (2007) *International Democracy Assistance for Peacebuilding: Cambodia and Beyond*. New York and Hampshire: Palgrave Macmillan.

Peou, Sorpong (2002–2003) 'Withering Realism? A Review of Recent Security Studies on the Asia-Pacific Region'. *Pacific Affairs* 75(4): 575–584.

Peou, Sorpong (2002) 'Regional Community Building for Better Global Governance',' in *The United Nations System in the 21st Century*, edited by Volker Rittberger. Tokyo: United Nations University Press.

Peou, Sorpong (2000a) *Intervention and Change in Cambodia: Toward Democracy*. New York, Singapore and Chiang Mai: St. Martin's Press, Institute of Southeast Asian Studies, and Silkworm.

Peou, Sorpong (ed.) (2000b) *Cambodia*. Aldershot: Ashgate.

Peou, Sorpong (1998) 'The Subsidiarity Model of Global Governance in the ASEAN-UN Context'. *Global Governance* 4(4): 439–459.

Peou, Sorpong (1997) *Conflict Neutralization in the Cambodia War: From Battlefield to Ballot-box*. Kuala Lumpur, New York and Singapore: Oxford University Press.

Phnom Penh Post (2013) 'Japan and Cambodia: Fast Facts', 23 December.

Phorn, Bopha (2013) 'Official Says "Strategic Partnership" With Japan Won't Irk China.' *The Cambodia Daily*, 18 December.

Pou, Sothirak (2012) 'Managing Poverty in Cambodia',' in *Cambodia: Progress and Challenges Since 1991*, edited by Pou Sothirak, Geoff Wade and Mark Hong. Singapore: Institute of Southeast Asian Studies.

Pou, Sothirak and Imagawa, Yukio (2012) 'Cambodian-Japan Relations',' in *Cambodia: Progress and Challenges Since 1991*, edited by Pou Sothirak, Geoff Wade and Mark Hong. Singapore: Institute of Southeast Asian Studies.

Prak, Chan Thul (2014) "Consumerism booms as Cambodia embraces once-forbidden capitalism." *Reuters*, 28 September. Available from: www.reuters.com/article/2014/09/28/us-cambodia-economyidUSKCN0HN0YJ20140928?feedType=RSS&virtualBrandChannel=11563.

Sam, Sam-Ang (1994) 'Khmer Traditional Music Today',' in *Cambodian Culture since 1975*, edited by May M. Ebihara, Carol A. Mortland and Judy Ledgerwood. Ithaca, NY and London: Cornell University Press, pp. 41–42.

SerMyo-ja (2009) 'Seoul, Phnom Penh Sign Agreements'. Available from: http://editorials.cambodia.org/2009/10/seoul-phnom-penh-sign-agreements.html?m=0.

Severino, Rodolfo C. and Hong, Mark (2012) 'ASEAN and the Cambodia Campaign',' in *Cambodia: Progress and Challenges Since 1991*, edited by Pou Sothirak, Geoff Wade and Mark Hong. Singapore: Institute of Southeast Asian Studies.

Thayer, Carlyle (2012) 'ASEAN's Code of Conduct in the South China Sea: A Litmus Test Community-Building?' *The Asia-Pacific Journal* 34(4) August. Available from: www.japanfocus.org/site/make_pdf/3813.

Thong, Khon (2012) 'Welcome Remarks at the Opening Ceremony of ASEAN+3 Joint Cultural Performances: Unity in Diversity – Siem Reap Angkor: Cultural City of East Asia 2012'. Siem Reap, 3 November.

Trading Economics (n.d.) Available from: www.tradingeconomics.com/cambodia/inflation-cpi.

UNDP (United Nations Development Program) (2013) *Human Development Index – The Rise of the South: Human Progress in a Diverse World*. Available from: http://hdr.undp.org/sites/default/files/Country-Profiles/KHM.pdf.

World Bank (2014) 'Cambodia – World Bank Expects Slower Growth in Developing East Asia Pacific in 2014'. Available from: www.worldbank.org/en/news/press-release/2014/10/06/cambodia-world-bank-expects-slower-growth-in-developing-east-asia-pacific-in-2014.

World Economic Forum (2013) *The Global Gender Gap Report*. Geneva: World Economic Forum.

Xinhua (2014a) 'Cambodia Attracts Some 460,000 Chinese Visitors in 2013, up 39pct', 4 February. Available from: www.shanghaidaily.com/article/article_xinhua.aspx?id=198122.

Xinhua (2014b) 'Cambodia's Trade with ASEAN Members Reaches $4.16 bln Last Year', 4 March. Available From: www.asean-cn.org/Item/10087.aspx.

Xinhua (2013) 'New Chinese Envoy Pledges to Further Enhance Ties with Cambodia', 25 July. Available from: http://news.xinhuanet.com/english/china/2013–07/25/c_132573145.htm.

Zhou Daguan (2007) *A Record of Cambodia: The Land and its People*, translated with an introduction by Peter Harris. Chiang Mail: Silkworm Books.

3 Indonesia

Maintaining a leading role in the making of the ASEAN and APT community

Mangadar Situmorang

> I envision a century-old Indonesia standing on the three great pillars that make up a great modern state: a strong and just economy, a stable and modern democracy, and a thriving civilization.
>
> President Susilo Bambang Yudhoyono (Strategic Review 2012)

Based on internationally accepted standards, Indonesia is the largest country in Southeast Asia. This brings about certain impacts on how it conducts its foreign relations. Its influence on the region is also remarkable. The regional dynamics of Southeast Asian countries partly in the form of activities in the Association of Southeast Asian Nations (ASEAN) and the likely development within the broader region of East Asia covering Japan, China and South Korea which altogether make up the ASEAN Plus Three Community, are likely to be influenced by individual countries like Indonesia.

In the interest of understanding the regional and international condition of Southeast and East Asia, the first step to be taken is to develop a comprehensive knowledge of every single country within the region. This does not necessarily mean to adopt hastily, without being critical to the classical realist paradigm which emphasizes the centrality of state in international relations. The important point made here is the sensibility of the approach as an easier way to get closer to the dynamics of foreign relations of a particular country and of the more complex regional and international relations.

This chapter discusses Indonesia's role in the making of the ASEAN and ASEAN Plus Three (APT) cooperation. The argument proposed here is that Indonesia's international and regional relations are built on the concept of concentric circles. It starts from a good relationship with neighbouring countries closest to Indonesia circled and centred at ASEAN. Following that are broader regional and inter-regional collaborations such as APT and Asia Pacific Economic Cooperation (APEC). This clearly shows the importance of ASEAN to Indonesia and to its broader foreign policies and cooperation. Djauhari Oratmangun, Director-General of ASEAN Cooperation, Indonesia's Ministry of Foreign Affairs, makes it very clear, 'For Indonesia, the East Asia or the Asia-Pacific Community would not happen without ASEAN as its foundation' (2010, iii).

1 Indonesia's national perspectives

Apart from its huge territory, another equally important characteristic of Indonesia as a country is its archipelagic shape. Consisting of approximately 18,000 islands, which are politically regarded as connected rather than separated by seas, Indonesia's 240 million population (2012 estimate) is dispersed across the islands. The western part (Sumatra and Java) is a densely populated area. It must be added that Java (including Bali), although it amounts to roughly only one-sixth of national territory, is the area where about 60 per cent of the national total population lives.

In terms of demographic configuration, Indonesia is one of the most heterogeneous countries in Southeast Asia and even the world. In religious context, the majority (88 per cent) are Muslim and this makes Indonesia a country with the largest Muslim community in the world, but it is known internationally as being moderate in nature. The rest are affiliated with other religious beliefs (Christianity, Catholicism, Buddhism, Hinduism, and Confucianism) in addition to local traditional faiths. Socially and culturally, there are about 300 ethnic and/or sub-ethnic groups with their own local languages, traditions, and values. The Javanese including Balinese, Sundanese, and Madurese make up the majority ethnic group, which consists of approximately 60 per cent of the national population, and consequently is the major culture which undoubtedly colours the way the state is ruled. Other major ethnic groups, though amounting to less than 10 per cent respectively are the Minangkabau (also called Melayu or Malay in terms of cultural identity), Buginese, Makassarese, Bataknese, Betawi, and Banjar. The ethnic Chinese group is widely viewed as a minority group (compared to indigenous national – the so-called *pribumi* – ethnic groups), even though the number is much larger than certain *pribumi* groups.

Indonesia's history prior to its independence on 17 August 1945 is frequently said to have contributed to forming the state of Indonesia. Shared experiences of having been a colonial state of Portugal, the Netherlands, and finally Japan have forced the heterogeneous people to become united. *Bahasa* Indonesia as the national and official language accompanied by a strong and centralized government has also played a significant role in building one single identity as *Bangsa Indonesia* (Indonesian nation).

The shared identity, however, is likely challenged by social and economic problems. Most of the people are classified as low- and middle-income-level communities. The last few decades have shown an increasing number of people living in urban areas due to industrialization and this has made the traditionally agricultural economy less attractive to the younger generation. Apart from contributing to the rise of the middle class (estimated to amount to more than 30 million out of the whole population) (Jakarta Post, August 5, 2013), the gradually increasing income per capita of up to approximately US $4,000 (in a 2013 estimate) is also indicative of the growing strength of the national economy and this made Indonesia the sixteenth largest economy in the world (2013) and currently the tenth by 2014 (Tempo, May 2014). Industrialization and modernization are continuing to progress which inevitably brings about problems that the country has to manage very carefully. Table 3.1 shows clearly the comparative leverage of Indonesia among other Asian countries.

All aforementioned issues have great impacts on how the country administers social and economic matters throughout the political system it adopts and how it perceives the region of Southeast Asia and its regional associations. Before discussing the latter in the following section, attention needs to be given to Indonesia's domestic politics first.

Up to the present, discourses on national politics have been predominated by the process of democratization. It started in May 1998 when President Suharto was forced to end his New Order regime which was marked by a highly centralized power and which was made possible with the support from the military, the bureaucracy, and the dominant quasi-party, *Golongan Karya* (*Golkar*). Following the Asian financial crisis in 1997–1998 and the Suharto administration's failure to escape from it, the wave of democratization across the nation forced Suharto to step down and conclude his authoritarian rule. The event marked the new agenda of political reform or what is called *reformasi* in Indonesian.

Table 3.1 Geographic and demographic size and GDP of Indonesia compared to other countries of ASEAN Plus Three

Country	Geographic area (in sq km – including land and water)	Demographic size (July 2012 est.)	GDP (PPP, 2011 est.)
Indonesia	1,904,569	248,645,008	$1.125 trillion
Singapore	697	5,353,494	$314.9 billion
Brunei Darussalam	5,765	408,786	$21.03 billion
Malaysia	329,847	29,179,952	$463.7 billion
Thailand	513,120	67,091,089	$602.2 billion
Myanmar	676,578	54,584,650	$82.68 billion
Laos	236,800	6,586,266	$17.41 billion
Cambodia	181,035	14,952,665	$33.82 billion
Vietnam	331,210	91,519,289	$300 billion
The Philippines	300,000	103,775,002	$391.1 billion
South Korea	99,720	48,860,500	$1.554 trillion
Japan	377,915	127,368,088	$4.444 trillion
China	9,596,961	1,343,239,923	$11.3 trillion
Timor Leste	14,874	1,143,667	$9.507 billion

Source: CIA, *The World Factbook.* www.cia.gov/library/publications/the-world-factbook, accessed 2 March 2014.

Reformasi evoked two main agendas which unfortunately were often neither integrated nor sequential processes. While the first agenda (namely to end Suharto's New Order authoritarian regime) was practically successful in time as Suharto stepped down in May 1998, the second agenda was widely perceived as unclear and really dangerous (Urbaningrum 1999; Alhumami 1999). At that time no one was quite sure whether post-Suharto Indonesia would move to a democratic country as the anti-Suharto movements called for or whether it might slide into disarray and disintegration as several scholars worried about (Brown 2003; Forrester and May 1998). Positive signs were slow to come to the surface. Under fuming public pressures, the then President B.J. Habibie who took over the reins from Suharto, managed to take a series of crucial actions. These included *inter alia* the release of political prisoners, offering freedom to the media, and acknowledging the freedom of political expression and association. In addition to the calls for military and party system reform, Habibie was also forced to immediately carry out general elections based on free and just principles, which were subsequently held in 1999.

Post-Suharto Indonesia from its beginnings to its recent stage continues to face multiple and complex issues. After the short transitional government of Habibie, the following governments under President Abdurrahman Wahid ('Gus Dur', 1999–2001) and Megawati Sukarnoputri (2001–2004) were vying to settle down the political euphoria brought about by the reform. At the same time, they had to tackle economic problems caused by the Asian financial crisis and to carefully handle social tension and conflicts in addition to maintaining national integration. In all these traditional issues a new but broad issue emerged, namely, the consolidation of democracy. As the three groups of issues (economic development, conserving national integration, and consolidating democracy) existed simultaneously in the post-Suharto era, the central question for discussion and further investigation is how Indonesia could manage them carefully and successfully (Aspinall and Mietzner 2010; Crouch 2010).

Indonesian national policies and programmes to bring social-economic development, conservation of national security and unity, and consolidation of the democratic system, according to many standards are on the right track (Aspinall and Mietzner 2010, Diamond 2010). The country was widely appreciated due to the administration of President Susilo Bambang Yudhoyono over almost a decade in power (2004–2009 and 2009–2014). The positive signs, however, are often disturbed by a set of serious problems. The greater freedom caused by *reformasi* or more precisely the reduction of state power and the decline of government authority in public affairs as enshrined in the amended constitution was accompanied by a trend of communal violence and conflicts. *Pancasila*, the national ideology, introduced for almost half a century in order to build social tolerance and harmony among the very diverse social groups, sometimes with force, was widely questioned. Instead of an increasingly cohesive and consolidated society, *reformasi* tends to highlight the heterogeneous character of the nation in terms of ethnicity, culture, and religion.

Since 1999, several fundamental groups have come to the surface and been involved in a number of violent acts. The groups are generally associated with radical Islam whose teachings are in contrast to the Islamic mainstream. The latter are known as moderate, tolerant, and showing respect to religious differences. The radical groups are allegedly anti-secularist, against Western culture and values, and aim to introduce Islamic laws, *Syariah Islam*, and to replace the Pancasila ideology (Yunanto 2003, Abuza 2007). Bomb blasts in Bali, Jakarta and other cities in the early years of political reform were widely reported as actions carried out by such radical groups.

Corruption was one of the main concerns related to the anti-Suharto movements. Combined with the demand to bring down Suharto, the *reformasi* supporters organized protests against all practices of corruption, collusion, and nepotism (*Korupsi, Kolusi, Nepotisme – KKN*). In short, the anti-Suharto movement was also viewed as being a fight against such illegal and undemocratic practices.

The critical impetus for the government to be clean, good, transparent, and accountable comes mainly from outside the judiciary institutions (the judges, prosecutors, and police). These include the media, NGOs such as Indonesian Corruption Watch (ICW) and Indonesian Transparency (IT), and are backed by public opinion (Daniri 2009). This does not necessarily mean to eliminate the role of the newly and democratically elected government and parliament members (Harjapamekas and Rukmana 2009). The establishment in 2001 of a national Commission for Corruption Eradication (KPK) has forced government agencies at all levels to be more accountable in managing the state budget for national development (Ibrahim 2009). In its development, 'Suharto's centralized network was partly dismantled,' Harold Crouch argued, 'but its fragmented remnants formed their own networks around sections of the bureaucracy, the newly liberated political parties and regional governments' (2010, 191). This means that constant, comprehensive and collective attempts to eliminate corruption are badly needed since such endemic practices are not limited to Suharto's network but are also unfortunately prevalent among the new generation, the *reformasi* generation.

The future destination of Indonesia is basically determined by all elements of the country. Whether there will be sustainable social and economic progress, a stable and harmonious community and a consolidated democracy, the national government and leaders, political institutions, societal organizations, and people at large must altogether be responsible. Political parties are seen to be at the centre of the processes and dynamics. Theoretically and normatively, they play significant roles in educating people about democratic values, articulating people's interests, communicating government policies, and also recruiting leaders for government and political positions. In general, political parties are crucial for keeping the nation stable, united and progressing.

Nevertheless, parties and the party system are still in a developing process to be the principal guardian of national unity, development and democracy. While the number is fluctuating, all parties are commonly grouped into two ideological mainstreams: secular-nationalist and Islamic-religious parties (Tomsa 2010, 152). And all general elections held during the reform era (1999, 2004, 2009, and 2014) showed that nationalist-secular parties performed better in terms of gathering votes and occupying more seats in the legislative body (DPR) than the Islamic parties. The results might rightly prove Indonesia to be a country with moderate Muslims (Sukma 2010, 63–67).

Having considered the main domestic characteristics of Indonesia, it is fair to say that Indonesia is still working hard to carefully nurture its national affairs. In this context, Indonesia tends to assume an inward-looking foreign orientation and policy. In other words, Indonesia's government and people are likely to pay attention to internal challenges more than international affairs. As will be discussed in the following part, the national perception of other countries in Southeast Asia and beyond is very much based on such a domestic configuration and whenever possible Indonesia's foreign policies are projected on the preservation of national interests.

2 Indonesia's involvement within ASEAN

In order to make Indonesia a great modern state with a strong and just economy, a stable and modern democracy, and a thriving civilization, as President S.B. Yudhoyono (2012) contends, they 'will be preserved by an extensive web of strong diplomatic relations with our neighbours and with the region, all within the confines of a dynamic and cohesive ASEAN Community'. He also asserts that 'Indonesia 2045 must be able to maintain a robust independent and active foreign policy, which involves maintaining constructive partnerships with major powers'.

Yudhoyono's vision of Indonesia's foreign relations is basically established upon a very generic, everlasting, and unchanging principle, namely *bebas aktif* which literally means being independent and active. In its broader interpretation, the *bebas* principle reflects the autonomous independence of the government *from* any kind of global political powers or the sphere of influence of state groupings and *to* take any kind of action which is seen as significant to meet national interests. Sovereignty in terms of being factual (*de facto*) and formal (*de jure*) is cautiously considered and maintained as it is a very central principle and sensitive issue as well to all elements of the country. Meanwhile, the *aktif* (or active) principle constitutes the state's initiative and intention to take part in every aspect of the global relations and issues relevant to national interests. The 'free and active' principle therefore indicates Indonesia's existence in the world with all its international rights and obligations or capabilities and responsibilities.

The *bebas aktif* principle partly reflects the Indonesian standpoint during the Cold War era where the world began to be divided into two ideological and political blocs following the end of the Second World War. In April 1955, for example, Indonesia hosted the first-ever international conference gathering countries from Asia and Africa. Widely known as the Asia-Africa

Conference, it is recognized as an embryo to the establishment of the Non-Aligned Movement (NAM) in 1960s. Nonetheless, the *bebas aktif* principle was also used to justify cases when Indonesia under Soekarno (1945–1966) was having a closer relationship with the Communist bloc and conversely under Suharto (1966–1998) when it was closer to the Capitalist-Liberalist bloc. In this context, national interests as they were perceived and formulated by the existing governments are the chief factor for the country to conduct its foreign policies and relations (Anwar 2010, Wanandi 2008).

According to the national constitution (*Undang-Undang Dasar 1945*), Indonesian national interests are to bring national welfare and prosperity, to provide protection to its people, and to take part in maintaining international security and peace. Referring to a modern understanding of security, the constitution emphasizes the importance of both state security and human security which are to be met simultaneously. The constitution also stipulates a firm conception of the interconnectedness between domestic and international affairs. For Indonesia to develop its national social and economic life, there has to be proper cooperation with other countries and international peace and security cooperative arrangements have to be maintained and promoted.

As mentioned before, the way Indonesia conducts its international cooperation and meets its constitutional objectives is basically determined by how the country perceives the world and the region. This is very clearly represented or characterized by the ruling regimes such as Soekarno's independence revolution, Suharto's authoritarianism, and the post-Suharto reform era (from Habibie to Abdurrahman, Megawati, Yudhoyono, and Joko Widodo 'Jokowi') where the latter focuses on economic development and democracy consolidation as well.

Indonesia's view of world politics under Soekarno was strongly characterized by the anti-colonialist attitude and policy. It was argued that international peace and order was founded on national independence and freedom. It was clearly stipulated in the national constitution that 'independence is the right of every nation, and therefore colonialism has to be abandoned from the world since colonialism is against the basic rights of human beings'. The anti-colonialist orientation was considerably influenced by the long history of Indonesia being under colonial rule mentioned above. It was fortified by the fact that following the defeat of Japan and the Indonesian proclamation of independence on 17 August 1945, the Netherlands, with support from her British ally, wanted to resume its authority over Indonesia with the pretext of the international convention of *status quo ante bellum*. It took four years for Indonesia to fight, suffering huge casualties against the Dutch, and for the latter to finally recognize Indonesia as a free and sovereign state on 27 December 1949.

The independence of Malaysia on 31 August 1957 had also certain impacts on the anti-colonial feeling among Indonesian elites and the common people. However, it was not the independence of Malaysia itself which generated anger among many Indonesian politicians and people, triggering Soekarno to launch the *Ganyang Malaysia* (Crush Malaysia) campaign. Instead, it was the perception of the role of the British colonial rule in the formation of the Federation of Malaysia which was seen as a new form of colonialism or neocolonialism. Soekarno's policy of *Konfrontasi Indonesia-Malaysia* (Indonesia-Malaysia Confrontation) in 1963–1966 was basically associated with the view that the UK and USA were behind Malaysia to incorporate North Borneo into its federation. Not only was Malaysia seen as a rival to Soekarno and Indonesia's leadership in the region, but the incorporation of North Borneo into the Federation of Malaysia was also perceived as a serious threat to Indonesian sovereignty (Ba 2009, 46–48).

The anti-colonial feeling would not be regarded as a stand-alone view. In a broader context, Indonesia perceives the world and Asia as not merely uncertain, unpredictable, or anarchic, but also as hostile, unfair, discriminative, and hegemonic. Such a negative world view was widely attached to the role played by Western countries and more specifically the USA. Further investigation is of course needed to understand whether such sceptical views were principally affected by the national historical background of extensive colonialism or whether it was more likely confined to government elites, including the military, influential journalists, think-tanks, and individual scholars for any kind of particular interests and reasons. But, it is quite clear that such views are to a great extent in line with the traditional realist paradigm as one Indonesian scholar put forth as follows: 'From the Soekarno era till the end of Soeharto's regime, Indonesia's world view was mainly dominated by the mainstream perspective, namely realism. It was built on the suspicious, distrustful attitude, defensive and reactive as well as "inward-looking" in nature.' The scholar continued to observe that, 'Indonesia perceived international politics as an anarchic and unfriendly world which was not only potentially threatened its national interest but could even be dangerous for its existence' (Agussalim 2013).

Soekarno's attitude of anti-*Nekolim* (New Colonialism and Imperialism), which to some degree was directed against the Western-capitalist powers, was followed by the initiative to form a 'Jakarta–Phnom Penh–Beijing–Hanoi–Pyongyang axis', demonstrating the other side of the world's bipolar system, the eastern-communist power. According to one source, although the Soviet Union was a major supplier of arms and economic aid to Indonesia in the 1950s, the relationship with China was becoming closer because of the growing influence of the Indonesian Communist Party (PKI) under Soekarno's regime (Frederick and Worden 1993). This clearly showed a significant shift from the initial stance of being just anti-colonialism to an anti-Western capitalism position. The Asia-Africa Conference as mentioned above which formed the foundation for the establishment of NAM, G-77 and the South-South Cooperation forum, was altogether likely to show a critical standpoint towards the Western-capitalist powers.

Towards the region of Asia and Southeast Asia, Indonesia has shown enthusiasm in part through the formation of Maphilindo (Malaysia, the

Philippines, and Indonesia) in 1963. According to Alice D. Ba (2009, 47), Maphilindo was likely to express the ethno-nationalist ideas of the region, so different from the previous Association of Southeast Asia (ASA) formed in 1961 which included Thailand. However, the formation of ASEAN in 1967 obviously demonstrated Indonesia's intention and commitment to collectively develop a more stable and secure region of Southeast Asia. This took shape when Suharto took national power in 1966.

2.1 Indonesia and the ASEAN Political and Security Community (APSC)

The brief historical review above may be indicative of how Indonesia perceives ASEAN in terms of political-security aspects, recently known as the first pillar of ASEAN Community. Indonesia strongly holds that national independence is the key to security and peace at the national, regional and international level. 'We love peace, but we love freedom more' was a popular expression during the independence revolution in the second half of the 1940s and it has continuously been adopted up to the present. This is in line with the internationally accepted conception of state sovereignty as the foundation of world peace and security. The principle is usually associated with the non-interference principle, another internationally accepted principle and universally practiced including through the UN mechanism. Showing respect for other states' national sovereignty has been the principle Indonesia consistently adopts and brings into effect either in guarding its national interests or guiding its international relations. In addition to such a 'negative' principle of non-intervention, Indonesia also holds the 'positive' view in maintaining security and positive international politics by conducting and developing international cooperation. Many of these are conducted through becoming a member of various international organizations such as the UN in 1950 and the resumption of its membership of the UN in September 1966, being a signatory or party to different international treaties, and a co-founder or active participant of a number of international organizations, and particularly in the making of ASEAN and its subsequent progress.

The formation of ASEAN which was based on individual sovereignty of states and non-interference principles very much befitted Indonesia's national interests. In the interest of having a stable region, Indonesia believed that national sovereignty must be respected. For the region to be strong and developed, it was said that it had to rely on national resilience and development. Indonesia made this very clear before the first ASEAN Summit in Bali (1976). By introducing the concept of national resilience, Indonesia strongly expressed the political view that a regional organization of Southeast Asia, ASEAN, must be founded on national sovereignty without any form of interference from other country members. In this context it is fair to say that ASEAN has functioned as an instrument to protect and secure national sovereignty. ASEAN is not a supranational organization that could interfere in domestic affairs of its country members. The principles of national sovereignty, national resilience, and non-interference endorsed by Indonesia seemed to have a positive impact on other countries in the region to join ASEAN. The positive impact began with the integration of Brunei Darussalam in 1984 and was followed by Vietnam in 1995, and Myanmar and Laos in 1997. The acceptance of Cambodia in 1999 accomplished the ASEAN Ten membership.

Indonesia's insistence of ASEAN based on national sovereignty and non-interference principles was also related to its interest in building a nation state. Alan Collins (2003, 128) is right in asserting that 'nation building is often a brutal business'. For this practice, he continued, 'the elite wanted to be able to implement their policies knowing that neighbours would not interfere in their domestic affairs. ASEAN was therefore established to ensure sovereignty remained firmly located at the national level.' As has been discussed before, when Suharto came into power, the main agenda was to stabilize the country free from any form of political contestation and instability, mostly from domestic political forces. Controlling all political groups, whether they were associated with a particular ideology, religion, or ethnic, regional and cultural identity, was seen as a top priority. It was in many occasions carried out without considering democratic principles or human rights norms. Formulated in his propaganda of development trilogy (*trilogi pembangunan*), namely, political stability, economic growth, and social welfare, Suharto with support from national military forces began to exert political oppression, co-opt critical forces, and eliminate political opponents in the interest of economic and social development. These policies and programmes constituted the authoritarian regime for around three decades. More importantly, all these kind of practices were carried out without any form of interference from ASEAN country members.

Indonesia is not the only one using ASEAN's principles. Almost all ASEAN's members have faced similar challenges in building their nation states. Characterized as post-colonial states (except for Thailand), almost all other countries including Thailand, Malaysia, the Philippines and the new members of CLVM have experienced many domestic problems not only in dealing with social and economic difficulties but also in maintaining their national stability and unity, including the challenge to settle various kinds of ethnic separatist movements.

Indonesia's endorsement of ASEAN's principles of national sovereignty and non-interference continued through the introduction and adoption of ASEAN as a Zone of Peace, Freedom, and Neutrality (ZOPFAN) in 1971 and the Treaty of Amity and Cooperation in Southeast Asia (TAC) in 1976. While one may judge ZOPFAN simply as an institutional instrument to limit, if not to prevent, any kind of intervention from extra-regional powers, the TAC may be seen as highlighting the idea of making regional security and stability grow in a more positive and active sense. The adoption of the non-interference principle is likely to be regarded as a voluntary action by countries to restrain themselves from getting involved in the domestic affairs of other countries. On the other hand, the adoption and signing of TAC is also considered to be providing opportunities for country members to help one another whenever needed and seen appropriately.

Another crucial importance of TAC is for country members to take peaceful mechanisms to solve disputes among them. Every single member is strongly encouraged not to use force or to take armed action in whatever problem may emerge. Resulting from the ASEAN's First Summit in Bali, known also as Bali Concord I, TAC is widely perceived as a regional code of conduct which is useful to suppress conflict or to control tension among countries within the region. Furthermore, by adopting TAC it was expected that the regional security, peace, and stability of Southeast Asia has to be founded on the capability of all ASEAN country members to work together to manage their own problems without any form of intervention from external powers.

The non-violence mechanisms in resolving disputes among ASEAN country members strengthened the way ASEAN has been making regional and organizational decisions. The general way of ASEAN to make decisions is through informal meetings and dialogues in order to reach compromises and consensus. The whole process is known as *musyawarah* that will end with *mufakat* which simply means dialogues to reach consensual decisions. Alan Collins proposes its practical implementation in three forms: 'first, decision-making is achieved through consensus; second, if a compromise cannot be found, then the issue is adjourned; and third, members are prepared to defer their own interests to the interests of the association' (Collins 2003, 133; Luhulima 2008, 89).

The centrality of national independence and sovereignty, the non-interference principle, the non-violent conflict resolutions, and the consensual decision-making procedures altogether constitute the regional code of conduct, popularly called the ASEAN Way. To a great extent, Indonesia has played a very significant role in the making of ASEAN which had previously been viewed as an association characterized by a strong state-orientation, driven by government elites, tending to be exclusive, and dominated by each country's ministry of foreign affairs (Luhulima 2008, 89). Based on those principles and characteristics, Indonesia took an active role in handling the conflict in Cambodia that occurred in 1979. Under ASEAN's framework, Indonesia took initiative to bring conflicting parties to the negotiation table through a series of informal meetings known as cocktail parties and Jakarta Informal Meetings. The negotiation process ran until 1990. Acting as co-chairs with France and with full support from other ASEAN countries, the conflict was finally ended with the Paris Peace Agreement of 1991.

Following the end of the Cold War era, ASEAN continued to advance its political and security arrangements. By 1992, ASEAN issued a joint declaration on the issue of the South China Sea. One point made was to oppose the use of force to settle the territorial claims made by China or other countries. Two years later, ASEAN held the first meeting of the ASEAN Regional

Forum (ARF) which includes ASEAN member countries and other regional major countries such as China, Japan, USA, Australia, and the like. This is a broader regional and multilateral forum covering Asian and Pacific countries. ARF was designated as a forum to develop among participating countries Confidence Building Measures (CBM), Preventive Diplomacy, and whenever possible, Conflict Resolution. By 1995, ASEAN members reached an agreement on the Treaty of Southeast Asian Nuclear Weapon Free Zone (SEANWFZ) which made ASEAN a nuclear weapon free region and came into effect in 1997.

The idea of the ASEAN Security Community (ASC) was initially put forward at the 9th ASEAN Summit in Bali, 2003. Before it changed to ASEAN Political and Security Community (APSC), there had been a growing concern about the concept of comprehensive security. Many parties within the region asserted, as ASEAN founders and leaders implicitly believed, that national or state security could only be met by achieving national social and economic development. In Indonesia, the concept received huge support following the economic crisis in 1997/1998 which forced Suharto to step down. Political democracy and respect for human rights were seen as integral parts of comprehensive security. Having experienced such a significant domestic political change, Indonesia became the main supporter of the ASEAN Political and Security Community (APSC).

APSC does not intend to change the principles and norms ASEAN has adopted since its formation or the practices upon which ASEAN has based its main characteristics. By incorporating APSC as an integral part of the ASEAN Community, Indonesia wants to see ASEAN becoming more capable of settling potential conflicts that may take the form of interstate or intrastate conflicts. In this context, Indonesia wants more flexibility in the implementation of ASEAN's longstanding principles. Apart from promoting a democratic system and respect for human rights among member countries, Indonesia proposes the formation of a regional peace-keeping force which could make ASEAN play a more influential role in maintaining peace in the region and at a global level. In addition, Indonesia also put forward the urgent need of the ASEAN Extradition Treaty (Luhulima 2008, 97).

Indonesia's proposal to form a kind of ASEAN peace-keeping force and to promote democracy might be partly affected by its own experiences in seeing ASEAN's insignificant role in assisting to restore security in East Timor following the popular consultation where the overwhelming majority of East Timorese preferred to reject integration with Indonesia in 1999 and in helping the implementation of the Helsinki peace agreement in Aceh in 2005 (Luhulima 2008, 91). Another part of the reason is that Indonesia wants to see ASEAN becoming more proactive in keeping regional peace and order. However, there is also the opinion that Indonesia should aim to restore its role and leadership within ASEAN that has been decreasing following the 1997/98 economic crisis and political turmoil.

The idea to build APSC was subsequently developed through the Vientiane Action Program (VAP) adopted in November 2004. For example, VAP approved several points of democratic principles and human rights norms. The increasing role of non-state entities in the form of Track-Two dialogue was also acknowledged and appreciated. In order to enhance 'peace, stability, democracy and prosperity in the region through comprehensive political and security cooperation', VAP recommended 'Strategic Trusts' which include political development, sharing and shaping norms, conflict prevention, conflict resolution, and post-conflict peace-building. All these points are perceived to be the foundations of APSC, to be brought into effect in 2015.

2.2 Indonesia and the ASEAN Economic Community (AEC)

In terms of economic issues, the general picture of Indonesia's perspective is marked by its integration into the global economy, which is primarily based on liberal and free-market principles. Such integration occurred long before the Dutch colonial power controlled Indonesia's territory for approximately three and a half centuries, when China, India, and other countries in the Middle East and Southeast Asia became its major partners in trading. However, it was the political and economic control of the Dutch which brought Indonesia into the international capitalist economic system.

Following national independence, Indonesia continued to be part of such an economic system. Although marked by Sukarno's nationalization programme of all the former colonial Dutch companies operating in Indonesia, it was not intended to insulate the national economy from the international system. Instead of implementing an isolationist economic policy, Indonesia continued its international economic transactions either with the Western or the Eastern economic block during the Cold War era.

The initiatives to have a stronger economic cooperation within the Southeast Asia region emerged when Suharto came to power. The establishment of ASEAN in 1967 was a very clear proof reflecting the call for regional economic cooperation. As mentioned above, the formation of ASEAN with its economic stress was in line with Suharto's policy, namely, making economic development the top priority freed from any kind of national political disturbances and/or external interference. It is worth noting, however, that apart from getting closer to the region, Indonesia severely needed foreign aid and investment to support national development programmes. With this interest in mind, Indonesia continued to maintain good relationships with the Western countries and furthermore took the initiative to establish in 1967 the Inter-Governmental Group on Indonesia (IGGI, then replaced by the Consultative Group on Indonesia, CGI, in 1992), where a number of country donors and IMF, WB, and ADB were involved.

The demand for a meaningful regional economic form of cooperation became more visible after the First ASEAN Summit in Bali 1976 when the regional leaders revealed policy guidelines and an action programme for ASEAN economic cooperation with food commodity, energy, industry, and trade taking priority (Dirjen Kerjasama ASEAN Kemlu 2000, 23). It was followed by the signing of the Agreement on ASEAN Preferential Trading Agreement (PTA) in Manila in 1977. For almost 10 years after the agreement, there was no significant progress or result. The Third ASEAN Summit in Manila in 1987 attempted to develop a more advanced and integrated ASEAN market. Economic regionalism in Europe, North America, and other parts of the world seemed to force ASEAN leaders to make ASEAN more prepared to deal with international economic competition.

Through the ASEAN Economic Ministerial Meeting (AEM) in Bali in 1990, Indonesia took several initiatives in order to materialize ASEAN cooperation. One of the initiatives was for ASEAN members to adopt the Common Effective Preferential Tariff (CEPT). This is a scheme to reduce tariffs and consequently to increase trade volume among ASEAN country members. At the Fourth ASEAN Summit in Singapore in 1992, Indonesia supported the Framework Agreement on Enhancing ASEAN Economic Cooperation. This summit also agreed on the idea to develop ASEAN Free Trade Area (AFTA) which would be implemented in 15 years based on the CEPT framework.

Considering the international and regional economic dynamics, the Fifth ASEAN Summit in Bangkok in 1995 decided to bring AFTA into effect a little more rapidly, from 2008 to 2003. This was accomplished by accelerating the trade tariff reduction from 5–10 per cent to 0–5 per cent and maximizing the number of products at 0 per cent in 2000. It was followed by the Second Informal Summit in Kuala Lumpur in 1997 which was specifically used to discuss the Asian economic and financial crisis and tried to build regional economic resilience. At this event, the ASEAN Vision 2020 was also revealed with a strong emphasis on ASEAN economic integration. The following meetings, the Sixth ASEAN Summit in Hanoi in 1998 and the Third Informal Summit in Manila in 1999 underlined ASEAN's commitment to economic liberalization and integration. Apart from focusing on economic recovery programmes, Indonesia showed support for the idea to build the ASEAN Economic Community in 2015.

Compared to political and security issues, Indonesia played a rather moderate role in ASEAN economic integration. Given the fact that Indonesia has the largest economy in the region and has proposed various initiatives for an integrated regional economic cooperation, Indonesia was 'not sufficiently active' (Narjoko 2014). At the Bali Summit in 2003 Indonesia endorsed the establishment of the ASEAN Economic Community (AEC), and again at the Bali Summit in 2011, Indonesia put forward the Regional Comprehensive Economic Partnership (RCEP). However, Narjoko (2014) writes, 'there are obstacles to Indonesian leadership in ASEAN'. Some key concerns he mentions are 'issues regarding infrastructure development, a high dependence on natural resources for generating income, a more rigid labor market, and continuing development gaps between regions within Indonesia'.

2.3 *Indonesia and the ASEAN Social and Cultural Community (ASCC)*

The Declaration of ASEAN Concord II (Bali, 2003) stipulated the establishment of the ASEAN Community by 2020, which was later accelerated to 2015. This clearly shows that Indonesia realized the importance of social and cultural aspects in order to attain the sustainable peace and security of the community. While the Cebu Declaration (the Philippines, 2007) maintained the acceleration of an ASEAN Community by 2015, the ASEAN Summit in Singapore in 2007 agreed on the development of the blueprint for the ASCC. It is said that the primary goal of the ASCC is to develop the ASEAN Community 'that is people-centred and socially responsible with a view to achieving enduring solidarity and unity among the nations and peoples of ASEAN'. Having a united people of ASEAN is expected to be achieved by promoting a regional common identity and building a caring and sharing society that is inclusive and harmonious where the well-being, livelihood, and welfare of the peoples are enhanced (ASEAN Social and Cultural Community Blueprint, 2009, 1).

In regard to the diversity of society and culture of ASEAN country members, the idea to have a common identity of ASEAN peoples may sound too ambitious and unrealistic. However, it would not be ASEAN without such idealistic and even romantic ideas. There have been views saying that ASEAN was built on formal ideas instead of materialized reasons (Ba 2009, 29). And, it is fair to say that the idea was very much influenced by how Indonesia's leaders perceive themselves as a state and a community as well. The process is never-ending.

Geographically, demographically, and culturally diverse, Indonesia has challenging tasks in managing its domestic and international affairs as well. The term 'imagined communities' coined by Benedict Anderson (1991) is fair to indicate that different groups share the imagination of being connected and even united within the Indonesian nation. National leaders and the government have been in the front line to introduce, conserve, and develop this feeling that communities living in Sabang (in the northwest of Sumatera) and Merauke (in the southeast of Papua province) and those inhabiting North Sulawesi and East Nusa Tenggara with their respective cultural identities are all integrated under the nation and state of Indonesia. In this context, there is no need for each group to know one another. Given the former colonial power which helped form national territory and garnered a shared historical experience, the government has struggled and continuously strives to develop a feeling of 'oneness' and internal cohesiveness. Introducing and promoting the 'nationalist catch-cry and oft-espoused Pancasila principle of unity in diversity' (Kingsbury 1998, 163; Ramage 1995) and other symbolic and unifying propaganda such as the national language, *Bahasa Indonesia*, the central government also attempted to nurture the nation based on the values of pluralism and tolerance through social and economic development programmes across the nation.

Indonesia's interest in pursuing ASEAN's ideal of a caring and sharing society might be partly inspired by the national experience of the demand for a united and cohesive society. It has been a growing understanding that the existence of strong government and the presence of security forces within communities may not enhance social tolerance and cohesiveness. Instead, it is social and economic development, a democratic system, and respect for human rights that are the key factors in creating a cohesive society.

Taking seriously into account the complexity of global interdependence as demonstrated by the interconnection of issues and multi-dimensions of national interests and the growing influence of international non-government entities, Indonesia acknowledges the increasingly important role of domestic non-government entities in carrying out its international relations. This is supported by the democratic transition in domestic politics. 'The foreign policy should reflect democratic transformation which has taken place at home. Hereafter, it is necessary to place an emphasis on the importance of support and participation from all stakeholders for the effective Indonesian foreign policy in strengthening its position at the international level' (Indonesian Ministry of Foreign Affairs, 2012).

3 Indonesia's involvement in the establishment of APT

None of the Indonesian national objectives highlighted above could be self-fulfilling. In other words, positive relations with the international community seem to be imperative. This cooperation covers a range of entities including individual or groups of states and international organizations, and in many cases, cooperation with private sectors and various societal associations is also inevitable.

In dealing with the opportunities and challenges offered by globalization, Indonesia has taken comprehensive steps that are generally in line with the concept of concentric circles, as previously mentioned. Considering the centrality of stability of surrounding countries to Indonesian national security and stability, Indonesia locates ASEAN at the centre of its concentric circles. Following that are the ASEAN Regional Forum (ARF) and ASEAN Plus Three (APT). There are also other circles, Asia Pacific Economic Cooperation (APEC) and Asia-Europe Meeting (ASEM) where ASEAN was said to be representing the association (ASEAN Ten) rather than individual members. While APEC (formed in 1989) is intended to develop economic cooperation between Asia and the Pacific countries, ASEM (established in 1996) aims at developing a constructive dialogue and cooperation between Asia and European countries. Given the fact that European countries (in the form of the European Union) have played and continue to play important roles in global economics, politics and security, Asian leaders see the importance of maintaining a good relationship between the two regions in issues related to security, economics and social development.

In line with the post-Cold War system, the idea to establish the ASEAN Regional Forum (ARF) was related to the collective awareness of China emerging as a superpower, not only in Asia but all over the world. By 1992, when the Chinese government made a public claim of territorial sovereignty over the entire South China Sea (SCS), it pushed ASEAN leaders to respond appropriately. The claim was seen as a sign of threat to the stability of the Southeast region, noting that several ASEAN country members (Brunei, Vietnam, the Philippines, and Malaysia) also have made claims over parts of SCS. At the same time, China is also viewed as having huge potential for the economies of the region. Based on these somewhat dilemmatic views and interests, ASEAN leaders considered the importance of having meaningful and intensifying dialogues with China, and other major powers in the region, such as the USA, Canada, Russia, Japan, South Korea, Australia, New Zealand, and other relevant countries.[1] The idea led to the conduct of the first meeting that officially marked the formation of the multilateral forum, the ASEAN Regional Forum (ARF), in Bangkok in 1994. Its primary objective was to find the best way to manage the international dynamics within the region in the interest of maintaining the region in peace and security and for the sake of economic development.

Like the centrality of ASEAN to Indonesia's foreign policies and relations, Indonesia strongly holds a similar view of the centrality of ASEAN within the ARF. Indonesia is consistently active in maintaining and nurturing the Forum which is grounded on the following unchanged principles: the non-negotiable principle of national sovereignty, non-interference, and consensual decision-making process. Since ASEAN has been viewed as a regional shield to secure national integrity and stability, ARF was also believed to be instrumentally important as the second regional protection of Indonesia's sovereignty. Underlying ARF as a forum for dialogues and constructive consultations, the forum is strategically important to discuss security issues within the region and to maintain the region as a stable and peaceful one. Such positive conditions will bring about benefits to national economic development and the region as well. This proposition is likely to reemphasize the comprehensive security concept that has been widely adopted by Indonesia and other ASEAN countries.

The ASEAN Plus Three (APT) cooperation began to take form in 1997. The establishment was also partly pushed by the economic crisis that devastated the region in 1997. It was accompanied by an understanding that the existing collaborations such as ASEAN and APEC had their own limits in dealing successfully with the economic damage and negative social-political consequences caused by the crisis. Simply put, the reason to establish APT was to have more resources from major countries within the region. On the other hand, the East Asian countries also saw the benefits of developing closer relations with the ASEAN countries (Stubbs 2002, 441–444).

While Indonesia shows consistent and positive contribution to the formation and development of ARF with its focus on preserving peace and security in the region, Indonesia also realizes the significant role of China, Japan, and South Korea in their national economic development as well as the role they play in the region. In this respect, Indonesia shows strong support for the establishment of APT which literally means ASEAN plus Japan, China, and South Korea. It is worth noting, however, that besides APT, ASEAN has built strategic partnerships with the respective countries individually. ASEAN and China have agreed on the ASEAN–China Free Trade Agreement (ACFTA) which was believed to be able to boost investment and the trade volume between the two entities. With Japan, there was the ASEAN–Japan Comprehensive Economic Partnership and with South Korea, the ASEAN–South Korea Partnership. The form of bilateral partnership is seen to strengthen the multilateral mechanism of APT.

Formed and convened for the first time at ASEAN's second informal summit in Kuala Lumpur in 1997, APT was expected to provide Asian regional solutions to the ongoing regional economic crisis. Indonesia, which was hit severely by the 1997 financial crisis, realized that Asian economic powers could do something to help solve the problem. This was partly caused by the view that the international economic institutions, such as the World Bank, IMF, and WTO, which are dominated by the USA and EU countries, made insufficient efforts to help Indonesia and other ASEAN countries to handle the problem. With this argument, Indonesia hand in hand with other countries in the region believed that Asian economic powers had the capability to deal with the damage caused by the crisis and to prevent similar repercussions in the future. Keeping this in mind, Indonesia showed full support for the Chiang Mai Initiative Multilateralization (CMIM) that was launched in May 2000. This CMIM was intended to manage regional short-term liquidity problems with economic support from Japan, China and South Korea to facilitate the work of the existing international financial institutions such as IMF, WB, and ADB. A decade later there is an opinion saying that 'as the CMI emerges as the major regional institution in its own right it is likely to remain, at least initially, light on surveillance and more focussed on building up its political independence from global institutions' (Rathus 2011).

Indonesia also showed appreciation for the adoption of the Asian Bond Markets Initiatives (ABMI) New Roadmap. The Initiative is expected to 'develop efficient and liquid bond markets in the region through a more efficient utilization of regional saving for regional investment' (www.asean.org). The adoption of CMIM and ABMI brings about significant achievement in both trade and investment values between ASEAN members and East Asia's countries.

There is no doubt that for Indonesia the forms of bilateral and multilateral partnership with the countries in East Asia are strategically important. Japan has been a most crucial country partner to Indonesia for investment and trade since the 1970s. The growing economic development of China and South Korea made them increasingly influential on Indonesia's economy. Although the USA and European Union are also essential and remain the traditional source of investment and financial assistance to Indonesia, countries in East Asia are increasingly important to Indonesia's sustainable economic growth.

The economic significance of East Asian countries to Indonesia's economy is frequently blended with their geographical proximity and the self-claimed commonalities in historical, social, and cultural values. These claims may constitute a shared sentiment of the ASEAN Way and Asian values. The consequence would be positive results. Thus, in addition to the growing trend in trade and other economic transactions, social and cultural interactions tend to intensify between ASEAN and the three countries. They cover various issues such as youth, environment, labour, and health. For example, 'In the area of youth, the APT countries have three regular forums for sharing information and discussing cooperation regarding youth, namely APT Ministerial Meeting on Youth (AMMY+3), the APT Senior Officials Meeting on Youth (SOMY+3) and the APT Youth Caucus' (www.asean.org). The 5th SOMY+3 held in September 2012 in Jakarta is just an example of how Indonesia fully supports an extended and deepened cooperation among groups of people in Southeast Asian and East Asian countries.

4 Conclusions

The structural-institutional approach applied in discussing Indonesia's domestic politics and international relations helps to identify several political forces and challenging issues. It has to be kept in mind, however, that the issues are very fluid in the sense that separation between the domestic and international context may well be misleading and even prove dangerous. In other words, there are always linkages between political, social, and economic issues at both domestic and regional or global levels which influence each other. The existence and significance of Indonesia to the region and *vice versa* must be perceived as the outcome of interaction between its domestic competence and international influence.

Since independence, Indonesia has shown changing perceptions of Southeast Asia, the Asian region, and the world in general. This is in part, if not mainly, caused by changes within domestic politics. It is also reasonable to argue that changes within the international political constellation and regional dynamics contribute significantly to the way Indonesia perceives the region and the world, and the way it manages its domestic affairs. This all has led Indonesia to have a more cooperative view of the region and the world, and at the same time, it has pushed Indonesia to develop a more democratic political system.

The reform (or post-Suharto) era generally shows Indonesia adopting a more positive view and deepening engagement with the construction and development of Southeast Asia and Asia's regional architecture. The government with the support from various groups that hold strong views on globalization tends to be in the front line to bring the country to the higher level of regional integration and community. Having adopted the democratic system and showed some progress in the consolidation of democracy, the post-Suharto governments from Habibie to Yudhoyono see ASEAN and the broader Asian regional cooperation in the form of ARF and APT as benefiting not only to

Indonesian national political and economic development but to all of the countries in the region. The newly elected President Joko Widodo (Jokowi) has promised that non-government entities will have more room to become involved in regional integration and globalization. It was argued that Indonesia's foreign policy should be based on people participation. Based on this argument, the future of the ASEAN Community through its three pillars of the ASEAN Political and Security Community (APSC), the ASEAN Economic Community (AEC), and the ASEAN Social and Cultural Community (ASCC) will also be shaped by the Indonesian people.

The advance of regionalization by including Japan, South Korea and China and the establishment of the APT Community is indicative of recognizing the crucial role of the three countries in strengthening Southeast and East Asia cooperation in political and security affairs and in economic and socio-cultural matters. Indonesia perceives the advance and inclusion of the three major powers to be highly likely to fortify the ASEAN Community. Bilateral relationships conducted by every ASEAN country member with each of the three East Asia countries are irrefutable and have to be appropriately taken into account for the mutual benefit of both ASEAN and East Asia Communities. Indonesia also believes that constructive multilateral and institutional conduct through ASEAN frameworks must be continuously nurtured and developed for a peaceful, advanced and prosperous community in Asia.

Note

1   The European Union was also involved. Other countries outside ASEAN members are India, Mongolia, and North Korea.

References

Abuza, Zachary (2007) *Political Islam and Violence in Indonesia*. London: Routledge.

Agussalim, Dafri (n.d.) 'New Trends in Indonesian's Foreign Policy Orientation and Practices: From Regional to Global Oriented'. Available from www2.gsid.nagoya-u.ac.jp/blog/anda/files/2011/08/56-dafri-agussalim_trends-in-indonesias-foreign-policy.pdf (accessed 11 January 2013).

Alhumami, Amich (1999) 'Paradoks-paradoks Reformasi' [The Paradoxes of Reform]. *Kompas*, 15 September.

Anderson, Benedict (1991) *Imagined Communities: Reflections on the Origin and Spread of Nationalism*. Revised edition. London: Verso.

Anwar, Dewi Fortuna (2010) 'Indonesia, the Region and the World'. Available from: www.eastasiaforum.org/2010/05/28/indonesia-the-region-and-the-world.

Anwar, Dewi Fortuna (1995) 'Twenty-Five Years of ASEAN Political Cooperation'. In *ASEAN in a Changed Regional and International Political Economy*, edited by Hadi Soesastro. Jakarta: CSIS, pp. 108–128.

'ASEAN Social and Cultural Community Blueprint, 2009', in *Roadmap for an ASEAN Community*. Jakarta: The ASEAN Secretariat Public Outreach and Civil Society Division.

Aspinall, Edward (2005) *Opposing Suharto: Compromise, Resistance, and Regime Change in Indonesia*. Stanford, CA: Stanford University Press.

Aspinall, Edward and Marcus Mietzner (eds) (2010) *Problems of Democratization in Indonesia; Elections, Institutions and Society*. Singapore: ISEAS.

Azra, Azyumardi (2011) 'Islam, Indonesia and Democracy'. *Strategic Review*, 1(1): 78–81.

Ba, Alice D. (2009) *[Re]Negotiating East and Southeast Asia: Region, Regionalism, and the Association of Southeast Asian Nations*. Stanford, CA: Stanford University Press.

Barton, Dominic (2011) 'Indonesia in the New World'. *Strategic Review*, 1(1): 63–72.

Brown, Colin (2003) *A Short History of Indonesia: The Unlikely Nation?* Crows Nest: Allen & Unwin.

Collins, Alan (2003) *Security and Southeast Asia: Domestic, Regional, and Global Issues*. Singapore: ISEAS.

Crouch, Harold (2010) *Political Reform in Indonesia After Soeharto*. Singapore: ISEAS.

Daniri, Mas Achmad (2009) 'Mekanisme Whistleblower dan Pencegahan Korupsi' [Whistleblower Mechanism and Corruption Eradication]. In *Korupsi Mengorupsi Indonesia*, edited by Wijayanto and Ridwan Zachrie. Jakarta: Gramedia, pp. 641–662.

Diamond, Larry (2010) 'Indonesia's Place in Global Democracy'. In *Problems of Democratization in Indonesia; Elections, Institutions and Society*, edited by Edward Aspinall and Marcus Mietzner. Singapore: ISEAS, pp. 21–49.

Eschborn, Norbert, Sabrina Hackel and Joyce Holmes Richardson (eds) (2004) *Indonesia Today – Problems and Prospects: Politics and Society Five Years into Reformasi*. Jakarta: KAS.

Forrester, Geoff and R.J. May (eds) (1998) *The Fall of Soeharto*. Bathurst: Crawford House Publishing.

Frederick, William H. and Robert L. Worden (eds) (1993) *Indonesia: A Country Study*. Washington, DC: GPO for the Library of Congress. Available from country-studies.us/indonesia.

Frigo, Michael (2013) 'Indonesia: A Rising Economic Power', *The Jakarta Post*, 5 August.

Hadiwinata, Bob S. (2004) 'Stirring from Beyond the Borders: International Actors and Democratization in Indonesia'. In *Indonesia Today – Problems and Prospects: Politics and Society Five Years into Reformasi*, edited by Norbert Eschborn, Sabrina Hackel and Joyce Holmes Richardson. Jakarta: KAS, pp. 11–32.

Harjapamekas, Erry Riyana and Aan Rukmana (2009) 'Dasar-dasar Strategi Pemberantasan Korupsi di Indonesia' [Bases of Strategy to Eradicate Corruption in Indonesia]. In *Korupsi Mengorupsi Indonesia*, edited by Wijayanto and Ridwan Zachrie. Jakarta: Gramedia, pp. 605–624.

Ibrahim, Farid M. (2009) 'KPK: Posisi Strategis, Problem, dan Prospeknya' [KPK: Strategic Position, Problem, and Its Prospect]. In *Korupsi Mengorupsi Indonesia*, edited by Wijayanto and Ridwan Zachrie. Jakarta: Gramedia, pp. 663–689.

Indonesian Ministry of Foreign Affairs (2012) Available from: www.kemlu.go.id/id/kebijakan/landasan-visi-misi-polugri/Pages/Ringkasan.aspx (accessed 12 March 2012).

Isra, Saldi and Eddy O.S. Hiariej (2009) 'Perspektif Hukum Pemberantasan Korupsi di Indonesia' [Legal Perspective in Eradication of Corruption in Indonesia]. In *Korupsi Mengorupsi Indonesia*, edited by Wijayanto and Ridwan Zachrie. Jakarta: Gramedia, pp. 553–603.

Kingsbury, Damien (1998) *The Politics of Indonesia*. Melbourne, Oxford and Auckland: Oxford University Press.

Laksmana, Evan A. (2009) 'Moulding a Strategic and Professional Indonesian Military: Policy Options for the Next Administration'. *The Indonesian Quarterly*, 37(3): 352–363.

Leifer, Michael (1995) 'ASEAN as a Model of a Security Community'. In *ASEAN in a Changed Regional and International Political Economy*, edited by Hadi Soesastro. Jakarta: CSIS, pp. 129–142.

Liddle, R. William (ed.) (2001) *Crafting Indonesian Democray*. Bandung: Mizan.

Luhulima, C.P.F. (2008) 'Regional Strategy for a Nuclear-Weapon Free Zone: The ASEAN Case' *The Indonesian Quarterly*, 36(2): 120–137.

Machfudz, Anas S. and Jalewari Pramodhawardani (eds) (2001) *Military without Militarism: Suara dari Daerah*. Jakarta: LIPI.

McDougall, Derek (1997) *The International Politics of the New Asia Pacific*. Boulder, CO: Lynne Rienner.

Nabers, Dirk (2006) 'The War on Terrorism and Security Cooperation in the Pacific'. In *Redefining the Pacific?: Regionalism Past, Present and Future*, edited by Jenny Bryant-Tokalau and Ian Frazer. Hampshire: Ashgate, pp. 67–88.

Narjoko, Dionisius (2014) 'Why Indonesia Needs to Lead in Economic Integration', *East Asia Forum*. Available from www.eastasiaforum.org/2014/03/03/why-indonesia-needs-to-lead-in-economic-integration (accessed 15 February 2014).

Nurhasim, Moch (ed.) (2003) *Praktek-Praktek Bisnis Militer: Pengalaman Indonesia, Burma, Filipina, dan Korea Selatan*. Jakarta: RIDEP Institute.

Oratmangun, Djauhari (2010) *ASEAN Selayang Pandang*, 19th edition.

Palmer, Norman D. (1991) *The New Regionalism in Asia and the Pacific*. Lexington, MA: Lexington Books.

Permanent Mission of the Republic of Indonesia to the United Nations, New York (2005) *Indonesia and the United Nations: Working Together for Peace and Development*.

Purdey, Jemma (ed.) (2012) *Knowing Indonesia: Intersections of Self, Discipline and Nation*. Clayton, Vic.: Monash University.

Ramage, Douglas E. (1995) *Politics in Indonesia: Democracy, Islam and the Ideology of Tolerance*. London: Routledge.

Rathus, Joel (2011) 'Chiang Mai Initiative: China Takes the Leader's Seat'. Available from www.eastasiaforum.org/2011/06/30/chiang-mai-initiative-china-takes-the-leader-s-seat (accessed 15 February 2014).

Samuel, Hanneman and Henk Schulte Nordholt (eds) (2004) *Indonesia in Transition: Rethinking 'Civil Society', 'Religion', and 'Crisis'*. Yogyakarta: Pustaka Pelajar.

Sekretariat Direktorat Jenderal Kerjasama ASEAN (Secretariat of Directorate General for ASEAN Cooperation) (2000) *ASEAN Selayang Pandang*, 15th edition, Jakarta: Kementerian Luar Negeri.

Soesastro, Hadi (ed.) (1995) *ASEAN in a Changed Regional and International Political Economy*. Jakarta: CSIS.

Soesastro, Hadi, 2009) 'APEC in 2010 and Beyond: An Agenda for East Asia'. *The Indonesian Quarterly*, 37(3): 375–384.

Stubbs, Richard, 2002, 'ASEAN Plus Three: Emerging East Asian Regionalism?', *Asian Survey*, 42(3) May/June: 440–455.

Sukma, Rizal (2010) 'Indonesia's 2009 Elections: Defective System, Resilient Democracy'. In *Problems of Democratization in Indonesia; Elections, Institutions and Society*, edited by Edward Aspinall and Marcus Mietzner. Singapore: ISEAS, pp. 53–74.

Suwasta, Putu (2013) *Menegakkan Demokrasi, Mengawal Perubahan* [Implementing Democracy, Guarding Changes]. Jakarta: Lestari Kiranatama.

Tay, Simon S.C., Jesus Estanislao and Hadi Soesastro (eds) (2000) *A New ASEAN in A New Millennium*. Jakarta: CSIS.

Tomsa, Dirk (2010) 'The Indonesian Party System after the 2009 Elections: Towards Stability?' In *Problems of Democratization in Indonesia; Elections, Institutions and Society*, edited by Edward Aspinall and Marcus Mietzner. Singapore: ISEAS, pp. 141–159.

Urbaningrum, Anas (1999) 'Mewaspadai Ranjau-ranjau Reformasi' [Taking Care of the 'Mines of Reform']. *Kompas*, 6 January.

Wanandi, Jusuf (2008) 'Strategic Trends in East Asia'. *Indonesian Quarterly*, 36(3–4): 312–326.

Wanandi, Jusuf (1995) 'ASEAN and an Asia Pacific Security Dialogue'. In *ASEAN in a Changed Regional and International Political Economy*, edited by Hadi Soesastro. Jakarta: CSIS, pp. 143–158.

Wijayanto and Ridwan Zachrie (eds) (2009) *Korupsi Mengorupsi Indonesia* [Corruption Corrupts Indonesia]. Jakarta: Gramedia.

Yudhoyono, Susilo Bambang (2012) 'Indonesia in 2045: A Centennial Journey of Progress'. *Strategic Review*, 1(1): 47–57.

Yunanto, S. et al. (2003) *Militant Islamic Movements in Indonesia and South-East Asia*. Jakarta: RIDEP Institute and FES.

4 Laos

Economic and social development towards the ASEAN Economic Community (AEC)

Phouphet Kyophilavong, Somchith Souksavath and Sengchanh Chanthasene

1 National perspectives

1.1 Historical perspective

The History of Laos is officially traced to the establishment of the kingdom of Lan Xang by Fa Ngum in 1353. Entering a period of decline in the seventeenth century, Lan Xang was controlled by Siam (now Thailand). During this period, the country was divided into three dependent states: Luang Prabang in the north, Vientiane in the centre, and Champassak in the south. Following its occupation of Vietnam, France also absorbed Laos into French Indochina via treaties with Siam in 1893 and 1904. During World War II, the Japanese occupied French Indochina. When Japan surrendered, Laos declared Laos independent, but by early 1946, French troops had reoccupied the country and conferred limited autonomy on Laos. During the First Indochina War, the Indochinese Communist Party formed the Pathet Lao (Lao Nation) resistance organization committed to Lao independence. Laos gained full independence on 22 October 1953. Growing American and North Vietnamese military presence in the country increasingly drew Laos into the Second Indochina War (1954–1975) (Stuart-Fox, 1997).

The Pathet Lao took total power on 2 December 1975. After 1975, Laos introduced planned economy like the Soviet Union and other communist countries. During that period, there was poor economic performance and Laos depended heavily on Soviet aid channelled through Vietnam up until the Soviet collapse in 1991. In the 1990s the communist party gave up centralized management of the economy and turned it into a market-oriented economy in 1986 called New Economic Mechanism (NEM) or 'Chinthanakanmai' in Lao. Under NEM, Laos was reformed in various areas leading to high economic performance (Goscha and Ivarsson, 2003). Since 1986, Laos has implemented various reforms under NEM, which include the following vital components: promotion of private production through improved incentives; upgrading institutional infrastructure to improve market economy operation; strengthening Laos' comparative advantage through trade liberalization and specialization; and the establishment of price stability through macroeconomic policy measures (Ljunggren, 1993).

Laos has integrated itself into globalization as indicated by its joining ASEAN (Association of Southeast Asian Nations), and AFTA (ASEAN Free Trade Area) in 1997 and 1998, respectively. Furthermore, it was granted full membership of WTO (World Trade Organization) in February 2013. In addition, Laos is a member of the Asia-Pacific Trade Agreement (APTA), East Asia Summit and La Francophonie.

Economic reforms, notably the introduction of the New Economic Mechanism, have played important roles in the promotion of political-security, economic and socio-cultural changes. As a member of ASEAN, Laos could benefit with the promotion of political stability. In addition, economic reforms and international and regional integration have also had a significant impact on Lao economy.

Laos was able to deliver high economic growth except during the Asian Financial Crisis of the late 1990s. Economic growth averaged about 8 per cent from 1990 to 2013. In 2013, Lao GDP was attributed by the agricultural sector (25.2 per cent), industrial sector (28.0 per cent), service sector (38.9 per cent) and others (7.9 per cent). In addition, the macroeconomic situation was stable. From 2011 to 2013, the average inflation rate was held to a single digit. The exchange rate was also stable during this period. GDP per capita also increased significantly. GDP per capita in 1980 was USD 310, which increased to USD 984 in 2010 and to over USD 1000 in 2012. These developments have led to Laos moving from a 'Low Income' status to a 'Low-Middle Income' category by 2012 according to the World Bank. Moreover, poverty has declined significantly.

Analysis of four Laos Expenditure and Consumption Surveys (LECS) from the World Bank and DOS (2009) showed that poverty has fallen significantly. In 2008, Laos poverty was 28 per cent in LECS 4. While poverty has gone down, inequality has gone up, especially in Vientiane and other urban areas. The Gini coefficient increased from 30.5 in LECS 1 (1992/93) to 35.4 in LECS 4 (2007/08). In Vientiane, the Gini coefficient increased from 29.7 in LECS 1 (1992/93) to 38.00 in LECS 4 (2007/08). Reforms and integration have reduced poverty significantly, but it has led to increased inequality.

For socio-cultural affairs, there was some restriction on beliefs and Lao tradition before the economic reforms in 1986. Since the economic reforms with the reintroduction of free trade and private enterprise, Lao beliefs and tradition have come back to life. Buddhism and traditional Lao festivals have been revived (Vatthana, 2006).

2 Involvement of Laos within the region

2.1 Contribution of Laos to regional cooperation

ASEAN leaders agreed to establish an ASEAN Economic Community (AEC) by 2020, later on expedited to 2015. The AEC includes existing economic programmes such as the ASEAN Free Trade Area (AFTA), the

ASEAN Framework Agreement on Services (AFAS), and the ASEAN Investment Area (AIA). The core concept of the AEC is to develop a single market and production base that is stable, prosperous, highly competitive and economically integrated with effective facilitation for free flow of goods, free flows of services, free flows of investment, free flows of skilled labour, and freer flow of capital by 2015.

One of the most important concerns in AEC is the development gap between older and newer members (CLMV: Cambodia, Laos, Myanmar, and Vietnam). Development gaps will hinder the progress of AEC. CLMV members are also different in terms of the pace of reforms and international integration as well as the socio-economic performances. CLMV has limited resources, limitations of knowledge, lack of practical experiences and small domestic markets. AEC will promote economic growth, narrow development gaps, and strengthen competitiveness and opportunities to learn and exchange in the development process of CLMV. However, the AEC may widen development gaps between the new and older members. For example, AEC may have negative effects on the environment and social aspect of CLMV. Laos is one of the CLMV countries having large development gaps when compared with old ASEAN members. Promoting economic growth and reducing poverty is a priority of the Lao government. Through reforms, Laos has achieved high economic growth and poverty has been reduced sharply. However, in order to maintain sustainable economic growth in the long run in catching up with other ASEAN countries, various economic issues need to be addressed.

Since 1975, the Lao People's Revolutionary Party has been ruling Laos. This single party has played important roles in the economic development, peace and prosperity for Laos. As noted earlier, in 1986, the Lao government introduced an economic reform policy called the 'New Economic Mechanism' or 'NEM' to shift from a centrally planned economy to a more open market-oriented one. Since the introduction of the NEM and the consequent opening of the economy, Laos has enjoyed relatively rapid economic growth, remarkable political, economic and social stability, improved living standards and has achieved gradual poverty eradication.

Despite its small land size, economy and population, Laos has contributed to regional cooperation in various ways. In economic terms, Laos has contributed to regional cooperation in four ways. Its first contribution is the promotion of investment in the region. Laos is one of the most resource-rich countries in Asia. More than 570 mineral deposits have been identified, including gold, copper, zinc and lead (DOG, 2008). This resource not only attracts foreign investment from ASEAN countries, but also attracts foreign direct investments from other regions. Foreign investments have been flowing to Laos significantly since 2003 (Kyophilavong and Toyoda, 2012; Kyophilavong, 2009). Its second contribution is its export and promotion of industrial linkage in Asia. Most of the products from the Lao natural resource sector are for export in terms of raw materials and finished goods to Asian countries. This provides opportunities for industries in Asia to use raw materials to produce goods for export to this region and the rest of the world. Cheap raw materials from Laos could promote more linkages of industries in this region. The third contribution is its contribution to energy security in this region. Energy plays an important role in economic development in ASEAN (Payne, 2010). However, most Asian countries face a shortage of energy. Laos has been known for its substantial hydropower potential, which is estimated at 26,000 MW (excluding mainstream Mekong); only 9 per cent of this capacity was being used in 2004 (Pholsena and Phonekeo, 2004). The development of hydropower will contribute to energy security in this region. In addition, it will also promote investment in energy development and more energy integration in this region. The fourth contribution is the promotion of connectivity and improvement of trade facilitation in the region. Connectivity is one of the important factors to promote economic growth in this region. In addition, poor trade facilities will hinder growth because of increased transaction costs in this region (ESCAP, 2015). Laos is a land-locked country which links with five countries (China, Myanmar, Thailand, Cambodia and Vietnam). It is a perfect location to promote connectivity in Asia. Infrastructure and connectivity have been developed in Laos by the Greater Mekong Subregion (GMS) supported by the Asian Development Bank (ADB). In addition, Laos has support from other countries and sources. Therefore, Laos plays an important role in improving the infrastructure, connectivity and trade facilitation to promote economic development in this region (Itakura, 2014).

Being located in the most dynamic region of the world, the Association of South-East Asian Nations (ASEAN)/ASEAN Free Trade Area (AFTA), and its special trade relations with several partners are important to Laos. ASEAN has now become more dynamic in establishing an ASEAN Community by 2015. The community consists of three pillars – the ASEAN Political-Security Community, the ASEAN Economic Community, and the ASEAN Socio-Cultural Community. Furthermore, ASEAN aims to strengthen its external relations. The achievements in economic cooperation have made a significant contribution to the economic development of ASEAN.

Laos' accession to ASEAN in 1997 is the fruit of its implementation of the consistent foreign policy of peace, independence, friendship, and cooperation aimed at contributing to the building of Southeast Asia as a region of peace, stability and cooperation for development. Its membership in ASEAN has contributed to further strengthening the socio-economic development of Laos and regional resilience. As a result of the accession to ASEAN, there has been an increase in trade, investment, and foreign tourist arrivals in Laos, contributing significant revenues to the country (Fukase and Winters, 2003; Menon, 1999). Moreover, the country has received assistance and technical support as well as help in human resource development from other member states, dialogue partners and other external partners of ASEAN.

Laos is not only gaining the benefits of becoming a member of ASEAN, it has also actively contributed to ASEAN activities. Its successful chairmanship of ASEAN in 2004–2005, for example, led to the ASEAN nations as well as other countries recognizing the role and capacity of Laos. Subsequently, the country was entrusted to contribute to the region by chairing and hosting various important regional and international meetings and events. In November 2012, for example, Laos was honoured to host the 9th Asia-Europe Meeting (ASEM) Summit and in 2016, Laos will assume the ASEAN chairmanship for the second time. The ASEAN Development Fund, established at the 38th ASEAN Ministerial Meeting held in Laos to support the projects of the Vientiane Action Programs (VAP), has received contributions from several international organizations and ASEAN partners, particularly Japan with the value of USD 70 million. Among others, Laos has also contributed to ASEAN as a coordinating country with partners including the European Union (EU) and India during the summits. This contribution from Laos has not only brought benefits to Laos, but also to the whole of ASEAN.

Another contribution is the Laos Pilot Program (LPP) for Narrowing the Development Gap in ASEAN. LPP is aimed at contributing significantly to ASEAN integration by establishing an effective tripartite cooperation mechanism among the government of Laos, the ASEAN Secretariat and Japan International Cooperation Agency (JICA) through the implementation of three cooperation components – tourism promotion, safety of agricultural products and environmentally sustainable cities. For instance, tourism development which is anticipated to contribute significantly to local communities, made use of the database already established in the Lao National Tourism Administration (LNTA) server, thus developing market-driven community-based tourism by making use of the accumulated know-how and experience. These developing tourist sites contribute to increasing tourism networks in ASEAN and the GMS (Greater Mekong Subregion) while taking into account the natural and cultural conservation of Laos. Other important examples consistent with the LPP's cooperation concept, 'Green, Clean and Beautiful Laos', contributing to ASEAN integration are: (1) Limestone Forest, which is a candidate for a World Heritage site, in Khammouane province; (2) Champhone Wetland which was registered in the Ramsar Convention, in Savannakhet province, and (3) Mekong River Dolphins, which were registered as an endangered species, in Champasak province.

In sum, Laos is not only benefiting from ASEAN but also playing an important role in economic, cultural and political development in the region.

3 Opportunities and challenges of regional cooperation

3.1 Political-security perspectives

In the increasingly integrated and interdependent world, cooperating with other countries across the region offers Laos opportunities for experience exchange, donor coordination, technical support, more market access, increasing investment, and various benefits. Another benefit for Laos in accessing ASEAN to work on political-security cooperation among member states, is a better political environment through a cohesive, peaceful, stable and resilient region. As Laos and most of ASEAN member states are facing challenging political and security issues in the region, including an arms race, corruption, the development gap and the impact of it, ethnic clashes and intolerance, human trafficking, human rights abuses, an illicit drug trade, migration, money laundering, social injustice, terrorism, territorial maritime disputes, and other forms of transnational crimes, a rules-based ASEAN Political-Security Community (APSC) would be established. In addition, there will be the ASEAN Economic Community (AEC) and ASEAN Socio-Cultural Community (ASCC) to ensure a harmonious political and security environment in the region.

The main components of the APSC are political development, shaping and sharing of norms, conflict prevention, conflict resolution, post-conflict peace building, and implementing mechanisms. Regional promotion of political-security development will ensure a peaceful, harmonious, and democratic environment for Laos. Based on the principles of democracy, the rule of law and good governance, promotion and protection of human rights and funda-mental freedoms as inscribed in the ASEAN Charter, APSC has put its effort to strengthen the regional political-security cooperation among ASEAN member states, and between ASEAN and its external partners.

To ensure that the peoples of the member states live at peace with one another and with the world at large in a democratic and harmonious envir-onment, all ASEAN members have been consistent in their efforts to main-tain and promote peace and stability in the region as well as the world at large through enhancing political-security cooperation within ASEAN and between ASEAN and its external partners. Rather than forming a primarily economic-focused organization, in the ASEAN Vision 2020 and the 2009–2015 roadmap and timetable for an ASEAN Community adopted by all member states, ASEAN also envisions establishing a fully functional political-security community. Some of the foundations for ASEAN's transition from a strictly economic community to a much broader security community have already been laid down as demonstrated by the adoption of the Declaration on the Zone of Peace, Freedom, and Neutrality (ZOPFAN), the Treaty of Amity and Cooperation in South East Asia (TAC), and the Treaty on the Southeast Asian Nuclear Weapon Free Zone (SEANWFZ). These achieve-ments have enabled ASEAN to continue promoting peace and stability, which is an important condition for development cooperation for all ASEAN members as well as between and among ASEAN members and their external partners through bilateral, sub-regional, regional and multilateral cooperation frame-works. This has contributed significantly to the socio-economic development of all ASEAN members, including Laos.

However, although ASEAN aims at achieving a much higher degree of political, security, and cultural integration among its member states, whether a stronger political community is possible appears to be questioned. The individual ASEAN members may also be one of the major problems slowing the progress towards building an APSC. This may be attributed to the insufficient power of the ASEAN Secretariat to coordinate, monitor and direct the policies, programmes and activities of ASEAN and member states in achieving the APSC. In order to overcome the issues and to promote the APSC with the aim to enhance good governance, the rule of law, and protect human rights, strengthen democracy, and fundamental freedoms, efficiently designing and directing the political and legal cooperation to integrate the political and legal systems of the member states are essential. For this purpose, adopting stronger conventions on anti-corruption and good governance, human trafficking, illicit drug trade, environmental protection, maritime disputes, extradition and mutual legal assistance, money laundering and other forms of transnational crimes should be considered.

Laos has contributed to the creation of the ASEAN political-security community with cooperation and support. First, economic development and poverty reduction are important factors maintaining political-security. The Lao government has established development goals and poverty eradication strategy to ensure sustainable economic development and graduate from Least Developed Country (GoL, 2004; GoL, 2010). Second, Laos also makes an effort to improve governance and environmental climate for business and investment. In addition, Laos also cooperates and coordinates with ASEAN members and external partners to maintain and promote peace and stability in the region.

3.2 Economic perspectives

ASEAN will implement the AEC in 2015. However, for Laos, joining the AEC will create both opportunities and challenges. First, ASEAN could be Lao PDR's biggest market, particularly Thailand, Lao PDR's biggest trading partner, with more than half of the Lao total exports and more than 30 per cent of the Lao total import each year. In terms of export, Lao PDR can increase exports to the ASEAN market based on the principle of free flow of goods of the AEC, which means no or zero restriction to trade for ASEAN member countries. In terms of imports, their prices will be cheaper and there will be more options for domestic consumers and investors from ASEAN countries. Second, for economic and trade negotiations at the international level with non-ASEAN states, particularly with more advanced and developed partners, joining ASEAN/AEC will strengthen the Lao PDR's bargaining power as part and parcel of ASEAN. Third, in terms of investment, again based on the principle of free flow of investment, more investment capital can be attracted to the country for economic growth. Fourth, in terms of services (banking, health care, education, telecommunication), the institutional and regulatory framework, services facilitation and services competitiveness of Lao PDR will be improved. Fifth, in terms of labour forces, based on the principle of free flow of labour, Lao PDR can have more labour migrants added to the Lao labour forces because Lao PDR is short of labour both in quantity and quality. Sixth, ASEAN offers Cambodia, Lao PDR, Myanmar and Vietnam (CLMV) the 'Initiative for ASEAN Integration' (IAI). The IAI framework covers a variety of human resource development programmes which contribute to the objective of integrating the four newer member countries (CLMV) into ASEAN. A training centre was set up in each of the four countries, and since 2002, the four cuntries have been conducting training courses for government officials in a wide variety of fields, including English language, information technology, public administration, trade and tourism. More than 20,000 officials have been trained so far.

However, the AEC also has challenges for Laos. The study conducted by ERIA (2012) on the scorecard for Lao PDR's preparation for AEC, by using the scoring approaches set by AEC criteria (score for full commitment is 100 per cent), showed the scores are in general very low. They are as follows: in terms of trade facilitation, only 39 per cent for customs modernization, 7 per cent for national single window; in terms of investment promotion and facilitation, 50 per cent for quality of investment promotion agencies, 46 per cent for investment promotion and facilitation strategy, 20 per cent for investment generation, 50 per cent for investment policy transparency; in terms of transport facilitation, 44 per cent for implementation of ASEAN Framework Agreement on the Facilitation of Goods in Transit (AFAFGIT), 25 per cent for implementation of ASEAN Framework Agreement on Multimodal Transport (AFAMT), 17 per cent for implementation of ASEAN Multilateral Agreement on the Full Liberalization of Passenger Air Services (MAFLPAS), and in general low scores for mutual recognition arrangement on professional services (architectural service, engineering service, dental practitioner service, medical practitioner service, nursing service), standards and conformance (cosmetic sector, electrical and electronic equipment, medical device, pharmaceutical sector, prepared foodstuff sector, rubber-based products sector, traditional medicine sector). The low scores for the progress of Lao PDR in preparation to join AEC means Lao PDR needs to make more efforts in preparing the institutional and regulatory frameworks as well as strengthening the country's capacity to fulfil its commitments to AEC.

Deepening integration within the context of AEC means, on the one hand, deepening cooperation, and on the other hand, deepening competition. Deepening competition, but weak competitiveness is the most critical challenge for Lao PDR. In particular, the business sectors will face hard competition because prices of imported goods from member countries will be cheaper and there will be more imported goods in the domestic market. Some domestic companies would even not be able to survive. In terms of competitiveness, Lao PDR has been ranked 167 out of the 183 countries by the IDC/World Bank on 'Doing Business 2014'. As a result, Lao PDR will gain less benefit in joining ASEAN/AEC, compared with other ASEAN member countries (WB and DOS, 2009). In terms of the social aspects, deepening economic integration will also change social relations and create more social problems such as drug trafficking, HIV-AIDS, crimes, migration, domestic cultural loss, etc. Even if the Lao PDR can reach the UN-MDGs by 2015, a large number of Lao people will remain poor and minimally educated. Take, for instance, the Lao score on the Human Development Index (HDI). It lags behind other ASEAN countries and is declining from 0.60 in 2005 to 0.57 in 2013. Strengthening human development is one of the most important factors for Laos (UNDP, 2014). Lao PDR will be disadvantaged in fulfilling its commitments to AEC.

3.3 Socio-cultural perspectives

To realize the goal of establishing a full-fledged ASEAN Community by the year 2015, a community harmonious in politics, unified in economics and responsible in socio-cultural affairs, it is essential for ASEAN to strengthen the cooperation in not only political, security and economic aspects but also socio-cultural affairs. Regarding regional socio-cultural cooperation, with a population of over 500 million, ASEAN is characterized by diversity in languages, cultures, and religions; but the member states live in peace and harmony with one another. All ASEAN members cooperate in development and continue to jointly implement cooperative activities to establish the ASEAN Socio-Cultural Community (ASCC) with the aim of building a caring and sharing society, promoting fine national traditions, and cultures of the respective member states.

Towards building an ASEAN Community (ASCC) by 2015, it would be assured that ASEAN is gradually becoming a stronger and broader grouping. ASCC has five key characteristics, including human resources development, social welfare, social justice and rights, environment stability ensuring, ASEAN identity building, and poverty alleviation.

Being a member of ASEAN, Laos will gain more sustained development by the following four core elements of the ASCC Plan of Action, of which about 80 per cent of the actions have been achieved with the remaining actions to be completed before 2015. The four core elements are: (1) Building a community of caring societies to address issues of poverty, equity and human development; (2) managing the social impact of economic integration by building a competitive human resource base and adequate systems of social protection; (3) enhancing environmental sustainability and sound environmental governance; and (4) strengthening the foundations of regional social cohesion towards an ASEAN Community in 2020.

Poverty reduction is primary for Laos' sustainable development goal. The sustainable development goal is the balance of the economic, environmental and social pillars (GoL, 2004). It is fundamental to the development of the human potential, allowing people to participate fully in the mainstream of economic life and contribute to society. As noted earlier, analysis of four Lao Expenditure and Consumption Surveys (LECS) from WB and DOS (2009) showed that the incidence of poverty has fallen since LECS 1, though it fell slowly from 1997–1998. The incidence of poverty fell from 46 per cent in LECS 1 to 39 per cent in LECS 2, and from 33.5 per cent in LECS 3 to 28 per cent in LECS 4. However, as mentioned before, inequality has increased, especially in Vientiane and other urban areas. The Gini coefficient increased from 30.5 in LECS1 (1992/93) to 35.4 in LECS 4 (2007/08). In Vientiane, the Gini coefficient increased from 29.7 in LECS1 (1992/93) to 38.00 in LECS 4. It shows that Laos has made achievements in the reduction of poverty but poverty is still high in Laos in comparison with other ASEAN countries. In order to reduce poverty and income inequality, the Lao government has implemented various programmes and projects which focus on poor districts, such as building infrastructure, improvement of health care and education and promotion of microfinance (GoL, 2004).

Through the ASCC, Laos is assured to benefit from being a member of ASEAN. In other words, Laos will have an opportunity to enhance its potential for production, consumption and wealth creation which are also desired by all ASEAN members, thus ensuring the benefits of regional integration. All ASEAN members will also strive, individually and collectively, to build caring societies, committed to, and capable of addressing fundamental issues of poverty, equity and human development.

Despite a few benefits, there are some negative effects as a result of integration. With globalization, many of the region's traditional societies, with their cherished cultural norms and practices, are facing new challenges. Although Laos benefits from accessing ASEAN cooperation in many aspects, there are potential challenges for the country. As ASEAN would promote more foreign direct investment (FDI) in Laos, especially in the natural resources sector, environment-related problems may arise. Environmental issues are at the centre of the welfare of over 80 per cent of the population of Laos, as negative environmental trends, such as illegal trade in wildlife and protected species, illegal logging and deforestation, land degradation, socio-environmental impacts of large-scale hydropower systems, and increased urban and industrial pollution directly threaten their livelihood and welfare (Lang, 2001; Dasgupta et al. 2003).

In addition, more regional cooperation would provide space for illegal migration and human trafficking. Despite its high growth rate, Laos is experiencing an increase in such issues. Among ASEAN countries, Thailand and some other member countries, with higher wages and standard of living, attract migrants and trafficking from Laos due to the ease of traveling across the border (Molland, 2010). Illegal migrants and trafficking from Vietnam also travel through Laos and Cambodia to reach Thailand, making Laos a transit country as well as a source country. Furthermore, due to its unique geographical situation at the crossroads of many ASEAN countries, Laos is likely to face an explosion of labour migration flows resulting from the ongoing regional cooperation, generating more demand for sexual and labour exploitation as well.

4 Involvement of Laos within East Asia (ASEAN Plus Three)

ASEAN has one of the highest shares of foreign investment among the major regional economic integration areas in the developing world. Foreign investment is a central driver of ASEAN's competitiveness and economic dynamism. As the region is the geographic centre of the world's growth corridor at present, expanding the cooperation is attractive to foreign investment and offers opportunities for the region. To enhance unity and mutually beneficial cooperation and provide a good experience for promoting more regional cooperation in Asia, ASEAN Plus Three (APT) was established in 1997 with the purpose to move towards the goal of an East Asian community as a result of the Asian financial crisis. APT, which is the latest development of East Asian regional cooperation, is a forum that functions as a coordinator of cooperation between ASEAN countries and the three East Asian countries, including China, Japan, and South Korea which are in the throes of a major economic transformation. With the identification of new and expanded cooperation in the region, APT, which has established the Chiang Mai Initiative, is credited with forming the basis of financial stability in Asia. The cooperation is one of the crucial ways forward in improving the regional attractiveness as an investment destination, deepen economic linkages intra-regionally and with the rest of the world, and regain its robust economic growth performance, and thereby improve further the regional growth (Hunda, 2003; Beeson, 2003).

To strengthen and deepen cooperation among the 13 member nations, there are several APT programmes. Laos is actively participating in various programmes.

4.1 Political-security perspectives

Due to the 1997 Asian financial crisis, the APT Summit in December 1998 proposed the formation of an 'East Asia Vision Group' (EAVG). The Group would be primarily composed of eminent intellectuals in charge of drawing up a vision for mid- to long-term cooperation in East Asia. It explored ways to expand and intensify mid- to long-term cooperation in political and social-cultural sectors, including economic ties to facilitate further development of the East Asian region. Its findings were submitted in a report to the APT Summit in 2001. Since the EAVG report was submitted to the APT Leaders, the East Asia Vision Group II (EAVG II) was established in October 2011 with the major aim of reviewing the APT cooperation over the past 15 years and providing a future vision of APT for the next decades. In addition, due to the essential role of cooperation, all APT countries reaffirmed at the 14th APT Summit in November 2011 in Bali that the APT process would continue as a main vehicle towards the long-term goal of building an East Asian community with ASEAN as the driving force.

Another notable area of political and security cooperation among the APT nations is actually the ASEAN Political-Security Community (APSC) established at the Summit in Kuala Lumpur in December 1997, to promote political development in adherence to the principles of democracy, the rule of law and good governance, fundamental freedoms, and promotion and protection of human rights, for the highest benefit of all member states. The APSC envisages the following three key areas which are inter-related and mutually reinforcing, and shall be pursued in a balanced and consistent manner: (1) rules-based community of shared values and norms; (2) cohesive, peaceful, stable and resilient region with shared responsibility for comprehensive security; and (3) dynamic and outward-looking region in an increasingly integrated and interdependent world.

The community is a means by which all members can pursue closer interaction and cooperation to create common mechanisms to achieve goals and objectives in the fields of political security. In this regard, Laos as well as other member nations can benefit through the regional promotion in which all sectors of society, regardless of gender, race, language, religion, or social and cultural background are encouraged to participate in, and benefit from the process of the integration. Furthermore, in the interest of preserving and enhancing peace and stability in the region, the community seeks to strengthen mutual beneficial relations between member nations and their dialogue partners by maintaining its centrality and proactive role in a regional architecture that is open, transparent and inclusive, while remaining actively engaged, forward-looking and non-discriminatory.

In addition, the APT process is able to offer an institutionalized way for facilitating compromises to produce a meaningful agreement and cooperation that is mutually satisfactory to all members. The cooperation has made significant progress as indicated by the frequent political exchanges and enhancement of traditional friendship and mutual trust assuring the political-security development for the member states, including Laos. To spread peace and prosperity in the region, APT has put in an effort to strengthen practical political-security cooperation in the region.

Despite the progress of the cooperation, APT faces some constraints and challenges, including diversity in political systems, economic and social conditions and ideologies, unresolved historical issues (result of wars and occupations during pre-colonial times), conflicting territorial claims, different alliances and character of relations with the big powers of the region, political mutual trust or the lack of it among member nations in the region, and rivalry among member nations and among dialogue partners that remain to be solved. The competitions in the form of competing regional and bilateral initiatives offered to ASEAN members by major powers such as competing free trade and economic partnerships, as well as shifting policies and bureaucratic priorities (as, for example, the case of Japan's foreign aid priorities that degrade China) are evident political challenges.

4.2 Economic perspectives

Underpinning the larger benefits from the cooperation, ASEAN Plus Three (APT) is now being pursued by many in political and non-traditional security, trade and economy, and society and culture. In terms of economics, given strong support for the cooperation facilitation, APT is regarded as one of the most successful stories of regional cooperation. It is one of the most dynamic integrated economic regions, which includes two economies with the highest GDP growth rates in the world, namely, China and Vietnam. Furthermore, almost all APT countries have export-oriented economic policies providing opportunities and advantages for foreign trade activities.

Facilitating the integration with the plus three nations, the regional vision to have free flow of goods, services, investment, skilled labour, and freer flow of capital could be achieved. Through APT cooperation, the following opportunities for socio-economic growth of the member states could be realized: (1) greater choice of goods and services for consumers through increases in trade; (2) larger economies of scale for businesses and industries, thereby increasing productivity while reducing production costs leading to more competitive pricing; (3) lowering of production costs can be passed onto consumers who can benefit from lower prices of goods and services; (4) greater demand for goods and services will create more jobs; (5) greater entrepreneurship and innovation in products and services through the increase in trade and investment; (6) higher growth and prosperity could be achievable through the stronger business networks; and (7) higher level of employment would contribute towards building a larger middle class, thereby reducing the gap between the rich and the poor and promoting social stability.

Substantive steps have been taken in the financial cooperation among the APT nations, as evidenced by, for example, the increase in bilateral currency swaps, and intra-regional economic and trade interdependence. With the aim to increasingly promote mutually beneficial economic cooperation, a breakthrough in the multilateralization process under the 'Chiang Mai Initiative' (CMI) has upgraded the financial cooperation in the region. The CMI is an important regional cooperation in Asia for swap lines and credits agreed to by the APT countries in May 2000. This initiative aims to prevent a crisis like the one in 1997–1998 and promote financial stability. Furthermore, the process of developing an Asian bond market is being accelerated (Park and Wang, 2005).

Although the international financial crisis and other world economic issues may challenge Laos as well as other countries in the region, with particular emphasis on pushing further economic integration, the APT nations have the confidence and determination to strengthen pragmatic cooperation, earnestly implement the consensus reached, improve their overall ability to respond to a crisis and any other related issues in order to sustain their status as one of the financially stable regions of the world. This indicates the efforts of APT cooperation in promoting sustainable development for the benefit of the people in the region.

Although APT has enjoyed significant economic growth, the community still faces common problems and challenges of unbalanced economic development among member nations. Notably, some countries still lag behind in economic and social development, particularly the newer members such as the CLMV (Cambodia, Laos, Myanmar, and Vietnam) countries. In addition, in spite of prospects of trade relations between APT and other regions, the imbalance in bilateral trade may have negative impacts like the creation of obstacles to market stability. However, since strengthening APT cooperation is the general trend and the common desire of all member countries, the economic integration process of APT has been continuously promoted to lead to maximum benefits for all member countries. In addition, APT has maintained a sound momentum of growth in the past decade with the establishment and improvement in multi-level dialogue and cooperation mechanisms, and identification of short-term and mid- to long-term areas of cooperation. Furthermore, implementing measures towards full economic integration by deepening and broadening internal economic opportunities, fostering effective cross-border facilitation to provide greater economies of scale and expanded market size, and nurturing dynamic linkages with the global supply chain and world economy by raising the competitiveness through connectivity, and attaining regional integration through effective implementation of various initiatives, has been promoted.

Lao economy has been integrated with APT countries in term of trade and investment. According to Jeong-Soo and Kyophilavong (2014), more than 90 per cent of the trade of Laos is from APT countries which shows the deep trade integration with these countries. In addition, more than 70 per cent of Foreign Direct Investment in Laos was from APT countries (Kyophilavong, 2009).

Despite its small economy, Laos plays important roles in APT integrations in three areas. First is promoting trade and investment with APT countries. Laos is rich in natural resources, including land, water and minerals (World Bank, 2010). These rich resources could promote investment and trade between Laos and APT countries and the rest of the world. Second is to promote and develop the infrastructure to link with the APT countries. As Laos shares borders with five APT countries, it plays an important role in connectivity. Third, Laos has rich water resources and has high potential hydropower development to produce electricity to support economic growth in APT countries (Pholsena and Phonekeo, 2004).

4.3 Socio-cultural perspective

In terms of socio-cultural development, APT cooperation has expanded to cover rural development, education, culture, social justice and rights, social welfare and protection, poverty reduction, environment management, natural resources, food security and safety, information and telecommunications technologies, science, infrastructure, elimination of illegal drugs, narrowing the development gap, and other related fields, showing the great contribution of APT to peace, stability, social progress, and common prosperity of the region.

Continuing the existing cooperation, APT has heightened cooperative efforts in social and human resources development together with alleviating economic and social disparities within and among member states. In order to ensure the benefits from the regional integration, APT has adopted the Declaration of ASEAN Concord II (Bali Concord II) where the link between ASEAN's economic and social agendas was notably highlighted. The Bali Concord II's commitment, particularly aims at investing more resources for basic and higher education, training, science and technology development, job creation, and social protection in the region as well as individual nations.

As Laos as well as many other member nations are still very much in the developmental stage, by accessing APT cooperation, these countries are assured of gains in the form of socioe-conomic development. On the other hand, with the contribution from mainly larger economies, APT will enhance the well-being and livelihood of the peoples of the member nations by providing them with equitable access to human development opportunities through promoting and investing in education and lifelong learning, human resource training and capacity building, encouraging innovation and entrepreneurship, promoting the use of the English language, and other related activities.

With APT's strategic objective and concrete plans to contribute towards sustainable socio-economic development in the region, the problems of persisting socio-economic disparities, and extreme poverty and hunger across member nations, for example, are to be addressed. Through implementation of mitigation and adaptation measures based on the principles of effectiveness, flexibility, equity, common but differentiated responsibilities, and respective capabilities, enhancing regional and international cooperation is achieved. In this regard, the issue of climate change and its impacts on socio-economic development, health and the environment is to be addressed. It is anticipated that this may bring significant benefits for all member nations.

Having supported the APT cooperation through a number of activities in human resource development of the member nations, the plus three nations of China, Japan and Korea have made important contributions in promoting socio-cultural development in the region. An example of the cooperation between ASEAN and the plus three nations for sharing of experiences in strengthening social security and social protection is the implementation of a series of annual China-ASEAN High-Level Seminars. The High-Level Seminars are essential and beneficial for ASEAN member states and China in terms of exchanging experiences in human resource development and social security, given the accelerating pace of economic liberalization in the region.

Some remarkable support from Japan for socio-cultural development in ASEAN is the establishment of the three-year ASEAN Program in Industrial Relations, the ASEAN-Japan Collaboration Program for Strengthening the

Basis of Human Resources Development in CLMV (2004–2007), and the labour-related development in the ASEAN-Japan Plan of Action adopted by the ASEAN-Japan Commemorative Summit held in 2003. In addition, since youth employment is an important concern for all the APT nations in terms of socio-cultural development, the Asian Conference on the Future of Youth was proposed by Japan with the aim of facilitating sharing of experiences of youth employment concerns and challenges in the region. Continuing the assistance to ASEAN member states, Korea has also contributed to APT through the annual Human Resources Development meeting and various socio-cultural programmes for officials of ASEAN member states.

Despite the least attention on the socio-cultural pillar, it is actually the most essential unit in APT since it is a place where numerous religious beliefs are espoused, and various ethnicities are embraced. Therefore, solving the socio-cultural issues in the region is crucial. On the other hand, unlike the political-security pillar and the economic one, although the significance of the social-cultural pillar can hardly be seen by the eye, ignoring it can affect the whole community. Other problems and challenges in socio-cultural cooperation in the region that the APT member nations have faced include unskilled labour mobility, unemployment, poverty, and socio-economic disparities. However, with the strong support for an ASEAN Community based on political-security, economic and social-cultural cooperation, the plus three nations of China, Japan and Korea are deeply interested to explore opportunities for collaboration with ASEAN to address priorities for developing and enhancing human resources as a key strategy in ensuring economic growth with equity while mitigating the negative effects arising from economic integration.

5 Conclusion

Laos had suffered as a result of colonization, invasion and war in the past. With Lao independence in 1975, a centrally planned economy was introduced. The New Economic Mechanism (NEM) replaced the centrally planned economy in 1986. With the NEM, Laos has been able to achieve high economic performance and poverty has been reduced significantly.

The Lao national development goal is to escape from the Least Developed Country (LDC) criteria by 2020. In order to achieve this goal, the Lao government has established the national development plan. The strategy is to harmonize three pillars of development, namely, the economic, social and environmental issues. Despite high economic growth during the past 20 years, Laos is still facing various economic, social and environmental issues. Macroeconomic conditions are still weak, and there is a lack of human resources and infrastructure. Social and environmental problems have been increasing over time.

Despite its small size in terms of population and economic power, Laos has been contributing to ASEAN in various ways. For instance, Laos contributes to the promotion of investment in this region because Laos is a resource-rich country and it can contribute to the export and promotion of industrial linkages in Asia. Laos also contributes to energy security in this region because Laos has substantial hydropower potential. In addition, Laos contributes to the promotion of connectivity and improvement of trade facilitation in the region because Laos has links with five countries.

The establishment of the ASEAN Economic Community (AEC) will bring various benefits to Laos in terms of trade, investment and technical transfer and deeper integration in ASEAN. However, there are still some concerns about development gaps between Laos and other ASEAN members and also emerging social and environmental problems. In order to overcome these issues, increasing the capacity of institutions and human resources might be one of the most important strategies.

References

Beeson, Mark (2003) 'ASEAN Plus Three and the Rise of Reactionary Regionalism', *Contemporary Southeast Asia: A Journal of International and Strategic Affairs*, 25(2): 251–268.

BoL (2012) *Annual Report. Bank of Lao PDR (BoL)*, Vientiane: The Bank of the Lao PDR.

Dasgupta, Susmita, Deichmann, Uwe, Meisner, Craig, Wheeler, David (2003) *The Poverty/Environment Nexus in Cambodia and Lao People's Democratic Republic*, World Bank Policy Research Working Paper 2960, Washington, DC: The World Bank.

Department of Geology (DOG) (2008) *Geological Strategy Development Plan in 2008-2010 and 2010–2011 (in Lao)*. Vientiane: Department of Geology, Ministry of Energy and Mines. Unpublished.

DoS (Department of Statistics) (2009) *Lao Expenditure and Consumption Survey 2007/08*, Vientiane: Department of Statistics, Ministry of Planning and Investment.

ERIA (2012) *Mid-term Review of the Implementation of AEC Blueprint*, Jakarta: Economic Research Institute for ASEAN and East Asia (ERIA).

ESCAP (2015) *Trade and Non-tariff Measures: Impacts in the Asia-Pacific Region*, United Nations Economic and Social Commission for Asia and the Pacific (ESCAP).

Fujita, Yayoi and Phanvilay, Khamla (2008) 'Land and forest allocation in Lao People's Democratic Republic: Commarision of case studies from community-based national resources management research. *Society and Natural Resources*, 21(2): 120–133.

Fukase, Emiko and Winters, L. Alan (2003) 'Possible Dynamic Effects of AFTA for the New Member Countries', *The World Economy*, 26(6): 853–871.

GoL (2004) *The National Growth and Poverty Eradication Strategy (NGPES)*, Vientiane, Laos: Committee of Planning and Investment.

GoL (2005) *The Industrialization Strategy towards 2020*, Vientiane, Laos: Committee of Planning and Investment.

GoL (2010) *Seventh National Socio Economic Development Plan (NEDP) for 2011 to 2015*, Vientiane, Laos: Ministry of Planning and Investment.

Goscha, Chrisopher E. and Ivarsson, Soren (2003) *Contesting Visions of the Lao Past: Lao Historiography at the Crossroads,* NIAS Studies in Asian topics, No. 32, Copenhagen: NIAS Press.

Hunda, Markus (2003) 'ASEAN Plus Three: Towards a New Age of Pan-East Asian Regionalism? A Skeptic's Appraisal', *The Pacific Review,* 16(3): 383–417.

Itakura, Ken (2014) 'Impact of Liberalization and Improved Connectivity and Facilitation in ASEAN. *Journal of Asian Economics,* 35: 2–1.

Jeong-Soo, Oh and Kyophilavong, Phouphet (2014) 'Impact of ASEAN-Korea FTA on poverty: the case of Laos', *World Applied Sciences Journal,* 28: 114–119.

Kyophilavong, Phouphet (2009) *Mining Sector in Laos,* BRC Discussion Paper Series No. 18, Bangkok Research Center (BRC), IDE-JETRO.

Kyophilavong, Phouphet (2008) 'SMEs development in Lao PDR,' in *Asian SMEs and Globalization, ERIA Research Project Report 2007,* edited by H. Lim. Jakarta: The Economic Research Institute for ASEAN and East Asia (ERIA).

Kyophiavong, Phouphet and Toyoda, Toshihisa (2008) 'Impacts of Foreign Capital Inflows on the Lao Economy,' in *Empirical Research on Trade and Finance in East Asia,* edited by Toshihisa Toyda. Hiroshima: Shudo University.

Lang, Christopher R. (2001) 'Deforestation in Vietnam, Laos and Cambodia.' In *Deforestation, Environment, and Sustainable Development: A Comparative Analysis,* ed. Dhirendra K. Vajpeyi. Santa Barbara, CA: Greenwood Publishing Group, Inc.

Leebouapao, Leeber (2008) 'Lao PDR Country Report', in *Developing Roadmap toward East Asian Economic Integration,* edited by Hadi Soesastro, ERIA Research Project Report 2007–2001-1, Chiba: IDE-JETRO.

Levine, Ross, Loayza, Norman and Beck, Thorsten (2000) 'Financial Intermediate and Growth: Causality and Causes. *Journal of Monetary Economics,* 46(1): 31–77.

Ljunggren, B. (1993) 'Market Economies under Communist Regimes: Reform in Vietnam, Laos and Cambodia,' in *The Challenge of Reform in Indochina,* edited by B. Ljunggren, Boston, MA: Harvard University Press.

Menon, Jay (1999) 'Transitional Economies in Free Trade Areas: Lao PDR in the ASEAN Free Trade Area', *Journal of the Asia Pacific Economy,* 4(2): 340–364.

Molland, Sverre (2010) '"The Perfect Business": Human Trafficking and Lao–Thai Cross-Border Migration', *Development and Change,* 41(5): 831–855.

Park, Yung Chul, Wang, Yunjong (2005) 'The Chiang Mai Initiative and Beyond. *The Word Economy,* 28(1): 91–101.

Payne, James E. (2010) 'Survey of the International Evidence on the Causal Relationship between Energy Consumption and Growth. *Journal of Economic Studies,* 37(1): 53–95.

Pholsena, Sommano and Phonekeo Daovong (2004) Lao Hydropower Potential and Policy in the GMS Context, United Nations Symposium on Hydropower and Sustainable Development, Beijing International Convention Centre.

Sachs, Jeffrey D. and Warner, Andrew M. (2001) 'Natural Resources and Economic Development – The Curse of National Resources.' *European Economic Review,* 45(4–6): 827–838.

Stuart-Fox, Martin (1997) *A History of Laos,* Cambridge: Cambridge University Press.

UNDP (2014) *Hum Dev Reports.* United Nations Development Programme.

Vatthana, Pholsena (2006) *Post-war Laos: The Politics of Culture, History and Identity,* Singapore: Institute of Southeast Asian Studies (ISEAS).

Warr, Peter (2010) 'Roads and poverty in rural Laos: An Econometric Analysis.' *Pacific Economic Review,* 15(1): 152–169.

Washington DC and Department of Statistics (DOS), Vientiane, Laos.

World Bank (2010) *Doing Business 2010*. Washington, DC: World Bank.

World Bank (2010) *Development with a Rapidly Expanding Natural Resources Sector: Challenges and Policy Options for Laos*, Washington, DC: World Bank.

World Bank (2004) *Lao PDR Country Economic Memorandum: Realizing the Development Potential of Lao PDR*, Vientiane: World Bank.

World Bank and DOS (2009) *Poverty in Lao PDR 1992/3–2007/8*, Washington, DC: World Bank.

5 Malaysia and the development of Asian regionalism

Nor Azizan Idris and Zarina Othman

1 National perspectives

Malaysia is geographically divided by the Malacca Straits into two parts: Peninsular Malaysia and East Malaysia. Peninsular Malaysia is located at the centre of Southeast Asia, at the southern tip of Thailand and surrounded by Malacca Strait waters on the west side and South China Sea on the east. East Malaysia consists of two states of Malaysia: Sabah and Sarawak on the island of Borneo. Malaysia is located strategically on the waters that connect the East and the West, which later contributed to the history of the nation being influenced by the merchants from around the world. The Malays came under the influence of the Indians from about the beginning of the Christian era. In the eleventh century, the Indian traders from the Langkasuka Kingdom came to the northwest of Malaya, bringing with them the religions of their ancestors, Hinduism and Buddhism. The historical remains can be seen at the archaeological site in Lembah Bujang, Kedah, in the northern tips of Peninsular Malaysia

Around the fourteenth century, the southern part of the peninsula was ruled by Majapahit, a Hindu Kingdom in Java, while the northern part was governed by Sukhotai and later by Ayudhya of Siam. Later in mid-fourteenth century, the Malacca Sultanate was founded by Parameswara, a prince from Palembang in the southern part of Sumatra who fled to Temasek (now Singapore) and finally reached Malacca where he established his kingdom (SarDesai 2003). Under Parameswara, Malacca became an important port that attracted Arab traders who introduced Islam. Malacca thrived as an important entrepot with a well-organized political and economic system with diverse languages, cultures and ethnic groups. Some of the traders stayed permanently and married the locals thus producing the Baba and Nyonya (mix of Malay and Chinese) culture. Malacca's independence was supported by the Ming rulers of China (SarDesai 2003). The Sultanate also became the centre of Islam in Southeast Asia.

In the early sixteenth century, the Portuguese founded a trading settlement in Goa, on the west coast of India and later invaded Malacca in 1511, after realizing the importance of Malacca's entreport and economic domination in

Southeast Asia, and planned to dominate the Spice Islands (the Moluccas); but this was countered by the Spaniards (SarDesai 2003). In 1641, the Dutch took control of Malacca until 1789. The British who aimed to protect their increasing trade with China first settled in Penang, on the west coast of the Malay Peninsula and in stages established their authority over the entire Peninsula (Andaya and Andaya 1982).

The Japanese occupied Malaya from 1942 until 1945 during World War II. After the war, the British immediately took control but later had to deal with guerrilla insurgents (SarDesai 2003). The communist insurgency led by the Communist Party of Malaya (CPM) began in 1948. Even when Malaya achieved independence in 1957, the communist problem remained a major concern for the country's newly independent government led by the country's first premier, Tunku Abdul Rahman. The 1955 Baling Talks between the CPM and the Malayan authorities showed that the latter had an advantageous position. Thus, it took 12 years for the British Army to defeat the communists.

The issue of independence began in 1948, with British plans for the transfer of power. Malaya was formed into a loose federation excluding Singapore, because of the fear that the Chinese in Singapore would dominate the federation. Independence was granted to the Federation of Malaya in 1957, earning them membership of the British Commonwealth. The first Supreme Head, who would be selected every five years from among the Malay rulers, was the Raja of Perlis (SarDesai 2003). Three years after Malaya's independence from British colonial rule, the Emergency was declared to have ended. However, the threat from the CPM was far from over because it remained a major concern of the government even in the 1960s and 1970s (Sidhu 2009, 4).

The bitter war with the communists left the greatest mark on Malaya's policymakers. It was not until the Emergency was officially ended in 1960 that Malaya would vote for China's admission into the United Nations (UN) (only on the basis of the two-China policy). It has been pointed out that because the communist insurgency was largely (Malayan) Chinese in initiative and composition, the government could not afford overtures to China while the insurrection was still in progress (Saravanamuttu 2010, 74).

Later in 1963, Singapore, Sarawak and Sabah joined the Federation and formed Malaysia, but Brunei opted out while Singapore joined the Malaysian Federation in 1963. The Malaysian leadership was apprehensive over the strength of communist political forces in Singapore and accepted it despite the racial imbalance this would cause due to Singapore's majority Chinese population. The inclusion of Singapore resulted in a bitter political competition between the People's Action Party (PAP) and the Alliance Government led by the United Malays National Organization (UMNO) (Tan 2004, 115). The tension between the Singapore Chinese and the Malays led to the withdrawal of Singapore from the Federation in 1965.

Security and stability are the main concerns for many states, especially for newly multiracial Malaysia. Realizing that political stability, economic development and social harmony are among the major ingredients for its survival, Malaysia, together with four other Southeast Asian states, namely, Thailand, Singapore, Indonesia and the Philippines, established a regional institution, known as the Association of Southeast Asian Nations (ASEAN). With a population of approximately 30 million people and a per capita gross national income (GNI) of $6,540, Malaysia has achieved the status of a newly industrialized country (NIC). The Malaysian success story is especially note-worthy because of the country's geographic and racial diversity. There is no more powerful force in Malaysian society than communalism, or the division of the country into racial communities: 51 per cent Malay, 26 per cent Chinese, 7 per cent Indian, and the rest smaller minorities and migrant populations. The Malays are Muslim, predominantly rural and agricultural, or *bumiputra* ('sons of the soil'). The non-Malays are urban and mostly non-Muslim, generally involved in industry and trade (Dayley and Neher 2010, 133).

Since the colonial period, the country has had to contend with three large and distinct groups, which mainly, due to history, could be identified most closely by their role and place in Malaysia's society and economy. In contrast to most developing countries, Malaysia's politics has been characterized by extraordinary continuity since its independence in 1957. That continuity has been based on the essential stability of the government, despite constant poli-tical tension and occasional upheavals. The government has taken the form of a semi-permanent coalition of representatives from the main communal groups. Unlike the shifting coalitions between rival parties that are common in other countries, the ruling coalition in Malaysia constitutes a distinct entity with its own constitution and rules. At its core is the alliance between the dominant Malay party, UMNO, and parties representing the non-Malay communities, of which the Malaysian Chinese Association (MCA) and Malaysian Indian Congress (MIC) are the most important (Crouch 1997, 32).

The *bumiputra* are further segmented into sub-groups such as the Malays predominant in West Malaysia, and the Melanaus, Bajaus, Kadazans, Iban and Muruts in Sabah and Sarawak. The Chinese likewise have their sub-groups based on clan identities such as Hokkien, Cantonese, Teochew, Hakka and Hainanese. Sub-groups in the Indian community are the Malayalees, Punjabis, Tamils and Bengalis. The existence of the diverse cultural and reli-gious beliefs poses a challenge for the Malaysian government to maintain peace and stability in order to develop the country.

Malaysia achieved its independence on 31 August 1957 at a time when not only was the international environment extremely unpredictable and volatile but the internal situation also was unstable due to the outbreak of a commu-nist insurgency in 1948. Externally, the onset of the Cold War after World War II divided the world into two camps, namely the Western capitalist camp led by the United States and the Eastern communist camp lead by the Soviet Union. Connected to this was the larger problem of the 'threat from the north' taking the form of communist expansion in the region. Furthermore, the outbreak of the Korean War (1950–1953) and the escalation of the war in

Vietnam with the United States' involvement only confirmed these concerns. As such, the domino theory that remained a major concern for most Western policymakers in the 1950s and 1960s also created anxiety amongst the Malaysian policymakers in some ways. Closer to home and in the region itself, other problems surfaced in the early 1960s when Indonesia attempted aggression on Malaysia – though in a limited fashion (Sidhu 2009, 2).

Apart from communism, communal tension, namely, race relations between the Malays and Chinese, was another major concern of the Malaysian government during the 1960s. While the 1960s remained relatively calm, the decade ended with an episode that almost shook the foundations of the nation. The outbreak of communal violence on 13 May, in the aftermath of the 1969 general elections, saw a bitter confrontation between the Malays and the Chinese, resulting in a number of deaths, mostly due to the socio-economic imbalances between the Malays and Chinese. The outbreak of the riots saw the extension of the emergency rule and the suspension of parliament for 21 months with the administration of the country taken over by the National Operations Council (NOC) headed by the Deputy Prime Minister, Tun Abdul Razak. The riots were indeed a watershed in Malaysian history because not only was political life refashioned, but also the whole notion of internal security took yet another dimension, namely, that based on race relations (Sidhu 2009, 4–5).

The government of the day had to rethink their development strategy in order to cater to the needs of a multi-ethnic society and alleviate the growing income disparity. In order to address the problem, the New Economic Policy (NEP) (1971–1990) was introduced with two main objectives: to eradicate poverty, and to restructure society in order to remove the identification of the ethnic groups with certain economic functions. This 20-year plan envisaged the redistribution of wealth based on growth where the indigenous people or the '*bumiputera*' would own 30 per cent of the nation's wealth by the year 1990. The restructuring of society includes affirmative action on behalf of the deprived indigenous Malays. Examples of these preferences are access to education, employment and economic subsidies in some sectors. Realizing that the development of a country depends largely on the need to have a good work force, emphasis was given to education. Despite its shortcomings, the policy has contributed positively to national unity and economic prosperity in the last 30 years (Faaland et al. 1990 and Norhashimah Mohd Yassin 1996). Two decades of sustained economic growth in Malaysia have resulted in significant reduction of poverty throughout the country. The national incidence of poverty dropped from 32.1 per cent in 1980 to 6.8 per cent in 1997, with a drop from 16.3 per cent to 2.4 per cent in urban areas and from 39.5 per cent to 11.8 per cent in rural areas over the same period (Economic Planning Unit, 1999). In 1991, Malaysia under Mahathir, launched VISION 2020, a goal to transform Malaysia into a fully developed nation in its own mould, by the year 2020.

The world was shocked with the incidence of the Asian financial crisis. Malaysia was one of the countries affected. The Malaysian government's initial response to the crisis, and especially Mahathir's responses, was one of a series of unorthodox interventions. Several direct steps were taken to insulate the domestic interest rate from capital mobility. The offshore, over-the-counter CLOB (Central Limit Order Book) in Singapore was stopped to prevent illegal short selling of Malaysian shares. There was also the step of banning the short selling of 100 blue-chip stocks and the plan to use funds of the Employees' Provident Fund (EPF) to shore up share prices. This was followed up, most importantly, by the announcement of capital controls on 1 September 1998. With such a move, Mahathir supposedly followed a proposal by MIT Professor Paul Krugman who had argued in an article in *Fortune* magazine that such capital controls could give crisis-ridden Asian economies breathing space to resume growth (Saravanamuttu 2010, 214–215).

Malaysian Prime Minister Mahathir Mohamad's 1 September 1998 announcement of capital controls was important in several regards. Whereas Thailand, South Korea and Indonesia had gone cap in hand – humiliatingly accepting conditions imposed by the International Monetary Fund (IMF) – in order to secure desperately needed credit, the Malaysian initiative reminded the world that there are alternatives to capital account liberalization (Jomo 2001: 199). The controls remained in place for almost eight years and were lifted only in July 2005 when the ringgit peg was removed. Mahathir and the government claimed that they made the difference in Malaysia's economic recovery when compared with the other crisis-stricken East Asian economies. In retrospect, it is true that by doing so, and in tandem with various other fiscal and monetary measures, Malaysia was able to avoid an IMF rescue package. By the middle of 1999, the Malaysian authorities were already trumpeting that the recovery was more evident, with the stock market showing signs of new life, indicated by the KLSE-CI breaching 800 points by August after a low of about 260 points at the nadir of the crisis. By August, regular monthly surpluses in the current account had also boosted Malaysia's international reserves to US\$31 billion, good for seven months of imports (Saravanamuttu 2010: 215).

2 Malaysia's role within ASEAN

ASEAN is the cornerstone of Malaysian foreign policy. It is both of geopolitical significance and economic relevance to Malaysia and also to the nations within this region. Its renunciation of the use of force and promotion of peaceful settlement of disputes has been the foundation to its peace, stability and prosperity in the region.

In the post-Cold War era which saw the emergence of competing regional economic groupings and uncertainty in the regional security environment, Malaysia believed that a strong and successful ASEAN is not only an economic necessity but also a strategic imperative. A prosperous, consolidated and stable ASEAN at peace with itself and with its immediate neighbours would provide the best guarantee for the security of the entire Southeast Asia and East Asia region.

Before the birth of ASEAN, there were other attempts to create regional organizations and it must be noted that Malaya has been playing an active role in regional initiatives. As early as April 1958, the Malayan premier, Tunku was reportedly toying with the idea of a defence treaty organization consisting of Malaya, Burma, Thailand, Laos, Cambodia and South Vietnam. Tunku discussed his plan with President Gracia of the Philippines in a visit in January 1959, at this stage denying reports that he was considering an anti-communist pact for Southeast Asian countries. The upshot was a surprisingly prompt announcement of a plan for the formation of the Southeast Asia Friendship and Economic treaty (SEAFET), an association with apparently only economic, trade, and educational objectives. However, the plan received lukewarm response except from Thailand and South Vietnam. SEAFET was eventually abandoned and in its place an Association of Southeast Asian States (ASAS, later, ASA) was proposed in July 1960, with Malaya, the Philippines, and Thailand as the sponsor nations. Malaysia was instrumental in the formation of the Association of Southeast Asia (ASA), the first truly indigenous association in the area in that all its members belonged to countries of Southeast Asia. ASA, formed in 1961, appears, however, to have been an offshoot of Tunku's effort at a broader grouping of non-communist Southeast Asian states (Saravanamuttu 2010, 65–66).

Another regional initiative that was short-lived is MAPHILINDO – a vague scheme of cooperation between Malaysia, the Philippines and Indonesia that was formed in 1963 as a result of consultations between the leaders of the three nations – Tunku (Malaysia), Macapagal (the Philippines) and Sukarno (Indonesia). This initiative did not take off because of the conflicting interest of the participating nations, especially the opposition of both the Philippines and Indonesia to the proposed formation of Malaysia.

The Association of South-East Asian Nations (ASEAN) was created by the governments of Indonesia, Malaysia, the Philippines, Singapore and Thailand through the Bangkok Declaration, which was signed by the deputy prime minister of Malaysia and the foreign ministers of the other four countries in August 1967. ASEAN replaced the earlier Association of Southeast Asia (ASA), comprising Thailand, the Philippines and Malaya, which had been created in 1961. This regional institution is an important platform to manage conflict and to create a stable and prosperous region.

Overall, Malaysian foreign policy discourse and practice have traversed the periods of six premierships, each with its own distinctive style, economic and political predilections. Throughout the six periods, ASEAN has paradoxically provided the common themes for Malaysian foreign policy as its central focus and instrumentality of practices as well as the source of new, definitive or altered versions of politics, initially proposed by Malaysia. During the Tunku Abdul Rahman period, the theme of rapprochement pervaded all intra-regional ASEAN relations.

After Tun Razak, Malaysia's second prime minister took over the reins of government; the drive for non-alignment and the neutralization of Southeast

Asia became ASEAN's prime concern, as much as they were Malaysia's own concerns. By being in ASEAN and taking into account the sensibilities of other ASEAN states, Malaysia was able to take its own schemes to a broader plane and provide them with a regional flavour. The Hussein Onn (the third prime minister) government arrived at the time of significant changes in ASEAN both in terms of intra-regional and extra-regional developments. Malaysia was able to anchor its foreign policies to ASEAN to mount effective actions vis-à-vis developments emanating from Indo-China. During the Mahathir administration (the fourth prime minister), ASEAN appears to have not escaped the spillover effects of the reformism of the Mahathir government, especially in its economic relations. This notwithstanding, ASEAN has remained pivotal for Malaysia as it has for other member states in respect of broad security policies towards the region and the world in general (Saravanamuttu 1997, 48).

Since its establishment, ASEAN has developed and refined various mechanisms and arrangements to promote trade, investment and other collaborative activities. Much of ASEAN's attractiveness to the outside world is built on the economic success of its member states and their potential for greater growth. As ASEAN confronted the various challenges such as international terrorism, economic slowdown, in the face of economic and financial crises, it is ASEAN's common effort that accounted for Malaysia's success in facing these challenges (Malaysia Ministry of Foreign Affairs 2014).

The expansion of the original ASEAN to include other Southeast Asian countries has made an even bigger contribution to developing national resilience, promoting economic growth, enhancing regional co-operation and ensuring regional peace and security. Malaysia believes that the existence of ASEAN has encouraged patterns of behaviour that reduce risks to security by enhancing bilateral relations as well as fostering habits of open dialogue on political and security matters including establishing confidence-building measures. The dialogue through the ASEAN PMC process and ASEAN Regional Forum (ARF), in which ASEAN functions as the core group, adequately serves the purpose.

To adapt itself to a changing regional landscape and future challenges, ASEAN came out with the ASEAN Charter. With the Charter, ASEAN has undergone transformational changes to become a rules-based organization with legal personality. It reiterates the common principles which bind all 10 ASEAN member states, i.e. rule of law, good governance, principles of democracy and constitutional government; shared commitment and collective responsibility in enhancing regional peace, security and prosperity; and enhanced consultations on matters affecting the common interest of ASEAN (Malaysia Ministry of Foreign Affairs 2014).

In the 1970s, Malaysia began to publicly profess its non-aligned status, pursue a posture of equidistance, and promote its concept of Southeast Asian neutrality. Whilst Tunku had openly embraced a staunch pro-Western and anti-communist stance to deal with external security threats and openly rejected non-alignment, the more pragmatic second Prime Minister, Tun Abdul Razak (1970–1976), on the other hand, decided to pin the country's hope on regionalism and non-alignment. In other words, there was a marked departure from the policy of conservative pragmatism followed by the Tunku to that of assertive activism under the leadership of Tun Razak.

As such, in 1970, Malaysia officially joined the Non-Aligned Movement (NAM) when Tun Razak attended the NAM meeting in Lusaka, Zambia, where the first call for the neutralization of Southeast Asia was made. About a year later, it was within this context that Malaysia enunciated a non-military approach to regional security unveiled in the concept of Zone of Peace, Freedom and Neutrality (ZOPFAN) in November 1971, at the Meeting of the ASEAN Foreign Ministers in Kuala Lumpur (Sidhu 2009, 6–7). The strategy of promoting a ZOPFAN in the region became the cornerstone of Malaysia's foreign policy in matters of defence and security. The scheme had its roots in Tun Dr Ismail's proposal of 1968, but it was officially publicized only in 1970 in Lusaka. The idea was to minimize the involvement of the Great Powers – namely the United States, Russia and China – and at the same time to guarantee ASEAN's neutrality. The emphasis then shifted to the ASEAN-initiated proposal of ZOPFAN or for some form of a 'neutrality system' (Saravanamuttu 2010, 149 and 155).

Before Malaysia assumed the chair of ASEAN in 2005, Malaysia had perceptibly pushed for a much higher level of collaboration with ASEAN. Among other things, Malaysia called for the regional body to explore possibilities of a common time zone, common travel document, and common currency. In the National Colloquium on ASEAN held in Kula Lumpur on 8 August 2004, Malaysia declared that it would try to work towards the following objectives:

- Prepare the groundwork or building blocks for the nucleus of the ASEAN Community idea.
- Strengthen ASEAN external relations, especially with respect to the ASEAN Plus Three relationship.
- Work towards the ASEAN Charter which would confer upon it 'an international legal personality'.

(*The Star*, 8 August 2004 in Saravanamuttu 2010, 250–251)

In December 2005, Malaysia hosted the ASEAN and East Asian Summits. When Abdullah, Malaysia's fifth Prime Minister, delivered the 2006 ASEAN Lecture on 8 August (ASEAN Day), he placed considerable emphasis on the importance of the ASEAN Charter as the instrument to carry the regional body forward. Arguing that while the cardinal principle of ASEAN has been 'non-interference', the concept required refinement and the regional body needed to update the enduring principle of the Treaty of Amity and Cooperation (TAC) in order to make it relevant and responsive to the changing needs of member countries (*Bernama,* 8 August 2006 in Saravanamuttu 2010, 251).

Pursuant to making ASEAN a more effective, closely integrated, rules-based, and people-oriented regional organization, ASEAN member states decided to formulate an ASEAN Charter which they eventually signed at the 13th ASEAN Summit in Singapore. The ASEAN Charter puts in place a new legal and institutional framework for ASEAN to improve its implementation, coordination, and decision-making process. The Charter came into force on 15 December 2008.

3 Malaysia and the ASEAN community

After more than three decades, ASEAN decided to transform the institution into a Community. It was first agreed for the Community to be established by the year 2020 but later the establishment was accelerated for the year 2015, five years earlier than its original plan. Thus, ASEAN will be the major architect for the regional integration. ASEAN is determined to accelerate the full implementation of the ASEAN Community's programme areas, measures and principles, with appropriate flexibility and at the same time recognizes the importance for ASEAN member states to adopt a balanced approach towards achieving all three pillars of the ASEAN Community.

With its dedicated Plans of Actions and Protocols, ASEAN will move closer towards its goal of building the ASEAN Community, characterized by greater political and security interaction and engagement, a single market and production base, with free flow of goods, services, capital investment and skilled labour and a caring society, focusing on social development, education and human resources development, public health, culture and information, and environmental protection.

ASEAN came out with the blueprints for the three community pillars, aimed to further strengthen cooperation and coordination among ASEAN member states' relevant sectoral bodies. The ASEAN Economic Community Blueprint was adopted by the ASEAN Leaders during the 13th ASEAN Summit in November 2007. In its foreign policy strategy, Malaysia continues to actively reaffirm its commitment and work within ASEAN to achieve peace, security and prosperity in the region. Malaysia also continues to work together with fellow ASEAN member states towards the establishment of the ASEAN Community by 2015. On a broader scale, ASEAN will encourage closer relations with other regional groupings on issues of common concerns and mutual benefits (Malaysia Ministry of Foreign Affairs).

Consistent with Bali Concord I and II, Malaysia's efforts would focus on creating an ASEAN Community by 2015 comprising three pillars, namely the ASEAN Political-Security Community, ASEAN Economic Community and ASEAN Socio-Cultural Community. Malaysia would continue to concentrate on enhancing the ASEAN mechanisms, the ASEAN Plus Three (APT), the ARF, bridging the technological and developmental gap between the newer and older ASEAN members and settlement of disputes in the South China Sea through diplomacy and dialogue (Malaysia Ministry of Foreign Affairs 2014).

4 Malaysia and the three pillars of ASEAN community

In 2003, ASEAN's chairmanship passed from Prime Minister Hun Sen's Cambodia to President Megawati Sukarnoputri's Indonesia. This was the first opportunity for a post-Suharto Indonesia leadership to play an important role in shaping the region's future. A Bali ASEAN Summit was capped by the signing of the 'Bali Concord II', signifying a rededication to the political, economic, and social goals expressed more than a quarter of a century earlier at the first Bali summit. The goal was to create 'a dynamic, cohesive, resilient and integrated ASEAN Community by the year 2020. It is potentially the most significant development in ASEAN since 1997. The three pillars are: an ASEAN Political-Security Community (proposed by Indonesia), an ASEAN Economic Community (proposed by Thailand), and an ASEAN Social-cultural Community (Solingen 2005, 20; Weatherbee 2009, 105).

ASEAN's push for the three forms of 'communities' – political-security, economic, and socio-cultural – has also been wholeheartedly taken on board by the Malaysian government along with the ASEAN Charter signed in November 2007 at the 13th ASEAN Summit in Singapore (Saravanamuttu 2010, 338).

4.1 ASEAN Political-Security Community (APSC)

The APSC idea focused on using ASEAN's existing mechanisms for resolving intramural disputes, and much closer collaboration on transnational security challenges including terrorism, narcotics- and people-trafficking, and maritime security issues. As envisaged in the Declaration of ASEAN Concord II at the October 2003 summit, the APSC reflected ASEAN's established collective emphasis on comprehensive security and the principle of non-interference, explicitly ruling out an ASEAN defence pact, military alliance or joint foreign policy (Huxley 2005, 18).

The nature of the APSC was spelled out in more detail in the Vientiane Action Programme (VAP), issued during the ASEAN Summit in November 2004, which listed five 'strategic thrusts' aimed at achieving results by 2010: political development (including the promotion of human rights and the prevention of corruption), the shaping and sharing of norms (notably efforts to adopt a regional code of conduct in the South China Sea, and various counter-terrorism measures), conflict prevention (including establishment of an ASEAN Arms Register and the promotion of maritime security cooperation), conflict resolution, and post-conflict peace-building (Huxley 2005, 18–19).

As a member of ASEAN, Malaysia had been actively engaged in multilateral defence institutions such as the ARF, the ASEAN Defence Minister Meeting (ADMM) and most recently, the ADMM Plus. The importance of defence diplomacy is even more pronounced considering Malaysia is not party to any military alliance. Participation in a multilateral setting is an important avenue for Malaysia to engage in regional discussion and management of security issues. The expansion of ADMM to ADMM Plus is a positive development in that it brings together the major powers and ASEAN, and it would be more functional compared to the ARF as the former has fewer members emphasized more on cohesiveness among ADMM Plus members.. At that point, the ADMM Plus appears to be following in the tracks of the ARF in avoiding the hard questions on substantive security issues. Issues and threats such as non-proliferation and territorial disputes are not yet on 'the table'. The inaugural ADMM Plus had identified five focus areas: disaster relief, counter-terrorism, maritime security, peacekeeping and military medicine. These 'safe' security issues are non-controversial and restate what regional member states have been doing in the last decade. It is also a modality that had served ASEAN and its partners well when it comes to security cooperation, with the strategy of downplaying controversial issues and using the incentive of 'low hanging fruits' to instil confidence and nurture future cooperation. This is an approach that is amenable to Malaysia. In the absence of an imminent threat, the urgency to push for cooperation in 'hard security' issues is lacking (Mun 2010, 25).

In the area of maritime security, the only trilateral security arrangement among ASEAN states is the coordinated patrol of the Straits of Malacca. In 2004, Malaysia, Indonesia and Singapore (the three littoral states) undertook the tasks of patrolling the Straits of Malacca. Although this operation has successfully contained the incidence of piracy, there are some problems, with the main issue being the lack of trust. Hence, with Kuala Lumpur's initiative, an agreement was reached on the coordinated patrol of warships and 'Eye in the Sky' aerial surveillance flights by the three states, which took effect on 13 September 2005. The operations are coordinated by Malaysian authorities, and Malaysia contributed most of the assets for the operations. Both operations have gone on as planned and the piracy incidence at the Straits of Malacca was reduced to almost 'nil'. On 21 April 2006, the Malacca Straits Sea Patrols and 'Eye in the Sky' were subsumed under one overarching framework called The Malacca Straits Patrol. Even though this security arrangement only actively involved three member states of ASEAN, the Malacca Straits Patrol operation has successfully shown that member states of ASEAN can work together to achieve regional security and stability. This operation can be the benchmark and future reference for any multilateral security arrangements within ASEAN (Redha @ Redo Abduh bin Abd Hamid 2010).

Despite some limited police cooperation and multiple statements condemning terrorism, ASEAN has not yet spearheaded a strong cooperative arrangement on terrorism, despite the common fear that terrorism could stifle foreign investment and economic growth – the pillars of an internationalization strategy. In 2002, Malaysia drafted a treaty to harmonize and coordinate legal systems to deny safe havens to terrorists. However, this was not an ASEAN initiative and its viability is not yet evident. In 2003, Malaysia inaugurated a Southeast Asian Antiterrorism Center in Kuala Lumpur, funded by the United States America (USA) (Solingen 2005, 19).

In the absence of an effective multilateral framework to deal with terrorist threat in Southeast Asia, bilateralism or sub-ASEAN regionalism has represented the ASEAN fallback position. In this context, Malaysia, Indonesia and the Philippines, most prone to Jemaah Islamiyah (JI) organization and attacks, signed an agreement, which provides for anti-terrorism exercises, combined operations, and sharing of information, including the setting up of a hotline between the three countries (Jong 2007, 20).

In terms of ASEAN integration, Malaysia also played an active role in the shape and composition of the ARF, ASEAN's post-Cold War regional security apparatus officially inaugurated at the 1994 Summit. The 22-nation forum provides Malaysia with a voice in the security agenda of the region. It was in line with Malaysia's foreign policy desire for the involvement of regional powers to guarantee regional peace. Given USA's membership in ARF, Malaysia foreign policy involvement was further in line with Malaysia coming to terms, albeit reluctantly, with the unipolar dominance of the USA in the aftermath of the demise of the Soviet Union. Thus, ARF has become the cornerstone of the nation's regional security concerns in the post-Cold War era (Dhillon 2009, 215).

4.2 ASEAN Economic Community (AEC)

The establishment of the AEC is the ultimate goal of economic integration as outlined in the ASEAN Vision 2020. The AEC is meant to be a single market and production base with a free flow of goods, services, investments and a freer flow of financial capital. The AEC would also promote equitable economic development, reduce poverty and socio-economic disparities, and strengthen the ASEAN institutional mechanisms, including the improvement of the Dispute Settlement Mechanism (ASEAN Secretariat 2003).

At the sub-regional level, increased efforts were made towards realising the benefits of the growth triangle concept such as the Brunei, Indonesia, Malaysia and Philippines-East ASEAN Growth Area (BIMP-EAGA). Such efforts would no doubt allow for prosperity to spread to the less developed areas, thereby, bringing meaning to the 'prosper-thy-neighbour-policy'. At the regional level, Malaysia will continue to push for the strengthening of ASEAN as a regional grouping. This includes support for a whole range of functional co-operation on a sub-regional basis (such as the ASEAN Mekong Basin Development Co-operation) or on an ASEAN-wide basis, the phasing in of AFTA and the implementation of the ASEAN Investment Area (Malaysia Ministry of Foreign Affairs 2014).

ASEAN has since adopted this philosophy and the member governments have made significant effort to establish an ASEAN Free Trade Area for the benefit of all those living in Southeast Asia. Malaysia was a prime mover in these initiatives since a market of almost 560 million people with a growing disposable income will enable Malaysia's manufacturers and exporters to increase revenues and profits. With the kind of collaboration and alliances that ASEAN-based companies can put together, truly ASEAN-wide enterprises can emerge that have the economies of scale to compete globally and generate employment opportunities across the region (Mahathir and Irwan 2007, 104).

The Malaysian private sector was actively encouraged to develop trade links and investment projects in these countries. It was felt that increased trade and investment would lead to increased employment, more wealth and rising consumption. Malaysian goods will then find their way into these expanding markets thereby bringing additional income to the Malaysian businesses that produce and export them. Rising prosperity for Malaysia and her neighbours is a virtuous cycle and would lead to a continually enhancing way of life for all (Mahathir and Irwan 2007, 104).

Another example of increased economic activity among ASEAN countries can be seen in the intra-ASEAN investment flows. As ASEAN is working towards establishing AEC, Malaysia is aiming to enhance trade and investment flows in the region which would contribute towards regional integration, growth and development. Malaysia is among the largest investors in ASEAN. The ASEAN region has much investment potential for Malaysian outward investment, and such opportunities will be expanded upon the implementation of ASEAN investment initiatives like the ASEAN Comprehensive Investment Agreement (ACIA) and the ASEAN Framework Agreement on Services (AFAS). In terms of trade, Malaysia is among the largest players in intra-ASEAN trade. In 2007, Malaysia's trade with ASEAN amounted to US $78 billion. In addition, ASEAN as a region is Malaysia's second largest trading partner, accounting for 25.1 per cent of its total trade (TIOS Consulting 2007).

4.3 ASEAN Socio-Cultural Community (ASCC)

The ASCC aims at raising the quality of life of the ASEAN citizens, to strengthen their cultural identity and to achieve a more sustainable use of natural resources. The ASCC Plan of Action, declared at the 10th ASEAN Summit in Vientiane consists of four core elements: to build a community of caring societies, to manage the social impact of economic integration, to enhance environmental sustainability and to strengthen the foundations of regional cohesion (Cuyvers and Tummers 2007).

The ASCC Blueprint narrows the focus of the region's socio-cultural development into six arenas: (a) Human Development; (b) Social Welfare and Protection; (c) Social Justice and Rights; (d) Ensuring Environmental Sustainability; (e) Building the ASEAN Identity; and (f) Narrowing the Development Gap.

The ASCC presents plans for building the ASEAN community through the promotion of 'greater awareness and common values in the spirit of unity in diversity at all levels of society' including 'engagement with community' and declares its aim to 'build a people-oriented ASEAN where people are at the centre of community building, through the participation of all sectors of society'. The implementation plans include the engagement of ASEAN-affiliated NGOs, as well as convening the ASEAN Social Forum (ASF) and the AAN Civil Society Conference (ACSC) on an annual basis (Tay and May-Ann 2009).

The first ASEAN Civil Society Conference (ACSC) was organized in 2005 by the Malaysian government as host of the ASEAN Summit. The organization also involved the following Malaysian CSOs: the ASEAN Studies Centre, University Tekonologi MARA (UiTM), Third World Network, Yayasan Dakwah Islamiah Malaysia (YADIM), Angkatan Belia Islam Malaysia (ABIM), Peace Malaysia and the Malaysian Environmental NGOs (MENGO). It was attended by more than 120 participants from ASEAN NGOs (Tay and May-Ann 2009, 8).

The statement from this 1st ACSC was presented to the Heads of State during the 11th ASEAN Summit in Kuala Lumpur, the first time that civil society was given direct access to the ASEAN process. The report was noted in the Chairman's Statement of the 11th ASEAN Summit, where ASEAN recognized the convening of the 1st ACSC, acknowledged the increasingly important role that civil society plays in the development of the ASEAN Community, and explicitly stated that they 'supported the holding of the Conference annually on the sidelines of the ASEAN Summit and its report be presented to the Leaders'. This convening of the first ACSC 2005 could be said to mark a shift in ASEAN's engagement with civil society (Tay and May-Ann 2009, 8).

Following the 1st ACSC held in Malaysia in 2005, new networks began to form in the civil society sector. A number of regional networks of NGOs developed from existing NGOs, such as the Solidarity for Asian People's Advocacy (SAPA), Forum-Asia, the Southeast Asian Committee for Advocacy (SEACA), the Third World Network (TWN) and AsiaDHRRA – the Asian Partnership for the Development of Human Resources in Rural Asia (Tay and May-Ann 2009, 9).

Despite ASEAN's emerging Community, ASEAN was also faced with issues such as the haze problem. Extensive forest and grass fires, leading to smoke pollution as well as a host of losses and costs, some less immediately visible and more lasting, have become regular events in Southeast Asia. With particular atmospheric conditions, this pollution has persisted for long periods, and has become known, somewhat euphemistically, as 'haze'. Previous episodes of the haze have occurred in 1982–1983, 1987, 1991, and 1994, but that of 1997–1998 was more extreme, costly, and in some localities, life threatening (Cotton 1999, 331).

ASEAN cooperation on the environment has a history of over 20 years, having started with the establishment of the ASEAN Expert Group on the Environment (AEGE) and ASEAN Senior Officials on the Environment (ASOEN). In June 1990, the ASEAN Ministers on the Environment endorsed the Kuala Lumpur Accord on the Environment and Development, which enunciated a common stand that could be described as generally 'pro-development', on the relationship between these two issues (Cotton 1999, 342).

Though 'transboundary pollution' was considered in the 1990 document, the Indonesian forest fires of 1994 prompted ASEAN to adopt measures specifically designed to meet this problem, in the form of the ASEAN Cooperation Plan on Transboundary Pollution, considered at the ASEAN Ministerial Meeting on the Environment convened in Kuching in October 1994. The first 'programme area' identified relates to 'regional haze incidents', and the strategy outlined to deal with these incidents emphasizes fire-fighting capability (including early warning fires) and the prohibition of burning during dry periods. Following from this agreement, a 'Haze Technical Task Force' was established by ASOEN in 1995, with the aim of sharing information on fire prevention and containment, including making available satellite data on actual fires (Cotton 1999, 343).

But even though ASEAN focused on the haze problem, the mechanisms established moved ponderously, although the crisis of 1997 mobilized ASOEN to meet three times in the year. Senior officials agreed to regional division of labour in November, with Singapore taking the lead in the monitoring of fire hazards, Malaysia concentrating on fire prevention, and Indonesia dealing with fire fighting. In addition, a ministerial-level meeting in December 1997 adopted a 'Regional Haze Action Plan' which focused squarely on the problem (Cotton 1999, 343).

In addition, ASEAN civil society groups have been involved in tackling the haze problem. There have been four major regional dialogues by CSOs on the haze. The first was in 1998, following an NGOs Policy Dialogue, held in Singapore and organized by the Singapore Environment Council and the Singapore Institute of International Affairs. Since then, there have been three haze dialogues held: in 2006, 2007, and 2009, organized by Singapore Institute of International Affairs working in collaboration with other think tanks and CSOs. The Singapore and Malaysian governments have also undertaken to work with local Indonesian authorities and communities in provinces affected by the haze (Tay and May-Ann 2009, 12).

ASEAN's role has also expanded to encompass economic and socio-cultural functions including health. ASEAN health ministers hold regular formal meetings. In 2000, the Yogyakarta Declaration on the Healthy ASEAN 2020 strategy was posited as the basis for cooperation between member countries, as well as with international health agencies (Barraclough and Phua 2007, 226).

The seventh ASEAN meeting of health ministers, hosted by Malaysia in 2004 with the theme 'health without frontiers', was particularly relevant for foreign affairs and health. This meeting endorsed continuing cooperation between members not only to counter infectious diseases but also to deal with the health ramifications of international trade agreements, and to encourage joint food standards and regulation. It was also agreed that ASEAN countries would work with World Health Organisation (WHO) and other UN agencies to examine recommendations of the Commission on Macroeconomics and

Health to monitor health-related Millennium Development Goals (Barraclough and Phua 2007, 226).

In April 2003, Malaysia played a prominent regional role in responding to the outbreak of Severe Acute Respiratory Syndrome (SARS). It hosted the first special meeting on SARS of the ASEAN Plus Three health ministers in Kuala Lumpur. At this meeting, participants agreed to take comprehensive trans-border action to contain the disease and to facilitate the exchange of information. They also affirmed their intention to follow WHO's travel guidelines and initiated the establishment of an ASEAN research centre on controlling communicable diseases. Two months later, Kuala Lumpur was the venue for WHO's international conference on SARS (Barraclough and Phua 2007, 227).

In December 2003, in the wake of the severe SARS epidemic, Brunei and Malaysia initiated bilateral health meetings. They agreed to establish working groups for future joint projects and for a memorandum of understanding to strengthen and formalize future cooperation not only on communicable diseases but also laboratory facilities, health surveillance, food safety, tobacco control and the cross-border movement of patients (Barraclough and Phua 2007, 227).

5 Malaysia and ASEAN Plus Three (APT)

As a founding member of ASEAN, Malaysia continues to emphasize the relevance and importance of ASEAN as the forum and catalyst for regional dialogues. ASEAN Dialogue Partnerships, ASEAN Regional Forum, ASEAN Plus Three (APT) and East Asia Summit (EAS) have allowed member states to engage leading powers on issues of global and regional importance. While Malaysia's Look East Policy has focused on Japan and South Korea, China is also important to Malaysia. The relations between the two countries normalized during the Cold War.

Malaysia's most important step towards neutralism actually came with the recognition and establishment of diplomatic relations with the People's Republic of China (PRC). Overtures of rapprochement with China became evident when Malaysia began to soften its China line soon after the termination of Konfrontasi (Saravanamuttu 2010, 123). Hence, Malaysia reversed its policy and began supporting the admission of the PRC into the UN and indicated the country's willingness to establish a dialogue with PRC, provided that the latter was willing to change its policy towards Malaysia and support Malaysia's policy of peaceful co-existence and non-interference (Sidhu 2009, 7). In the 1971 U.N. General Assembly (UNGA), Malaysia voted for the Albanian resolution which allowed for the seating of China and, consequently, Taiwan's expulsion. There followed in October 1971 a 19-man trade mission to China, led by Pernas Chairman, Tengku Razaleigh, to establish direct trade links with the PRC. Subsequent missions followed, paving the way for unofficial negotiations on recognition and diplomatic ties. Then on 27 May 1974, a Malaysian entourage, led by Prime Minister Tun Abdul Razak, left for the PRC in the first high-level official contact of the two governments since Malaya's independence in 1957. On 31 May, Malaysia and China announced the normalization of relations to be followed by an exchange of ambassadors. At the same time, Malaysia terminated diplomatic (consular) relations with Taiwan (Saravanamuttu 2010, 124–125).

Malaysia's Prime Minister Mahathir Mohamed played an important role in introducing the idea of regionalism in East Asia, back in 1991. He suggested that the region should cooperate to establish what was then known as the East Asian Economic Grouping (EAEG), which included all ASEAN states, China, Japan and South Korea. Mahathir's overall disappointment with ASEAN's inability to move decisively in the economic sphere prompted his EAEG, and subsequently, the East Asia Economic Caucus (EAEC) idea. Mahathir made a policy speech about the EAEG idea to the Hong Kong Foreign Correspondents' Club on 14 October 1992. According to Mahathir, 'the EAEG or EAEC should neither be a formal grouping like ASEAN nor should it be a trade bloc like North American Free Trade Area (NAFTA) or the European Community (EC). As it is dedicated to world free trade, it cannot be protectionist and give its members preferential treatment in intra-regional trade. Its chief purpose is to provide a strong voice for East Asian countries in trade negotiations with the rest of world, particularly the EC and NAFTA' (*New Straits Times*, 15 October 1992 in Saravanamuttu 2010, 190–191).

Although it received a lot of criticism, his ideas stimulated new thinking about regionalism in East Asia. EAEC is more like a forum to discuss common economic problems, enhance economic cooperation, promote and protect free trade, accelerate economic growth, promote open regionalism and to contribute to the multilateral trading system (Shibata 2006).

Mahathir's idea on East Asian regionalism was further promoted by the Institute of Strategic and International Studies (ISIS) which became the think tank representing Malaysia in the ASEAN-ISIS second track diplomacy. As a consequence of Malaysia's advocacy of East Asian regionalism under Mahathir, ISIS created the East Asian Economic Centre (EAEC) with the same name to Mahathir's proposal since 2003. The EAEC engages in independent policy-oriented studies, conferencing and networking, and hosting the East Asian Congress, an annual quadripartite gathering of policymakers, scholars, the private sector, and the media (Saravanamuttu 2010, 42).

Later in 1997, APT was established with EAC as the long-term project of APT. Mahathir's idea of promoting this Asian regionalism can be traced back to the country's Look East Policy (LEP). The LEP was proposed by Mahathir Mohamed, as the key to the political, economic and social development of the country. He suggested that Malaysians should emulate qualities such as industrious work ethics, a strong sense of public commitment and respect for social order from Japan, as features that are generally considered to be based on the Confucian moral code. The Prime Minister argued that the rapid development of East Asian countries, notably Japan and South Korea, was brought about by their appreciation of these qualities – the so-called Asian Values – and Malaysia should follow these exemplars. From the outset, this LEP has been regarded as a relatively successful case of international educational cooperation. Under the LEP, educational links between Japan and Malaysia have been expanded. In this process, however, the aspects of 'culture' and 'values' have become less prominent than the initial advocacy for the LEP. Instead, looking East and learning from Japan have worked as powerful metaphors for political aspirations for Asian regionalism (Shibata 2006, 650).

For political change, the LEP worked as a powerful metaphor for denouncing the Western colonial legacy and the consolidation of nations in the Asian region. Mahathir tried to develop the concept of an East Asian Community – a kind of political, economic and cultural consortium in the region. In the face of political, economic and education consolidation within free trade blocs in Europe, such as the EC and the NAFTA, Mahathir suggested that countries in East and Southeast Asia should be more cohesive and unified so that they could play a meaningful role in the global economy (Shibata 2006, 653).

Although Asians had APEC, the Asia-Pacific Economic Cooperation, it did not fit in with Mahathir's parameters. Its formation was a disappointment for him, because it seemed to him to be influenced by the USA and its Western allies. Instead, Mahathir proposed the formation of 'ASEAN+3', an enlargement of ASEAN with the inclusion of Japan, South Korea and China. Mahathir's vision for the EAEC is a reduced version of APEC through the exclusion of Australia, New Zealand and the USA. For him, Asian countries needed to restore their cultural sovereignty that for a long time had been encroached upon by Western powers. Mahathir's idea eventually evolved into the creation of an East Asian citizenship and the formation of an East Asian Community (Shibata 2006, 653–654).

As the fifth prime minister after Mahathir, Abdullah Badawi has also largely maintained the thrust of Malaysian foreign policy vis-à-vis ASEAN and East Asian relations. ASEAN remains the anchor of Malaysia's overall orientation towards the rest of the world, but he continued to push for greater East Asian regional integration via the Asian Plus Three grouping. Several meetings finally led to the First East Asia Summit (EAS), held in Kuala Lumpur in 2005 when Malaysia assumed the 39th ASEAN Standing Committee Chairmanship in July and played host to the 11th ASEAN Summit. The KL Summit was guided by the motto of 'One Vision, One Identity and One Community'. In his speech at the Second East Asia Congress in Kuala Lumpur on 21 June 2006, Abdullah called for the establishment of an East Asian Community (EAC) based on 'six cardinal imperatives', namely, egalitarian and democratic; omni-directional and embracing, turning its back on no one; caring and mutually beneficial; committed to global empowerment; devoted to economic prosperity, and, obsessive about regional peace and friendship (Saravanamuttu 2010, 251; Azhari Karim 2007, 110).

The prime motivation for regionalism is often economic benefits and this appears to the case of APT. For Malaysia, the APT will form a crucial component of its long-term economic and political strategy. While Malaysia's top trade partner in 2005 was the US (16.63 per cent), Japan and China accounted for 11.67 per cent and 8.79 per cent of its total trade respectively. Sino–Malaysian trade has been on the rise in the past few years and is expected to continue its upward trajectory. In the meantime, trade and investment relations with Japan continue to be an important contributor to the Malaysian economy. What the APT offers is a unique platform for Malaysia to maintain and further its trading ties with China and Japan without favouring one or the other. By aligning itself with China and Japan, Malaysia is hoping to ride on the economic coat tails of the two largest economies in the region (Tang 2006, 203).

The political calculus is somewhat different. The rapid rise of China's economic fortunes in the last decade poses a strategic dilemma for its neighbours, including Japan and Malaysia. Kuala Lumpur and Tokyo had repeatedly brushed aside the 'Chinese threat' and focused on the positive effects of the economic transformation of China whose diplomatic mantra of a 'peaceful rise' seems to be successful. Although both countries are wary of an emergent China, the APT allows Malaysia and Japan to engage China through trade and investment in the hope that strong economic ties will spill over to political cooperation (Tang 2006, 204).

6 Conclusion

It became rather logical that the post-Konfrontasi years would bring about a new political development in Southeast Asia by way of renewed regional cooperation, heading to the formation of ASEAN. Since the inception of the grouping, Malaysian leaders have put a priority on ASEAN as a vehicle for the internationalization of its national aspirations. Its foreign policy since gaining independence in 1957 has been predicated upon riding on the back of ASEAN while at the same time maintaining a grip on the grouping and steering it towards a direction that will benefit Malaysia and the region as a whole and if needed to, even beyond. Malaysian middlepowermanship may be said to have emerged in this period which saw a shift of statecraft from the national to the regional as ASEAN increasingly became the conduit for collective statecraft and policy orientations of engaging the major hegemonic powers, and the instrument for bringing about a new regional order.

Malaysia has proved time and again that it can play a significant role, if it wishes to, in influencing and at times leading regional co-operations. Being a founder member of ASEAN, Malaysia has played a key role in building it into the regional force that it is today. Almost all past Malaysian Prime Ministers have devoted significant efforts and time in pursuing the dream of building a more cohesive and strong regional co-operation via ASEAN. They have also played important roles in shaping ASEAN foreign policy and economic co-operations. Today, ASEAN comprises all nations in Southeast Asia, an objective that Malaysia worked hard to achieve and a triumph of consensual negotiations based on mutual respect.

Malaysia has determined what its identity is from the beginning of its existence as an independent country since 1957, and has attempted to secure its national interest by making ASEAN the instrument for achieving its foreign policy goals. In part, she has been greatly assisted by having the right leaders at the right time to take the mantle of leadership. Successive prime ministers from Tunku Abdul Rahman, Tun Razak, Tun Hussein Onn, Tun Mahathir Mohamad, Abdullah Ahmad Badawi and now Najib Tun Razak have chosen the path of constructivism by which to steer the country forward.

As emphasized in the discussion of Malaysia's foreign policy, regional cooperation has always been its major preoccupation. ASEAN remains its cornerstone. In this respect, Malaysia attaches vital importance to relationships with countries in the Southeast Asian region. ASEAN will continue to be the cornerstone of Malaysia's foreign policy and the predominant forum for maintaining regional peace and stability through dialogue and cooperation. The peace, prosperity and stability that Malaysia enjoys today are to a large extent due to ASEAN's role as an organization that fosters trust and confidence amongst its member states.

References

Andaya, B.W. and Andaya, L.Y. (1982) *History of Malaysia*. London: Macmillan Press.

ASEAN Secretariat (2003) Declaration of ASEAN Concord II (Bali Concord II), Bali, 7 October. Available from: www.aseansec.org/15159.htm.

Baginda, Abdul Razak (ed.) (2007) *Malaysia Foreign Policy: Continuity & Change*. Singapore: Marshall Cavendish.

Baginda, Abdul Razak (ed.) (2009) *Malaysia Defence & Security Since 1957. Continuity & Change*. Singapore: Marshall Cavendish.

Barraclough, Simon and Phua, Kai-Lat (2007) 'Health Imperatives in Foreign Policy: The Case of Malaysia'. *Bulletin of the World Health Organization* 85(3): 161–244.

Cotton, James (1999) 'The "Haze" over Southeast Asia: Challenging the ASEAN Mode of Regional Engagement'. *Pacific Affairs*, 72(3): 331–351.

Crouch, Harold (1997) *Government and Society in Malaysia*. New York: Cornell University Press.

Cuyvers, L. and Tummers, R. (2007) 'The Road to an ASEAN Community: How Far Still to Go?' Centre for ASEAN Studies (CAS) Discussion Paper 57 (December). Antwerp, CAS & Centre for International Management and Development.

Dayley, Robert and Clark D. Neher (2010) *Southeast Asia in the New International Era*. 5th edition. Boulder, CO: Westview Press.

Dhillon, Karminder Singh (2009) *Malaysia Foreign Policy in the Mahathir Era 1981–2003*. Singapore: NUS Press.

Economic Planning Unit (1999) *Mid-Term Review of the Seventh Malaysia Plan (1996–2000)*. Kuala Lumpur: Economic Planning Unit.

Faaland, Just, J.R. Parkinson, Rais Saniman (1990) *Growth and Ethnic Inequality*. Kuala Lumpur: Dewan Bahasa dan Pustaka.

Huxley, Tim (2005) 'Southeast Asia in 2004: Stable, but Facing Major Security Challenges'. *Southeast Asian Affairs.* Singapore: ISEAS.

Jomo, K.S. (2001) 'Capital Controls'. In *Malaysia Eclipse: Economic Crisis and Recovery,* edited by K.S. Jomo. London and New York: Zed Books Ltd.

Jong, Kim Hyung (2007) 'ASEAN Way, Its Implications and Challenges for Regional Integration in Southeast Asia', *JATI,* 12: 17–29.

Karim, Azhari (2007) 'ASEAN-Association to Community: Constructed in the Image of Malaysia's Global Diplomacy'. In *Malaysia Foreign Policy: Continuity & Change,* edited by Abdul Razak Baginda. Singapore: Marshall Cavendish.

Ministry of Foreign Affairs (2014) 20 June. Available from: www.kln.gov.my.

Mirzan, Mahathir and Fazil Irwan (2007) 'Malaysia's Role in ASEAN Regional Cooperation: A Look at Foreign Policy Themes', *Asia-Pacific Review,* 14(2): 97–111.

Mohd. Yasin, Norhashimah (1996) *Islamisation/Malaynisation: A Study on the Role of Islamic Law in the Economic Development of Malaysia 1969–1993.* Kuala Lumpur: A.S. Noordeen.

Othman, Muhammad Fuad and Zaheruddin Othman (2010) 'The Principle of Non-Interference in ASEAN: Can Malaysia Spearhead the Effort towards a More Interventionist ASEAN'. Proceedings of Seminar on National Resilience (SNAR), Political Management and Policies in Malaysia, Langkawi, Malaysia, 13–15 July.

Redha@ Redo Abduh bin Abd Hamid (2010) 'ASEAN Security Cooperation: Challenges and the Way Ahead. *The Journal of Defence and Security,* 1(1): 52–64.

Saravanamuttu, Johan (1997) 'ASEAN in Malaysian Foreign Policy Discourse and Practice, 1967–1997', *Asian Journal of Political Science,* 5(1): 35–51.

Saravanamuttu, Johan (2010) *Malaysia's Foreign Policy: The First Fifty Years.* Singapore and Petaling Jaya: Institute of Southeast Asian Studies (ISEAS) and Strategic Information and Research Development Centre (SIRD).

Sar Desai, D. R. (2003) *Southeast Asia: Past and Present,* 5th edition. Boulder, CO: Westview Press.

Sar Desai, D. R. (2006) *Southeast Asian History: Essential Readings.* Boulder, CO: Westview Press.

Shibata, Masako (2006) 'Assumptions and Implications of Cross-National Attraction in Education: The Case of "Learning from Japan'. *Oxford Review of Education,* 32(5): 649–663.

Sidhu, Jaswant S. (2009 'Malaysia's Defence and Security since 1957: An Overview'. In (ed.) *Malaysia's Defence & Security Since 1957,* edited by Baginda, Abdul Razak. Kuala Lumpur: Malaysian Strategic Research Centre.

Solingen, Etel (2005) 'ASEAN Cooperation: The Legacy of the Economic Crisis', *International Relations of the Asia-Pacific,* 5(1): 1–29.

Tan, Andrew T. H. (2004) *Security Perspectives of the Malay Archipelago.* Cheltenham: Edward Elgar.

Tang Siew Mun (2006) 'Japan's Vision of an East Asian Community: A Malaysian Perspective', *Japanese Studies,* 26(2): 199–210.

Tang Siew Mun (2010) 'Malaysia's Strategic Outlook and Developments in its Defence Policy'. In the National Institute of Defense Studies, Japan. *Asia Pacific Countries' Outlook and Its Implications for the Defense Sector.* NIDS Joint Research Series No. 5.

Tay, Simon and May-Ann, Lim (2009) 'Assessment and Overview: ASEAN and Regional Involvement of Civil Society'. Singapore Institute of International Affairs, November.

TIOS Consulting International (2007) 'Interview with Datuk Jalilah Baba, Director General of MIDA'. Available from: www.ipfa-group.com/assets/files/interviews/mida_Malaysia (accessed 20 June 2014).

Turnbull, C.M. (1999) 'Regionalism and Nationalism'. In , ed. *The Cambridge History of Southeast Asia, Vol. 2, Part 2*, edited by Tarling, Nicholas. Cambridge: Cambridge University Press.

Volkmann, Rabea (2008) 'Why does ASEAN Need a Charter? Pushing Actors and their National Interests', *ASIEN*, 109: 78–87.

Weatherbee, Donald E. (2009) *International Relations in Southeast Asia, The Struggle for Autonomy*, 2nd edition. Singapore and New York: ISEAS and Rowan & Littlefield Publisher Inc.

6 The Republic of Union of Myanmar and the ASEAN and APT processes

Maung Maung Soe

1 National perspectives: A historical narrative of different voices in the national identity formation

The early history of Myanmar began in the eleventh century. Those days were called the golden age of a united Bagan dynasty. The first king of Bagan was King Anawrahta, who set up Myanmar under his monarchy. He worshiped Buddha and Buddhism became the national religion in his era. Bagan was the first capital in Myanmar history. Bagan is also called City of Pagodas. The last kingdom was ended by King Thibaw from the Konbaung dynasty, and Mandalay was the last capital in Myanmar history before the British colonization.

The British colonial authorities had practiced the divide and rule method in Myanmar. Before making Myanmar a colony, the British had fought Anglo-Burmese (Myanmar) wars for more than 60 years. They occupied Myanmar completely in 1886. After making Myanmar a colony, it became one of the provinces under India. Myanmar has numerous ethnic groups like the Shan, Kachin, Kayin, Mon, Myanmar, Yakhain, Kayar, and Chin. They provided the British with the conditions to adopt a divide and rule strategy. However, the first protests by Myanmar intellectual classes and Buddhist monks were launched against British rules and regulations in the 1920s. The outbreak of the Second World War created opportunities to bring about the independence of Myanmar. Myanmar finally became independent on January 4, 1948, at 4:20 am. That time was selected as a result of the agreement between the British and Myanmar. Ten years after independence, the democratic government of Myanmar was challenged by communist and ethnic groups who felt under-represented in the 1948 constitution. Prime Minister U Nu was then removed by General Ne Win, one of General Aung San's followers. From 1962 to 1988, the country was closed to the outside world and very isolated. The political system then was based on the Burmese Way to Socialism. In July 1988, Ne Win announced his retirement as the head of state, and on August 8, Myanmar was ruled by the State Law and Order Restoration Council (SLORC), later renamed as State Peace and Development Council (SPDC). On March, 30 2011, the political system was moved to a multiparty democracy format. U Thein Sein became President of the State with more collaboration with international organizations. Notably, ASEAN is seen to be one of the associations that could play a vital role in assisting progress in Myanmar. Myanmar became the chair of ASEAN in 2014.

1.1 Political security perspectives

1.1.1 The kingdom era

The Bagan kingdom was the first kingdom in Myanmar history. The Bagan dynasty spanned from the mid-eleventh to the thirteenth century under 55 kings. The first king of the Bagan dynasty was King Anawrahta (1044–1077), who consolidated control over the kingdom, unified its diverse peoples, and made Theravada Buddhism, introduced by Buddhist missionary Shin Arahan, central to the kingdom. Besides laying the foundations of Bagan's greatness as a dynasty, King Anawrahta is often seen as a central figure in Myanmar history.

The Bagan dynasty ended in 1287, when Mongols invaded and destroyed it. After the Mongol invasions ended in 1365, Myanmar was divided politically, separating into two regions, upper and lower Myanmar, each of which gave rise to a kingdom. In upper Myanmar, the Inwa dynasty was started by King Thadominbya, and its 19 kings ruled from 1365 to 1552. In lower Myanmar, the Hanthawady kingdom (Bago dynasty) was begun by King Ba-nya-Oo as the Bago dynasty under 11 kings who reigned from 1369 to 1528.

Between 1386 and 1422, the Inwa and Hanthawady kingdoms fought. The Hanthawady King Bayintnaung reunited the Hanthawady empire and rebuilt it on a grand scale between 1552 and 1581, and is known as the Lord of the White Elephants. The Inwa Dynasty of upper Myanmar was ruled at that time by King Nyaungyan between 1598 and 1606, and the Nyaungyan dynasty ruled upper Myanmar under 10 kings.

Turmoil in the Bago dynasty in 1752 ended the Hantharwady kingdom. In its place, the new Konbaung dynasty arose in upper Myanmar, and its 11 kings ruled from 1752 to 1885 as the last kingdom in Myanmar history. The Konbaung dynasty had several capitals, from its first in Shwebo, then to Inwa, next to Amarapura, and finally ending in Mandalay. King Mindon ruled from Mandalay, the last capital of the Konbaung dynasty, which ended with king Thibaw in 1886.

1.1.2 The British colonial era

Britain began its colonial forays into Myanmar from 1826, and had fully colonized the country by 1886. Under this system, Myanmar was ruled from 1887 by a Chief Commissioner in the name of Lieutenant Governor, a position that was upgraded to Governor status in 1923. Up to 1937 Myanmar was ruled as part of the British India colonial system. In 1937, the House of Representatives was set up, and it ruled independently from the India Governor.

During the Second World War, from 1943 to 1945, Myanmar was occupied by Japan. This occupation was opposed by several organizations that were led by the Anti-Fascist People's Freedom League (AFPFL), with General Aung San as its first president. After the war ended, Britain restored its colonial rule in Myanmar until 1947. The AFPFL party remained active during this period and negotiated independence for Myanmar with the British government, resulting in the Aung San-Attlee Agreement signed on January 27, 1947.

1.1.3 After independence

On January 4, 1948, Myanmar became independent from Britain, and adopted a constitution which made it a quasi-federal Union, with the states of Kachin, Kayah, Kayin and Shan becoming parts of the system of governance under a bicameral legislature consisting of a Chamber of Deputies and a Chamber of Nationalities. After independence, insurgent unrests and the arrival of Kuomintang forces which had fled China resulted in violence in Myanmar.

1.1.4 The caretaker government

In 1958, a Caretaker Government emerged in Myanmar run by a small group of military officers, led by General Ne Win as Chief of Staff, and a few brigadiers. General Ne Win was appointed head of the Caretaker Government by the parliament on October 28, 1958, due to budget allocation problems and divisions in the ruling AFPFL party. Control over Myanmar thus shifted to General Ne Win, whom they trusted to conduct fair and free parliamentary elections for the sake of the nation.

Elections were held on February 6, 1960 and the state authority was handed over from General Ne Win to the winning Pyi Daung Su Party, on April 4, 1960. Political turmoil followed rapidly in the country, and with the Pyi Daung Su Party divided, U Nu became the Prime Minister. The country was full of confusion and misunderstandings among various groups. There were public dissatisfactions with government policies, and criticisms about changing the Buddhist State and the failure to start a federated state. On March 2, 1962, a coup by General Ne Win led him to take control of the country, and removed U Nu from his role as Prime Minister. Although U Nu still believed himself to be the legitimate leader and wanted to form an interim government, General Ne Win prevented him from doing so. Simultaneously, ethnic groups in several states formed organizations to oppose the new military government.

1.1.5 Revolutionary council

In this situation, a military council led by General Ne Win took over the state on March 2, 1962. The coup gave rise to a Revolutionary Council which aimed to secure and administer the nation. He also formed two committees at the ward and village level, aiming to restore stability to the nation. On April 1, 1963, the Revolutionary Council announced in a Declaration of General Amnesty that it would start negotiating with various insurgent groups. In this regard, it concluded an agreement with Kayin Revolution Council on March 12, 1964. Referring to the Burma Constitution of 1947, which was drawn up based on socialist principles, General Ne Win created the Burmese Socialist Program Party (BSPP), which became the government's single dominant party.

The BSPP created the Pyithu Hluttaw (similar to a parliament). Together, the BSPP party and Pyithu Hluttaw became the supreme state organ, enacting laws and appointing members to the executive and the judiciary bodies as part of a new state system. The BSPP was organized by the notion of democratic centralism, and it ran the national economy by centrally organized economic plans. The BSPP was supported mainly by two class organizations, the Peasants Asiayon (a farmers' association) and Workers Asiayon (a labor organization). Its government formed the Lanzin Youth Organization Committee which included young people from local areas. In 1973, the BSPP government mapped out a 20-year economic plan. The long-term plan was divided into five medium plans (each four years long) and short-term plans (each a year long) and it sought to double the GNP per capita in 20 years.

Although the national economy was run in a centrally planned way, it was poorly administered, breeding and leading to social discontent, and socio-economic unrests. The protests in August 1988, known as the 8888, soon spiraled out of control, leading to chaos around the country. This led the military government taking charge on September 18, 1988, announcing the formation of the State Law and Order Restoration Council (SLORC) as the national government. The Chief of Staff, General Saw Maung, was later given a new title and promoted as Senior General and Chairman in the state constitution. Senior General Than Shwe succeeded Senior General Saw Maung, when the latter retired on April 23, 1991, after serving four years as Chairman of the SLORC government.

1.1.6 Renamed SLORC as State Peace and Development Council (SPDC)

The SLORC was reorganized as the State Peace and Development Council (SPDC) on November 15, 1997 in order to efficiently and effectively make Myanmar into a modern and developed nation. The SPDC would focus on foreign affairs, and sought to participate in international activities, and become more accessible to foreign visitors. The SPDC attained membership for Myanmar in the ASEAN community, when it joined the regional body in July 1997. Although ASEAN had earlier offered Myanmar a chance to join as a member, Myanmar was isolated and rejected the offer at the time. This situation changed in the 1990s, as the SPDC vigorously courted ASEAN membership. Myanmar also joined a number of other regional groupings at the same time. These included the following:

- The Greater Mekong Sub-region Economic Cooperation Project, 1992.
- ASEAN member, July 23 1997.
- BIMSTEC (Bangladesh, India, Myanmar, Sri Lanka, Thailand, Economic Cooperation), 1997.
- Attendance at the Conference on Regional and Development in Kunming (known as The Kunming Initiative) with China, India, and Bangladesh, discussing ways to improve communications among all countries on the Silk Road between Assam and Yunnan, August 1999.
- ACMEC: Irrawaddy, Chao Phraya, Mekong Economic Strategy Group, 2003.

1.1 Economic perspectives

Under British colonization, the Myanmar economy became commercialized, and rice became the major crop for export. Myanmar remains a leading rice exporting country. The economy was dominated by British firms such as the Burma Oil Company (BOC), Steel Brothers, and the Bombay Burma Trading Company. When the British colonial rule ended, Myanmar started to organize a national economy based on a planned economic system.

After independence, the ruling AFPFL party started a liberal socialist economic policy from 1952, using an eight-year plan called Pyi Daw Tha Se Mum Kaing, which aimed to establish a new welfare state. That plan was not completed due to the lack of planning experiences.

From 1962 to 1988, the Myanmar economy was controlled by a state planning system run by a command economy. The military Revolutionary Council was the ruling institution, led by the BSPP party, and managed by Ne Win. Even though the BSPP started as a very small group at the beginning, it gradually expanded into a mass party, and became the most powerful institution in Myanmar by its second decade in power. Unfortunately, the BSPP failed in achieving its goals, and the economy was depressed under the autocratic command and controlled system. In 1988, national power shifted to the military again in the form of the SLORC, consisting of 19 high-ranking military officers. The SLORC Chair, General Saw Maung, and most ministers in SLORC government, were military officers. The cabinet at the time had to face relationship problems with international organizations owing to administrative measures enforced by the junta's policies. Chairman Senior General Than Shwe sought to change the economy to an agro-based industrial country from an agricultural country, and to provide peasants agricultural land rights. This transformation in Myanmar's economy shifted the economic policy of the BSPP based on the centrally planned approach to one directed by the market. This was done by relaxing former restrictions on private industries and trade, by offering incentives to attract foreign direct investment (FDI), and by offering more opportunities to capitals from overseas. Tourism has become a booming part of the Myanmar economy, with 1996 named as Visit Myanmar Year.

Within the country, the SLORC started major construction programs, including the building of bridges, roads and highways, railway lines, which sought to improve transportation and communication. Dams and reservoirs were built to encourage cultivation, and new satellite towns and better housing were planned to improve national living standards. Myanmar sought to practice an independent non-aligned foreign policy, by participating in UN-related programs and activities, and cultivating friendly relationships with other countries, especially neighboring Southeast Asian countries. This non-aligned foreign policy led Myanmar to join ASEAN. Myanmar's economic development was also aided by better border trade with neighboring China and Thailand, encouraging the private sector and loosening restrictions on some exported items. The SLORC issued a major foreign investment law which promised to protect foreign investments from nationalization after November 3, 1988. This encourages more entrepreneurs to plunge into private business ventures. In the late 2000s, foreign investments concentrated on the extractive industries such as oil, gas, minerals, timber, and fisheries. It remains to be noted that business and manufacturing activities are frequently run directly by the relevant ministries, and some ministries have extensive joint ventures with foreign firms.

1.2 Socio-cultural perspectives

Under the ruling of kings in Myanmar, a static feudal society prevailed with limited change. The society was customary, and shaped by traditions, making it very conservative. Life in Myanmar was focused on peace and tranquility without much concern for economic progress. The peoples and their kings shared common ethnic backgrounds and religions.

Under the colonial era, some national movements started to emerge after 1897, when the British colonial government formed an appointed advisory council in Myanmar. In 1906, the Young Men's Buddhist Association (YMBA), followed by the General Council of Burmese Association (GCBA) were formed. These two associations helped generate national movements and advocate constitutional advancement in the 1920s. In 1923, there was a University Boycott protesting against the restrictive University Act. And along with the formation of Dobama Asiayon (Myanmar Association) in 1930, Sayar San led a peasants' rights protection organization, and paved the way for a nationalist movement which became more radical. In 1938, "The Revolution of the Myanmar 1300" began as a strike in the oil fields of Chauk-Yenangyaung, and gave rise to a broader national movement. Throughout the colonial era, including the Japanese occupation, most of the peoples of Myanmar struggled for their survival, and had little hopes of improvement or development. During this time, the colonial government threatened the security of peoples' lives, and people lived with little hope for a better future. Food supply for half of the population was not secured and there was a deep human security crisis, affecting food, health, education, livelihood, and personal well-being.

From the end of the colonial period until 1962, internal conflicts and competition among political parties for votes in elections were substantial. In the political turmoil, insurgency also created more social instability. All these factors contributed to a coup. In 1962, the Revolutionary Council conducted a coup d'état, and in the following socialist era, society was run by a centrally planned system, guided by BSPP, and managed by General Ne Win. Although the country was run by planning via a command economy, social well-being declined, and Myanmar society entered the group of nations with the lowest developmental level. Then, the 8888 Peoples' Demonstration threatened the regime of General Ne Win.

When, on September 18, 1988, the military transferred power to the SLORC, as a "coup by consent," the SLORC was designed to continue the military rule from the older to the younger generation. The SLORC focused on maintaining the political integrity of the Union of Myanmar, aiming to integrate and unify the state, and to consolidate its national sovereignty. The SLORC took action and held peace talks with insurgent groups which have been in disagreement with the state since independence and concluded agreements and compromises on cease-fires with the armed ethnic groups. In addition, the SLORC also established a separate ministry for the development of border areas to extend and intensify their development and drug eradication programs.

Myanmar has strengthened relations with China, its major border trade partner, and provider of development assistance and infrastructure construction. Myanmar has also tried to improve goodwill with other neighboring countries like Thailand, India, and Bangladesh. Under the SPDC regime, the government gave permission to set up foreign direct investment banks and to open indigenous banks to provide capital accumulation in the domestic economy. Foreign investors are interested and concentrated mainly on mineral exploration, especially crude oil and natural gas. However, as a transitional economy, Myanmar has recently changed from a centrally planned economy to a market economy, which has provided foreign investors many opportunities to work on business ventures with low wages and surplus labor. Myanmar gas has started to be exported in 2008. It has joint ventures with France, US, and Thailand, producing gas for export by pipeline from offshore areas in the west, moving it to Thailand and to China in the east. At the end of 2008, Myanmar authorities have allowed 422 foreign investment projects and inward investments were over US$ 15 billion.

One of the probable motivations behind Myanmar joining ASEAN in July 1997 was the prospect of greater opportunities to attract investments from the region. After the Asian financial crisis of 1997 that started in Thailand, Myanmar had more opportunities.

Table 6.1 Major historical events of Myanmar

	Time Frame	Major Historical Events
The Kingdom Era	2nd century B.C.	Appearance of first city-states
	1044–1297	First Myanmar Empire founded by Anawratha of the Bagan Dynasty Period of Anawratha's Kingdom 1044–1077
	1297–1599	Second Myanmar Empire founded by Bayintnaung of the Toungoo – Hanthawady Dynasty Period of King Bayintnaung 1552–1581
	1599–1885	Third Myanmar Empire, founded by King Alaungpaya of the Konbaung Dynasty Period of King Alaungpaya's Kingdom 1752–1760
The Colonial Era	1824–1826	First Anglo–Myanmar War
	1852	Second Anglo–Myanmar War
	1885	Third Anglo–Myanmar War
	January 1st, 1886	British annexation
	August 1, 1943	Grant of nominal independence by Japanese
	March 27, 1945	Start of Anti-Fascist Resistance
	October 16, 1945	Reestablishment of British administration
The Socialism Era	March 2, 1962	State Power assumed by Revolutionary Council
		Foundation of Burma Socialist Program Party (BSPP)
		Handover of power to BSPP government (1974)
SLORC and The Road to Democracy	September 18, 1988	Emergence of State Law and Order Restoration Council (SLORC)
		Multiparty Democratic General Election (May 1990)
		Reorganized as State Peace and Development Council (SPDC in 1997 November 15)
Multiparty Democracy	March 30, 2011 to present	Multiparty Democracy

Source: Compiled by author based on Myanmar: Facts and Figures 2002 (Myanmar Printing and Publishing Enterprise), Ministry of Information (2002).

2 Involvement of Myanmar within the region (ASEAN)

2.1 Introduction

The size encompassed by the Association of Southeast Asian Nations (ASEAN) countries is 4.46 million sq. km, or 3 percent of the world's land area. More than 600 million people live in the ASEAN region, or about 8.8 percent of the world's population. In 1961, before ASEAN took shape, the Association of Southeast Asia (ASA) was formed by the Philippines, Malaysia, and Thailand in 1961 and Maphilindo was set up by the Philippines, Malaysia, and Indonesia in 1963. Eventually, the ASEAN Declaration was announced in Bangkok in 1967 to form the regional organization. Today, ASEAN consists of 10 member countries.

2.2 Political-security perspectives

ASEAN was established on August 8, 1967 in Bangkok, Thailand. The founding members were Indonesia, Malaysia, Philippines, Singapore, and Thailand. Although Myanmar was one of the countries offered ASEAN membership from the start, Myanmar was inward looking and its economy was run under a command and control system. As such, Myanmar did not accept the membership, and it lost a great opportunity to be one of ASEAN's founding members. New members joining ASEAN include the following: Brunei Darussalam on January 7, 1984, Vietnam on July 28, 1995, Laos and Myanmar on July 23, 1997, and Cambodia on April 30, 1999. Currently, ASEAN has 10 member countries and they form the ASEAN region.

The ASEAN Community focuses on three key dimensions, namely, the Political-Security Community, the Economic Community and the Socio-Cultural Community. Each pillar has its aims and each is tied to the Initiative for ASEAN Integration (IAI).

Myanmar needs to enhance its collaboration within the member countries and the region, not only for enhancing its national economic growth, but also to promote its social progress and cultural development. It has been a rewarding experience to join ASEAN, whose first priority, as stated in the ASEAN declaration, is to accelerate the economic growth, social progress and cultural development of countries in the region through joint endeavors conducted in the spirit of equality and partnership in order to strengthen the foundation for a prosperous and peaceful community of Southeast Asian nations.

Before becoming an ASEAN member, Myanmar was a very isolated country and its political, social, and economic life were still under a centralized autocratic authority. While Myanmar's development requires peace, stability, and prestige, it also needs to move toward democracy. The law and order system of Myanmar must be established in harmony with the countries of the region and in adherence to the principles of the United Nations

Charter. As an ASEAN member, Myanmar has greater access to various opportunities due to ASEAN's aims to promote active collaboration and mutual assistance in areas of common interest across the economic, social, cultural, technical, scientific, and administrative fields. Myanmar can learn ways to improve the training of its people in educational and technical fields by borrowing experiences from ASEAN. The key aims of ASEAN are in line with the needs of Myanmar. Notably, ASEAN has emphasized greater utilization of cultivated lands, and promoted agricultural trade policies. As an ASEAN member, Myanmar will benefit.

According to the proverb that "man does not live by bread alone," Myanmar needs to have greater familiarity with the cultures of Southeast Asian and international society, and maintain patterns of beneficial cooperation in the ASEAN region. ASEAN provides rewarding opportunities to all members including Myanmar with goodwill and benevolence. Regarding fundamental principles, ASEAN member countries would adhere to the Treaty of Amity and Cooperation (TAC) in Southeast Asia of 1976. As Myanmar becomes a full member of ASEAN, it will create mutual benefits to ASEAN and Myanmar.

Although Myanmar is in Southeast Asia, it shares boundaries with China and India. If ASEAN finds it difficult to deal with some critical circumstances related to these two Asian powers, Myanmar may be able to help ASEAN solve some of the difficult areas and demarcation disputes. As such, Myanmar and ASEAN as a community would become a driving force for the peace and prosperity in the region.

All over the world, the independence, sovereignty, and territorial integrity of some countries could be threatened. This is especially true for isolated countries which are weak and could not exert themselves. As a result, it may be better for them to stay with either a region or a bloc rather than remain isolated. In the case of ASEAN, it retains the basic principles of non-interference in the internal affairs of seeking peaceful solutions to all problems and rejecting the threat or use of force. All of these principles align with those of Myanmar. Thus, China, a key partner of Myanmar, may use Myanmar to advance its interests in the Southeast Asian region if Myanmar were not a member of ASEAN. However, as an ASEAN member, Myanmar can take steps to avoid overdependence on China, and follow ASEAN's aims and policies.

Within the region, Myanmar can seek cooperation and experiences from ASEAN member countries, learning from other transitional economies like Vietnam, Cambodia, and Laos, and even from Indonesia's pro-democracy activities.

Since the ASEAN Political Security Community (APSC) aims to ensure that all member countries in the region remain at peace with each other in a democratic and harmonious environment, Myanmar would support it. While there may be intra-regional differences among member countries, ASEAN has a common vision and objectives to work through peaceful processes.

ASEAN has developed ASEAN standards, thus preventing conflict and enhancing peace-building among its members. Myanmar shares the values and norms of ASEAN for peaceful development, mutual respect, and shared responsibility, and seeks integration with its members.

2.3 Economic perspectives

The ASEAN Economic Community (AEC) will provide a new economic foundation for its member countries. Myanmar will have the opportunity to play a key role in a single market and production base in AEC. It has confidence in competition within the economic zone, and is open for an equitable path of economic development, and economic integration in the region. The AEC will provide Myanmar with access to areas of cooperation, where there may be assistance for human resources development and capacity building. Its citizens can also use their professional qualifications in the AEC, and Myanmar may integrate its industries across the region to promote outsourcing utilization. Myanmar's development will benefit if ASEAN is transformed into a region with free movement of goods, services, inwards and outwards capital flows, and easy job hunting for its professional and skilled labor.

"Moving forward in unity toward a peaceful and prosperous community" is the ASEAN motto, and it reminds all that Myanmar needs to maintain its momentum of ASEAN integration. Since ASEAN hopes to achieve full political, economic, and social integration in 2015, Myanmar should try to implement more economic reforms and to progress in the areas of human rights, religious freedom, and green economic activity. All of these factors are controversial and how they are resolved will affect ASEAN's effectiveness. To enhance progress in the socio-economic arena, Myanmar must balance its relationships with fellow ASEAN members and extra-regional powers, particularly with China and the United States.

Myanmar authorities have said that three more border trade points will be open in 2015, making it a total of 15. According to a Ministry of Commerce announcement, two of the new border points will connect Myanmar with Thailand, with one located in the southern Tanintharyi Region, and the other in Kayah State. The third trade point will be located in Chin State, connecting Myanmar to India. Myanmar's most lucrative border trade points are Muse, Lweje, and Chin Shwe Haw for China, Myawaddy for Thailand and Tamu for India. According to official data, more than US$ 3 billion was traded at Muse in the 2013–2014 fiscal year.

Myanmar can reap economic benefits from the AFTA program which does not apply a common set of external tariffs on imported goods as the EU does. As such, ASEAN members may impose tariffs on goods entering from outside ASEAN according to their national schedules. On the other hand, goods originating in the ASEAN region may receive a tariff rate of zero to 5 percent from ASEAN member countries. Cambodia, Laos, Myanmar, and Vietnam, the CLMV countries, may have additional time to implement this tariff-reduction rate. This Common Effective Preferential Tariffs (CEPT) scheme will permit Myanmar to have time to prepare for it. The CEPT scheme provides options to ASEAN members in three areas, namely, in the temporary exclusive list, in sensitive agricultural products, and in some general exceptions. The temporary exclusive list refers to products for which tariffs will ultimately be lowered within the zero to 5 percent, but are being protected temporarily by a delay in tariffs reductions. Sensitive agricultural products involve some commodities and exports items like rice, beans, and pulses, whose tariff levels could be reduced from zero to 5 percent over a certain period. General exceptions are only available to produce which an ASEAN member country is permitted to protect for national security reasons or for the promotion of public morals and social ethics, or the protection of human, animal, or plant life (environmental protection green economies) and public health. These exceptions also extend to other items that have artistic, historic, and archaeological value to the country concerned. All have agreed to these statements and enacted zero tariffs rates on these imports by the original signatory countries, except for the CLMV countries, which will have to abide by this practice by 2015.

Myanmar benefits from the maritime security policy of ASEAN since Myanmar has sea areas in its south and southwest territories. ASEAN is applying the laws of Safety of Maritime Navigation (known as SUA Convention) by improving the national legislation to address questions about sea level problems. This issue is important to suppress unlawful acts against the SUA Convention. Five countries, Brunei Darussalam, Myanmar, Philippines, Singapore, and Vietnam are aligned in this action.

In 2014, ASEAN economic ministers met in Myanmar's capital Nay Pyi Taw and discussed issues related to economic progress in the region. The four-day meeting saw ministers talking about issues regarding the ASEAN Economic Community (AEC) to be implemented in 2015, economic cooperation among the member states, easing of regional taxes and tariffs and establishing trade regulations. Other subjects included ASEAN relations with ASEAN Plus Three. Representatives from the United States, Australia, New Zealand, India, and Russia were invited to participate in the meetings and trade agreements were signed with Australia, New Zealand, and India. Myanmar took the rotating chair of ASEAN in 2014, and set the theme of "Moving Forward in Unity to a Peaceful and Prosperous Community for ASEAN."

As an ASEAN member, Myanmar has been able to attract investments from its member states, notably Thailand. Thus Thai Tee Entertainment Company has reached an agreement with Myanmar's local conglomerate Shwe Than Lwin Media Co. Ltd, which operates Sky Net television, to manage the production and co-manage the strategy, operation, and marketing of the new joint-venture company, Tee International Myanmar. The two companies had previously reached an agreement in relation to the broadcasting of English Premier League Football matches, for which Sky Net is the authorized broadcaster in Myanmar. Thai Tee Entertainment company has said that it is planning to invest heavily in international markets in the future, and is also looking at opportunities in Laos and Cambodia.

In addition, under the scope of ASEAN Economic Community (AEC), Thai banks are leading the way in the race to obtain banking licenses awarded by the Central Bank of Myanmar. An increasing amount of Thai businesses and goods will arrive in Thailand's neighboring countries like Myanmar, and they will require help from banks. Myanmar currently has 35 foreign banks with representative offices in the country, with four large Thai banks, namely, Bangkok Bank, Krung Thai Bank, Siam Commercial Bank, and Kasikorn Bank. Thailand is Myanmar's second largest foreign trading partner, after China, and offers huge trading potential because of the large border area between the two countries. The Central Bank of Myanmar has said that it will allow a handful of foreign banks to begin limited banking operations by the end of 2014.

Muang Thai Life Assurance Public Company has opened a representative office in Yangon. This is the first Thai life insurance company to operate in Myanmar. The insurance industry is currently off-limits to foreign companies in Myanmar, but a number of international insurance companies have opened representative offices in the country. In 2013, the Myanmar government granted private insurance licenses to 12 local companies, allowing life, motor, fire, cash, and fidelity insurance services. Foreign insurance companies were not allowed before the opening of Muang Thai Life Assurance Public Company.

Thailand's military junta has said that the Thai government will initiate talks with Japan in an attempt to re-start work on the Dawei Special Economic Zone, in the south of Myanmar. This industrial zone would give a significant boost to logistics in Southeast Asia, as traders could avoid the Malacca Strait, one of the world's busiest shipping lanes.

The Thai firm PTT is conducting a feasibility study on a liquefied natural gas (LNG) distribution facility in Myanmar, which would allow onshore LNG transportation to Myanmar. If it goes ahead, the facility will have an annual capacity of five million tonnes and will be located close to the Dawei Special Economic Zone, a multi-billion dollar project which was stalled but which the Thai government has shown enthusiasm to re-start.

Vietnam has planned to invest up to US$ 1.5 billion in Myanmar by 2015, making it one of the top foreign investors in the country. Vietnam wanted to ensure further increases in bilateral trade between the two countries and encourage more Vietnamese tourists to Myanmar. Vietnam hopes Myanmar will accelerate the process for tenders by Vietnamese companies in fields like agriculture, energy, textiles, and banking. Currently, there are seven Vietnamese projects in Myanmar, amounting to more than US$ 500 million in investment. Vietnamese company Hau Giang Pharmaceutical (DHG) has decided to invest in a joint venture company, Anh Sao Viet Pharmacy Joint Stock Company (ASV Vietnam), in Myanmar.

Indonesia's state-owned construction firm, Wijaya Karya (WIKA) has signed an agreement with Noble Twin Dragon PTE Ltd, a Singaporean-Myanmar consortium, for the construction of "world-class office space and luxurious condominiums" in Yangon. The project, Pyay Tower and Residences, is expected to cost US$ 125 million in investment and work will begin soon.

2.4 Socio-cultural perspectives

Myanmar has had a chance to associate with the ASEAN Social and Cultural Community (ASCC). It aims to contribute to realizing an ASEAN community, together with the people and their societies. The ASCC seeks to share cultural values with unity among the people and ASEAN members. If one country knows the cultural values of other countries, it can build friendship and goodwill among those countries. This is because the ASCC is focused on nurturing the human, cultural, and natural resources for sustained development in a harmonious and people-oriented ASEAN. The goals of the ASCC are people-centered and socially responsible, and the goals are identical within the hearts of the Myanmar people. Therefore, Myanmar may bridge domestic and regional concerns based on a unity of purpose.

Myanmar may serve as a bridge between two great nations, India and China. Its role for the sake of security and stability may affect directly India, China, and ASEAN. For this reason, ASEAN should strengthen Myanmar's relations with both Asian powers and provide crucial guidance to balance extra-regional presence. This is a good strategy and it will retain ASEAN's centrality and delicate balancing game in Southeast Asia and the region.

The Myanmar government is trying to move toward a democracy that benefits Myanmar. As the second largest country in Southeast Asia, Myanmar is rich with abundant natural resources. On the other hand, Myanmar is also an ethnically diverse nation, having various regions, various races, different beliefs and cultures. All of these factors would affect the development of Myanmar and its progress.

Since Myanmar has joined ASEAN, the latter has taken a keen interest in Myanmar's development and created a Myanmar discussion group. In this caucus, ASEAN seeks to deal with issues related to Myanmar and its development. As ASEAN moves toward organizing an integrated economic community in 2015, Myanmar will have to speed up its activities. The ASEAN chairman status has now moved for the first time to Myanmar. This position will give Myanmar a good opportunity to show how it deals with power in the international arena. Myanmar will have to deal with challenges of controversial and problematic issues in a greater ASEAN context tactfully. As chairman of ASEAN, Myanmar should push among other things, to end regional problems like drug and human trafficking.

When Myanmar joined ASEAN in 1997, it was ruled by a military government called the SPDC, but in 2011 Myanmar was encouraged to develop democracy. Thus, since March 2011, Myanmar has begun a set of reforms, and it is clear that Myanmar's government recognizes the challenges it faces, and is striving to address them. ASEAN has helped Myanmar gain political legitimacy around the world. It also offers the state the opportunity to be seen as a responsible member of the international community. In the domestic arena, if the Myanmar government is successful in arranging ceasefires with groups representing the most populous ethnic minorities, and in pursuing ethnic reconciliation and preventing sectarian violence, its prospects for long-term stability and democratization will improve.

Myanmar has a chance to control transnational crimes in the ASEAN region. ASEAN ministers and particularly the interior and home affairs ministries have endorsed the ASEAN Declaration on Transnational Crime, mandating coordination with other ASEAN bodies like the ASEAN Law Ministers and Attorneys General, the ASEAN Chiefs of National Police, the ASEAN Finance Ministers, the Directors-General of Immigration and Emigration, and the Directors-General of Customs Duties. Trade investigations, prosecution, and rehabilitation of perpetrators of transnational crimes, including international terrorism are deliberated at the ASEAN Ministerial Meeting on Transnational Crime (AMMTC). In conjunction with the Declaration, Myanmar has attempted to organize several training programs in psychological operation and warfare for law enforcement officials and on intelligence procuring, bomb explosive detection, post-blast investigation, airport security and travel document security, immigration matters and cross-border controlling. This helps to make Myanmar a part of the regional institutional frameworks on transnational crime.

Myanmar has been cooperating with other countries or groups of countries against piracy and smuggling. It has also been working with the ASEAN Regional Forum (ARF) which provides assistance in the areas of law enforcement and intelligence gathering, the suppression of terrorist financing, the strengthening of border security involving the movement of people, goods, and documents, and other types of transportations.

3 Involvement with East Asia (ASEAN Plus Three)

3.1 Introduction

The ASEAN plus Three (APT) process began in 1997. It focuses on cooperation among ASEAN countries and China, Japan, and South Korea in the political and security arenas, as well as areas in transnational crime, trade and investment, financial flows, tourism, agriculture, fishery, forestry, mining, small and medium enterprises, information and communication technology, energy, environment and sustainable development, poverty alleviation, development for vulnerable groups, culture and tradition, education, science and technology, public health, and disaster management. At the 11th APT Summit in November 2007, held in Singapore, the APT provided the guideline for the

future direction of APT cooperation in what is known as the APT Cooperation Work Plan (2007–2017). This ATP guidance was endorsed again at the
APT Directors-General Meeting on July 3, 2009 in Seoul. There are gaps
between the plans and their implementation as noted in the review by the
APT Foreign Ministers Meeting on June 30, 2013. As a result, the APT set up
a new timeframe of 2013–2017 to address the gaps in the implementation of
goals. This revised Work Plan will be discussed again at the 16th APT
Summit on October 10, 2014 in Bandar Seri Begawan. It should be noted that
the "East Asia Vision Group" (EAVG) of ASEAN was proposed as The
Vision Group of the APT in December 1998. This vision targets mid- to long-
term cooperation areas in East Asian countries for economic collaboration,
political and socio-cultural activities, in the early twenty-first century. The
EAVG II, established by APT Leaders and East Asian Leaders, will provide
future vision on the APT in coming decades. APT is the new challenge for the
central role of ASEAN in expanding regional capacity building. It is a test to
see if the APT cooperation could continue to support the central role of
ASEAN and pave the way toward regional integration, both in Southeast
Asia and more broadly in East Asia.

To be sure, the APT countries reaffirmed their strong commitment to deepening and broadening the APT process as a key vehicle toward achieving an
East Asian community when they met at the APT Commemorative Summit
in November 2012. The APT leaders expressed their continued support for
the central role of ASEAN in the evolving regional architecture and reiterated
that the APT cooperation would continue to support the realization of the
ASEAN Community and assist in regional integration efforts. Myanmar's
support for the APT is mainly reflected in its bilateral interactions with three
East Asian Countries, namely, China, South Korea, and Japan.

4 The China–Myanmar relationship

Myanmar and China have a long history, extending back to the pre-colonial
era, when the military of the Qing dynasty entered into the kingdom of the
time. Later, the defeated Chinese Nationalist Kuomintang (KMT) troops
penetrated into the northern Shan State in 1949. After 1988, China and
Myanmar's relationship was strengthened for diplomatic, political, and
security reasons. China is the major supplier of goods to Myanmar for consumption and production. China regularly imports from Myanmar raw
materials such as timber and natural gas. It also has a large amount of economic cooperation with Myanmar in the areas of public utility and energy.
The current relationship between China and Myanmar is based more on ties
between the two governments than on the development of Myanmar's economy. Notably, Myanmar has been tied down with a large amount of national
debts which it must repay to China. In addition, Myanmar's long border line
with China, more than 2227 kilometers, is longer than that with any other
country. Sino-Myanmar relations have long been based on the five principles

for peaceful coexistence, including mutual respect for each other's territorial integrity, sovereignty, and mutual non-aggression. Nowadays, China and its enterprises are heavily involved in Myanmar's economy, especially in the manufacturing, agriculture, forestry, infrastructure, mining, natural gas, and energy arenas. China, as a member of the ASEAN Plus Three, will have more opportunities to participate in APT Programs centered on economic cooperation with other member countries like Myanmar.

China is the main importer of Myanmar's exports, consisting of timber, agricultural products, marine products, minerals, and natural gas. Border trade provides a direct route connecting central Upper Myanmar to Yunnan Province in China. China's long-term loans with low interest rates aim to assist Myanmar's businesses, but they have also added to the national debt. This suggests that Myanmar's economy is now heavily dependent on economic ties with China. This brings up a potential concern in that Chinese firms may shift their import sources from Myanmar to another country. Probably, such a transfer would benefit Myanmar in the short term, but not in the long term.

It should be noted that China Union Pay International (China UPI) has announced that it is working in cooperation with Myanmar's Cooperative Bank (CB Bank) to introduce its EASi Travel Union Pay card for the first time in Myanmar. This card can be used in Myanmar and internationally. It will be available from September 2014. This card requires deposits in Myanmar kyats and is accepted in more than 140 countries. In addition, China UPI signed a joint-venture agreement with CB Bank to install ATM machines in December 2012. It has also reached an agreement with Myanmar Payment Union regarding points-of-sale terminals. ATM machines were introduced for the first time in late 2012, just as payments via Master Card and Visa.

5 Myanmar and South Korea under the APT

Working under the APT, the joint committee on Economic Cooperation of Myanmar and South Korea agreed on a $500 million loan to Myanmar for the period from 2013 to 2017. The loan was funded by the Economic Development Cooperation Funds. The joint committee discussed ways to use these loans on infrastructure development and to promote services and sports tournaments. Among the private sector collaboration between South Korea and Myanmar, there is a memorandum of understanding (MOU) on economic cooperation for manufacturing and energy projects. The MOU made possible the Foodstuff Manufacturers Association and South Korea SMEs Association Exhibition which was held in Yangon in 2013, with 76 Korean companies participating. South Korea launched a IT center called Information Access Center (IAC) in Nay Pyi Taw to help Myanmar's national development. This will permit a leading sector to become a part of an e-government system.

The South Korean International Cooperation Agency (KOICA) provides Myanmar with a road network and a way of developing a dry zone as part of the Greening the Central Zone project. This project will include reforestation and giving water access in dry zone areas, especially in the Nyaung Oo, Bagan, and Mandalay Region, and in central areas of Myanmar. The South Korean government plans to build a friendship bridge that will cross the Yangon River near Dala township, Yangon division, where there is plenty of land and labor to permit South Korean companies investment opportunities as an industrial park. One reason for such smooth cooperation between South Korea and Myanmar is that the former lacks energy and natural resources, while the latter is rich in natural resources.

Myanmar's people are Buddhist, but South Korean people have been influenced basically by Confucianism. In other social features, both societies respect elders, love their families, and value their local communities. Such features have facilitated the setting up of about 170 South Korean enterprises in Myanmar. According to the FDI ranking, South Korea is the fourth most important investor in Myanmar after China, Thailand, and Hong Kong.

The largest cargo company of South Korea, CJ Korea Express has announced that it will serve as the international partner with Myanmar government to develop a distribution center in Yangon. This company will sign a joint-venture agreement with the Road Transport Administration Department in Myanmar to develop the 13,000 square-meter center and will operate it for 20 years. The company is planning to finalize the agreement by the end of 2014, and says it will establish seven distribution bases, operating more than 200 trucks to deliver supplies that include cement, agricultural products, and building materials in Myanmar. It also plans to launch global delivery services in the future. The company has highlighted Myanmar's strategic importance close to India, China, and the ASEAN nations as a good location for logistics operations.

6 Myanmar and Japan under the APT

Japanese–Myanmar relations have a long history. Myanmar was occupied by the Japanese in 1943, and on August 1 of that year, the Japanese military declared the independence of the state of Myanmar. As a result of that declaration, Dr Ba Maw became the Head of the State of Myanmar under a new constitution drawn up by the Japanese military. Nonetheless, in 1945, Myanmar fought against Japan's occupation, and continued the struggle until gaining its independence in 1948. Since achieving independence, Myanmar has tried to remain neutral, but at times is affected by China's shadow. Japan has tried to support Myanmar but without success, partly due to the many demands made by Japan and also due to Myanmar's failures including failures to fulfill its promises. The situation in Myanmar has been changing and it is leading toward a more democratic system. Finance Minister and Deputy Prime Minister Taro Aso has indicated that Japan would cancel Myanmar's debt to Japan and develop the Thilawa Special Economic Zone. In addition, it plans to do the following:

- Waiving 300 billion yen of the 500 billion yen (US$ 5.74 billion) of Myanmar's outstanding debt.
- Covering the remaining debt of 200 billion yen by a bridging loans from private banks.
- Making a US$ 900 million bridging loan to cover the US$ 500 million debt due to the ADB and US$ 400 million debt due to the World Bank, so that ADB and the World Bank could restart lending to Myanmar.
- Making available a new 50 billion yen loan to develop the 2,400 hectare Thilawa industrial estate by a Japanese consortium of Mitsubishi, Marubeni, and Sumitomo Corporations.

Japan is seeking to deepen economic relations with Myanmar by offering Official Development Assistance (ODA) to Myanmar to improve its infrastructure. Japan believes this is an efficient and effective strategy, and will lead to an improvement of Myanmar society. By improving the infrastructure, Japan hopes to increase its investment in Myanmar and attract more FDIs into Myanmar. Myanmar has asked Japan for support to promote vocational training and agronomy education. Although Japan would like to see greater democratization in Myanmar, it needs to consider how to persuade Myanmar to act fully to move onto the right track. Japan has promised under the cover of the APT to support Myanmar's economic and political reforms both in the private and the public sectors, and provide technical assistance, infrastructure expertise, and interest-free or low interest loans that will improve connectivity in the APT region.

To be more specific, Japanese firms KDDI Corp and Sumitomo Corp have reached an agreement with state-owned Myanmar Posts and Telecommunications (MPT) to operate mobile phone services in the country. The joint venture (JV) will improve MPT's prospects in competing with Telenor and Ooredoo, two international firms granted licenses to operate in the country. These two have promised to invest substantial capital in the communication sector. As such, MPT is not the only telecoms operator in the country, and Telenor and Ooredoo will roll out their services in Myanmar's communication sector.

In addition, a Japanese company, Marubeni, plans to build to a 2,000 Megawatt coal-fire power plant in Myanmar's Tanintharyi Region. The company plans to form an agreement with a Thai company, PTT, the state-owned Electricity Generating Authority of Thailand (EGAT), as well as other interests from Myanmar and Thailand for the project. Eighty percent of the output of the power plant will go to Thailand. Total investment for the project is expected to reach almost US$ 3 billion.

Regarding the hosting of meetings related to ASEAN and APT, Japan has offered Myanmar a low-interest loan of US$ 105 million to help improve the country's communication network in the major cities namely, Yangon, Mandalay, and Nay Pyi Taw. The loan was offered by Japanese Foreign Minister Fumio Kishida. Japan will also help Myanmar with the development of its postal sector, offering technical support and training in the same three cities. Japan's government, particularly under current Prime Minister Shinzo Abe, has formed close ties with Myanmar's reformist government, offering various financial loans and grants as Myanmar builds its infrastructure amid a raft of economic and political reforms. According to Myanmar's Ministry of National Planning and Economic Development, Japan would give Myanmar almost US$ 200 million in aids in the second half of the 2013–2014 fiscal year.

Finally, it should be mentioned that Japan has granted an Official Development Assistance (ODA) loan to Myanmar to implement four development projects in the country. The loan, worth an estimated US$ 630 million, will be used for the upgrading of Phase 1 of the Yangon-Mandalay railroad, a water supply system for Yangon, Phase 2 of infrastructural development at Thilawa Port, and the development of irrigation facilities in Bago Region.

7 Conclusion

This chapter has presented Myanmar's development, focusing on its place within the ASEAN environment. The three sections have stressed Myanmar's history, Myanmar's roles in ASEAN, and Myanmar's role in the APT. Each section considers political security, economic development, and socio-cultural perceptions.

The first section gives an overview of Myanmar's political, economic, and socio-cultural history, while the second section looks at Myanmar's ties to ASEAN in the same areas; the last section outlines the impacts and consequences of ASEAN and APT on Myanmar.

Since 1997, when Myanmar acceded to the ASEAN, Myanmar's political, economic, and socio-culture life has become more integrated with the ASEAN region and mutual rewards. As such, this chapter addresses the question of "how can Myanmar benefit from its membership in ASEAN?" Previously, Myanmar suffered from Western economic sanctions and was highly influenced by neighboring countries such as China. This chapter shows that Myanmar has escaped from isolation and received mutual respect from other countries once it became part of ASEAN. It has also learned from interactions in the APT.

During the 1990s, China, Japan, and Korea (CJK) became part of ASEAN Plus Three, but individual CJK states have long been related to ASEAN through trading and other types of relationships. It would be argued that the APT grew from the ASEAN Regional Forum. It could also be influenced by the 1994 Asia Pacific Economic Cooperation summit in Bogor, Indonesia.

The year 1997 was important for Myanmar and ASEAN, both because in that year Myanmar joined ASEAN and also ASEAN established ASEAN Plus Three (APT). These developments permitted cooperation in various arenas, including politics and security, transnational crime, trade and FDI, finance, tourism, food, agriculture, fishery, forestry, minerals, and mining. In addition, Myanmar was able to work with more partners in the areas of SMEs, information and communication technology, energy, environmental and sustainable development, poverty alleviation, development of vulnerable groups, culture and heritage, education, public health, and transportation. The significance of all of these developments for Myanmar can be seen through the items covered in this chapter.

References

Aung, Hla Tun (2003) *Myanmar: The Study of Processes and Patterns*. Ann Arbor: University of Michigan Press.

Central Statistical Organization (1997) *Agricultural Statistics. Department of Agricultural Planning*. Yangon: CSO Press.

Cole, David C. and Betty F. Slade (1998) "The Crisis and Financial Sector Reform." *ASEAN Economic Bulletin*, 15(3): 338–346.

Drengson, Alan and Duncan Taylor (1997) *Ecoforestry: The Art and Science of Sustainable Forest Use*. Gabriola Island: New Society Publisher.

Fiorino, Daniel J. (1995) *Making Environmental Policy*. Berkeley: University of California Press.

Korea Development Institute (2002) *Knowledge Partnership Project: Recent Trends of Agricultural Development in the Union of Myanmar*. Jeollanam-do: Korea Rural Economic Institute.

Mankiw, Gregory N. (2012) *Principles of Economics*, 6th edition. Mason, OH: South-Western Cengage Learning.

Ministry of Agriculture and Irrigation (1999) *Information on Myanmar Agriculture. Department of Agricultural Planning*. Yangon: Myint Myitta Press.

Ministry of Agriculture and Irrigation (2008) *Myanmar Agriculture in Brief. Department of Agricultural Planning*. Yangon: Myint Myitta Press.

Ministry of Information (2002) *Myanmar: Facts and Figures 2002*. Union of Myanmar: Myanmar Printing and Publishing Enterprise.

Mya Than and Joseph L.H. Tan (ed.) (1990) *Myanmar Dilemmas and Options: The Challenge of Economic Transition in the 1990s*. Singapore: ISEAS.

Roscoe, Philip (2014) *The True Cost of Economics: I Spend, Therefore I Am*. London: Penguin.

Shin, Tun (2013) *Why Invest in Myanmar? And Other Notable Legal Articles*. Yangon: Wisdom House.

Steinberg, David I. (2013) *Burma/Myanmar: What Everyone Needs to Know*. 2nd edition. New York: Oxford University Press.

Thura Swiss Ltd (n.d.) 'News Letters, Economic Research Centre,' Shwe Hinthar B 307 6 1/2 Miles Pyay Road 11 Qtr. Hlaing Tsp. Yangon, Myanmar.

Torado, Michael P. and Stephen C. Smith (2011) *Economic Development*, 11th edition. London: Pearson.

United Nations (2003) *Economic and Social Commission for Asia and the Pacific: Guidelines on the Integration of Energy and Rural Development: Policies and Programs*.

Wilson, John S. and Benjamin Taylor (2008) 'Deeper Integration in ASEAN: Why Transport and Technology Matter for Trade.' *Trade Facilitation Reform Issue Brief*. Washington, DC: World Bank.

World Bank (2010) *Doing Business 2010*. Washington, DC: World Bank.

Zhang, X. (2006) 'The Rise of China and Community Building in East Asia.' *Asian Perspective* 30(3): 129–148.

7 The Philippines
Everything in place

Jose Rhommel B. Hernandez

1 History and the colonial experience

Archaeological excavations in the island of Palawan reveal human remains dating back to 45,000–42,000 B.P. (i.e., Before Present or Before A.D. 1950) More recent excavations in the north of Luzon unearthed human remains dating back to 67,000 B.P. The first, more commonly called the Tabon Man, which recent measurements reveal as a woman, has become the main evidence of the claim that the Philippines had its own core population prior to the Austronesian Migrations (Jocano 1975). Further research is recently being conducted on the so-called Callao Man found in the Callao Caves in Cagayan, north of Luzon.

By 4,000 B.P., a group of people, now called Austronesians, began populating the islands. Linguists and archaeologists alike believe that the Austronesians came from the southern part of China and then migrated to Taiwan and then to the Philippines (Bellwood 1997; Tanudirjo 2004, 83–103). All the native languages in the Philippines belong to the Austronesian family of languages making it a part of the largest linguistic family in the world. Besides language, the Austronesians also brought with them agricultural techniques, technology, and religion. The group therefore provided a base culture that served as the foundation not only of the Philippines but of Maritime Southeast Asia as well.

Christianity came to the Philippines as a consequence of Spanish colonization which started with the arrival of Ferdinand Magellan in 1521. Magellan, however, was killed by the chieftain Lapu-lapu of the Island of Mactan. Several expeditions followed in the years 1525, 1527, and 1541 but full colonization came under the leadership of Miguel Lopez de Legazpi in 1565 when he settled in Cebu. By 1572, he was able to occupy Manila with forces from the Visayas after an alliance with Sikatuna who was just waiting for the right time to attack the city. By this time, Islam has already taken root among many people in Mindanao. The first Muslim missionaries reached Sulu in 1380 led by the Arab trader Karim ul'Makhdum. By 1390, the Prince Rajah Baguinda of Minangkabau, Sumatra arrived in the islands with his followers and preached Islam in the islands thus partially Islamizing Palawan, the Visayas and Luzon by the sixteenth century. The first mosque in the Philippines was established in Simunul, Tawi-tawi at about the same time. This mosque is now called the Sheik Karimal Makdum Mosque (Majul 1999, 56–88).

The encounter with these world religions would permanently change the Philippine landscape. The conversion of the Filipinos to Catholic Christianity would be the only legitimizing reason behind the *Conquista*. The Spaniards would thus concentrate all their efforts to this end. The *Encomienda* system, for instance, despite its being economic by nature would acquire a religious meaning inasmuch as the *Encomenderos* were tasked to teach Christian Doctrines to the Filipinos in exchange for their labor and economic support. Those in the highlands would be transferred, sometimes by force, to settlements called *Reducciones* under the watchful eye both of the *encomendero* and the missionary. Later on, these *reducciones* would evolve into the *Pueblo* or town centered on the *Poblacion* with a Church and a Plaza at the center (Hernandez 2010, 67–80). Meanwhile, the Muslims in Mindanao as well as different ethno-linguistic groups would resist Spanish colonization and therefore, Catholic Christianity. The usual trading activities of the Sultanates with the Visayan Islands and Luzon were banned by the Spaniards in Manila which, in effect, construed all Muslim attempts to secure a place in commerce as piratical. The only legal trade took place between Manila and Acapulco through the Galleons plying the Pacific route with all other ports in the Philippines bringing their goods to Manila.

The difficulties brought forth by these changes would have a deep repercussion on the Filipinos. The period from the second half of the sixteenth century until the last decades of the nineteenth century was replete with rebellions demanding reforms in the political, religious, and agricultural realms and/or the expulsion of the Spaniards from the islands. The first rebellion was in 1574 under the leadership of the Rajahs Lakandula and Soliman, two years after the settlement of Spaniards in Manila. The biggest rebellion followed in 1587–1588. Tagged as the "Tondo Conspiracy," the rebellion was led by Magat Salamat together with several Datus from Tondo (de Marquina, 1990, 85–97). Both rebellions ended up with the Spaniards instituting reforms by allowing Filipinos to hold various positions in the colonial bureaucracy. Later rebellions such as that of Bankaw in Leyte and Tamblot in Bohol from 1621 to 1622 were religious uprisings demanding the return of the people to the religion of their ancestors. Other rebellions followed in other parts of the islands like the agricultural revolts of 1745 and 1822 as well as the revolt in Bohol led by Francisco Dagohoy from 1744 to 1815. The first decades of the nineteenth century saw the uprisings related to the monopolies being imposed by the colonial government. In the 1840s, a rebellion commenced in Tayabas, eastern Luzon, led by Apolinario dela Cruz or Hermano Pule as his followers call him. Dela Cruz organized a brotherhood or a *Cofradia* which earned the ire of the local priest inasmuch as the said brotherhood did not accept Spaniards or Mestizos (half breeds), whether they be Spaniard or Chinese. This led to a military action that resulted in the massacre of the members, including Hermano Pule.

Meanwhile, the Spanish authorities in Manila were trying to institute reforms for the islands. New policies were being introduced due to the different political developments in Spain. However, the fluidity of the events in Spain, i.e., the quick and abrupt changes in the administration between the conservatives and liberals brought Spanish administrators in the Philippines without any knowledge of the country. As a result, the more experienced Indio was marginalized and bypassed by inadequate and incompetent Spaniards. The last Galleon for Acapulco sailed in 1815 and the colonial government shifted its focus on the development of agriculture in the country with Friars owning vast *haciendas*. Despite the rise of a new middle class led by the *Inquilinos* or those renting the lands, much poverty still ensued and many decided to go rogue and become *Tulisanes* raiding the towns for their subsistence. In response, the Spanish government founded the *Guardia Civil*, who in their own right committed abuses that further aggravated the situation.

Perhaps the more lasting effects could be credited to the Educational Reforms of the 1860s. By a series of decrees, the Spanish colonial administration introduced reforms in the educational system foremost of which is allowing Indios access to higher education. Many young Filipinos were sent by their economically viable parents to study in the prestigious schools in Manila and Europe. One of these young men was Jose Rizal, who later on would lead the demands for reforms in the Philippines (Schumacher 1991, 16–34).

Born in 1861, Rizal benefited from the best educational institutions in the Philippines and Spain. Acquiring degrees both in Philosophy and Medicine, he effectively expressed liberal ideas through his writings, especially in his novels *Noli Me Tangere* and *El Filibusterismo*. His historical works clearly called for a history and a society autonomous from all the impositions of identity created by the Spaniards. His "Tripartite View of Philippine History" as opposed to the "Bipartite View" from the Spaniards asserted the flourishing culture and civilization of the Filipinos before the Spaniards who claimed that everything good in the Philippines was brought by them. Taking a cue from this, Andres Bonifacio organized the Katipunan, the society aiming for total and radical independence from Spain. Thus, the ground was set for the first Republican Revolution in the whole of Asia.

The Revolution led to the declaration of Philippine Independence in June 12, 1898. The United States of America however declared war against Spain and soaked their hands in the Philippine frontier. The Filipinos, having just emerged from the Revolution were forced to declare war against the US which did not recognize the June 12 declaration. The inadequacy of arms on the side of the Filipinos forced them to initiate guerrilla warfare by November 1899 lasting until 1913 at the Massacre of Bud Bagsak in Mindanao. On the side of the Americans, the Anti-Sedition Law was passed in 1901, the Anti-Brigandage Law in 1902, and the Flag Law in 1907 prohibiting the display of the Philippine flag. Every battle or skirmish after 1902 was, for the

Americans, simply a part of the insurgency and banditry. By 1918, the Philippine elite had already started parliamentary and diplomatic struggles for the recognition of Philippine Independence. The Philippine Legislature created the Commission on Independence in order to study matters related to the negotiation and organization of Philippine Independence from the US. Eleven senators led by Manuel L. Quezon and Sergio Osmeña presented independence as the national ideal of the Filipino people.

The first Parliamentary Mission went to the US in 1919 resulting in Woodrow Wilson's recommendation to the US Congress to legislate for the Independence of the Philippines. These Missions continued into the following years, namely, 1922, 1923, 1924, and 1925. Nothing came out of these except for the 1919 recommendation of Wilson. Sergio Osmeña and Manuel Roxas or the Os-Rox Commission of 1931–1933 succeeded in securing the passage of the Hare-Hawes-Cutting Act which was signed into law on January 17, 1933. Manuel L. Quezon however, moved that this law be vetoed and went to the US in November of the same year. Quezon was able to secure the Tydings-McDuffie Law which set a 10-year transition period starting from 1935 toward an independent Philippines by 1946. The Philippine Commonwealth was thus proclaimed on November 15, 1935 with Manuel L. Quezon as President and Sergio Osmeña as Vice-President.

The US joined the world war with the Philippines in 1941. Upon the defeat of Philippine and American forces in April and May, 1942 in Bataan and Corregidor, the Japanese forced the surrendering army to march from Bataan to Tarlac leaving 7,000–10,000 dead or murdered along the way. Quezon with Osmeña were evacuated to the United States early on and Douglas McArthur was ordered to Australia. Heroic resistance, however, did not stop. Thousands of Filipinos with some American officers joined the guerrilla movement which was able to control most of the Philippine provinces leaving the Japanese with only 12 out of 48 toward the end of the war. Meanwhile, a Japanese-sponsored Republic was established with Jose P. Laurel as President. Laurel did whatever he could in order not to allow the Filipinos to be conscripted into the Japanese army.

McArthur's forces landed in Leyte in October of 1944. He was accompanied by the President of the Commonwealth Sergio Osmeña, who succeeded Quezon after the latter's death in August 1944. Fighting continued until the Japanese surrendered in September 1945. Elections were held in early 1946. This time, Manuel Roxas was elected President and Elpidio Quirino as Vice-President. By July 4, 1946, Roxas and Quirino took their oath of office as the new President and Vice-President of the Republic of the Philippines and the United States declared its recognition of Philippine independence.

2 The Philippines in the United Nations and ASEAN

The nineteenth century gave birth to an educated group of young men more commonly called the *Ilustrados*. As a product of the series of educational reforms in the 1860s, these young men were highly educated in the Spanish and European system of education. Jose Rizal, the foremost of these "enlightened ones," is a shining example of what an Ilustrado should be. Having studied in Europe, Rizal was able to enjoy the benefits of the reforms after the French Revolution of 1789 and the liberalist philosophy it carried. Meanwhile, the Philippine experience had already evolved an indigenous system of government based on the concept of *bayan* and *bansa*.

The revolutionary Andres Bonifacio, for his part, attempted to retrieve these concepts in his *Haring Bayang Katagalugan* (Supreme Nation of Katagalugan). Katagalugan here would mean the entire population of the Philippines. It would apparently be a synthesis of the Nación concept from Rizal and the indigenous *Bansa*. Attached to this is the agenda of a national renewal of internal bonds toward freedom and self-determination. Bonifacio was, however, marginalized by the elite sector of the *Katipunan*. This sector came from the tradition of Spanish patronage which was strengthened by the Spaniards for fear of uprising since the Tondo Conspiracy of 1587–1588.

Against this backdrop, the Philippine nation-state was born on June 12, 1898 and recognized by the Americans after almost 50 years of colonization and a war against the Japanese in July 4, 1946. Despite the difficulties at its birth, the Philippine nation-state continues at present in its struggle for freedom, progress, and self-determinism.

With this intent, the Philippines has become one of the active participants in the promotion of these goals both within its borders and in the world arena. The Philippines is one of the founding members of the United Nations Organization, which would become the United Nations (UN) in 1946. In 1954, Manila hosted the meeting for the Southeast Asia Collective Defense Treaty which laid the foundations for the Southeast Asia Treaty Organization (SEATO) in 1955. In the month of April of the same year, the Philippines was a participant in the Asian-African Conference or the Bandung Conference organized by several heads of state of new nations led by President Sukarno of Indonesia, with the heads of state of Burma, Pakistan, Ceylon, and India in their effort to oppose colonialism or neo-colonialism by the United States and the Soviet Union. This conference later on developed into the Non-Aligned Movement, founded in 1961 in Belgrade. In its effort to unite the Philippines with the Malay World, the then President of the Philippines Diosdado Macapagal convened a summit in Manila in 1963 paving the way to the proposed MAPHILINDO (Malaysia, Philippines, Indonesia). This did not push through, however, because of certain disagreements among the involved countries.

The goal of working together toward a better Southeast Asia would be realized in the founding of the Association of Southeast Asian Nations (ASEAN) on August 8, 1967 by Indonesia, Malaysia, The Philippines, Singapore, and Thailand. Membership in the association later on expanded to include Brunei Darussalam (1984), Vietnam (1995), Laos (1997), Burma (1997), and Cambodia (1999). Timur Leste has already submitted its application in 2011 to become the 11th member of the ASEAN, while Papua New Guinea currently enjoys Special Observer Status since 1981.

3 The Philippines in the ASEAN and the ASEAN+3

The Association of Southeast Asian Nations (ASEAN) originally came out from the alliance between the Philippines, Malaysia, and Thailand back in 1961. It was then called the Association of Southeast Asia (ASA). August 8, 1967 was the date of the establishment of the ASEAN when the foreign ministers of Indonesia, Malaysia, The Philippines, Singapore, and Thailand met in Bangkok to sign the ASEAN Declaration or the Bangkok Declaration. The five foreign ministers, who are considered as the founding fathers of the ASEAN are the following: Adam Malik of Indonesia, Narciso Ramos of the Philippines, Abdul Razak of Malaysia, S. Rajaratnam of Singapore, and Thanat Khoman of Thailand. Part of the Declaration states that the aims and purposes of the Association are: (1) to accelerate the economic growth, social progress, and cultural development in the region through joint endeavors in the spirit of equality and partnership in order to strengthen the foundation for a prosperous and peaceful community of Southeast Asian nations, and (2) to promote regional peace and stability through abiding respect for justice and the rule of law in the relationship among countries in the region and adherence to the principles of the United Nations Charter.

The First ASEAN Summit took place in Bali, Indonesia on February 23–24, 1976 with President Suharto as the host leader. Dubbed as the Treaty of Amity and Cooperation in Southeast Asia, the leaders of each member country agreed that their actions would be guided by the following principles: (1) Mutual respect for the independence, sovereignty, equality, territorial integrity, and national identity of all nations; (2) the right of every State to lead its national existence free from external interference, subversion, or coercion; (3) non-interference in the internal affairs of one another; (4) settlement of differences or disputes by peaceful manner; (5) renunciation of the threat or use of force; and (6) effective cooperation among themselves (Declaration of ASEAN Concord, 1976). By 1997, members of the ASEAN, particularly the Prime Minister of Malaysia, Mahathir Mohamad felt the need of integrating into the group the economic powers of Asia, namely, China, Japan, and South Korea. This gave birth to the expression ASEAN+3 which in the future may become ASEAN+6, including, Australia, New Zealand, and Russia.

In 2006, leaders of the ASEAN states initiated its transformation into becoming the ASEAN Community. This was laid down by a meeting of the ASEAN Eminent Persons Group (ASEAN-EPG) which provided the guidelines for the drafting of the ASEAN Charter. The ASEAN-EPG is composed of former heads of states or eminent statesmen from each of the member countries. The following are the members of the said group: 1) H.E. Dr. Aun Porn Moniroth (Kingdom of Cambodia); 2) H.E. Nguyen Manh Cam

(Socialist Republic of Vietnam); 3) H.E. Professor S. Jayakumar (Republic of Singapore); 4) H.E. Ali Alatas (Republic of Indonesia); 5) H.E. Tun Musa Hitam (Chairman, Malaysia); 6) H.E. Fidel V. Ramos (Republic of the Philippines); 7) H.E. Khamphan Simmalavong (Lao People's Democratic Republic); 8) H.E. M.R. Kasemsamosorn S. Kasemsri (Kingdom of Thailand); 9) H.E. Dr. Than Nyun (Union of Myanmar); 10) H.E. Pehin Dato Lim Jock Seng (Brunei Darussalam). The said group identified the three pillars of ASEAN Cooperation which has become the basis for drafting a blueprint for the Charter. The three pillars identified by the EPG are the following: 1) Political Security Community; 2) Economic Community; 3) Socio-cultural Community (ASEAN 2006).

Within these realms, the Philippines participated and continues to participate in the ASEAN both as a founding member and close ally to every member state. Continuously, the Philippines, since the end of World War II until the founding of ASEAN, has been struggling to keep up with the demands of a nation state in the community of nations. A proof of such conviction would be the provisions on human resources development and unhampered movement of business persons, professionals, talents, and labor on the pages of the ASEAN Charter. The Philippines also contributed provisions on the criteria for admitting new member states plus the refinements on the roles and functions of the Committee of Permanent Representatives in Jakarta as well as the strengthening of the role of the Secretary General. No doubt, the Philippines will continuously be committed on matters of calamity response, piracy, and terrorism within the region. Issues on overseas migrant workers will always be a priority as well as the peace process and problems of insurgency.

3.1 The political security pillar

The ASEAN member states in November 2003 made a milestone in declaring the creation of an ASEAN Community by 2020, later accelerated to 2015. In the Declaration of ASEAN Concord II, or the Bali Concord II, the leaders of the member states declared "the need to further consolidate and enhance the achievements of ASEAN as a dynamic, resilient and cohesive regional association for the well being of its member states and people." For this ideal, it was deemed necessary that the ASEAN Community shall be comprised of three pillars, namely, the ASEAN Economic Community (AEC), the ASEAN Political Security Community (APSC) and the ASEAN Socio-Cultural Community (ASCC). Originally, the APSC is simply the ASEAN Security Community but the Philippines in 2008 sought to rename it as the ASEAN Political Security Community. Such "renaming" would imply not only the goal of providing security for the state but also of the people (Hernandez and Kraft 2012, 1–10).

There are at least five areas in which security problems are being addressed in the APSC Blueprint. First and foremost is the area of democracy and human rights. Second, the APSC provides for post-conflict peace-building measures. Third, besides focusing on safety of navigation, the APSC also obliges cooperation in maritime safety and search and rescue activities. Fourth, provisions are set for ASEAN countries to address non-traditional security issues like problems of human trafficking, especially of children and women, human smuggling, drug trafficking, and transnational crimes like piracy. Last but not the least, there is a need for cooperation in terms of natural disaster management and emergency relief.

The Philippines deals with natural disasters annually. Besides having the highest annual tropical cyclone frequency within the region, the country also has to deal with floods, landslides, earthquakes, and drought. The annual average number of typhoons in the Philippines is 19–20. The highest number of typhoons entering the Philippine Area of Responsibility in recent history was in 1993 with a total of 32 and the lowest was in 1998 with only 11. Nineteen typhoons entered the Philippines in 2011 alone. Together, these typhoons caused 1,541 casualties with 9.87 million people affected and destroyed a total of around 38,088 houses and other properties. From the National Disaster Risk Reduction and Management Council (NDRRMC), there was an estimate of 26.5 billion pesos of total damage to properties.

Recently, disaster preparedness was once again put to the test in the wake of the typhoon Haiyan, a.k.a. Yolanda, when it hit the Philippines on November 8, 2013. For over a period of 16 hours, sustained winds of up to 195 mph swept through six provinces affecting 10 percent of the more than a hundred million people. The hardest hit areas were the coastal communities of Leyte and the southern tip of eastern Samar. In these areas, Yolanda knocked out power, telecommunications, food, and water supplies. Two weeks after the typhoon, the Philippine government reported an estimate of 13.7 million people affected with more than 3.45 million displaced. More than 240,000 of these were housed in 1,096 evacuation areas. A total of 792,000 people had already been evacuated prior to the arrival of the storm. But still, by November 25, 2013, there were an estimated 5,000 deaths and 1,600 missing (Lum and Margesson 2013, 2). All these figures are still fluid and subject to change.

As a response, the Philippine government, through the National Disaster Risk Reduction and Management Center (NDRRMC) and the Department of Social Welfare and Development (DSWD) immediately planned and administered disaster relief operations. The path of destruction which Yolanda left, however, prevented help from arriving immediately. Different Philippine government agencies like the Armed Forces, the Office of Civil Defense, and the Department of Health were all involved in the relief operations. In the lead is the NDRRMC, together with the Local Disaster Risk Reduction Management Councils (LDRRMCs), DSWD, the local government units, and other agencies.

The Philippine response to this kind of situation is the Climate Change Act of 2009 and the National Risk Reduction and Management Act in 2010. In addition, the Senate of the Philippines has submitted to the Office of the

President the bill titled as the People's Survival Fund. If the bill becomes a law, this would provide funds financing initiatives from the local government to adapt to climate change. The Philippine government, as a response to Yolanda's destruction has formed a high-level national task force to ensure a rapid transition from relief operations to rehabilitation and rebuilding of affected areas.

State security remains the ultimate goal of providing comprehensive security for ASEAN member states. This goal could also be seen in the efforts of the Philippines with respect to the Economic and Socio-Cultural pillars.

3.2 The economic pillar

As of 2010, the Philippines ranks number five among the ASEAN states in terms of the size of its economy or the Gross Domestic Product and number six in terms of its per capita income. Growth rates in the past are around 3–5 percent per year which occasionally went up to 6–7 percent. A drastic shrinkage of the economy came by 1984–1985. A negative 7 percent per year was registered after the assassination of Benigno S. Aquino, Jr. in August 1983 (Broad and Cavanagh 1988, 202–204). A less than negative 1 percent per year was registered in 1991 and a slight decline in 1998 as a result of the Asian Financial Crisis (Nanto 1998). It grew over 1 percent by 2009 in the aftermath of the global banking crisis when economies suffered recessions.

It was not always like this. In fact, the Philippines was viewed as having one of the most advanced economies at the end of the Second World War. The latter part of the 1950s until the early 1980s, however, was dominated by corruption in government, protectionist policies, and control of a few over the economy resulted into a slow economic growth. The Philippines was thus overtaken by her neighboring economies such as Hongkong, Taiwan, Singapore, and Korea. Still, corruption and inefficient bureaucratic institutions prevent a better competitive edge of the Philippine economy. The Philippines has also been considered as one of the most promising industrializing economies in Southeast Asia. Several leaders from the late 1940s until the early 1950s made industrialization a priority side by side with the agricultural development of the countryside. By the 1970s to the early 1980s, Philippine GDP came largely from the industrial sector. Dollar flight after 1983, however, forced it to shift to the service sector and as of 2011 the agricultural sector contributed only 12 percent of the GDP despite its having one-third of the labor force.

Main exports from the Philippines are semiconductors and electronic products, transport equipment, garments, copper products, petroleum products, coconut oil, and fruits. These products are shipped to the United States, Japan, China, Singapore, South Korea, Netherlands, Hong Kong, Germany, Taiwan, and Thailand. Manufacturing is confined to processing and assembly operations by subsidiaries of multinational corporations. Earnings from this sector reached around 48 billion dollars in 2011.

Since its shift to the service sector, remittances from the overseas Filipino workers reached a total of 23 billion dollars in 2011. Added to this, the Information Technology and Business Process Outsourcing (IT-BPO) Industry earned 8.9 billion dollars in 2010 with an annual growth of 30 percent. Currently, the Philippines is the third largest player in the IT-BPO industry after India and Canada. The growth of Philippine service export of 3.6 percent per year is more than the yearly average of Asia which is 1.5 percent. The coming ASEAN Economic Community with its liberalization of service trade would thus benefit the Philippines.

The Philippines ranks fifth among the 10 ASEAN member states in the total value of its trade with other ASEAN countries. Singapore, Malaysia, and Thailand are the most active in this intra-ASEAN trade. The Philippines ranks eighth among the member states with a percent share in GDP of 58 percent in terms of its outward economy with Singapore as the most outward with a percent share of GDP of 314 percent and Myanmar as the most inward with 27 percent. The Philippines is not much involved with intra-ASEAN trade. As of 2010, 87 percent of intra-ASEAN trade was contributed by four countries namely, Singapore, Malaysia, Thailand, and Indonesia. The Philippines only has 5.35 percent of the total (Philippine Statistics Authority-National Statistics Office 2014).

The 40 years of ASEAN's pursuit of regional cooperation has not resulted in closer regional economic ties for the Philippines. As early as the 1950s, the Philippines had been in relative isolation among its neighboring countries in Southeast Asia as a result of its trade partnership with the United States. Malaysia and Singapore had the strongest trading and interdependent relations since the 1960s with Indonesia and Thailand following to a certain extent. These four countries have the highest trading rates with China, Japan, and South Korea. For the Philippines, the top trading partner is Japan, second is United States and third is China for the first half of 2012.

Several elements hamper economic growth in the Philippines which is ranked as one of the most difficult countries to do business in after Cambodia and Laos PDR. Besides corruption and inefficient bureaucracy, the country has inadequate infrastructure. For this, the solution of the national government is to promote the public–private partnerships on infrastructure development. Only 3 percent of the Philippine GDP is spent on infrastructure development while the ASEAN average is 5 percent. Around 2010–2011, the government presented to potential investors 17 billion dollars of infrastructure projects. By 2012, the government had prepared plans for 16 infrastructure projects of public–private partnerships including airports, roads, railroads, and water projects. The Philippines is currently regarded as one of the emerging economies with laws and structure to make public–private partnership projects attractive to investors. In addition, the Philippines has established the Public-Private Partnership Center of the Philippines under the National Economic and Development Authority (NEDA) to accelerate the financing, construction, and operation of key government infrastructure projects.

Recently, the Philippines scored 60.1 in the 2014 Index of Economic Freedom (Miller et al. 2014). This made the Philippines the 89th country in terms of economic freedom in the world and 16th out of 42 countries in the Asia-Pacific Region. Since 2010, the Philippines has registered a 5 percent annual growth increase. The government has legislated reforms to enhance the investment environment with incentives for job growth. However, deeper commitment to reforms is needed, and while the perceived level of corruption has decreased, more anti-corruption measures need to be firmly institutionalized.

Future economic growth in the ASEAN region is promising. Currently, it is estimated that member countries are expected to increase their overall GDP by 1.7 percent. There is an estimated $105 billion increase in the economic welfare of member states. The Philippines is projected to become the 16th largest economy in the world by 2050, overtaking the rest of the region.

3.3 The socio-cultural pillar

The Filipinos have yet to feel the effects of the modest economic development being experienced by the Philippines in the past decades. As of 2012, the Philippines has the highest rates of unemployment, i.e., 6.9 percent and underemployment which is 19.3 percent among the ASEAN 5. The goal of establishing an ASEAN which is "people-centered and socially responsible" as stated in the Socio-Cultural Blueprint, aims to ensure that economic growth in the region goes hand in hand with an increasing quality of life. Unfortunately, the Philippines seem to have made no progress at all.

The Philippines is the poorest among the ASEAN 5 with 30 percent of the population living below the poverty line. It is also the only member state with a slow progress toward the Millennium Development Goal 1 of minimizing by half the proportion of people living on less than a dollar a day. The rest of the ASEAN 5 has reached this target while Laos and Cambodia are making steady progress and are on track to meeting these goals by 2015.

Needless to say, poverty alleviation is the primary goal in order to improve the standard of living. Attached to this is the popular view of education as a solution to poverty. The Philippines has one of the highest adult literacy rates in the region, second only to Singapore. The primary education participation rate, however, has become less outstanding. Some decades ago, the Philippines outranked other ASEAN member states with a 99 percent net enrollment ratio in primary education. This dropped to 90 percent by 2002 and remains the lowest in the region second to Laos.

In the academic year of 2012–2013, the government launched one of the flagship projects of the Aquino Administration. This is the K-12 education program which adds mandatory kindergarten education plus two additional years of senior high school. Attached to the additional years of basic education is the reform of the curriculum which places greater importance on subjects like Mathematics, Science, and English. Criticisms, however, are not wanting and the Department of Education has identified the triad of People, Resources, and Curriculum as the main problems ailing the system.

The Philippines has one of the highest, next to Cambodia, pupil–teacher ratios in primary and secondary education in the ASEAN. At 35–37:1, it lags far behind Brunei with 11–13:1, which is the lowest in the region. The Philippines also has an estimated shortage of 74,000 teachers. This is on top of the shortages of classrooms, textbooks, chairs, and sanitation facilities. A shortage of at least 50,921 classrooms which causes overcrowding is further aggravated by occasional natural disasters, especially flooding.

The education budget of 2012 was higher from the last by 31 billion pesos. Unfortunately, this is only 2.1 percent of the GDP which is, in fact, lower than the previous year's 2.3 percent. The United Nations recommends that the education budget should at least be 6 percent of the GDP and the Department of Education itself is asking the same from the government. Within the ASEAN 5, the Philippines is only fourth in terms of national government budget allocation for education vis-à-vis the GDP. The highest allocation for education of 3.2 percent of the GDP happened only in the academic year of 1997–1998. Since then, there is a steady decrease together with the quality of education, especially the quality of primary education. In a span of three years, Philippine ranking in terms of this indicator has dropped from 72 in 2008–2009 to 110 in 2011 (National Statistics Office 2014).

The same problems can be found within the national health services of the Philippines. The Philippines has one of the lowest health expenditures in terms of percentage of GDP after Indonesia, Brunei, and Myanmar. There have been significant increases in the health budget from 24.65 billion pesos in 2010 and 31.82 billion in 2011 to 42.15 billion in 2012. The increases however are below the standard set by the World Health Organization of 5 percent of the GDP (Department of Health 2015).

The Philippines ranked as average within the ASEAN with most of its health indicators. Measles immunization and successful treatments of Tuberculosis cases are slightly below the regional average. After Brunei, Malaysia, Singapore, Thailand, and Vietnam, the ratings for life expectancy at birth, maternal mortality, neonatal and infant mortality are all ranked average within the region. Maternal mortality is on the rise, even if it is still within the ASEAN average. The documented 162 maternal deaths in 2009 had steadily risen to 221 after two years and much blame is given to the lack of access to health facilities and family planning. A positive health indicator is that the Philippines has one of the lowest estimated number of adults having HIV after Singapore and Laos PDR. Recent data however, shows an increase of new cases. Starting from 2011, the number of new cases has risen to 92 percent compared to the previous year (Crisostomo 2014). The National AIDS Council of the Philippines has drafted various action plans and campaigns to address this alarming growth of cases.

Being a state heavily dependent on remittances from overseas workers has also affected the public health sector. Health workers, i.e., nurses, midwives, and doctors are leaving the country to find higher paying jobs elsewhere. A big number of health workers have already left the country where only 62 percent of births are attended by a skilled medical professional. The ratio of physicians and nurses however, remain within the average of the ASEAN. But the exodus has resulted in the closing of over a thousand hospitals all over the country.

3.4 ASEAN Plus Three (APT)

The ASEAN Plus Three (APT), i.e., ASEAN member states plus South Korea, Japan, and China, was formed against the backdrop of the Asian financial crisis in 1997. It was institutionalized in 1999 when the country leaders issued the Joint Statement on East Asia Cooperation in the Third ASEAN+3 Summit held in Manila. Currently, ASEAN+3 cooperation has deepened and broadened to include almost every aspect of life in the member states. These aspects include cooperation in the areas of political security; transnational crime; economic; finance; tourism; agriculture and forestry; energy; minerals; small and medium-sized enterprises; environment; rural development and poverty eradication; social welfare; youth; women; civil service; labor; culture and arts; information and media; education; science, technology, and innovation; and public health.

The Philippines has long been a partner of the Plus Three countries of South Korea, Japan, and China. Attracted by the low cost of English language education and housing, South Koreans, as of 2013, number around 88,102 all around the country. Most of these Korean expatriates are concentrated in Metro Manila, Cebu, Iloilo, Bacolod, Davao, and Cagayan de Oro. As of 2011, the Philippine Bureau of Immigration showed that many of these Koreans in the Philippines are university students. Numbering about 6,000, they are twice more than the Chinese and Iranians.

Philippine bilateral relations with South Korea started in 1949 when the Republic of Korea was recognized as a sovereign state by the Philippines. The Philippines was one of the first states which recognized the sovereignty of South Korea and is the first ASEAN member state to do so. Currently, South Korea is also the sixth biggest trading partner of the Philippines, while, as of 2011, it is also considered as the third most attractive Southeast Asian country for South Korean investors. Attached to this bilateral relation is the military aspect. Military relations between the two countries started during the Korean War when the Philippines sent troops to strengthen the Allied Campaign against North Korea. South Korea is now one of the active arms suppliers of the Armed Forces of the Philippines. Besides selling varied small arms, South Korea also donated some fighter jets and trainer planes to the Philippine Air Force.

Relations between the People's Republic of China and the Republic of the Philippines have significantly improved over the years since the time of the former President Ferdinand E. Marcos. Recent developments in the South China Sea, however, have put some strain on this relationship.

Over the years, there have been several bilateral agreements between the two countries. These agreements are the Joint Trade Agreement in 1975; Scientific and Technological Cooperation Agreement (1978); Postal Agreement (1978); Air Services Agreement (1979); Investment Promotion and Protection Agreement (1992); Agreement on Agricultural Cooperation (1999); Tax Agreement (1999); and Treaty on Mutual Judicial Assistance on Criminal Matters (2000).

China and the Philippines signed the Joint Statement between China and the Philippines on the Framework of Bilateral Cooperation in the Twenty First Century in 2000 confirming the establishment of a long-term and stable relationship on the basis of good neighborliness, cooperation, mutual trust, and benefit. In 2005, the state visit of President Hu Jintao to the Philippines established the determination of the two countries toward the strategic and cooperative relations that aim for peace and development. This was further deepened during Premier Wen Jiabao's official visit in 2007. Both countries issued a joint statement reaffirming their commitment in taking more steps to deepen the strategic and cooperative relationship for peace and development.

Post-World War II relations with Japan were established in 1956 when a war reparations agreement was concluded. Japanese companies and individual investors began returning to the Philippines toward the end of the 1950s. A Treaty of Amity, Commerce and Navigation was signed between the Philippines and Japan in 1960. This, however, did not take effect until 1973 when the legislature was abolished by Marcos under Martial Law. Japan replaced the United States as the main source of investment in the Philippines by 1975. It remains as a major source of funds for development, trade, investments, and tourism at present.

4 The Philippines and ASEAN integration

The Declaration of Asia Concord II mandated the establishment of an ASEAN Community. At the heart of the document is the declaration that the three pillars of political security, economic and socio-cultural cooperation would be the foundation of the ASEAN Community as noted earlier. Of utmost importance to the member states have been the political security and economic cooperation pillars.

For its part, the Philippines is leading the preparations for the Socio-Cultural Community Plan of Action. The Philippines also proposed an ASEAN Convention for the Protection of the Rights of Migrant Workers. Other States, especially Indonesia and Vietnam actively supported this call. Singapore and Malaysia which receive a large number of these workers were not as supportive. The discussions were continued, however, upon the request of the Philippines during the 2007 ASEAN Summit in Cebu. Instead of a Convention, Malaysia suggested a declaration which gave way to the Cebu Declaration or the Declaration for the Protection and Promotion of the Rights of Migrant Workers.

Understandably, the Philippines consistently pursued a legally binding document on migrant workers in the region. Since it shifted to the service sector, migrant labor has already played a major role in the Philippine economy. As of 2011, the Philippines has received a total of 21.3 billion dollars in remittances from overseas workers equivalent to as much as 12 percent of the country's GDP. Within the ASEAN, there are over 180,000 Filipino migrant workers. This figure represents 4 percent of the four million Overseas Filipino Workers (OFWs) around the globe.

The inclusion of migrant workers in the ASEAN Socio-Cultural Community Blueprint gave an assurance that this concern would be on the ASEAN agenda. Different backup mechanisms have already been established to complement this. These are the ASEAN Forum on Migrant Labor and the ASEAN Committee on Migrant Rights. In order to track the progress of member states toward the 2015 goal of establishing the ASEAN Community, the ASEAN Secretariat adopted the ASEAN Economic Community Scorecard. Included, as one of the scorecard categories, is the "Free Flow of Services."

5 Conclusion

The history of the Philippines could be characterized as a history of a continuous struggle for self-determination. When the first colonizers came, they had never really placed the archipelago in their total control. The Spanish colonial period in the Philippines was obviously riddled with rebellions which in general would demand for freedom and independence. In the end, the country got it via a Revolution. Toward the end of America's reign in the Philippines, World War II intervened with much damage and destruction. Still, the Philippines would fight for its freedom and independence even when stripped of arms. Filipinos would endure everything for a better day to come.

The Philippines in its own way has contributed to the progress of the ASEAN. From its founding until now at the threshold of its establishment as a community, the Philippines is always present to assist the ideal of unity and progress. These may have been elusive for a long time, but the Philippines has not lost its focus despite the many setbacks it has gone and has been going through. It may have all the weakness of a fragile state, but it always has the enthusiasm of exploring things which are for the common good. From the times when ancient Filipinos worked and built their fields as a community, to the times when they would leave to earn for their family, the Filipinos have consistently shown their resilience to whatever setbacks or disasters they encountered. History shows that Filipinos are a people who will never give up on their country or on each other.

References

Abad, M.C. (2011) *The Philippines in ASEAN: Reflections from the Listening Room.* Manila: Anvil Publishing.

Association of Southeast Asian Nations (2006) *Report of the Eminent Persons Group on the ASEAN Charter*. Kuala Lumpur: ASEAN EGP.

Association of Southeast Asian Nations (2009) *Roadmap for an ASEAN Community, 2009–2015*. Jakarta: ASEAN Secretariat.

Bellwood, Peter (1997) *Prehistory of the Indo-Malaysian Archipelago*. Honolulu: University of Hawaii Press.

Broad, Robin and John Cavanagh (1988) 'Things Fall Apart: The Rise of Debt, the Fall of Marcos and the Opportunity for Change' in Robin Broad. *Unequal Alliance: The World Bank, the International Monetary Fund and the Philippines*. Berkeley: University of California Press, pp. 202–239.

Chow, Jonathan T. (2005) "ASEAN Counterterrorism Cooperation Since 9/11." *Asian Survey*, 45(2): 302–321.

Crisostomo, Sheila (2014) 'DOH: 2013 HIV/AIDS Cases Almost 5000' *The Philippine Star*, 29 January 2014.

De Marquina, Esteban (1990) 'Tondo Conspiracy of 1587–1588.' *Documentary Sources of Philippine History*, edited by Gregorio F. Zaide. Manila: National Book Store, pp. 85–97.

Dempwolff, Otto (1938) *Vergleichende Lauttehre des Austronesischen Wortschatzes*. Berlin: Dietrich Eeimer (Andrews U. Steiner).

Department of Health (2015) *Annual Report 2014, Department of Health Philippines*. Manila: Department of Health. pp. 23–24.

Fifth ASEAN People's Assembly (2007) *The Role of the People in Building an ASEAN Community of Caring and Sharing Societies: Report of the 5th ASEAN People's Assembly, Manila, Philippines, 8–10 December 2006*. Quezon City: Institute for Strategic and Development Studies.

Final Communique of the Asian-African Conference of Bandung (1955) Bandung, Indonesia.

Gardner, Fletcher (1906) 'Philippine (Tagalog) Superstitions.' *The Journal of American Folklore*, 19(75): 191–204.

Gugler, P. and Julienne Chaisse (2010) *Competetiveness of the ASEAN Countries: Corporate and Regulatory Drivers*. Cheltenham: E. Elgar.

Heng Keng, Chiam (2009) *The Three Pillars of the ASEAN Community: Commitment to the Human Rights Process*. Bangkok: 5th Roundtable Discussion on Human Rights in ASEAN.

Hernandez, C.G. and H.J.S. Kraft (eds) (2012) *Mainstreaming Human Security In ASEAN Integration: Human Security and the Blueprints for Realizing the ASEAN Community*. Quezon City: Institute for Strategic and Development Studies. pp. 1–10.

Hernandez, Carolina G. and Gina R. Pattugalan (eds) (1999) *Transnational Crime and Regional Security in Asia-Pacific*. Quezon City: Institute for Strategic and Development Studies.

Hernandez, Jose Rhommel B. (2010) 'Reduccion: Ang Pag-uwi sa Diskurso ng Pananakop at Pakikipagtunggali,' *Malay*, 23(1): 67–80.

Hew, Dennis (ed.) (2005) *Roadmap to ASEAN Economic Community*. Singapore: Institute of Southeast Asian Studies.

Jocano, F. Landa (1975) *Philippine Prehistory: An Anthropological Overview of the Beginnings of Filipino Society and Culture*. Quezon City: Philippine Center for Advanced Studies, 1975.

Jones, D.M. (2006) *ASEAN and East Asian International Relations: Religion Delusion*. Cheltenham: E. Elgar.

Lum, Thomas and Rhoda Margesson (2013) *Typhoon Haiyan (Yolanda): U.S. and International Response to Philippines Disaster.* Washington, DC: Congressional Research Service.

Majul, Cesar Adib (1999) *Muslims in the Philippines.* Quezon City: University of the Philippines Press.

Miller, Terry, Anthony B. Kim and Kim R. Holmes (2014) *2014 Index of Economic Freedom.* Washington, DC: The Heritage Foundation and Down Jones and Company, Inc.

Nanto, Dick K. (1998) *The 1998–98 Asian Financial Crisis.* Washington, DC: Congressional Report Service.

National Statistics Office (2014) *The Philippines in Figures 2014.* Manila: National Statistics Office. pp. 35–41.

Salazar, Zeus A. (2006) *Ang Pilipinong Banua/Banwa sa Mundong Melano-Polynesiano.* Lungsod Quezon: Palimbagan ng Lahi.

Salazar, Zeus A. (1998) *The Malayan Connection: Ang Pilipinas sa Dunia Melayu.* Lungsod Quezon: Palimbagan ng Lahi.

Schumacher, John (1991) *Rizal in the Context of Nineteenth Century Philippines in John Schumacher. The Making of a Nation, Essays on 19th Century Filipino Nationalism.* Quezon City: Ateneo de Manila University Press. pp. 16–34.

Tanudirjo, Daud Aris (2004) 'The Structure of Austronesian Migration in Island Southeast Asia and Oceania.' *Southeast Asian Archaeology: Wilhelm G. Solheim II Festschrift,* edited by Victor J. Paz. Quezon City: The University of the Philippines Press, pp. 83–103.

Tiwani, S. (2010) *ASEAN: Life After the Charter.* Singapore: Institute of Southeast Asian Studies.

8 Singapore

The dynamics of city state development and relations with ASEAN and APT

Kong Chong Ho

1 Introduction: Singapore as a small city state in Southeast Asia

Within the ASEAN cooperative framework, member countries deliberate and agree on a number of initiatives critical to the region, offer financial and other resources which allow such initiatives to take root and blossom, and take turns to host meetings that support the socio-economic and political development efforts. This collaborative and collective orientation, long recognized as the hallmark of ASEAN's success, makes it important to understand the uniqueness of a member country's contribution. The focus of this chapter is thus on an examination which allows us to see the unique or the comparative advantage of Singapore's contributions. To understand Singapore's role in ASEAN, we should look at the relationship between a country's attributes and the distinct ways in which it relates to ASEAN. This relationship can be undertaken in two broad ways. The first is to look at how Singapore's historically derived attributes of being a small state as well as a port city shape its orientation towards the region and beyond. This first point allows the reader to understand how historical and structural features of the country shape its relationship with the rest of the world. The second look involves an understanding of the developmental features of Singapore as a city state from which we can deduce a comparative advantage in terms of the nature of contributions.

The size of a country matters. In the book *Small States in the World Market*, Katzenstein (1985) shows that participation in regional groupings has allowed small European states to pool their interests, exert a larger voice on a range of collective interests and gain a stronger bargaining position against a stronger state. Nuemann and Gstöhl (2004, 17) argue that because material resources are limited, this structural factor 'may predispose small states to favour discourses that institutionalize rules and norms, such as international law, international regimes, and international institutions'.

We can extend the small country and its inherent lack of resources argument to the nature of economic development. Saul (1982) argues that the lack of natural resources also predispose small countries to move into niches which may be less attractive or paid less attention by larger countries. Moreover, governments are pushed to become more interventionist in developing the economy because of the constraints of size. Within this framework, trade becomes an important niche as opportunities are capitalized and skills developed within the small country.

These historical and structural dynamics certainly apply to Singapore. Singapore's development as a port city by the British created an entrepôt niche which included not just the infrastructure in terms of the harbour and a set of services oriented to trade, but also an outlook which is focussed on the immediate sub-region and to markets in Europe, India and China (Wong 1960, 160). And when Malaysia's export economy around tin and rubber expanded, the trading economy centred in Singapore grew proportionately (Buchanan 1972, 22) One of the colonial economic legacies has been the creation of an excellent entrepôt infrastructure (habour, warehouses, transport and communication facilities) along with a well-developed layer of business and trading services (banks, trading houses, wholesalers, and transport and communication services). Since decolonization, the port city function continues to be significant in Singapore's economy as it is a major port of Southeast Asia. With stronger government intervention, other economic activities, an industrial base which is dependent on overseas foreign direct investment (beginning with electronics and more recently pharmaceuticals and chemicals) has built on this early economic layer. In turn, Singapore continues to look outwards in its economic outlook and is sensitive to the interplay between international relations and economic relations.

Aside from this broad historical and structural perspective, we should also look more in-depth into the nature of Singapore's development to examine the agencies of development and to see how these shape the nature of Singapore's development. All countries move at a different pace for different sectors and understanding which sectors Singapore is ahead in will allow us to establish Singapore's unique contribution.

2 The nationalist perspective: the process of nation building and identity-formation in Singapore

Examining the short history of identity-formation in Singapore, three stages can be determined. The laissez faire policy developed by the British under the colonial period resulted in a situation where economic priorities prevailed over social concerns. The maintenance of the physical infrastructure of trade was of paramount importance in ensuring the surplus which accrued to British interests. This imbalance of priorities is aptly summarized by Edwin Lee (1989, 40):

> The British in Singapore measured success by the amount of trade secured and the miles of roads paved. But what about schools, hospitals, and low-cost housing? In the matter of schools and hospitals, the government invoked laissez-faire principles and expected philanthropic contributions from private individuals who had benefited from the free trade system.

It is important to point out that this disregard for social and community expenditures was only possible because the government was kept in place by the effective threat of force rather than the popular support of the people. In such a situation, the concerns of society and state only overlapped with regard to a narrow set of economic issues. Any social improvement schemes were left to various local communities. Such an ethnic community-based model in turn meant that popular support tended to be mobilized and therefore confined within respective communities and never expanded past these boundaries. While the communities did achieve some success, particularly in the area of education, their efforts tended to be limited and sporadic because they depended on the resources and energies of a few prominent individuals. Such a system did not adequately meet the communities' needs in areas such as health and housing, which required more resources and systematic planning. In such an environment, identity formation is largely restricted to within the community as mobilization and social support is organized from within rather than at the societal level.

After World War II, there was a willingness on the part of the colonial administration to prepare for the gradual transfer of power to an independent government, while at the same time attempting to safeguard British interests (Stockwell 1986, 83–88). Education was expanded with the aim of creating new civic loyalties and training as preparation for self-government (Tan 2001). As Ong (1975, 74) suggested, the next step for Singapore after self-government was complete independence from the British and the merger with Malaya seemed the surest way to independence and at the same time allowed Singapore to have access to the Malayan hinterland. The merger was brief: proposed by the Prime Minister of Malaya in 1961, became a reality in 1963 and was dissolved when Singapore was separated from Malaysia in 1965. Whether the separation was due to the differential politics and aspirations between Singapore and Malaya (Parmer 1966, 111) or the racial nature of the power struggle between Malaya and Singapore (Milne 1966, 175), had Singapore continued with the Federation, nation-building and identity-formation would have taken a different route.

The move to a nationalist model therefore began afresh with Singapore's independence. And in the 1960s, when the People's Action Party (PAP) gained a majority in the Singapore parliament, it put in place the infrastructure which made a national model possible. With growing support stemming from its programmes, a strong state infrastructure and concerns with nation building following independence in 1965, Singapore embarked upon a centralized model of identity building. As schools became nationalized and curriculum developed through the Ministry of Education, new generations of school-going children and youth became socialized into a Singaporean identity. National service for Singaporean males reinforced emergent nationalist identity through a common mission to serve the country. A comprehensive system of community centres and resident committees developed in public housing estates enabled Singaporean families of different religious and ethnic backgrounds to interact and form a common bond.

Attempts at a more participative identity-building model in partnership with the government began after two decades of socio-economic development. The identity-building effort in the first two decades of independence was largely a state-driven initiative, spearheaded by the government in a concerted effort to build a national identity on top of a strong ethnic identity, changing essentially a pluralist society to a nation. As Velayutham (2004, 12) observes, while Singapore's economic progress constituted a source of support for the government, there is a lack of a more full-fledged emotive nationalism.

The participative model was in part a reaction to globalization and the worry that Singaporeans will lose their Singaporean roots built painstakingly through a nation building effort. While the government embraced inevitability of globalization and saw Singapore's role in harnessing its benefits in terms of economic gains through trade, tourism and services, as well as in terms of the innovations which can be adopted, it also saw globalization as eroding the Singaporean identity through the increased mobility of Singaporeans, their increasing share of non-local ties through friendships and marriage, and a growing marketplace of ideas.

Thus, under Prime Minister Goh Chok Tong, three social bonding exercises were conducted: the Next Lap in 1991, Singapore 21 in 1999, and Remaking Singapore in 2002. In the 2002 Remaking Singapore project, Prime Minister Goh said that the exercise was an attempt to find ways of rooting Singaporeans to the country, adding that 'when we proclaim that we are Singaporeans, we are expressing our belief in the Singapore way of life, and in our shared values' (*Straits Times*, 19 August 2002). The objectives of these exercises were to create a new consensus beyond the pragmatic goal of making a living (*Straits Times*, 18 July 2004). The new participative model of national identity launched in the 1990s attempts to counter the relentless pull of the external world by engagement at the following levels (a) the identification and strengthening of a set of core values; (b) the reaffirmation of the family as a social anchor; and (c) recognizing, perhaps for the first time, that an active citizenry is needed, implying that with globalization and an educated society, a sustainable identity model for Singapore can only be the result of active stake-holding. When Lee Hsien Loong took over as PM and unveiled his first budget in 2005, the budget was aimed at not only promoting a vibrant economy, but also fostering a stronger sense of community among Singaporeans (*Bernama*, 18 February, 2005).

In the 2011 general elections, the People's Action Party (PAP) had its share of votes decline from 66.6 per cent in 2006 to 60.14 per cent. Significantly, two senior PAP ministers were among the casualties, as the Aljunied Group Representation Constituency was captured by the Workers Party, which emerged as PAP's main rival. This raised the possibility of a two-party system as the Workers Party established itself (Tan 2012). The day after the election, Prime Minister Lee was quoted as saying it was a watershed election, with a different electorate with different concerns and a desire to 'see more opposition voices in the Parliament to keep a check on the PAP government' (*Straits*

Times, 8 May 2011). Later in the month, Prime Minister Lee pledged to engage all segments of society in inclusive dialogue (*Straits Times*, 22 May 2011). A year later, a new government ministry, the Ministry of Culture, Community and Youth was created to 'strengthen community bonds, promoting volunteerism and philanthropy, engaging youth and developing sports. Additionally, it will promote harmonious communal relations, amid an atmosphere of simmering anxieties over the influx of new citizens' (*Straits Times*, 1 August 2012).

In 2013, the nation-building exercise termed the 'Singapore conversation', was aimed at engaging Singaporeans in identifying a set of issues and solutions. As Mr Heng Swee Kiat, the Education Minister in charge of the project puts it, the Singapore conversation hopes to foster deeper understanding among Singaporeans, identify their key concerns, and reach consensus on some areas that will form the basis of policies and programmes (*Straits Times*, 9 September 2012). Introduced at the 2012 National Day Rally, Prime Minister Lee framed the Singapore Conversation in the following way: 'What future do we see for Singapore? What kind of home do we want for our children? I believe all of us want to be proud to be Singaporeans, and to live in a successful country that meets our aspirations. What does this mean?' The process is as important as the outcome. The ground up involvement of Singaporeans to create a common understanding is the goal. For citizens, it is developing an awareness of the policy constraints faced by the government. For the government, it is an opportunity to solicit systematically the views of different segments of society, their aspirations and problems and working to come up with solutions. More importantly, the opportunity to participate may create what Velayutham (2004, 11), borrowing from Hage (1996), terms 'governmental belonging', a more active form of citizen identity which comes about from active involvement.

3 Political security perspectives

3.1 Development of democracy, politics and governance in Singapore

The path of political development in Singapore marked an initial period of civil unrest and a struggle for domains among several political parties after the British colonial government initiated the process of local self-rule after World War II (Turnbull 1969). The People's Action Party (PAP) eventually came into power through a range of measures aimed at neutralizing the left wing opposition parties including preventive detention measures (Gamer 1972) and changes within the civil service aimed at controlling the influence of oppositional left wing elements and working with moderates who identified with the modernization and development programmes initiated by the PAP (Seah 1976).

Keeping the opposition from making inroads with the electorate also required PAP to create jobs and provide schools and housing as essential means of winning the electorate. Significantly, the PAP created a set of new organizations to manage various developmental tasks such as investment promotion, tourism development, industrial development and public housing while leaving policy and housekeeping functions to the government ministries (Ho 2009). The British colonial government had focussed on port development and neglected social expenditures. A 1947 housing survey has found that out of the population of 938,000 residents in Singapore, 72 per cent were housed within the Central Area of Singapore, leading to an over-congested city core, with slums developing around the city fringe (Ho 1993). The PAP's record of developing public housing estates in the 1960s made a significant mark on the electorate as the following account shows:

> Public housing is probably the most visible and demonstrative project in the Republic. Its success had assured support for many other government policies. It is perhaps not a pure coincidence that results of the study on the level of satisfaction with public housing are similar to the result of the 1972 election in which the People's Action Party received 70% of the popular vote and won all the seats in the parliament.
>
> Yeh and Pang 1973 (quoted in Hassan 1976, 240)

As the housing problem tapered by the late 1970s, the next key focus was on developing a health system which incorporated features of co-payment for those who can afford it but at the same time, through the state's direct control of the health system, the PAP has been able to provide quality health care for lower income and elderly patients through a comprehensive system of clinics at public housing estates and government managed hospitals (Chiu et al. 2012).

Through such provision of public goods such as housing and health, the PAP has been able to build an effective social contract with the electorate.

The 1980s also saw the building of a more active civil society among an increasingly educated society. For example, the organization of the women's movement received a significant boost with the formation of the Singapore Council of Women's Organisation in 1980 as a non-governmental umbrella organization overseeing local women's organizations. This was followed in 1985 with the formation of the Association of Women for Action and Research (AWARE) (Wee 1987). AWARE works to promote participation and rights for women and also works with government on developing a range of amenities (e.g. child-care centres) benefits (e.g. on health benefits) and legal protection (for victims of rape and domestic assault). And with the rise of the internet in the 1990s, and later social media, this meant new avenues of participation. The government saw the internet as an important technological and educational tool and promoted this in schools and universities. This easy availability among an educated population created the opportunity for opinion making and mobilization through internet blogs such as Mr Brown and the Temasek Review. In an early review of citizenship participation under conditions which were more restrictive, Ho (2000, 448) pointed out that 'the Constitution guarantees the liberal rights of Singaporeans, and hence the mechanisms for citizenship participation are in place. The failure to practice or implement these principles and structures, however, is an administrative and political rather than legal one.' This suggests that a more educated society, a government that is slowly open to a more participative society in order to achieve governmental belonging, the growth of civil society groups which work alongside the government (see previous section), and the stable presence of internet opinion making, will create an emergent infrastructure that supports citizen political participation.

The general election in 2011 saw an important change in electoral politics with an increase in the number of Workers Party (an alternative political party) members being voted into Parliament. The 2015 general election saw an increase in vote share going back to the PAP in part due of some of the measures the PAP developed after the 2011 election which signalled a greater responsiveness from the government. The anticipated gains for the opposition did not materialize but the Workers Party was the only other political party with members voted into parliament. And so while the possibility of a two-party system in Singapore may be premature, there will certainly be a more engaged parliamentary debate on a range of social issues.

3.2 Human rights

As a city state, Singapore has had to depend on foreign workers to augment key sectors in construction, health care and home care. This segment of the non-local workforce has grown to represent about 33.6 per cent of the Singaporean workforce in December 2012 (Straits Times, 21 April 2013). As foreign workers on temporary contracts, the most significant human rights challenge in Singapore is with migrant workers; their safety from industrial accidents, being exploited by their employers, and their general welfare especially in the area of housing. Non-government organizations like the TWC2 (Transient Workers Count Too) actively campaign for the rights and protection of a large migrant worker population in Singapore. According to Lyon (2005: 217–218, 224, 232), the TWC2 modelled its practices along other successful groups in two ways. It focussed its attention on building alliances with other local groups such as AWARE, the Singapore Council of Women's Organizations (SCWO), a state-sponsored group, and the Catholic group Commission for Migrants and Itinerant People (CMI) as well as with the embassies representing foreign worker home countries. And second, it focuses its attention on public education and improving the employment conditions. The Ministry of Manpower has also pushed for workers rights[1] and also employer responsibility, seeing the issue of worker rights as a partnership to be forged. Since 2005, the Ministry of Manpower (MOM) has taken enforcement action against 7,660 employers for failing to provide acceptable housing for their foreign workers. As a result, more than 50,000 foreign workers were relocated to better housing (Today, 19 December 2012). In doing its duty, the MOM works with civil society migrant rights groups like TWC2 and HOME (Humanitarian Organization for Migration Economics), by receiving referrals from them. In the last two years (2011, and 2012), MOM received more than 900 cases from these two agencies (Today, 5 February 2013).

3.3 Corruption

According to the Transparency International's 2012 Corruption Perceptions Index, Singapore is in the ranks of the least corrupt countries in the world (Reuters, 5 December 2012). According to Davinder Singh, a senior counsel and member of parliament, having a strong value system that is against corruption, protection against whistle blowers, and an effective enforcement arm are critical elements in the fight against corruption (*Straits Times*, 15 December 2005). On the issue of enforcement, Sam (2005, 56) points out that the enforcement arm, the Corrupt Practices Investigation Bureau whose Director is answerable only to the Prime Minister, has powers to arrest and search investigated persons in public and private sectors, regardless of the positions they hold. In the case of Singapore, the presence of a strong anti-corruption culture, the importance of a legal framework that is clear with regard to the types of corruption abuses, an effective enforcement agency that works to bring suspects, often powerful individuals to the courts, and a fair hearing, are indicative of the structural progress made in the eradication of corruption.

4 Economic perspectives: Development in the city-state

4.1 Economic development

Unlike the other member states of ASEAN, Singapore does not have an agricultural sector. Its economic history, as outlined briefly in the last section, has been its development as a port city. For the period between internal self government in 1959 and formal independence in 1965, a number of important agencies have been created to spearhead economic development. The Economic Development Board (EDB) was formed in 1961 to oversee economic development. This organization later split into the Jurong Town Corporation, an agency responsible for developing industrial estates, and the Development Bank of Singapore which focussed on financing projects. With this new division of labour, the EDB was left with the all important task of investment promotion in developed countries such as United States, Germany and Japan. Significantly, this specialized role indicated two very important features of its development. Unlike Korea and Taiwan which pursued a strategy of relying on its local companies to drive industrial growth, Singapore, because of its very small population and because of its trade orientation, felt it did not have the local capacity to grow the economy through industry. Instead, through the EDB, it opted on a strategy of relying on established large multinational companies looking for an overseas production base. Thus, the government essentially played a house-keeping function of ensuring that local conditions, the key elements being infrastructure, regulations, manpower, were well developed to support the needs of its overseas partners. This strategy of marshalling its limited resources in developing elements the government can control ensured a continuous investment in infrastructure such as transportation, communications, industrial estates and business parks, as well as a keen interest in making sure education and training can keep up with the pace of development. The result of this strategy was a well-developed education system and urban infrastructure.

The second consequence of a reliance on overseas investment, a strategy Singapore never abandoned but instead become better at doing, was an orientation to the rest of the world. In pursuing this strategy, the EDB set up a vast network of overseas offices that are in major centres of business and industrial activities. By the 1980s, the EDB had dedicated offices in 14 key cities world-wide, developing new offices in areas of new growth such as China in the 1990s (Ho 2009). This network allowed Singapore to tap economic opportunities in the rest of the world. Significantly, this reliance is not only international but also regional. As Singapore became more expensive in terms of land and labour, the city state looked towards its immediate neighbours, Malaysia and Indonesia as partners for industrial development. This cooperation is best illustrated by the growth triangle policy which saw the three countries developing Southern Johor (Malaysia), the Riau Islands (Indonesia) and Singapore as an integrated growth sub-region where multinational companies can move different parts of their operations, production as well as management and business services operations in the three areas. It is this reliance which also shaped Singapore's model of international relations in ways that Katzenstein (1985) and Nuemann and Gstöhl (2004) described, an approach which focussed on cooperation with major political and economic powers as well as international and regional regimes, based on norms and standards which are widely supported.

4.2 Tourism

Two other developments are to become important in understanding Singapore's role in ASEAN. Like industrial development, when the decision was made to develop tourism in the city state, there was little in terms of natural and cultural attractions. Lim (1979, 52, 80–81) noted that in the 1950s and early 1960s, there was little to see and do in Singapore and as a result, tourism in Singapore was incidental and visitors to the city were usually on route to somewhere else.

This was the context in which the Singapore Tourism Board (STB) was formed in 1964. While a long description of STB's role and successes is unnecessary, a number of points which are relevant to this essay need to be highlighted. First, like the EDB, the STB also built an important network of offices overseas in its efforts to promote the city state. This network again underscores Singapore's reliance on the rest of the world for its development. Second, Singapore's search for a variety of products to attract and keep tourists has increasingly moved to urban tourism attractions, amenities which a 'world class city must have' (arts development, malls, gardens, even casinos are planned as integrated entertainment complexes). This shift to urban attractions is significant because the appeal is across a broad range of consumers rather than just tourists, making these amenities linked to the lifestyle of the city. Thus Singapore's approach to tourism development allowed for a growth in the attractiveness of the city for tourists, visitors and locals alike. Linked to this set of attractions are well-developed air-routes and meetings and conventions facilities. Thus, the eco-system created features a strong air travel network (in terms of price and connections), a good set of meeting facilities and a broad range of attractions which appeal to different ages. This in turn becomes an important feature for Singapore in its attempts to host workshops and meetings related to ASEAN.

The other tourism-related development again arises from Singapore's small size which requires the city state to cooperate with other neighbouring countries to develop a more comprehensive tourism product. In this context, it is already recognized as a major air-hub for Southeast Asia. As early as the mid-1990s, the International Civil Aviation Organization (ICAO) indicated that of the 9.19 million air passengers landing in Southeast Asian cities, 37.5 per cent landed at Singapore's international airport (Rimmer 1996, 90). Pearce's (1997) study of the tourism potential of Sarawak, Malaysia (about four hours' flight time from Singapore) recognized Singapore not as a competitor to the niche that Sarawak tourism was based on, but that Singapore can act as a gateway and complementary destination. In the 1990s, Silkair was developed as a regional airline to ferry passengers to regional cities and resort areas in Southeast Asia. This was soon followed by a number of budget airlines operating in the region, notably Tiger airlines, Jetstar and Air Asia. These have the tendency to intensify air travel patterns in the region and integrate the region through tourism. Thus, what was started as a regional strategy has been developed further by the budget regional airlines; the effect is creating tourism cooperation between cities and regions.

4.3 Education

There is a close link between industrialization and education. The period from the 1970s to 1990s was when Singapore experienced the strongest pace of industrial development. The education system in Singapore underwent two phases of transformation to adjust to the demands of the industry. To grow the industrial workforce in the first phase of the industrial period (1960s to mid-1970s) technical education was initiated. Vocational schools were started in 1964 with an enrolment of 4,910 students (Goh and Gopinathan 2006, 15). The Technical Education Department was set up within the Ministry of

Education in 1968, which later became the Industrial Training Board in 1973. Technical education was expanded in secondary schools with the introduction of a technical stream in the curriculum. The number of students in this stream expanded from 12,000 in 1971 to 18,000 by the end of the 1970s (Cheung 1994).

In this early phase of industrialization, Pang and Low (1994) pointed out that the generally low education levels of the workforce did not slow down Singapore's economic development because the labour-intensive industrial activities during this period generally required low skills. It was after Singapore had achieved full employment in the mid-1970s that a higher skilled labour force was needed to sustain the manufacturing sector. Under such a context, existing workers had to receive further training in order to maintain their jobs and entrants to the workforce were required to possess more sophisticated working skills than the previous generation in order to enter the employment market. In 1979, the Vocational and Industrial Training Board was thus created and the Continuing Education and Training scheme it launched helped retrain 60,000 workers per year (Law 1996, 11). Significantly, the Institute of Technical Education (ITE) was created in 1992 to provide an integrated platform of industrial training for post-secondary education, part-time continuing education for workers as well as more specific industrial training offered by employers (through apprenticeship schemes and on-the-job training schemes) and skills certification programmes. Law Song Seng, the chief executive officer of the ITE, wrote that 'the most important challenge is to ensure that the training system remains relevant and responsive to the nation's changing skilled manpower needs' (1996, 20).

This point assumes greater relevance in an urban economy, where flows of economic activities in and out of the city occur at an accelerated pace. In a global economy, companies often move manufacturing and services activities to new and emerging markets with lower production costs and a large and cheaper labour pool. And as dominant industries fade out and new industries are attracted to the city as replacements, the task of human capital management is the anticipation of changing skill sets in the wake of a dynamic economy, and the timely response which is needed from the education system to help the city cope with such rapid restructuring to its urban economy.

This shift from manufacturing to services was due in part to the movement of manufacturing activities to Malaysia and also to China. Faced with rising manufacturing costs, since the 1980s, Singapore switched to a service-led strategy of promoting itself as the base for regional headquarters of multinational corporations (Dicken and Kirkpatrick 1991; Perry 1992) while at the same time continuing to upgrade its manufacturing base.

As Singapore has become a world city with an enlarged set of producer and consumer services, education development has taken several new paths different from that of its rivals. First, unlike Hong Kong which has gradually abandoned its manufacturing sector, Singapore's steadfast commitment to manufacturing suggests that it intends to continue to rely upon its technological edge to maintain the competitiveness. Human capital development could no longer be retained at the vocational level, which served the Republic quite well in the 1980s. The new form of human capital development has to depend on a close partnership between universities and industries for research and development, in which engineers and research academics could collaborate on new product design and innovative research. Under such a trend, in the past decade, the National University of Singapore and the Nanyang Technological University were transformed into research universities with a cluster of research institutes (Gopinathan 1999). The government has also created a number of research programmes and initiatives managed by the Ministries of Health, Education and Trade and Industry, along with the Agency for Science, Technology and Research to spearhead science and technology research (Sidhu et al. 2014).

Second, there has been a significant development of business and management studies in Singapore. This included the development of a third smaller specialized management university (the Singapore Management University), as well as the attraction of well-known business schools such as INSEAD to host their programmes in Singapore (Olds and Thrift 2005). As Olds and Thrift point out, the development of this institutional system will expose Singaporean educational institutions to competition (thereby forcing them to upgrade), and to produce (in discursive and institutional senses) a 'global education hub' that would be attractive to students from around the Asia-Pacific region.

This is also a higher education and research system that can support ASEAN in a number of ways, in terms of the leveraging on its scientific research especially in clean water technologies; the training of mid-career officials in public policy; and a high standard of English education for youths from ASEAN member states and also from the Plus Three partners.

4.4 The link between economic, social and political development

Singapore as a global city characterizes a development pattern which creates general economic prosperity but also incorporates problems such increasing income inequality, the need to adapt to changing skill sets for the young as new opportunities emerge and to compensate for sunset industries, and greater diversity as new migrants (workers, students, and families) come to the city state in search of economic, educational and quality of life opportunities.

Besides ensuring a dynamic economy and improving quality of life, problems which are associated with rapid economic development have to be managed. Moreover, as discussed in the previous sections, economic progress and higher education also create the conditions and a desire for increased citizenship participation. And so alongside the agencies which drive education, economic and technological development, of equal importance are the agencies for integration, necessary for creating a national identity out of an increasingly heterogeneous society. Alongside this layer of specialized government agencies are a range of civic and religious organizations which together support the socio-cultural development of the city state. Singapore's emerging role as a global city also makes it home to relief agencies which use Singapore as a base to support Southeast Asian operations.

As will be seen in the next section, Singapore's progress (through state and non-state efforts) in managing an increasingly diverse population fed by immigration, redistribution mechanisms to counter a growing income inequalities, and efforts to grow a built environment which is capable of delivering a high quality of life, allows it to make significant contributions to ASEAN's Socio-Cultural Community Pillar.

5 Involvement of Singapore within ASEAN

The success of ASEAN can only be sustained if individual member countries see value in the regional grouping. Kurus (1993, 820) points out that ASEAN provides two sets of benefits to member countries. First, it functions as a means for its members to obtain tangible and intangible benefits vis-à-vis external parties. And second, as a regional grouping, ASEAN can also provide a source of collective intra-regional benefits to individual members.

In this regard, Singapore has benefited in both general and specific ways. An example of the first type of benefits is illustrated through the exercise of ASEAN bloc politics. ASEAN and Australia was locked in a dispute in the late 1970s over Australia's International Civil Aviation policy which restricted the ability of ASEAN states' airlines to pick up passengers mid-route. As Kurus (1993, 823) points out, this dispute was really between Singapore and Australia because other ASEAN airlines were still too small to be immediately affected by this policy. Other ASEAN states supported the Singapore position and reacted as a bloc, eventually moving Australia to change its position.

Benefits can also accrue through internal processes. Southeast Asia is a region with internal political differences and potential conflicts between neighbours and the history of ASEAN is one with a number of examples where a common ASEAN stance and resolve has worked to preserve regional stability. For example, Indonesia took the leadership in mediating the Malaysia-Philippines dispute in 1968–1969, a year after ASEAN was formed (Rau 1981, 102–103). The settlement of the 1978 Vietnamese invasion of Cambodia by the early 1990s was another victory for ASEAN (Kurus 1993, 821; Acharya 1997, 323). These early successes paved the way for members to work together. The building of consensus through consultations and the sensitivity of members to each other's interests explain why Indonesia and Malaysia have taken the position at the Organization of Islamic Countries that the issue of Muslim minorities in Thailand and the Philippines represents the internal affairs of the two countries (Kurus 1993, 826).

And as countries in ASEAN receive these two types of benefits, there is also an expectation that the sustainability of ASEAN also requires individual member countries to contribute to ASEAN. In this respect, the argument made at the beginning of this chapter was that within the ASEAN community, each member country contributes to collective projects that improve the community. The general spirit of cooperation should not mask unique contributions of each member state; unique because their particular socio-economic development allows the particular member state to deliver a contribution that may be more advanced, more comprehensive, or of higher quality.

This section of the chapter considers Singapore's situation as a city state and a global city and argues that these conditions allow the Republic to make unique contributions to the ASEAN community. Of the three pillars, I chose to focus on the contributions in terms of the ASEAN Socio-Cultural Community Blueprint.

I believe that Singapore can play a unique role in human resource development. With Singapore's development as an education hub in higher education, this infrastructure can be harnessed to allow for human capital development of youths as well as for different types of shorter-term training, for example, of civil servants and professionals.

Another role is in terms of Singapore's facilitating access to applied Science and Technology again through the research facilitated by its universities. A parallel development of Singapore as an education hub is also its role in developing applied technologies in partnership with universities and industry. One promising application is in terms of environmental technologies like desalination, water re-use and waste water management.

Another feature which stands out is Singapore's good infrastructure in health and medical services. This infrastructure plays two general roles. The Health Promotion Board in Singapore plays an important public education role through the promotion of healthy lifestyles. This can certainly be expanded to a regional focus as workshops, seminars and programmes can be developed between health professionals in the ASEAN region, allowing healthy lifestyles to be attained in the region.

We examined migrant workers' rights in the previous section of the chapter. ASEAN can be seen as a region of senders and receivers as a significant flow of migrant workers find work within ASEAN. And while Singapore's focus has been confined to efforts to help migrant workers working in the Republic, a more coordinated effort through the protection and promotion of the rights of migrant workers can be promoted within ASEAN.

A longer economic history of industrial development, research and development and technology transfer in Singapore also means that Singapore can contribute in terms of environmental technologies in terms of waste water treatment, desalination, and water security. In this respect, Malaysia (*Straits Times*, 3 September 2011) and Indonesia (*Straits Times*, 18 November 1990) and Singapore have a long history of collaboration in the building of reservoirs and managing water reserves in Johor and Batam respectively.

Being a developed city state, Singapore can also play an important role in the promotion of quality living standards in ASEAN cities and urban areas. Our experience in the management of housing estates, the development of parks and green areas represents key planning experiences which can be shared with mayors of large cities in ASEAN. CEOs of major companies based in Singapore were asked in 2012 about key features of a liveable and sustainable city and whether Singapore has met such features. The City Development President mentioned the development of green buildings, the MD of Panasonic Asia Pacific mentioned partnering the government to build an eco new town that leads the way with energy solutions, and the managing partner of KPMG mentioned recycling and water conservation. In terms of information technology, the VP of the Enterprise Group highlighted having micro sensors and smart meters to enable utilities companies to maximize efficient resource usage while the country president of Schnieder Electric mentioned software which results in smart homes and buildings (*Business Times*, 18 June 2012). Singapore's Centre for Livable Cities set up in 2008 can play an important role in researching and discussing urban solutions and disseminating such information.

A related facet of Singapore's global city status is its well-developed arts infrastructure, a result of the government growing a set of amenities associated with its global city status (Chang 2000). Its development as a city for the arts has resulted in strong infrastructure, well-known arts events calendar, but because of its small size, an under-developed layer of arts talent. This situation makes Singapore an attractive venue for the performers in the region. And with the development of schools of music and the performing arts, Singapore may become an emerging destination for the training of such new talent in ASEAN.

6 Singapore's involvement in East Asia (China, Japan, South Korea)

We live in a time where the region is being intermittently placed under threat of communicable diseases. The ASEAN plus Three countries represent an important way forward for cooperation on communicable and infectious diseases.[2] As infection knows no boundaries, the development of a regional platform for information sharing and field epidemiology training are vital. Singapore's expertise in combating infectious diseases can certainly play an important role. This potential contribution is best captured by Philippe Huinck, the Regional Managing Director of International SOS, who had this to say in a 2012 interview:

> The real test for a highly urbanized and densely populated city like Singapore is healthcare infrastructure, particular when an epidemic hits ... the government's ongoing drive to make Singapore a multi-faceted regional medical hub has been key in developing a strong healthcare infrastructure that provides state-of-the-art services to patients along with training, research and collaboration opportunities for medical professionals.
>
> (*Business Times*, 18 June 2012)

The second and perhaps more important point is Singapore's economic engagement with ASEAN, East Asia and beyond. On this note, a 2014 opinion piece by Singapore's Ambassador-at-Large and former permanent secretary at the Ministry of Foreign Affairs, Bilahari Kausikan, noted that 'the important decisions are going to be made in Washington and Beijing, not in ASEAN capital or even in Tokyo, New Delhi, Seoul or Canberra. Still it is better to play even such a secondary role than just be a helpless spectator. Whether ASEAN can continue to play even such a role depends on whether it can remain relatively neutral and that in turn depends on the future of its integration project, particularly economic integration.' And to this end, Singapore, as a small city state, has placed more importance and perhaps invested more of its energies in this endeavour. At the time of this publication, two important areas are worth repeating. The first is Singapore's offer to host the ASEAN-plus-three Marcoeconomic Research Office (AMRO) created to operate a $120 billion currency sway scheme with the objective of managing future regional financial crises. AMRO has similar functions to the International Monetary Fund (IMF), in activities such as the monitoring and providing short-term liquidity to countries experiencing financial difficulties. Iwan Aziz, head of the Asian Development Bank's office of regional economic integration was reported as saying 'The day AMRO is in operation, to me, the Asian Monetary Fund is born' (Kyodo, 4 May 2011). The second major area of economic cooperation, one which was highlighted by Prime Minister Lee as a good example of inter-country economic ties is the Regional Comprehensive Economic Partnership (RCEP), a free trade pact the ASEAN 10 are negotiating with six partners – Australia, China, India, Japan, New Zealand and South Korea. The RCEP will incorporate almost half the world's population and about a third of its gross domestic product (*Straits Times*, 11 October 2013).

It should also be noted that Singapore's emphasis on regional economic integration does not imply that it is committed to an exclusive regional economic bloc. Thus, at the 2013 ASEAN plus Three summit, Prime Minister Lee called for the partnership between ASEAN and China, Japan and South Korea to be strengthened but also argued that it must stay connected to the rest of the world. He was quoted as saying 'stability and growth depends on us being open to other regions and organizations' (*Straits Times*, 11 October 2013). This openness to the rest of the world has been a hallmark of Singapore's economic position in ASEAN, primarily because as noted by Rau (1981, 107) 'the city-state needs access to markets'.

And on the role of AMRO, although some partner countries have a negative view of the IMF because of the treatment they received from IMF in the 1997 financial crisis and saw AMRO as a way to reduce the dependence of the region on IMF (Kyodo, 4 May 2011), Prime Minister Lee was clear in seeing AMRO as strengthening relations with IMF including combining regional resources with that of the IMF's in times of a financial crisis (*Straits Times*, 10 October 2013). The position of developing economic ties with different regions in the world served Singapore well in the 1997 financial crisis when it was able to leverage its economic ties outside of the region to weather the crisis (Ho 2003, 433–434).

7 Conclusion

The main point developed in the chapter is that each member state has both common and unique contributions to the ASEAN community. In the case of Singapore, its unique role as the only ASEAN member that is a city state, along with its socio-economic and political development, has resulted in Singapore being a planned city and a hub for education, research and development, arts and culture. This suggests that its primary role has meant that Singapore can contribute to the ASEAN through dissemination of planning, health practices, environmental technologies, and as a venue for education and training.

While the chapter does not deal with the two other pillars, the Political-Security Community Pillar as well as the Economic Community Pillar in any great detail, the last section should at least suggest the ways in which Singapore can contribute in these two spheres. Perhaps on the Political-Security Pillar, Singapore will support many of the issues and will let the larger member states take the lead on fostering peace and security in the region. And on the Economic Pillar, Singapore is likely to push for free flows of goods, services, investment and capital since these are likely to be flows that sustain a global city. Its investment in member states as well as direct cooperation in the growth triangle allow for confidence in working with member states on cooperative projects.

The ASEAN story is never completed. As the potentials and problems which are part and parcel of the global age we live in encompasses regions rather than single countries, ASEAN will have to continue to exploit potentials and manage problems. Climate change, terrorism, the increasing economic volatility of the world order, along with the spread of infectious disease are going to dominate the agenda of ASEAN. ASEAN can look to its list of impressive achievements – the institutions which have been built, the infrastructure laid, and the policies and agreements already in place – to provide the confidence that it can tackle these issues.

Notes

1 *Straits Times*, 2012, 'Singapore will do more for foreign workers: Minister', 19 December.
2 www.asean.org/?static_post=asean-plus-three-cooperation-2, accessed 1 May 2016 (see point 30).

References

Acharya, A. (1997) 'Ideas, Identity and Institution-building: From the ASEAN Way to the "Asia-Pacific Way"?' *The Pacific Review* 10(3): 319–346.

Bernama Daily Malaysian News (2005) 'PM Lee Unveils Budget Aimed at Remaking Singapore', 18 February.

Buchanan, I. (1972) *Singapore in Southeast Asia*. London: Bell and Sons.

Business Times (2012) 'Living in the City', 18 June.

Chang, T.C. (2000) 'Renaissance Revisited: Singapore as a Global City for the Arts'. *International Journal of Urban and Regional Research* 24(4): 818–831.

Channel NewsAsia (2013) 'ASEAN to Build Strong Foundation Ties with China, Japan and S Korea', 10 October.

Cheung, P. (1994) 'Educational Development and Manpower Planning in Singapore'. *CUHK Education Journal* 21(2)–22(1): 185–195.

Chiu, S., Ho, K.C. and T.L. Lui (2012) 'Reforming Health: Contrasting Trajectories of Neoliberal Restructuring in the City-States'. In *Locating Neoliberalism in East Asia: Neoliberalizing Spaces in Developmental States*, edited by B.G. Park, R.C. Hill and A. Saito. Chichester: Wiley-Blackwell, pp. 225–256.

Dicken, P. and C. Kirpatrick (1991) 'Services-led Development in ASEAN: Transnational Regional Headquarters in Singapore'. *Pacific Review* 4(2): 174–184

Gamer, R. (1972) *The Politics of Urban Development in Singapore*, Ithaca, NY: Cornell University Press.

Goh, C.B. and S. Gopinathan (2006) 'The Development of Education in Singapore Since 1965'. Paper prepared for the Asia Education Study Tour for African Policy Makers. Available from http://siteresources.worldbank.org/EDUCATION/Resour ces/278200–1121703274255/1439264–1153425508901/Development_Edu_Singapore _draft.pdf (accessed 15 April 2011).

Gopinathan, S. (1999) 'Preparing for the Next Rung: Economic Restructuring and Education Reform in Singapore'. *Journal of Education and Work* 12(3): 295–308.

Hage, G. (1996) 'The Spatial Imaginary of National Practices: Dwelling-Domesticating/ Being-Exterminating' *Environment and Planning D: Society and Space* 14(4): 463–485.

Hassan, Riaz (1976) 'Public housing'. In *Singapore: Society in Transition*, edited by Riaz Hassan. Kuala Lumpur, Malaysia: Oxford University Press, pp 240–268.

Ho, K.L. (2000) 'Citizen Participation and Policy Making in Singapore: Conditions and Predicaments'. *Asian Survey* 40(3): 436–455.

Ho, K.C. (1993) 'Issues on Industrialization and Urban in Literature: Public Housing in Singapore'. In *Malaysia and Singapore: Issues in Industrialization and Urban Development*, edited by B.H. Lee and K.S.S. Oorjitham. Kuala Lumpur: University of Malaya Press, pp. 369–392.

Ho, K.C. (2003) 'Attracting and Retaining Investments in Uncertain Times', *Urban Studies* 40(2): 421–438.

Ho, K.C. (2009) 'Competitive Urban Economic Policies in Global Cities: Shanghai Through the Lens of Singapore'. In *Shanghai Rising: State Power and Local Transformations in a Global Megacity*, edited by X.M. Chen, Minneapolis: University of Minnesota Press, pp. 73–91.

Ho, K.C. (2011) 'Arrested Agglomeration: The Spilling Out of Singapore's Economic Activities into the Surrounding Sub-region', *Seoul Journal of Economics* 24(2): 151–170.

Katzenstein, P.J. (1985) *Small States in World Markets*. Ithaca, NY: Cornell University Press.

Kurus, B. (1993) 'Understanding ASEAN: Benefits and Raison d'Etre'. *Asian Survey* 33(8): 819–831.

Kyodo News (2011) 'New E. Asian Financial Body Expected to be Asian IMF',' 4 May.

Law, S.S. (1996) 'Dynamics and Challenges of a Vocation Training System – The Singapore Experience' (ITE Paper No. 2). Singapore: Institute of Technical Education. Available from: www.ite.edu.sg/about_ite/ITE_Conference_Papers/Dynamics%20and%20Challenges%20in%20Vocational%20Education%20and%20Training%20-%20The%20Singapore%20Experience.pdf (accessed 1 May 2016).

Lee, E. (1989) 'The Colonial Legacy'. In *Management of Success: The Moulding of Modern Singapore*, edited by K.S. Sandhu and P. Wheatley, Singapore: Institute of Southeast Asian Studies, pp. 3–50.

Lim, C.H.V. (1979) 'A History of Tourism in Singapore 1950–1977'. Unpublished academic exercise, University of Singapore.

Lyon, L. (2005) 'Workers Count Too? The Intersection of Citizenship and Gender in Singapore's Civil Society'. *Sojourn* 20(2): 208–248.

Milne, R.S. (1966) 'Singapore's Exit from Malaysia: the Consequences of Ambiguity'. *Asian Survey* 6(3): 175–184.

Nuemann, I.B. and S. Gstöhl (2004) 'Lilliputians in Gulliver's World? Small States in International Relations'. Centre for Small States Studies, Working Paper 1–2004.

Olds, K. and N. Thrift (2005) 'Assembling the "Global Schoolhouse" in Pacific Asia: The Case of Singapore'. In *Service Industries, Cities and Development Trajectories in the Asia-Pacific*, edited by P.W. Daniels, K.C. Ho, and T.A. Hutton. London: Routledge, pp. 199–215.

Ong, C.C. (1975) 'The 1959 Singapore General Election.' *Journal of Southeast Asian Studies*, 6(1): 61–86.

Pang, Eng Fong and S. Yeh (1973) 'Housing Employment and National Development: The Singapore Experience'. *Asia* 31: 8–31.

Parmer, N.J. (1966) 'Malaysia 1965: Challenging the Terms of 1957'. *Asian Survey* 6(2): 111–118.

Pearce, D.G. (1997) 'Competitive Destination Analysis in Southeast Asia'. *Journal of Travel Research*, 35(4): 16–24.

Perry, M. (1992) 'Promoting Corporate Control in Singapore'. *Regional Studies* 26(3): 289–294.

Rau, R.L. (1981) 'The Role of Singapore in ASEAN. *Contemporary Southeast Asia* 3(2): 99–112.

Reuters (2012) 'FACTBOX-Transparency International's Global Corruption Index,' 5 December.

Rimmer, P. (1996) 'International Transport and Communications Interactions between Pacific Asia's Emerging World Cities.' In *Emerging World Cities in Pacific Asia*, edited by F.C. Lo and Y.M. Yeung. Tokyo: UN Press, pp. 48–97.

Sam, C.Y. (2005) 'Singapore's Experience in Curbing Corruption and the Growth of the Underground Economy'. *Sojourn* 20(1): 39–66.

Saul, S.B. (1982 'The Economic Development of Small Nations: The Experience of North West Europe in the Nineteenth Century',' in *Economics in the Long View*, edited by C.P. Kindleberger and G. Tella. London: MacMillan, pp. 111–131.

Seah, Chee-Meow. 1976. 'The Singapore Bureaucracy and the Issues of Transition', in *Singapore: Society in Transition*, edited by Riaz Hassan. Kuala Lumpur, Malaysia: Oxford University Press, pp. 52–66.

Sidhu, Ravinder, K.C. Ho, Brenda S.A. Yeoh (2014) 'Singapore: Building a Knowledge and Education Hub', in *International Education Hubs: Student, Talent, and Knowledge-Innovation Models*, edited by Jane Knight. Dordrecht: Springer, pp. 121–143.

Stockwell, A.J. (1986) 'British Imperial Strategy and Decolonisation in Southeast Asia 1947–1957,' in *Britain and Southeast Asia*, edited by D.K. Bassett and V.T. King, 79–90. Centre for Southeast Asian Studies Occasional Paper No. 13. Hull: University of Hull.

Straits Times (1990) 'Batam: Growth has Taken Root', 18 November.

Straits Times (2002) 'Singapore is the Sum of Our Dreams, Our Fears, Our Sweat', 19 August.

Straits Times (2004) 'The Difference PM Goh Made', 18 July.

Straits Times (2005) 'Corporate Governance, Singapore Style', 15 December.

Straits Times (2011) 'GE: "We hear all your voices", says PM Lee', 8 May.

Straits Times (2011) 'No Longer Politics as Usual', 22 May.

Straits Times (2011) 'The Water Story', 3 September.

Straits Times (2012) 'Govt Seeks to Forge Stronger Ties among Citizens, and with Them', 1 August.

Straits Times (2012) 'S'pore Conversation to Involve Thousands', 9 September.

Straits Times (2012) 'Framing the Singapore Conversation', 15 September.

Straits Times (2013) 'Foreign Workers: No Further Plans to Tighten Policy', 19 April.

Straits Times (2013) 'Asia Cooperation Will Help East Asia Thrive: PM', 11 October.

Straits Times (2014) 'Opinion: The Idea of Asia', Bilahari Kausikan, 8 November.

Tan, J. (2001) 'Education and Colonial Transition in Singapore and Hong Kong: Comparisons and Contrasts,' in *Education and Political Transition: Implications of Hong Kong's Change of Sovereignty*, edited by M. Bray and W.O. Lee, Comparative Education Centre (CERC), The University of Hong Kong, pp. 157–166.

Tan, K.P. (2012) 'Singapore in 2011: A "New Normal" in Politics?' *Asian Survey* 52(1): 220–226.

Today (2012) 'MOM "Making Things Better" for Foreign Workers: Ministry Taking Enforcement Action in Wage Disputes, Relocating Workers to "Acceptable Accommodation"', 19 December.

Today (2012) 'MOM Mulls New Body to Tackle Workplace Disputes', 5 February.

Turnbull, C. Mary (1969) 'Constitutional Development 1819–1968',' in *Modern Singapore*, edited by Jin-Bee Ooi and Hai-Ding Chiang. Singapore: Singapore University Press, pp. 181–196.

Velayutham, S. (2004) 'Affect, Materiality, and the Gift of Social Life in Singapore', *Sojourn* 19(1): 1–27.

Wee, Vivienne (1987) 'The Ups and Downs of Women's Status in Singapore: A Chronology of Some Landmark Events (1950–1987)'. *Commentary* 7: 5–12.

Wong, L.K. (1960) 'The Trade of Singapore 1819–1869',' *Journal of the Malayan Branch of the Royal Asiatic Society* 33 [192, part 4]: 1–315.

9 Thailand

Political, economic, and social development towards a closer community[1]

Pinn Siraprapasiri

1 Introduction

Thailand, previously known as Siam, is among the five founding members of the Association of Southeast Asian Nations (ASEAN) and has played key roles in fostering closer cooperation within East Asian region. This chapter will assess Thailand's contribution to the development and success of regional cooperation such as ASEAN and ASEAN Plus Three (APT). The second section introduces Thailand's historical accounts, particularly Thailand's political, economic, and social identities and development. The third section discusses Thailand's current settings. The fourth section explores Thailand's involvement in regional organizations such as the Indonesia–Malaysia–Thailand Growth Triangle (IMT-GT) and the Greater Mekong Subregion (GMS). The fifth section analyzes Thailand's contribution to ASEAN's Political-Security, Economic, and Socio-Cultural Communities. Thesixth section goes beyond ASEAN to explore the APT arrangements which started after the 1997 Asian Financial Crisis that had crippled many countries in the region and forced policymakers and practitioners in the financial world to reassess the liberalized approach to economic development. The last section provides a conclusion to Thailand's overall relation and contribution to ASEAN and APT with an analysis of the country's key strengths and challenges. It is through a better understanding of national development and differences and similarities among ASEAN and APT member countries, that a closer community can be achieved.

2 Thailand's political, economic, and social identities and development

Thailand is strategically situated at the heart of the Southeast Asia region. It borders Myanmar, Laos, Cambodia, and Malaysia, with access to the sea through Andaman Sea on the west and the Gulf of Thailand on the east. Thailand has a total area of 513,115 square kilometers with a population of approximately 64.78 million people in 2013 according to the Official Statistics Registration Systems, with over 8.5 million now residing in Bangkok, the capital city. Apart from Bangkok, Thailand's most populated provinces include Chiang Mai and Chiang Rai in the North, Nakornratchasima,

Udonthani, Ubonratchathani, and Khon Kaen in the Northeast, Chonburi in the East, and Nakornsrithammarat and Suratthani in the South (Department of Provincial Administration 2013).

The geographical location of Thailand renders it the center of political, security, economic, and cultural concerns. Tracing back to the colonial period of the nineteeth century where France and Britain were dominant Western powers in the Southeast Asian region, Thailand served as a buffer state, with British India on the west in Myanmar and French Indochina on the east in Cambodia, Laos, and Vietnam. Its political significance could not be overlooked. In July 1893 the French and the British agreed that it was necessary to have a neutral zone between their possessions. An agreement was reached between the two Western powers in 1896 which guaranteed the "inviolability of Chao Phraya River basin" (Chandran 1977). King Chulalongkorn's scheme for state reform and diplomatic skills led Thailand to be the only country in Southeast Asia that had never been colonized by the Western powers.

Thailand's contemporary political, economic, and social history is said to begin during King Chulalongkorn's reign. During his time, the country was shifting towards a "Modern State" through the implementation of a state reform which laid out the foundation for the country's later development. A series of government centralization policies with the introduction of ministries, a civil service system with remuneration, and provincial administrations was introduced. A taxation system was also established during the reform with the creation of the Revenue Department to streamline the tax collection. Moreover, there was a reform of the legal and court system which saw the establishment of the Ministry of Justice that brought about the centralization of all Courts of Justice in 1892. On the security front, a modern military system that replicated a Western system was adopted and state boundary demarcation was undertaken (Baker and Phongpaichit 2005).

During the nineteenth and the first half of the twentieth century, not only was the international environment not conducive for regional collaboration, situations in Thailand were also not stable enough for the government to take on regional initiatives. Thailand was undergoing constant political turmoil after having peacefully switched to democracy in 1932 during the reign of King Prajathipok. The country experienced a long and troubled transition period, with power grabbing, coup d'état,[2] and political and social divisions. Even after the Second World War, communication with neighboring countries was still limited as Thailand made an alliance with the United States to discourage communist infiltration.

Thailand's foreign policy during the 1950s up until the time of the inception of ASEAN in 1967 and well into the 1970s with the fall of the Indochina neighbors to Communism can be seen as a result of a political discourse on the Southeast Asian Mainland and external powers. Under the government of Field Marshal Thanom Kittikachorn, Thailand had allied itself more with the United States and the Southeast Asia Treaty Organization (SEATO), an international organization for collective defense in Southeast Asia created by the 1954 Southeast Asia Collective Defense Treaty, or the Manila Pact. Financial aid geared toward the military complex from the US government was mounting during the Vietnam War, with a record high for military aid of US$123 million in 1969 (Baker and Phongpaichit 2005).

A shift in the country's foreign policy came about after a push toward a true democracy was materialized in the "October 1973 Uprising" that brought an end to Field Marshal Thanom Kittikachorn's military regime. With a civilian government in a more democratic setting, Thailand began to reach out to its neighboring countries for better relations. Under the leadership of Mom Rajawongse Kukrit Pramoj (1975–1976) Thailand's foreign policy shifted from "Pro-West" to becoming friends with all countries regardless of their political ideologies. The practice of non-interference in internal affairs of other countries helped Thailand to establish diplomatic relations with China in 1975, at the peak of the Cold War in the Southeast Asian region.

3 Political, economic, and social settings

Thailand's government is a constitutional monarchy with His Majesty King Bhumibol Adulyadej, the ninth king of the Royal House of Chakri, as the Head of State, who delegates the people's power to the three separate branches of government: the executive, the legislative, and the judiciary. The executive branch is headed by the Prime Minister and the cabinet. The legislative power is vested in the Parliament and exercised through a bicameral National Assembly consisting of the House of Representatives and the Senate. According to the latest Constitution (B.E. 2554), the House of Representatives consists of 500 members serving four-year terms. Out of 500 members of the House of Representatives, 375 are directly elected by eligible voters. The other 125 members are from a party list election, representing different political parties in accordance with the proportional popular votes each party receives (Thai National Assembly 2013). The Senate consists of 150 members – 77 elected members, one from each of the 77 provinces, and 73 appointed members (Thai National Assembly 2013). Judicial power is exercised through courts: the Court of First Instance, the Court of Appeal, and the Supreme Court. As the country is in the process of writing a new constitution, some of these provisions may be altered; the fundamental principle, however, can be expected to remain the same.

Thailand in contemporary times has undergone a number of phenomenal waves. The first wave is the abolition of slavery which was initiated by King Chulalongkorn in 1874. This is considered to be a major shift in Thai society for it completely overhauled the entire social and economic structure of the country for the better. Political, economic, and social power previously held exclusively by the ruling classes was being redistributed among the people. Unlike the abrupt abolition of slavery in many countries around the world, the process in Thailand was carefully planned and gradually carried out. It began with the prohibition on entering anyone born in 1897 onwards into the slavery system. Eventually, slavery was abolished entirely in 1912.

The second wave that hit Thailand came from outside the country. The Great Depression that started in the United States in October 1929 seriously affected Thailand's economy. The economic downturn played a big role in fueling a movement toward democracy among the young, foreign-educated Thais called "Khana Ratsadorn" or "The People." The form of government was changed peacefully from an absolute monarchy to a constitutional monarchy on June 24, 1932, when King Prajathipok handed Khana Ratsadorn the power to design Thailand's democratic regime. Phraya[3] Manopakorn Nititada, a lawyer, became the first Prime Minister of Thailand. The road toward democracy, however, quickly ran into obstacles with a coup in April 1933, then again in June of the same year, signifying a problematic power-sharing structure of the country.

Eight decades later, Thailand is still not without political problems. From 1932 to 2014, the country has had 29 Prime Ministers and 18 constitutions, and has continually faced discontent that disrupts political development. One of the impediments to Thai political development and political stability is military interference, notably by staging a coup or asserting influence in the political arena through various channels. Reasons cited for such acts include to preserve democracy, to eliminate corruption, or to mediate conflicts (McCargo 2005, 2006).

Frustration with regard to the share in political power and misconduct by those in power have led to a number of movements and protests. The first of the major protests took place in October 1973, or often called "October 14 Incident," in which more than 500,000 people, led by university students, protested against Field Marshal Thanom Kittikachorn, Prime Minister, claiming him to be a corrupt military dictator. The incident ended with the Prime Minister stepping down, and Sanya Thammasak, then Rector of Thammasat University, appointed as civilian Prime Minister. A new constitution was written and an election was scheduled for January 1975. For a very short period of time democracy seemed to triumph. The root cause of the political problems, however, was not solved in this incident. The political condition in Thailand was further complicated with the fear of communist infiltration as its neighboring countries were won over by communism. In 1976, the "October 6 Incident" in which many young lives were lost took place. Many student activists and union leaders went underground, some joined communist insurgents fighting in various parts of the country. The communist problems became the country's foremost concern and justified the military's presence in government and politics. When General Prem Tinsulanonda became Prime Minister in 1980, he issued the Prime Minister's Order 66/2523, adopting "Pro-politics Military" scheme as a strategy to fight the Communist Terrorists Regime (The Prime Minister's Office 1980). The policy proved to be successful as it could gradually win over communist sympathizers leading to the dissolution of the Communist Party of Thailand.

After Prime Minister Prem Tinsulanonda left office in 1988, the country soon witnessed more waves of political turmoil as evidenced by the coup of 1991 and the Black May Incident in 1992. It was thought that the 1992 coup would be the last one since the Black May Incident brought about a major political reform which overhauled the Thai political system (McCargo 2006). A new constitution known as the "People's Constitution," drafted by representatives elected by the people, and nominees by academic institutions, was promulgated in 1997. To correct the flaws in the political system in the past, this Constitution sought to give the people more power to protect their rights and greater opportunity to participate in the political process, and to set up stronger political parties. There are provisions that aim to protect and promote human rights and religious freedom, and provisions that establish the Election Commission, the Inspectors of State Affairs of Parliament, the National Human Rights Commission, and the National Counter-Corruption Commission, hoping to make political institutions more transparent.

The 2001 election, the first held under the 1997 Constitution, led to an elected government with a strong majority. Prime Minister Thaksin Shinawatra initiated a number of populist schemes which had an immense impact on Thai political system as they created a new middle class through a process of de-agrarianization and de-peasantization (Satitniramai and Mukdawijitra 2013; Thabchumphon and McCargo 2011; and Walker 2012). However, as the government grew stronger, Thaksin was increasingly accused of corruption and authoritarianism, among many other charges. The society was split into Thaksin's supporters and the People's Alliance for Democracy, or the Yellow Shirt. There were clashes between the two groups and finally in September 2006, a military junta led by General Sonthi Boonyaratglin, the army's commander-in-chief, ousted Thaksin while he was abroad and took control of the government. In 2011, Thaksin's sister, Yingluck Shinawatra won the election and became Prime Minister. People were once again divided, and a real crisis began when Yingluck's government tried to pass an Amnesty Bill which triggered a protest by those who perceived it to benefit certain individuals and thus was not an effective means to bring about a true reconciliation among the people having different political views. This led Prime Minister Yingluck to dissolve the parliament in December 2013. After six months of peaceful protests, violence started. On May 22, 2014, General Prayuth Chan-ocha, the army's commander-in-chief, launched a coup d'état against Yingluck's caretaker government with the hope to overhaul the entire political, economic, and social system. Evidently, the root of the conflicts is so deep and so grave that it cannot be removed simply by a general election or a constitutional amendment.

The fourth big wave that has tremendously changed the landscape of Thailand's economy and led the country to become more closely tied with its neighbors is the 1997 Asian Financial Crisis. Following the Washington

Consensus on trade and financial liberalization, Thailand was, however, unprepared to devise an effective surveillance mechanism and a strong enough safety net to keep Thailand's economy as a whole above water in case of economic or financial mishaps. Thailand was not equipped with necessary and effective tools to regulate capital flows, and thus was unable to detect signs of financial catastrophe which threw millions out of work and caused dozens of financial companies to collapse with a colossal amount of non-performing loans. Short-term debt problems were magnified when the Bank of Thailand announced a change in the exchange system from a fixed exchange rate system to a managed floating rate system in July 1997. The Thai baht before the crisis was fixed at 25 baht per 1 US dollar; after the shift, it went down to about 50 baht per 1 US dollar.[4] In retrospect, the 1997 financial crisis has brought ASEAN countries closer together and led to stronger ties with China, Japan, and South Korea and the establishment of ASEAN Plus Three (APT). These led to initiatives such as Chiang Mai Initiative (CMI), Economic Review and Policy Dialogue (ERPD), and Asian Bond Markets Initiative (ABMI) that aim to create economic and financial stability in the region.

The above-mentioned waves are a few key events that have led to changes in Thailand's political, economic, and social systems. There are also other ripples that demand attention or policy adjustments during the course of Thailand's development and integration with other countries.

4 Regional engagement

On August 8, 1967, Thanat Khoman, Thailand's Foreign Affairs Minister under Field Marshal Thanom Kittikachorn's government, signed the Bangkok Declaration that established the Association of Southeast Asian Nations (ASEAN). Thailand is considered not only as one of the founders of ASEAN but also its home. It was during the height of political instability in the region and confrontation with communism that the five founding members namely Indonesia, Malaysia, the Philippines, Singapore, and Thailand, pledged to promote a better understanding and closer political, economic, and social ties among them.[5]

Altogether, the Bangkok Declaration is a step forward from other existing regional inter-state organizations such as the Association of Southeast Asia (ASA), established in 1961 among Malaysia, the Philippines, and Thailand, and MAPHILINDO, established in 1963, among three Malay-speaking countries, namely, Malaysia, the Philippines, and Indonesia, aiming at uniting Malay people separated by the geographical setting of the countries. Given the organizations of which Thailand was a member during the height of the Cold War, it can be argued that Thailand's involvement in regional affairs has partially been influenced by external actors, such as the United States and multilateral organizations such as the United Nations, rather than purely by its own initiative. The decision to join an organization was calculated not only on the basis of benefit that could be reaped from such an organization, but also on the speculation of negative externalities and the danger of not joining.

ASEAN in its early years suffered from member countries' domestic instability as well as infiltration from major powers that used the region as a chess board like in the Vietnam War. Thailand was no exception. From one military-ruled government to another, Thailand was so preoccupied with its domestic politics that there were no concrete policies toward ASEAN.

Despite the gloomy setting, ASEAN members managed to push through a seven-day free visa system for ASEAN members by the end of 1968. To keep the engine going, in 1969, it was agreed that each capital was to host a committee. Jakarta took food production and supply. Singapore took care of civil air transport. Manila looked after commerce and industry. Kuala Lumpur was responsible for meteorology. Bangkok took charge of shipping (Hagiwara 1973).

It was not until after the end of the Cold War that Thailand as well as other Southeast Asian countries were perceived to be joining an organization for the sake of economic benefit with less international politics involved. In 1993, a sub-regional economic cooperation was established among Indonesia, Malaysia, and Thailand. The leaders of the three countries saw an opportunity to reduce transaction costs through a joint effort for technology transfer and a better infrastructure connection, and decided to create the Indonesia-Malaysia-Thailand Growth Triangle Development Project (IMT-GT). Since its formation, the IMT-GT has grown in geographic scope and activities to encompass more than 70 million people. It is now seeing the development of 14 provinces in southern Thailand, eight states of Peninsular Malaysia, and 10 provinces of Sumatra in Indonesia. Through the IMT-GT, the three countries can improve their economic and social settings, promote sharing of economic resources, such as labor, capital, and natural resources, and promote technology transfer, investment, and co-production to become more competitive in the world market. To achieve the objectives, non-tariff barriers are reduced, a single declaration form introduced, a single inspection policy enforced, and information regarding border issues shared among the three countries.

Thailand is also an active member in the Greater Mekong Subregion (GMS) that is sponsored by the Asian Development Bank (ADB). This cooperation was established in 1992 among the six Mekong River riparian countries, namely, Cambodia, China, Laos, Myanmar, Thailand, and Vietnam. The main objective of the GMS is to strengthen sub-regional connectivity which will lead to stronger communities. A major achievement of the GMS Program is improved transport connectivity in the sub-region as exemplified in the main GMS economic corridors: the East–West, the North–South, and the Southern. In the energy sector, the GMS Program has helped lay the basis for grid interconnection in the sub-region. A number of major hydropower projects with private sector participation were developed under the program framework (Asian Development Bank 2013).

However, both opportunities and challenges are present for the GMS cooperation. While the arrangement promotes close economic ties, it has left out the sensitive issue of water usage and the dam constructions on the Mekong River. Disputes among the upstream and downstream countries regarding the dams have become more serious as the riparian states revive their plans to build hydroelectric dams on the river's mainstream (International Rivers 2013). Negative impacts such as declining fisheries, low water level, and changing natural borders have been felt downstream. While there exists the Mekong River Commission (MRC), established in 1995 to handle development projects of the Mekong River (Mekong River Commission 2013), with only the lower riparian countries as members, and China and Myanmar as dialogue partners, little has been done to establish a mechanism to safeguard the river.

Apart from collaboration at the sub-regional level, Thailand has also been an active member of many inter-regional collaborations. In 1994, Thailand hosted the first ASEAN Regional Forum (ARF) with the objectives to foster constructive dialogue and consultation on political and security issues of common interest and concern; and to make significant contributions to efforts toward confidence-building and preventive diplomacy in the Asia-Pacific region (ASEAN Regional Forum 2013). It also plays a crucial role in the Asia-Europe Meeting (ASEM), an informal process of dialogue and cooperation of the European Union member states, two European countries, and the European Commission with 20 Asian countries and the ASEAN Secretariat, which was first held in Bangkok in 1996 (Asia-Europe Meeting 2013). In 2012, the Tenth ASEM Finance Ministers' Meeting was held in Thailand with the theme "Strengthening a Dynamic Partnership, Sharing a Dynamic Growth" (Asia-Europe Meeting 2013). The aims were to learn from the EU's experience and find a mechanism to prevent the financial crisis, and to stimulate growth in Asia, Europe, and other parts of the world. It can be said that ASEM carries much of ASEAN's spirit in that it is informal and multidimensional in nature and it also aims to foster people-to-people connections for a better understanding among the peoples.

In summary, Thailand has been involved in many sub-regional collaborations and is an active member when it comes to inter-regional collaborations. During the Cold War, however, the focus was mostly either within the country or on the communist threat. It was not until the end of the Cold War that Thailand was able to openly and constructively interact with its neighboring countries in all dimensions.

5 Thailand and ASEAN

In a speech made by Abhisit Vejjajiva, then Prime Minister of Thailand, to commemorate the 42nd anniversary of ASEAN on August 8, 2009, he viewed

ASEAN as a strong and growing regional arrangement among member countries that has changed from what critics used to comment on as a talk shop to a forum with concrete agreements, implementations, and results. ASEAN now has representatives not only from the parliaments, but also from civil society organizations that together better represent the ASEAN peoples.[6] He envisaged a community where the rights of ASEAN citizens will be respected; their needs attended to; and their future filled with peace and prosperity. Given the political, economic, and social development of Thailand and the regional context, the following sections will explore Thailand's role and contribution toward the ASEAN Community.

5.1 *Thailand and ASEAN Political-Security Community*

Countries in the Southeast Asian region were divided during the Cold War and many were struggling to find their own balance in terms of political and security dimensions. Nevertheless, attempts to reunite them in the political-security aspect were evident. On November 27, 1971, in Kuala Lumpur, Malaysia, the five founding members of ASEAN signed the Zone of Peace, Freedom, and Neutrality Declaration (ZOPFAN). The main purpose of ZOPFAN was to keep the region free from interference by external powers and to create a sense of collective security, for they believed that once security was established, there would be a spill-over effect over other areas of cooperation. It is considered to be ASEAN's first attempt to draw normative boundaries vis-à-vis major powers (Ba 2010). However, due to the conflict between Cambodia and Vietnam and an incident that involved Thailand, ASEAN became a "party to the Sino-Soviet conflict" (Hänggi 1991), and thus the objective was compromised.

As the war in Vietnam was coming to an end, and communist victories were spreading in Indochina, the domino effect was becoming more real for Southeast Asia and this invited interventions by super powers. Mom Rajawongse Kukrit Pramoj, Thailand's Prime Minister, proposed a way to stay clear from falling victim of either camp. In 1976, ASEAN attempted to create a regional political and security order by introducing the Treaty of Amity and Cooperation (TAC)[7] that established ground rules for conducting international relations among the five countries as well as their partner countries. The Treaty has now been signed by many countries outside ASEAN including China, Japan, South Korea, India, Russia, the United States, and the European Union.

At the fifth ASEAN Summit held in Bangkok in 1995, ASEAN members took a step forward in signing the "Southeast Asian Nuclear Weapon-Free Zone Treaty". Among the key obligations are for ASEAN members "not to develop, manufacture or otherwise acquire, possess or have control over nuclear weapons or test or use nuclear weapons anywhere inside or outside the treaty zone" (Nuclear Threat Initiative 2013). The region, however, faced one obstacle to attain a nuclear weapon-free zone, that is, none of the nuclear powers – the United States, the United Kingdom, France, China, and Russia – was willing to sign the Protocol that vows to respect the Treaty. The nuclear powers are against the unclear Protocol and the inclusion of continental shelves and EEZ and the "restriction on the passage of nuclear-powered ships through the zone vis-à-vis the issue of the high seas as embodied in the UN Convention on the Law of the Sea (UNCLOS)" (Nuclear Threat Initiative 2013). It became apparent that ASEAN would have to tidy up its treaties and organizational structures to secure external players' partnership, especially in the political-security dimension.

Another initiative which Thailand has supported is an international peace mediation workshop which was recently organized by the European Commission (EC) and the Crisis Management Initiative (CMI) in Jakarta to promote cooperation between ASEAN and the European Union (EU) on conflict mediation and prevention in the region. During the Cold War, it was clear that ASEAN lacked an effective tool to manage interstate disputes and civil conflicts. While critics cite the ASEAN Way and the non-interference norm to be the causes of ineffective conflict management, or the lack thereof, it can also be explained through the lack of experience and guidance in such areas. In November 2012, with the help of the EU, ASEAN set up the ASEAN Institute for Peace and Reconciliation (AIPR) in Indonesia (EU-Asia Center 2013). Among the key questions that emerged was how to promote ASEAN as an effective vehicle for peace mediation. The EU has been responsible for a number of initiatives to strengthen its mediation and dialogue capacities in this field, and ASEAN is now taking steps to model itself on best practices from other regions in order to develop itself as a leader in peace building.

The ASEAN Political-Security Community (APSC) blueprint provides a number of recommendations for conflict management put forward by the regional grouping. The blueprint envisages three characteristics. The first characteristic aims for a rule-based community of shared values and norms. The second one envisages a cohesive, peaceful, stable and resilient region with shared responsibility for a comprehensive state of security. The third one aims for a dynamic and outward-looking region in an increasingly integrated and interdependent world. The blueprint outlines ASEAN's commitment to conflict prevention, preventive diplomacy, and post-conflict peace building. It also provides an action plan to achieve targets in these areas through research, cooperation, and development of an institutional framework to deal with regional conflict and security issues (Wandi 2010).

Under the new cooperation framework, Thailand will benefit from the APSC in many aspects. First, Thailand will enjoy a stronger community where members share values and norms. With a higher level of integration comes a higher level of trust, and, therefore, unity and peace. Second, there will be a regional conflict management mechanism that can quickly solve intra-regional disputes. While there is no regional court of justice, the Community serves as a stimulant for countries in conflict to solve their problems peacefully. The Community will allow ASEAN members to collaborate with non-ASEAN members on many issues such as conflict management, disaster management, and transnational crimes. In addition, it will make ASEAN stronger with more leverage in the international community. While the benefits from establishing the ASEAN Community are numerous, ASEAN members should also exercise caution as transnational crimes such as illicit arms trade, human trafficking, and drugs smuggling may be exacerbated as the borders get more porous. Moreover, the road toward APSC is not without hurdles. Domestic politics, different levels of development as well as diverse interests and priorities can delay the integration process. ASEAN members will have to solve existing intra-regional discords and existing domestic problems in order to have an effective and sustainable Community.

5.2 Thailand and ASEAN Economic Community

Thailand's contribution toward a closer economic community started when Prime Minister General Chatchai Chunhawan (1988–1991), declared a more engaging foreign policy toward its neighboring countries. Wars in Indochina and the widespread mistrust and enmity, as well as the presence of external powers from different political ideologies, made countries in Southeast Asia uneasy. It was difficult to form and foster any kind of cooperation among countries at war. It was General Chunhawan who proposed a policy of turning a battlefield into a marketplace. From economic collaboration, he hoped to see a spill-over of such friendly relations into other areas. His policy is considered to be a breakthrough, as Thailand had often adopted a reserved and inward-looking foreign policy. He also spearheaded a negotiation with Australia to help fund the first Thai–Lao Friendship Bridge over the Mekong River to foster more economic and social interactions between the two countries. The bridge was proven to be such a success that three more bridges were later built to stimulate more exchanges across the Mekong River.

A broader and larger economic cooperation took shape in 1992, at the ASEAN Summit in Singapore, when His Excellency Anand Panyarachun, Thailand's interim Prime Minister, proposed setting up ASEAN Free Trade Area (AFTA). The idea was to reduce trade barriers in goods, services, and financial services among member countries to stimulate a more efficient national production and intra-regional trade. Ideally, the vision was to have ASEAN as a single production unit; but due to different levels of economic and social development, the member countries started off with the Agreement on the Common Effective Preferential Tariff (CEPT) Scheme for AFTA which required each member to eliminate restrictions and other non-tariff barriers among themselves to 0–5 percent within 15 years starting from January 1, 1993. In 1995, the ASEAN members agreed to adopt the GATT Transactions Value System of Customs Valuation and an ASEAN Framework Agreement on Trade in Services. Under this framework, a number of sectors, including telecommunications, tourism, financial services, construction, and maritime transport were negotiated and prepared to be liberalized. As the result of the economic cooperation, trade values between Thailand and other ASEAN member countries have continuously increased (Tables 9.1–9.3 and Figure 9.1).

Another collaboration among ASEAN members in promoting greater economic efficiency, productivity, and competitiveness is the adoption of the ASEAN Framework Agreement on Intellectual Property Cooperation in 1995. This paved the way for better cooperation in the field of intellectual property rights (IPR) among government agencies, private sectors, and professional bodies of ASEAN. The ASEAN Intellectual Property Right Action Plan 2004–2010 served as a starting point for ASEAN member countries to foster collaboratively the development of a culture of learning, innovation, and creativity in ASEAN, optimizing on the diversity of member countries, to develop a regional identity and profile in IP and IPR generation, registration, commercialization, protection, and enforcement; and to encourage cross-border collaboration and networking for the widening and deepening of the ASEAN Science and Technology base and Research and Development activities, and the registration and commercialization of their results and outputs (ASEAN 2012). The issue of IPR, however, still requires stronger measures and a more effective mechanism to cope with the widespread IPR violation in Thailand and other Southeast Asian countries.

A more outward-looking economic policy was adopted during the time of Prime Minister Thaksin Shinawatra, a business man, who was elected to office in 2001. Thailand was in need of investment to stimulate economic growth to repay the International Monetary Fund after the 1997 financial crisis. He was the first leader to merge economic policy with foreign policy to

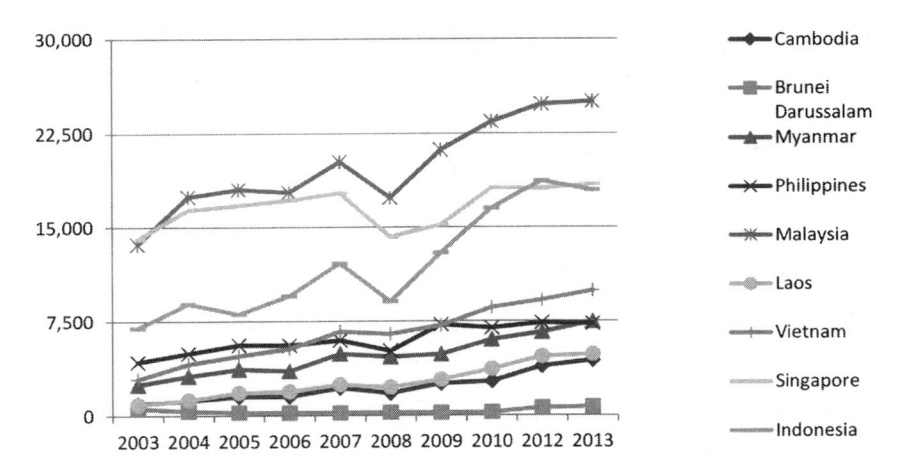

Figure 9.1 Trade values (import and export) between Thailand and ASEAN countries: 2003–2013 (in million US dollars)
Source: Thailand Trading Report, Ministry of Commerce, 2014.

Table 9.1 Trade values (import and export) between Thailand and ASEAN countries: 2003–2013 (in million US dollars)

	2003	2004	2005	2006	2007	2008	2009	2010	2012	2013
Cambodia	943.83	1,189.73	1,510.18	1,512.43	2,188.53	1,768.04	2,535.47	2,706.62	3,893.13	4,361.36
Brunei Darussalam	559.73	344.26	248.72	222.23	220.12	243.80	224.28	254.67	614.32	684.33
Myanmar	2,463.92	3,134.24	3,673.65	3,533.55	4,883.91	4,644.63	4,863.49	6,012.22	6,604.49	7,444.11
Philippines	4,248.07	4,938.14	5,595.64	5,573.29	5,964.32	5,131.41	7,215.59	6,947.58	7,354.41	7,277.26
Malaysia	13,647.21	17,444.54	18,040.24	17,795.85	20,258.60	17,378.88	21,202.75	23,431.19	24,790.57	25,004.52
Laos	874.79	1,252.83	1,827.29	1,921.26	2,467.62	2,249.67	2,860.68	3,688.22	4,671.40	4,851.11
Vietnam	2,908.11	4,084.75	4,731.12	5,297.68	6,662.88	6,467.88	7,161.79	8,583.98	9,176.07	9,923.07
Singapore	14,042.67	16,390.45	16,770.85	17,169.28	17,767.99	14,228.75	15,205.96	18,176.40	18,111.63	18,453.59
Indonesia	6,961.81	8,895.38	8,066.74	9,516.27	12,134.03	9,057.09	12,970.97	16,537.89	18,723.87	17,954.49

Source: Thailand Trading Report, Ministry of Commerce (2014).

Table 9.2 Values of imports by Thailand from ASEAN countries: 2003–2013 (in million US dollars)

	2003	2004	2005	2006	2007	2008	2009	2010	2012	2013
Cambodia	34.77	39.68	41.34	52.77	93.98	83.11	214.69	167.90	243.76	341.25
Brunei Darussalam	488.68	258.44	150.43	121.89	92.79	118.76	96.89	125.46	430.11	527.47
Myanmar	1,703.71	2,247.29	2,772.12	2,500.96	3,513.31	2,999.25	2,812.51	3,328.47	3,588.13	3,865.34
Philippines	1,947.98	2,366.18	2,539.38	2,330.03	2,364.40	1,914.90	2,374.50	2,577.49	2,662.48	2,512.25
Malaysia	6,983.72	10,166.06	10,166.46	9,371.42	10,093.60	9,227.71	10,746.54	11,755.73	12,800.73	12,705.51
Laos	144.09	285.16	617.27	509.22	642.86	498.25	747.99	1,077.77	1,208.82	1,302.92
Vietnam	552.71	1,122.86	1,077.78	1,207.98	1,503.47	1,492.12	1,397.32	1,937.00	2,917.48	3,124.75
Singapore	5,230.26	6,764.14	6,814.69	6,833.75	7,379.12	6,167.26	6,309.29	7,427.14	7,654.16	7,835.39
Indonesia	2,924.00	3,928.64	4,123.09	4,329.69	5,633.48	4,090.90	5,694.22	7,041.73	7,903.02	7,722.29

Source: Thailand Trading Report, Ministry of Commerce (2014).

Table 9.3 Values of exports from Thailand to ASEAN countries: 2003–2013 (in million US dollars)

	2003	2004	2005	2006	2007	2008	2009	2010	2012	2013
Cambodia	909.05	1,150.05	1,468.84	1,459.66	2,094.55	1,684.93	2,320.78	2,538.72	3,649.38	4,020.10
Brunei Darussalam	71.05	85.82	98.29	100.34	127.33	125.05	127.39	129.21	184.21	156.87
Myanmar	760.21	886.94	901.53	1,032.60	1,370.59	1,645.39	2,050.97	2,683.75	3,016.36	3,578.77
Philippines	2,300.09	2,571.96	3,056.26	3,243.26	3,599.92	3,216.52	4,841.09	4,370.09	4,691.93	4,765.01
Malaysia	6,663.49	7,278.48	7,873.78	8,424.43	10,165.00	8,151.17	10,456.21	11,675.46	11,989.83	12,299.02
Laos	730.71	967.67	1,210.01	1,412.04	1,824.76	1,751.42	2,112.69	2,610.45	3,462.58	3,548.19
Vietnam	2,355.40	2,961.89	3,653.34	4,089.70	5,159.41	4,975.76	5,764.47	6,646.99	6,258.58	6,798.32
Singapore	8,812.41	9,626.31	9,956.16	10,335.53	10,388.87	8,061.49	8,896.68	10,749.26	10,457.47	10,618.20
Indonesia	4,037.81	4,966.75	3,943.65	5,186.58	6,500.55	4,966.18	7,276.76	9,496.16	10,820.84	10,232.19

Source: Thailand Trading Report, Ministry of Commerce (2014).

arrive at an "economic diplomacy" in handling relations with neighboring countries. Thailand was able to repay the IMF's loan ahead of schedule.

Thailand's strengths and weaknesses must be realized and managed for the country to be prepared for the changes and to enjoy the benefits brought by the ASEAN Economic Community. Strengths such as its strategic position, sound financial institutions, good basic infrastructure, and capable skilled labor have drawn in foreign investments. The government together with the private sector should continue to ensure a sound and inviting economic environment.

Thailand is currently developing its connectivity plans with neighboring countries. In 2013, the country opened up 25 border check points; six with Cambodia, six with Myanmar, two with Malaysia, and 11 with Laos (Ministry of Foreign Affairs 2013) and has recently completed its fourth friendship bridge with Laos which has helped stimulate exchanges of not just goods but also knowledge for a better understanding among the peoples.

While the strengths mentioned above make Thailand attractive to investors, tourists, and workers, the country has been suffering from political instability, corruption, and now social divide. At the micro level, problems such as intellectual property rights violations and low English language skills are not addressed adequately. These will have to be fixed so that Thailand will have a stronger foundation and a greater potential for economic development.

The opportunities and challenges the ASEAN Economic Community will bring must also be analyzed in order for Thailand to reassess its own endowments and developmental status to prepare itself for the changes that may occur. Some of the opportunities are: first, Thailand will enjoy more foreign investment as it has much less strict regulation toward foreign ownership of a company compared with other countries. Second, with advanced technologies, Thailand can serve as a hub for value-adding activities for primary and secondary products. Third, the Board of Investment actively promotes the car industry, information and communication technology, and tourism which will draw in more investment. Fourth, Thailand will also benefit from the preparation process in political, economic, and social dimensions.

Nevertheless, Thailand will have to consider challenges stemming from a closer economic integration. First, with an increased minimum wage to 300 baht per day introduced in early 2013, Thailand may experience a decrease in investments from foreign companies that use unskilled labor as the overhead increases. Second, there have been a few concerns regarding the standards of skilled workers who will be able to secure jobs in ASEAN countries and also regarding the "brain drain" situation in Thailand where skilled labor choose to work in other countries where they can gain higher income. Third is the challenge from the liberalized market which may bring back memories of the 1997 financial crisis. Fourth is the judgment and political will of the government to support the projects which will be beneficial to the people of the ASEAN Community as a whole.

The ASEAN Economic Community has been promoted the most by the Thai government, organizations, and media and is the most well-received among the people. With an increased awareness of the economic integration and its benefits as well as its costs, Thailand can effectively engage in the activities laid out in the Roadmap (ASEAN 2009).

5.3 Thailand and ASEAN Socio-Cultural Community

Thailand has played an active role in promoting social integration among the peoples of ASEAN. With the ASEAN Socio-Cultural Community, Thailand aims to follow the roadmap that lays out six areas of cooperation: Human Resource Development, Social Security, Social Justice, Sustainable Environment, ASEAN Identity Building, and closing down the development gap. During the fifth ASEAN Summit in Thailand in 1995, it was the first time that ASEAN leaders showed a strong commitment to improve living standards of peoples in the region and to narrow the development gap within each country as well as among countries. The 1995 Bangkok Declaration outlines measures that will bring about unity. The spirit was later carried out in the 1996 meeting in which Thailand helped push forward the ASEAN Vision. The ASEAN Vision covers a wide range of regional cooperation. Among the most celebrated one is the ASEAN Foundation, proposed by then Vice Prime Minister and Foreign Affairs Minister Amnuay Veerawan, to support regional education and social learning projects.

Another initiative led by Thailand is the establishment of the ASEAN University Network in 1995 according to the agreement reached during the fourth ASEAN Summit. The objective is to create an ASEAN identity and to develop ASEAN human resources through collaboration among existing universities. The AUN office, located at Chulalongkorn University, Bangkok, Thailand, serves as a network hub for information exchanges as well as a venue for academic activities. Some of AUN's accomplishments include the ASEAN Studies program, joint research projects, ASEAN Youth Forum, student and faculty exchange programs, and joint effort to improve the quality assurance system for ASEAN universities.

Apart from the attempt to create an infrastructure for a better connectivity among peoples of East Asian countries, there is also an initiative by Thailand under the project "Community of East Asian Scholars: CEAS" to develop and promote educational collaborations in the form of a book project as well as plans for faculty and student exchanges. The project is among the largest for the East Asian academic communities that meet twice a year to complete a series of books to be used preliminarily by students in the APT countries. It is hoped that the project can help instill a regional identity through a better understanding of one another.

In terms of the human security issue, Thailand is the first country in Southeast Asia that has been a member of the Human Security Network (HSN) since it was launched in 1999 (UN Office for the Coordination of Humanitarian Affairs 2013). As a result, the Ministry of Social Development and Human Security was created in 2002 with the aim to promote social development and equality and social justice in the country. This also allows Thailand to be an active member in this regard as it plays an important role in protecting human rights and women and children's rights. Thailand was chair in drafting the Term of Reference for ASEAN Commission for the Promotion and Protection of the Rights of Women and Children (ACWC). The goal of this Commission is to serve as a mechanism that safeguards human rights as well as the rights of women and children in ASEAN. During the first ACWC meeting in February 2011 in Indonesia, Thailand was selected to be the chair of ACWC for a three-year term. Under Thailand's chairmanship, the Commission drafted Rules of Procedures (ROP) and a five-year plan that stressed the importance of elementary school education and domestic violence against women and children. Regarding this issue, Thailand offered to host a meeting on Violence Against Women and Children in 2012.

Thailand encourages the ASEAN Community to be a people-centered community by supporting a new mechanism created by the ASEAN Charter to take active roles in bridging gaps between ASEAN and other social organizations. In 2009, during the 15th ASEAN Summit in Thailand, ASEAN Intergovernmental Commission on Human Rights (AICHR) was established. AICHR serves as the newest regional arm in handling the promotion of human rights. Among its achievements are various workshops held among governmental officials, academia, and civil society organizations to raise awareness and to share experience in topics such as justice and human rights.

Another contribution by Thailand in the socio-cultural dimension is the creation of the Tripartite Core Group (TCG) which is comprised of Myanmar, ASEAN, and the United Nations. TCG is set up to support Myanmar after the country was severely hit by the Nargis cyclone. Post-Nargis Recovery and Preparedness Plan (PONREPP) is a three-year plan (2009–2011), supervised by the former Secretary General Surin Pitsuwan from Thailand. The Plan focused on creating social safety nets, improving infrastructure, and promoting education, among other areas. Her Royal Highness Crown Princess Sirindthorn also contributed to the projects to help Myanmar recover from the natural disaster.

Apart from the above-mentioned initiatives and roles played to help foster a better ASEAN Community, Thailand also supports other regional projects aimed at promoting sports, eradicating the use of drugs, and building awareness toward epidemics. It is hoped that through more communication and collaboration, member countries of ASEAN can grow more trust toward one another and develop shared values and norms that will in turn help stimulate a closer integration.

6 Thailand in ASEAN Plus Three

Throughout history, China has remained Thailand's leading trade partner. The two countries officially established diplomatic ties while Mao Zedong and Chou En-Lai and Mom Rajawongse Kukrit Pramoj were in office in

1975. Since then Thailand and China have enjoyed an amicable relationship. Thailand was among the first group of countries to invest in China in 1979. The Thailand-China Free Trade Agreement was signed in June 2003 and came into effect in October 2003. Among Thailand's top exported products to China are rubber, sugar, and plastic, and imported products from China include electronic parts, steel, and textile. In 2012, the trade value between Thailand and China was around US$64 billion (Table 9.4 and Figure 9.2) and more than 2.8 million Chinese tourists came to visit Thailand while more than half a million Thai tourists paid a visit to China (Thailand Business Information Center in China 2013).

Thailand and Japan also have a long relationship. The two countries formally established diplomatic ties in 1897 with exchanges of resident ambassadors. Since then there have been exchange visits between the royal family members as well as high-level officials. The Japan-Thailand Economic Partnership Agreement was signed in April 2008 and came into effect in November 2008. Japan's investment and foreign aid have allowed many government development projects to be realized. Some of the largest Japanese multinational corporations that invest in Thailand are Toyota, Honda, Nissan, Hitachi, and Toshiba. Among the top imported products from Japan are automobile parts and engines while the leading exported products to Japan are automobile, motorcycle, plastic, and rubber (Department of International Trade Promotion 2013). Apart from being trade partners, both countries have collaborated in the area of development. Japan International Cooperation Agency (JICA) has been working with the Thai government in areas such as social security, natural resources and energy, and environmental management (Japan International Cooperation Agency 2013). From a donor country, Japan is now Thailand's partner in providing assistance to other countries.

Thailand and South Korea developed relations when Thailand sent troops to South Korea during the Korean War from 1950 to 1953. Official diplomatic ties were later sealed in October 1958. Economic ties between the two countries are promoted through the Joint Trade Commission (JTC) and the trade value between Thailand and Korea has grown from US$59 million in 1975 to US$13 billion in 2012 (Table 9.4) (The Royal Thai Embassy in Seoul, Korea 2013). South Korea has become a popular destination especially for Thailand's younger generations. Statistics from the Korea Tourism Organization shows that the number of Thai people visiting South Korea ranks the fourth, just below Japan, Taiwan, and Hong Kong. Tourism is also an indicator of the close relations the two countries share.

As mentioned earlier, Thailand's bilateral relations with China, Japan, and South Korea had started long before ASEAN was established in 1967 and the ties have grown stronger in all dimensions after the region has gone through a series of common threats, both natural and man-made. The ASEAN Plus Three arrangement began soon after Thailand, Malaysia, Indonesia, and South Korea had been hit hard with currency speculations that exposed unsound financial structures resulting in the 1997 Asian Financial Crisis. In

Table 9.4 Trade value (import and export) between Thailand, South Korea, China, and Japan: 2003–2013 (in million US dollars)

	2003	2004	2005	2006	2007	2008	2009	2010	2012	2013
South Korea	6,840.49	7,716.81	9,323.03	8,970.34	10,916.20	8,840.01	11,650.15	13,091.30	13,411.30	12,978.04
China	19,228.67	25,510.07	30,234.43	33,614.87	37,583.18	35,465.73	45,438.22	53,813.70	62,196.79	61,874.00
Japan	45,081.46	51,555.46	50,302.70	50,404.00	55,563.28	43,625.17	57,918.33	62,735.54	71,107.18	60,245.30

Source: Thailand Trading Report, Ministry of Commerce (2014).

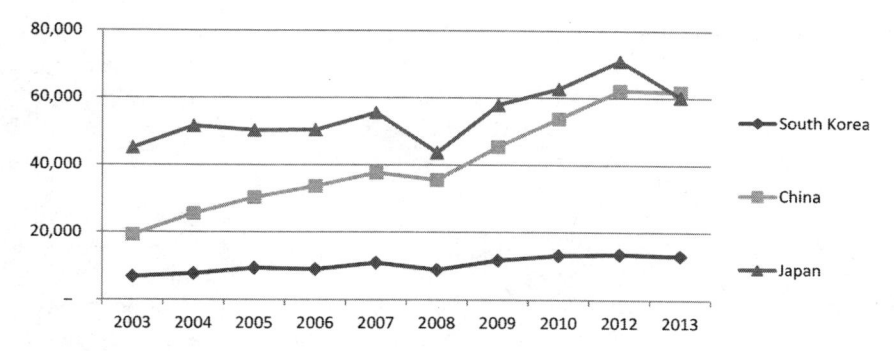

Figure 9.2 Trade value (import and export) between Thailand, South Korea, China, and Japan: 2003–2013 (in million US dollars)
Source: Thailand Trading Report, Ministry of Commerce 2014.

most of the countries, banks were burdened with a large amount of non-performing loans, partly due to a sharp decline in property prices, and partly due to the sharp currency depreciation. As a result, Thailand experienced excessive foreign debts and the international reserves fell by 31 percent to US $27 billion in 1997. Thailand quickly requested assistance from the IMF and sought bilateral loans from outside the region.

In December 1997, ASEAN leaders along with leaders from China, Japan, and South Korea met in Kuala Lumpur to discuss the remedies and the possible preventive mechanism to tackle the financial crisis. Under the ASEAN Plus Three (APT) umbrella, Japan proposed to have the Asian Monetary Fund for countries in the region to handle regional financial and monetary matters themselves and in order to respond to the problems more swiftly. The scheme, however, was opposed by the United States and did not receive China's support. In its place, along came a financial crisis prevention measure called the Chiang Mai Initiative (CMI), a regional foreign exchange liquidity support mechanism designed to be closely linked to the IMF. The CMI arrangement is not a new concept. In 1977, the original five ASEAN members established the ASEAN Swap Arrangement to fix short-term liquidity problems. However, the size of the available fund was inadequate to address the severe 1997 Asian Financial Crisis, and thus most ASEAN countries had to turn to the IMF for bail-out packages. In order to improve and strengthen the existing framework, the APT countries expanded the CMI arrangement to include all 13 countries and designed it to be responsible for monitoring capital flows, regional surveillance, swap networks, and training personnel. The term CMI, however, is mostly associated with a network of bilateral currency swaps.

In 2010, financial cooperation among the APT countries moved to a new stage when they officially implemented the Chiang Mai Initiative Multilateralization (CMIM), which replaced the existing network of bilateral agreements with a reserve pooling arrangement totaling US$120 billion (Aizenman et al. 2011).

Apart from collaboration to help strengthen regional financial and monetary systems, the APT initiatives also expand to cover collaboration in food and energy security, financial cooperation, trade facilitation, disaster management, people-to-people contacts, narrowing the development gap, rural development and poverty alleviation, social welfare, human trafficking, labor, communicable diseases, environment and sustainable development, and transnational crime, including counter-terrorism (ASEAN 2012). Moreover, in order for the collaboration between ASEAN and the APT to go hand in hand, the Guidelines to Implement the Second Joint Statement on East Asia Cooperation and the ASEAN Plus Three Cooperation Work Plan (2007–2017) were endorsed at the 13th APT Directors-General Meeting on July 3, 2009 in Seoul. Under this Work Plan is the ASEAN Plus Three Cooperation Fund (APTCF) with endowments of US$3 million to facilitate activities that support the APT cooperation.

Apart from the currency swap and technical assistance, the APT also wishes to create a closer community. In 1999, an East Asia Vision Group (EAVG) was set up to study the possibilities for the East Asian Community. The Vision Group was composed of eminent intellectuals charged with the task of drawing up a vision for mid-to-long term cooperation in East Asia for the 21st century. Its findings were submitted in a report to the APT Summit in 2001 (ASEAN 2012). After one decade since the EAVG submitted its report to the APT leaders, the East Asia Vision Group II (EAVG II) was established in October 2011 with the purpose of reviewing the APT cooperation over the past 15 years and providing future vision of the APT for the next decade. The EAVG II met four times in October 2011, February 2012, May 2012 and September 2012. The EAVG II Report was finalized and submitted to the 15th APT Summit in Cambodia in November 2012. Among the key findings are that there remain many challenges for the APT to tackle such as territorial disputes, arms races, the proliferation of weapons of mass destruction, and other non-traditional security issues. The report also talks about new economic challenges such as the shrinking demand from outside the region and instability of the international financial market after the 2008 global financial crisis (Ministry of Foreign Affairs 2012a).

The APT countries continue to learn from the past crises in order to develop an effective surveillance mechanism to detect possible financial and monetary crises and to create a functioning safety net that can help alleviate the impact. While the proposed Asian Monetary Fund was not materialized, other measures such as CMIM, ASEAN Plus Three Cooperation Fund, and the attempt to establish the East Asian Community point to a continuous effort at fostering a stronger community.

7 Conclusion

This chapter provides a brief overview of Thailand's political, economic, and social development as well as its role in and involvement with regional cooperation especially ASEAN and ASEAN Plus Three arrangements. While Thailand enjoys its strategic location and its relatively sound economic condition to the point that it emerges from an aid recipient to a donor, it is not without weaknesses. As mentioned earlier, Thailand has undergone major waves and ripples that have sometimes strengthened domestic institutions and at times weakened the foundation and morale of the country. Naturally, a country needs to fix problems at home before joining hands with others, but it cannot neglect the growing importance of international interdependence. Despite its preoccupation with unstable domestic politics, due to relatively short terms of the Thai Prime Ministers and, therefore, frequently interrupted government policies, Thailand has been considerably active in international and regional cooperation especially in the past few decades.

Toward a closer ASEAN Community, Yingluck Shinawatra's government laid out a list of policies to help strengthen Thailand's position in the region as well as in the world with plans to expedite the promotion and development of relations with neighboring countries "by enhancing cooperation between the public sector, private sector, people and the mass media in order to cultivate mutual understanding and instill closeness among all sectors" and to create unity and promote cooperation among ASEAN countries and other Asian countries (Ministry of Foreign Affairs 2012a).

Thailand's position in ASEAN and APT will depend on whether it can realize its strengths and lessen its weaknesses and create opportunities from the existing collaborations. Domestic politics and corruption are cited as the most prominent impediments by most national polls. Thailand should stress the importance of education and knowledge of ASEAN and APT, their histories, structures, activities, and benefits as they will help bolster a positive aspiration toward the integrations. ASEAN and APT are made up of member countries. With strong members, stronger communities can be achieved.

Notes

1 The author would like to acknowledge Attasit Pankaew, Professor at the Faculty of Political Science, Thammasat University for his valuable contribution on Thailand's political development and Thailand's trade statistics, and Prajak Kongkirati, Professor at the Faculty of Political Science, Thammasat University, for his insightful comments on Thai politics.
2 A list of coup d'état in Thailand, both the successful ones and the failed attempts, can be found at the Social Institute, Office of the Basic Education Commission.
3 Phraya is a rank conferred to commissioned officers who served as Permanent Secretary of Ministry, Director-General, Mayor of Important City, Commander-in-chief, and Chancellor of Royal Office.
4 For more information on Thailand's experience in the 1997 Asian Financial Crisis, see Waiquamdee, Disyatat, and Pongsaparn (2005) and Lauridsen (1998).
5 The members aim to accelerate the economic growth, social progress, and cultural development in the region through joint endeavors in the spirit of equality and partnership in order to strengthen the foundation for a prosperous and peaceful community of South-East Asian Nations; to promote regional peace and stability

through abiding respect for justice and the rule of law in the relationship among countries of the region and adherence to the principles of the United Nations Charter; to promote active collaboration and mutual assistance on matters of common interest in the economic, social, cultural, technical, scientific, and administrative fields; to provide assistance to each other in the form of training and research facilities in the educational, professional, technical, and administrative spheres; to collaborate more effectively for the greater utilization of their agriculture and industries, the expansion of their trade, including the study of the problems of international commodity trade, the improvement of their transportation and communications facilities and the raising of the living standards of their peoples; to promote South-East Asian studies; and to maintain close and beneficial cooperation with existing international and regional organizations with similar aims and purposes, and explore all avenues for even closer cooperation among themselves.

6 ASEAN. Special Lecture on "Thailand's Role in ASEAN" by His Excellency Mr. Abhisit Vejjajiva, Prime Minister of the Kingdom of Thailand to Commemorate the 42nd Anniversary of ASEAN, Saturday, August 8, 2009, Vithes Samosorn, Ministry of Foreign Affairs.

7 Treaty of Amity and Cooperation (1976): mutual respect for the independence, sovereignty, equality, territorial integrity, and national identity of all nations; the right of every State to lead its national existence free from external interference, subversion or coercion; non-interference in the internal affairs of one another; settlement of differences or disputes by peaceful means; renunciation of the threat or use of force; and effective cooperation among themselves.

References

Aizenman, Joshua, Yothin Jinjarak and Donghyun Park (2011) "Evaluating Asian Swap Arrangements." ADBI Working Paper Series No. 297.

ASEAN (2009) 'ASEAN Roadmap 2009–2015.' Available from: www.asean.org/resour ces/publications/asean-publications/item/roadmap-for-an-asean-community-2009-2015 (accessed April 2013).

ASEAN (2012) 'The ASEAN Declaration (Bangkok Declaration).' Available from: www. asean.org/news/item/the-asean-declaration-bangkok-declaration (accessed January 2013).

ASEAN (2012) 'ASEAN Intellectual Property Right Action Plan 2004–2010.' Available from: www.asean.org/news/item/asean-intellectual-property-right-action-p lan-2004-2010 (accessed April 2013).

ASEAN (2012) 'ASEAN Plus Three.'. Available from: www.asean.org/asean/externa l-relations/asean-3/item/asean-plus-three-cooperation (accessed April 2013).

ASEAN (2012) 'Treaty of Amity and Cooperation in Southeast Asia Indonesia, 24 February 1976.' Available from: www.asean.org/news/item/treaty-of-amity-and-coop eration-in-southeast-asia-indonesia-24-february-1976-3 (accessed January 2013).

ASEAN Intergovernmental Commission on Human Rights (n.d.) Available from: www.aichr.org/category/activities/thailand (accessed April 2013).

ASEAN Regional Forum (n.d.) Available from: www.aseanregionalforum.asean.org (accessed April 2013).

Asia-Europe Meeting (n.d.) Available from: www.aseminfoboard.org (accessed April 2013).

Asia-Europe Meeting (n.d.) Available from: www.aseminfoboard.org/events/10th-asem -finance-ministers-meeting-finmm10 (accessed April 2013).

Asian Development Bank (n.d.) 'Greater Mekong Subregion.' Available from: www.adb.org/countries/gms/overview (accessed April 2013).

Ba, Alice D. (2010) 'The Association of Southeast Asian Nations' in *The Routledge Handbook of Asian Security Studies*, edited by Ganguly, S., Scobell, A. and Chinyong Liow, J.. New York: Routledge.

Baker, Chris and Pasuk Phongpaichit (2005) *A History of Thailand*. Cambridge: Cambridge University Press.

Chandran, Jeshurun (1977) *The Contest for Siam, 1889–1902: A Study in Diplomatic Rivalry*. Kuala Lumpur: University of Malaya Press.

Department of International Trade Promotion. Ministry of Commerce. 'Japan's Trade Performance in the First Quarter of 2013.' Available from: www.ditp.go.th (accessed November 2013).

Department of Provincial Administration (2013) 'Population Statistics.' Available from: http://stat.bora.dopa.go.th/stat/y_stat55.html (accessed November 2013).

EU-Asia Center. Available from: www.eu-asiacentre.eu/pub_details.php?pub_id=89 (accessed April 2013).

Hagiwara, Yoshiyuki (1973) 'Formation and Development of the Association of South East Asian Nations', *The Development Economies*, 11(4): 443–465.

Hänggi, Heiner (1991) 'ASEAN and the ZOPFAN Concept', Pacific Strategic Papers. Institute of Southeast Asian Studies.

Indonesia-Malaysia-Thailand Growth Triangle. Available from: www.imtgt.org (accessed April 2013).

International Rivers. Available from: www.internationalrivers.org/campaigns/mekong-mainstream-dams (accessed April 2013).

Japan International Cooperation Agency (JICA) (2013) 'Thailand'. Available from: www.jica.go.jp/project/english/area/asia/018_1.html (accessed November 2013).

Korea Tourism Organization (2014) Available from: http://kto.visitkorea.or.kr/eng/tourismStatics/keyFacts/KoreaMonthlyStatistics.kto#search (accessed February 2014).

Lauridsen, Laurids (1998) 'The Financial Crisis in Thailand: Causes, Conduct and Consequences?' *World Development*, 26(8): 1575–1591.

McCargo, Duncan (2005) 'Network Monarchy and Legitimacy Crises in Thailand.' *The Pacific Review*, 18(4): 499–519.

McCargo, Duncan (2006) 'The 19 September 2006 Coup – Preliminary Thought on the Implication for the Future Directions of Thai Politics.' Asia Research Institute, National University of Singapore.

Mekong River Commission. Available from: www.mrcmekong.org (accessed April 2013).

Ministry of Commerce (2014) 'Thailand Trading Report.' Available from: www2.ops3.moc.go.th (accessed February 2014).

Ministry of Foreign Affairs (2002) *Thailand's Foreign Policy: Forward Engagement: Collection of Speeches by Dr. Surakiat Sathirathai*. Bangkok: Ministry of Foreign Affairs.

Ministry of Foreign Affairs (2012) 'Report of the East Asia Vision Group II.' Available from: www.mfa.go.th/asean/contents/files/asean-media-center-20130312-112418-758604.pdf (accessed April 2013).

Ministry of Foreign Affairs (2012) 'Policy on Foreign Affairs and International Economic.' Available from: www.mfa.go.th/main/en/policy/9868-Foreign-Policy.html (accessed November 2013).

Ministry of Foreign Affairs (2013) 'ASEAN: A Regional Perspective',presented by Mr. Surapong Tovichakchaikul.

National Identity Board Office of the Prime Minister (2000) *Thailand into the 2000's.* Office of the Prime Minister.

Nuclear Threat Initiative. Available from: www.nti.org/treaties-and-regimes/southeast-a sian-nuclear-weapon-free-zone-seanwfz-treaty-bangkok-treaty (accessed April 2013).

Ockey, James (2000) 'The Rice of Local Power in Thailand: Provincial Crime, Election and Bureaucracy.' in   *Many and Power in Provincial Thailand*, edited by McVey, Ruth. Singapore: ISEAS Press.

Satitniramai, Apichat and Yukti Mukdawijitra (2013) *Re-examining the Political Landscape of Thailand.* Chiangmai: The Universities for Healthy Public Policy.

Terwiel, Berend Jan (2011) *Thailand's Political History: From the 13th Century to Recent Times.* Bangkok: Riverbooks.

Thabchumphon, Naruemon and Duncan McCargo (2011) 'Urbanized Villagers in the 2010 Thai Redshirt Protest: Not Just Poor Farmers?' *Asian Survey,* 51(6): 993–1018.

Thai National Assembly (2013a) 'Constitution and Acts.' Available from: www.parliam ent.go.th/ewtadmin/ewt/parliament_parcy/download/parliament_law/2319-2556-0.pdf (accessed November 2013).

Thai National Assembly (2013b) 'Constitution and Acts.' Available from: www.pa rliament.go.th/ewtadmin/ewt/parliament_parcy/ewt_w3c/ewt_dl_link.php?nid=8337 (accessed November 2013).

Thailand Business Information Center in China (2013) 'Thailand-China Relations.' Available from: www.thaibizchina.com/thaibizchina/th/thai-china (accessed November 2013).

The Prime Minister's Office (1980) 'Prime Minister's Order 66/2523.' Available from: www.opm.go.th (accessed November 2013).

The Royal Thai Embassy in Seoul, Korea (2013) 'Thailand-Korea Relations.' Available from: www.thaiembassy.org/seoul/th/relation (accessed November 2013).

Tipparat, Pranee (ed.) (2002) *ASEAN in the New Millennium.* Bangkok: Institute of Security and International Studies.

UN Office for the Coordination of Humanitarian Affairs (2013) Available from: http://unocha.org/humansecurity/about-human-security/human-security-un (accessed December 2013)

Waiquamdee, Atchana, Disyatat, Piti and Pongsaparn, Runchana (2005) 'Effective Exchange Rates and Monetary Policy: The Thai Experience', Bank of Thailand Discussion Paper.

Walker, Andrew (2012) *Thailand's Political Peasant: Power in the Modern Rural Economy.* Madison: The University of Wisconsin Press.

Wandi, Agus (2010) 'Can ASEAN be a Peace Mediator?' *The Jakarta Post,* 13 August . Available from: www.thejakartapost.com/news/2010/08/13/can-asean-be-a-peace-m ediator.html-0 (accessed April 2013).

10 Vietnam in ASEAN Plus Three

Cooperation for a better future

Nguyen Hong Son

1 National perspective

The history of Vietnam, according to mythology, dates back more than 4,000 years. The first Vietnamese people were descended from the Dragon Lord Lac Long Quan and the Immortal Fairy Au Co. Lac Long Quan and Au Co had one hundred sons before they split. Fifty children went with their mother to the mountains, and the other 50 went with their father to the sea. The eldest son became the first in a line of early Vietnamese kings, known as the Hung kings. Hung kings established their country, located on the Red River delta in the north of present-day Vietnam.

Reliable archaeological sources, however, indicate that the first country of the Vietnamese people dates to some 2,700 years ago (Quynh et al. 2006). The history of Vietnam is a story of struggle for national independence and unification. For most of the period from 111 B.C. to the early tenth century, Vietnam was under the direct rule of China. It regained its autonomy in 939 A.D., and had complete independence a century later. Since then, while Vietnam remained a tributary state of the Chinese empire, it made every effort to repel the repeated attempts by successive dynasties from that large neighbor to annex it once again. The country was first officially named Vietnam in the early nineteenth century (Quynh et al. 2006).

Vietnam's independent period temporarily ended in the mid-nineteenth century, when it was colonized by France. In 1930, the Vietnamese Communist Party was formed by Ho Chi Minh, a national hero, and his comrades to struggle for the national independence of Vietnam. During the Second World War, the Japanese occupied Vietnam from September 1940, though they retained French administrators during their occupation until March 1945 when they toppled the French administration and replaced it with a Japanese-backed government. In August 1945, Ho Chi Minh and his Communist Party successfully seized the administration and declared Vietnam an independent state on September 2, 1945. After the Second World War ended, the French reasserted their control to colonize Vietnam once again. This led to a nine-year resistant war against the French colony and ended with the major victory by Ho Chi Minh and his Communist Party in Dien Bien Phu. In the same year of 1954, major powers concluded the Geneva Accord and agreed to temporarily partition Vietnam into two parts at the 17th parallel. In the northern part of Vietnam, there was a Communist regime, whereas in the southern part, there was a regime supported by the United States. The Second Indochina War (1954–1975), known in the US as the Vietnam War and in North Vietnam as the American Resistance War, cost around two million Vietnamese lives (Thach and Khang 2008, 436), and ended with the victory of North Vietnam and the reunification of the country in 1975.

Vietnam came out of the war with a devastated economy and immediately had to face the new enemy: poverty and backwardness. This "internal enemy" seemed harder to fight against. The centrally planned economic system, which was helpful during the war, became inappropriate in peace time, and dragged the economy into a state of shortage. At the same time, Vietnam was bogged down in the Cambodian conflict, and isolated from the international community because of the US embargo. To sustain the economy, Vietnam had to rely on assistance from the Soviet Union and other members of the Communist bloc in Eastern Europe.

The call for economic reforms toward market mechanism was not easily accepted due to the ideological constraint of the Cold War era. In addition, the reform motivation was not strong because of the illusion about a nation who could defeat the superpower, would soon become a developed socialist country. In the mid-1980s, Vietnam was in a severe socio-economic crisis that threatened the ruling power of the Communist regime. In contrast, the 1980s was a glorious time for many Asian economies. Thailand, Malaysia, Singapore, and Indonesia, despite the fact that they had a similar starting point of development of their economy to South Vietnam during the 1960s, had emerged as the Asian dragons or tigers. In China, Deng Xiaoping already led the Chinese Communist Party to initiate the reforms in the late 1970s after the devastating Cultural Revolution. In a very difficult moment, Vietnam realized that it was already left behind and would be left further behind its neighboring countries without a comprehensive reforms of the socio-economic and political system.

In 1986, the Sixth National Congress of the Vietnamese Communist Party (VCP) launched the *Doi Moi*[1] (Renovation) with an aim to bring Vietnam out of socio-economic crisis by abandoning the command economic system, introducing the market economy, and integrating Vietnam into the international community. The success of the reforms was vital for the sustainability of the regime in the face of the crisis that occurred in the Soviet Union and Eastern Europe, and later brought down the communist system in these states.

During the War, North Vietnam made every attempt to balance relations with its two major allies, the Soviet Union and China. This became harder when the former and the latter parted ways. As Vietnam leaned toward the Soviet Union after the reunification, Vietnam–China relations deteriorated, falling to a trough by the outbreak of a short border war in 1979.

Normalizing the relationship with the powers, including China and the US, and promoting regional integration were Vietnam's priorities in the beginning of the open-door period and this was the first step that brought the country out to the external world. The *Doi Moi* came along with a rapid policy change, from *"more friends less enemies"* in the late 1980s to *"befriending all members of the international community"* in the early 1990s, then *"dynamic and active international economic integration"* in the mid-2000s and *"dynamic and active international integration"* at present (VCP 1988, 1991, 2001, 2006, 2011a). The latter policy guideline implies that there would not be an effective integration of just a single area while the others remain outside the process. Instead, a comprehensive and multifaceted integration of the whole country into the world is inevitable.

Vietnam only emerged from international isolation after it completely withdrew its troops from Cambodia in 1989. The early 1990s witnessed Vietnam's major achievement in advancing its diplomatic relations. In 1991, China reestablished full diplomatic ties with Vietnam after more than a decade of hostility. In 1994, the US lifted the economic embargo against Vietnam, and one year later the two countries normalized their relationship. The breakthrough in the relationship with the US allowed Vietnam to quickly improve its relations with the countries in Northeast Asia and Western Europe, and at the same time, to expedite its regional integration project.

Vietnam became the seventh member of the Association of Southeast Asian Nation (ASEAN) in 1995. The admission of Vietnam into the ASEAN marked an end of the divisive era when the Southeast Asian region was split into two hostile blocs of different ideologies. It was an important condition for peace, stability, integration, and development in Southeast Asia. For the first time in its history, ASEAN could carry out the expansion project envisioned by its founding fathers to include all 10 countries in Southeast Asia into one regional community, sharing a common identity and norms.

The membership of ASEAN has brought to Vietnam a great deal of benefit in the fields of politics, security, economics, culture, social affairs, and external relations. Within a few years after the accession to ASEAN, Vietnam was able to develop a new status in the international and regional arena. Located in the Southeast Asian peninsula, sharing the border with China and facing the East Sea, Vietnam is in a position to serve as the bridge between Southeast Asia and Northeast Asia as well as between China and India. Having a strategic position, abundant resources, a big market, and fast-growing economy, Vietnam quickly became a focal point in the foreign policy of major powers.

Vietnam was admitted to the Asia-Pacific Economic Cooperation Forum (APEC) in 1998. It joined the common efforts of ASEAN to extend the group's ties with large economies in East Asia, including China, Korea, and Japan. In 2005, Vietnam attended the inaugural East Asia Summit. As an ASEAN member, Vietnam was committed to implementing the agreement between ASEAN and its partners such as ASEAN-China Free Trade

Agreement, ASEAN-Korea Free Trade Agreement, and ASEAN–Japan Economic Partnership Agreement. Vietnam has also made a strong commitment to the construction of the ASEAN community and its three pillars: ASEAN Political and Security Community (APSC), ASEAN Social and Cultural Community (ASCC), and ASEAN Economic Community (AEC) that were agreed by the ASEAN leaders in their 2003 summit.

In 2007, Vietnam became a member of the World Trade Organization (WTO). Vietnam has also established the strategic partnership relation with Japan in 2006, the comprehensive strategic cooperation partnership relation with China in 2008, and strategic cooperation partnership relation with Korea in 2009. Close ties with China, Japan, and Korea are crucial for Vietnam's contribution to the establishment of the ASEAN Plus Three community.

Since 1992, Vietnam has participated in the Greater Mekong Subregion (GMS) Development Cooperation Program that involves Yunnan Province of China, Myanmar, Lao PDR, Cambodia, Thailand, and Vietnam. Vietnam is also an active member of other subregional cooperation schemes, such as the Thai Government-initiated Ayeyawaddy-Chao Phraya-Mekong Economic Cooperation Strategy; the Development Triangle Initiative; the West-East Economic Corridor Development; and the bilateral program with China on "Two Corridors-One Economic Belt."

Although Vietnam was seen as one of the less developed ASEAN members (in the CLMV group), it has made great efforts to narrow the development gap within ASEAN. Since the *Doi Moi*, Vietnam has recorded major achievements in market reforms, poverty reduction, and international integration. The high growth rate of the Vietnamese economy contributed to the dynamic economic growth of East Asia. In addition, situated in the economic growth hub of East Asia, Vietnam can enjoy the positive spillover effect from the growth of major economies such as China, Korea, Japan, and India.

1.1 Political-security perspective

The politics of *Doi Moi* can be viewed from different theoretical angles. The Marxian perspective locates economic changes at the starting point of the *Doi Moi*, and sees that changes in the economic base produce changes in the superstructures, or political and social institutions. The structural "second image-reversed" perspective tends to see changes in domestic political structure as the consequence of the international politics and international economy (Gourevitch 1978). The conduct of the *Doi Moi* is thus shaped by the external forces of globalization, and by the deliberate emulation of foreign countries that have already succeeded. However, internationalization can change the preferences of domestic actors toward policies and policy-making institutions, and change policies and institutions which may shape domestic actors' policy preferences (Milner and Keohane 1996, 5). In this regard, as Vietnam becomes more integrated into the global economy, the course of reforms leads to mounting pressure to further open up the economy, society, and political system.

In reality, unlike the economic sector, political reforms in Vietnam take place with more caution. There is a concern about political instability, particularly the collapse of the regime that has already happened in the Soviet Union and Eastern European communist states. Although political reforms in Vietnam take place slowly, changes have already occurred in three intertwined processes: institutionalization, decentralization, and democratization.

Institutionalization where formal politics and formal relationship regularly prevail over informal politics and informal relationship (Tsu 2002, 102) is the most visible and important change. An attractive economic environment needs a strong legal and facilitating administrative system. It also requires a greater degree of transparency and public participation in the policy-making process. This was also the requirement for Vietnam when it wanted to receive international assistance from the donor community as well as when it joined the international organizations such as ASEAN, APEC, and WTO.

The economic reforms also require a new team of leadership. The old revolutionary leaders have retired and were succeeded by young technocrats who are more familiar with the economic issues and committed to reforms and hold a more proactive view toward international and regional integration. Leadership succession in the reform era of Vietnam proved very smooth. The orthodox Communist tradition which allowed the top leader to stay in power until his death was replaced by a two-term tenure leadership after the Sixth Party Congress. The Ninth Party Congress abolished the advisory position of the retired party leaders in 2001.

For many years, there has been a discussion on the trade-off between the "red" and the "expert" within the VCP. In the past, the red was given priority before the expert. However, in handling the issues of reforms and integration, the party realizes that its legitimacy is built on not only political ideology but also performance, and there is a need to adopt a more pragmatic view. In 2006, the Tenth Party Congress decided to open the party organization to admit all social classes, including private entrepreneurs, and permit party members to enter the private sector. The VCP is now not only the party of the working class but also of the middle class and all people.

Economic decentralization requires political decentralization for the state to have prompt responses to the market, and appropriate economic policy. There is the realignment of the cumbersome party and state organizations to give more autonomy to the lower level of the government, and simplify administrative and political process. There is also a re-demarcation of the functional and organizational boundary between the state and party. The party now claims to be in charge of the political leadership, and the state is in charge of the management. The National Assembly, which had a limited role in the past, also becomes more active in oversight and law-making activities. Nonetheless, Vietnam does not adopt the "separation of powers" principle.

Democratization emerges as a new demand of the reform era. For the first time, the Ninth Party Congress declared democracy as an objective of development and socialism as enshrined in famous slogan: *"prosperous people, strong country, democracy, equality and civility"* (VCP 2001). It was followed by the efforts to transfer the political power from the state to the society and allowed for a more active political role of societal forces. There is greater democracy at the grass-roots levels in which local elections, e.g. at the commune level, have become competitive, and local residents can participate more freely and actively in the policy-making process. Participation of local residents is a prerequisite to implement the projects which need to mobilize the resources from the community.

Compared to the period before the *Doi Moi*, there is larger room for various voices to criticize the government officials although the media is still under the control and censorship of the government. The policy discourse has a much wider scope, ranging from the privatization of state-owned enterprises (SOEs), environmental degradation, gender discrimination, urban-rural migration, state monopoly and red tape of the administrative system to corruption scandals.

The Tenth Party Congress brings the issue of "societal critique" – the task of civil society, to the fore of public discussion. Societal critique is said to be the implementation of socialist democracy, and people's rights and responsibility. It is a requirement in leading and managing the state (VCP 2006, 182–183) because critique from society will help to correct the mistakes in guidelines, policy, and plans of the party and state. This notion also fits well into the Marxian philosophy of dialecticism which implies that the habit of monologue is alien to the Communist Party which has a "blood and flesh" relationship with the people.

Although the political system has undergone significant changes in the reform period, those changes occur within the constraints of the party-state institutions. In implementing the *Doi Moi*, the VCP confirms the upholding of socialism on the basis of Marxism-Leninism and Ho Chi Minh thought, and emphasizes the party leadership as a determinant of the socio-economic achievement (VCP 2001). There is also the protection of the unique leadership of the Communist Party, and of the Party's line according to the principle of democratic centralism: that is, "individual submits to organization; minority submits to majority; subordinate submits to superordinate; and local authorities submit to central authority" (Ho Chi Minh 1996, 268). The communist ideology in Vietnam is associated with patriotism. National independence associated with socialism has been the central theme of the VCP's propaganda since its birth. The VCP maintains that it was the only force that had successfully led the revolution in Vietnam to victory, and it continues to successfully lead the reform process (VCP 2011b).

1.2 *Economic perspective*

Economic reforms are the essence of the *Doi Moi* with the objective of transforming the Soviet-style command economic system to a market-oriented economy. Once the government let the market decide production, there came the abandonment of the rationing system, and introduction of the price system determined by the market.

Before the *Doi Moi*, the command mechanism and the rationing system seriously obstructed the incentive of production because everybody received the same reward regardless of their efforts. In the mid-1980s, there was a severe socio-economic crisis. The inflation rate reached the three-digit level. There was a shortage of commodities. The economy had to rely on foreign aid, which was cut off after the collapse of the communist system in Eastern Europe. The economic reforms restored the production incentive and brought back efficiency to the economy. In 1989, Vietnam began to export rice after being a net rice importer for a long time. By the early 1990s, inflation was reduced from the three-digit level to the one-digit level. The economy began to have a positive growth rate. The threat of commodity shortage was alleviated. In the mid-1990s, the Vietnamese economy was able to emerge from the crisis and experience a high growth rate.

The introduction of the market economy is a prerequisite for Vietnam to expand its external economic relations. From a closed economy which only traded with the communist bloc, the Vietnamese economy has opened up for trading with and receiving investment from all countries. International economic integration became a policy priority of the government. Before 1990, Vietnam had trading relations with only 40 partners. By 2012, Vietnam established diplomatic relations with more than 170 countries, and signed trade agreements with over 80 countries and regions, including all advanced economies (GSO 2012). From an isolated economy, Vietnam is now an important member of various regional and international economic organizations.

Since the 2000s, Vietnam's foreign trade has grown around 20 percent per year, and reached over 150 percent of the GDP in 2011, placing the Vietnamese economy among the ones that have highest level of openness. From a negligible figure in 1986, total registered foreign direct investment (FDI) into Vietnam reached $200 billion in 2011 and became a vital capital source of the economy. Japan, Korea, China, and ASEAN 6 are major trading partners of and investors in Vietnam (GSO 2011).

Vietnam's perspective of international economic integration has changed dramatically from a conservative to a more liberal trend. In the early 1990s, there was still a worry that the "open door" could allow "mosquitoes" and "flies," implying negative impacts from outside, to come in. International integration was restricted to economics. The approach to international economic integration was reactive as Vietnam was committed to it as less as possible and delayed its implementation as long as possible. The WTO accession has brought Vietnam to a more proactive approach to economic integration. It has been recognized that delay in implementing commitments can cause delay of the reforms and loss of the opportunities that occur in economic integration.

In the process of economic liberalization, the government encourages the development of multi-economic sectors, including the private sector, and recognizes it as the engine of economic growth. At the same time, the government pushes hard to reform the non-performing state-owned enterprises. Prior to the reform period, the state sector accounted for 90 percent of the economy in the north and 60 percent of the national economy. By 2010, the non-state sector (i.e. the private sector, foreign-invested sector, and collective sector) has accounted for more than 70 percent of the national economy (GSO 2010).

Since the mid-1990s, Vietnam has conducted economic industrialization and modernization with the objective of becoming a modern industrialized country by 2020. The share of the agricultural sector to GDP dropped from above 40 percent in 1990 by half in 2011 (GSO 2011). More importantly, the economic structure has been modernized. The service sector, which was viewed as "unproductive" and restrained before the *Doi Moi*, has become the leading sector of the economy. The face of the country has been modernized with a rapid process of urbanization.

From the recession in the 1980s, Vietnamese economy has emerged as one of the fastest growing economies in Asia since the mid-1990s. The GDP has doubled every 10 years since 1990, raising the hope for Vietnam to catch up with ASEAN 6 in a few decades. High economic growth has contributed to reducing poverty significantly. Per capita income rose from merely $250 in 1986 to over $1300 in 2011. Since 2010, Vietnam has become a low-middle-income developing country. The poor household ratio dropped from 70 percent in 1980 to 12 percent in early 2012 (or three million households) according to the adjusted poverty line (GSO 2012). The Human Development Index (HDI) increased 37 percent over the past 20 years, reaching 0.728 in 2011 (UNDP 2001, 2011). By 2006, 20 million Vietnamese, or almost a quarter of the total population, have been brought out of poverty, making Vietnam one of the most successful countries in the world in the war against poverty (MPI 2009).

At present, Vietnam's economic reforms are still incomplete. Market institutions have not been firmly established, even missing in many areas. The SOE reforms have not gone far enough. There is still a state monopoly in various sectors such as energy, mineral resources, oil, pension, railway, postal services, etc. The recent collapse of Vinashin, a state-owned shipbuilding corporation, presented a partial failure of the government's pilot scheme on establishing economic giants. The banking sector is another Achilles heel of the economy because of the non-performing loan problem which is mostly caused by the debt of the SOEs. Although Vietnam pursues an export-oriented strategy, there is a chronic huge trade deficit that places the economy in a state of serious imbalance. There is also concern about the weak value of the Vietnam Dong that leads to the dollarization of the economy and the accumulation of gold in the population.

The economic boom for many years has relied on the natural resource-intensive industrialization, and it causes serious environmental degradation. The adverse impact of environmental degradation is magnified because

Vietnam is a country that is likely to be seriously affected by the global climate change. Vietnam's economic productivity has not increased on par with the neighboring countries. The quality of labor force is still very low. The average educational level of the population is at about the sixth grade. In 2011, only 16.3 percent of the active labor force have been trained in their skills (GSO 2012). Despite more than 25 years of reforms, there is lingering red tape in the administration that worries the investors. Since 2008, serious macroeconomic issues such as high inflation, low liquidity in the banking system, increased public debt and budget deficit that have been accumulated over the past years of rapid but unsustainable growth have slowed down the growth rate of the economy.

Weak institutions, low-quality human resources, and poor infrastructure have become the bottlenecks of the Vietnamese economy. Vietnam is facing an urgent need for economic restructuring to ensure its future development and prosperity. This requires harsher reforms and stronger determination.

1.3 Social-cultural perspective

The *Doi Moi* has made Vietnamese people wealthier and happier. At present, Vietnam has completed most of the Millennium Development Goals (MDGs) set for developing countries in 2015. Among countries of similar rank of GDP per capita, Vietnam is seen as achieving major success in terms of social welfare.

Yet, there was a dark side of the economic boom and market economy. Economic growth creates a widening gap between the rich and the poor, and between urban and rural areas, making these major obstacles that Vietnam has to deal with to achieve socialism. The fruit of economic growth has not been equally distributed in the society. Most of it stays in the cities and those who live there, and only has a trickle effect on the rural areas. The infrastructural projects, factories, service economy, and high-income jobs arrive first in the urban areas. Due to the disadvantageous terms of trade, farmers accounting for almost 70 percent of the total population benefit less from the reforms. It is strikingly surprising that in 2011 the GDP per capita in Ho Chi Minh City is around $3,100, but the ethnic people in some hamlets of the mountainous areas only earn around $1 a day (GSO 2011).

The poverty gap is even sharper between different geographic locations such as the upland and lowland, and between the Kinh majority and numerous ethnic minority groups. While the rates of rural poverty are kept around 10 percent in the lowland areas (e.g. the Southeast and Red River Deltas), the rates of rural poverty usually exceed 50 percent in upland provinces and districts (e.g. the Central Highlands and the Northern Mountains). While the rural poverty rate for the Kinh majority has fallen from 30 percent to less than 5 percent during the past decade, poverty reduction has rarely occurred amongst the ethnic minorities, with nearly two-thirds of them still classified as poor (MARD 2012, 7). There are multiple factors that contribute to the pertinent poverty in the remote and mountainous region and among the ethnic minority, including disadvantageous locations, under-developed physical infrastructure, low education and low skill levels, limited access to support services, and prevailing social and cultural taboos of the indigenous communities.

The above economic gap is likely to create a divisive society, a situation in which the city exploits the countryside, and the rich exploit the poor. This becomes a potential source of social tension and instability.

Corruption is a severe problem in the reform era. Economic reforms provide ample opportunities for the corrupt officials to plunder state resources in the government-funded projects, trading of monopolized licenses and properties of privatized SOEs, and impose high taxes and fees on local residents. Low income makes accepting small graft a normal social habit among a number of state officials. Graft not only becomes widespread among low-ranking officials but also touches the high level of the government. The VCP recognizes that corruption within the state and party's apparatus is a vital threat toward the regime since it reduces the legitimacy of the party and state. Anti-corruption becomes a high political objective. The highest party and state leaders in Vietnam have repeatedly proclaimed "party rectification" and declared that there was no "forbidden zone" in the war against corruption (Truong 2006).

Another important source of social instability is the tension mounting from issues such as land, migration, unemployment, and labor rights. Land is one of the most tenuous issues in the reform era. Urbanization raises land prices rapidly and having a piece of land becomes a fortune for many families. Yet, land is not private property and can be appropriated by the government for public projects. There are many cases where local farmers resent the forced displacement and inadequate compensation. The protest occurs not only among individuals but also the entire local community.

There is a large number of laborers working in the informal sector. This is also a typical characteristic of the transitionary economy. The Labor Force Survey in 2007 (General Statistical Office 2007) reports that the informal sector accounts for almost 11 million jobs out of a total of 46 million in Vietnam. This represents nearly a quarter of all main occupations (23.5 percent) (Cling et al. 2011, 17). Poor labor conditions, low wage and dangerous jobs in the informal sector contribute to widespread inequality and even anger by the exploited groups in the society.

Demographic increase also creates heavy pressure on the government in terms of employment and social welfare policy. Each year, approximately 1.5 million young people join the workforce but not all of them are able to find jobs and only a small part of them are able to find appropriate jobs. There is a gap between the educational system and the labor market. According to the survey by the Ministry of Education and Training in 2011, approximately 63 percent of the graduated students are unable to find jobs and the rest have to be trained for new jobs (Ngan 2012).

The above tension occurs in the middle of the transition from a traditional society to a modern one. In this emerging society, individuals are related to one another not only by their relation to the party-state, but also to a variety of independent groups. As such, there is the important role of not only the masses but also the middle class.

The middle class in Vietnam can be defined as those who live in the urban areas, have higher income and are more educated. They have more opportunities to travel, access to various kinds of information, participate in social activities and exercise a democratic culture. These are the characters of the salaried bureaucrats, urban proletariats including the white-collar workers, workers in foreign-invested sectors, petite bourgeoisie, and high-income retired people. Scholars often regard the middle class as the agent of change and a force of democratization (Moore 1966). It is a part of society that embraces the value of civic culture and civil society.

The Vietnamese civil society is different from the West and bears many "Asian characters." From the liberal perspective, the primary objective of civil society is to influence and check the abuse of power by the state, or even contest against state power (Alaggapa 2004). The neo-Tocquevillian tradition also refers the quality of civil society to the density of voluntary associations or the degree of social capital that increases the social trust (Putnam 1993).

While most Vietnamese citizens belong to at least one organization – a rate which is higher than some other Asian countries such as China and Singapore (Dalton et al. 2003, 4), these memberships may not reflect the quality of participation. Membership in the social groups does not necessarily produce the bond of trust and reciprocity that the theory of social capital suggests because the traditional agrarian and Confucian traditions encourage trust in a relatively narrow circle of family and close friends (Dalton et al. 2003). According to a survey result, social trust is low among those who do not belong to any social group but dips to its lowest level among those who belong to many organizations (Dalton and Ong 2003).

Thus, the popular perspective in Vietnam tends to incorporate various kinds of state-led organizations, including the mass organizations (e.g. Fatherland Front, Ho Chi Minh Red-scarf Teenager, Ho Chi Minh Communist Youth Union, Women's Union, Veteran Association) into civil society (Duong et al. 2003). This perspective tends to see civil society as the "organizational weapon" – an instrument for mobilization to support state activities, or a medium for the state to detect, mitigate and solve tensions in society.

2 Involvement of Vietnam within the region (ASEAN)

2.1 Political-security perspective

In 1995, Vietnam became the 7th member of the ASEAN. Regional integration created the structural pressure for change in Vietnam's political institutions and foreign policy, including those toward its neighbors. Vietnam's old concepts of national interest, security, national independence, and autonomy were redefined to suit the new context. From a country that was regarded as the outpost of Communism in Southeast Asia and the security threat for ASEAN, Vietnam has become an active and responsible member of the regional community. From a country that implemented a "leaning toward one side" policy, i.e. the Soviet Union in the Cold War era, Vietnam has restored the balance in its relationships with all major powers (i.e. China, US, Russia, and EU).

By participating in all ASEAN agreements and mechanisms such as the Treaty of Amity and Cooperation (I and II), Southeast Asian Nuclear Weapon Free Zone Treaty, ASEAN Declaration on the South China Sea, Declaration on the Conduct of Parties in the South China Sea, ASEAN Regional Forum, and the future APSC, Vietnam becomes an important factor that contributes to peace and stability in the region. The presence of Vietnam in ASEAN contributes to increasing the power of ASEAN vis-à-vis major powers. In return, Vietnam has used the collective force of ASEAN to increase its relative strength vis-à-vis major powers.

The territorial dispute in the East Sea is a potential conflict within ASEAN and between some ASEAN countries and China. As one of the parties of the conflict, Vietnam has consistently attempted to seek peaceful solutions and called on other parties to restrain from the use of force to resolve the conflict. Vietnam has also called for proper implementation of Declaration on the Code of Conduct in the East Sea and the approval of the Code of Conduct in the East Sea by all involved parties. This effort has contributed to peace and security in Southeast Asia and has been appreciated by the international community.

Vietnam's current foreign policy recognizes the important role of APSC in promoting peace, stability, and cooperation in the Southeast Asian region. It also acknowledges that Vietnam's participation in APSC will serve its national interest, and creates a favorable external environment for its socio-economic development. However, in the process of building APSC, ASEAN will step into a number of areas which are considered "sensitive" in Vietnam's foreign policy such as democracy, human rights, the establishment of peace-keeper forces, ASEAN human rights mechanism and a common parliament, etc. because these may allow foreign intervention into Vietnam's domestic affairs. Furthermore, the escalating tension in the territorial disputes in the East Sea causes Vietnam to be cautious about the effectiveness and success of the APSC project even though this can be seen as the driving force that pushes ASEAN countries closer to each other to resolve the conflict.

2.2 Economic perspective

ASEAN economic integration is always an important part of Vietnam's foreign economic policy. Right after joining ASEAN in 1995, Vietnam has implemented its commitments to ASEAN Free Trade Area (AFTA-CEPT), which has now been incorporated into the ASEAN Trade in Goods

Agreement (ATIGA). Vietnam is also actively participating in the conclusion and implementation of the ASEAN Framework Agreement on Services (AFAS) and ASEAN Comprehensive Investment Agreement (ACIA).

Trade and investment relations between Vietnam and ASEAN have been improved significantly along with active and responsible participation of Vietnam into ASEAN. Among others, ASEAN became the major trade and investment partner of Vietnam. Trade turnover between ASEAN and Vietnam has increased from merely USD 4.8 billion in 1996 to nearly USD 40 billion in 2012 (Figure 10.1). Accumulated (registered) FDI from ASEAN to Vietnam during the 1990–2009 period was USD 40 billion (1,517 projects),

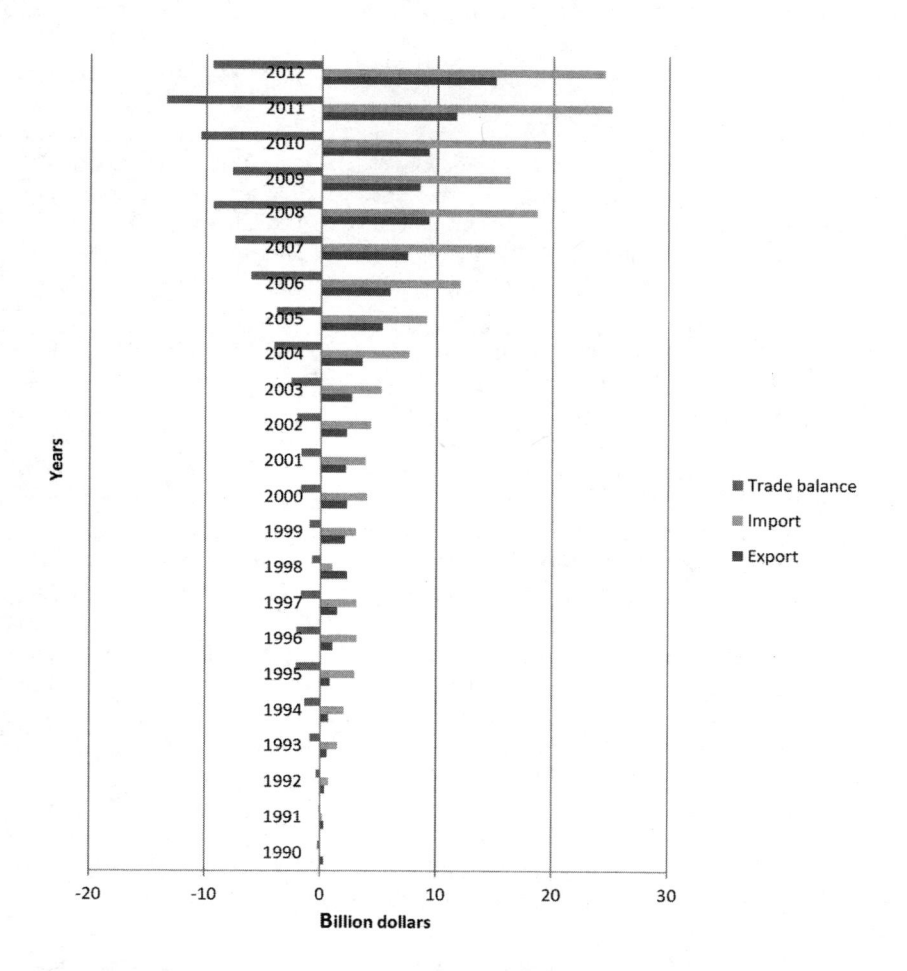

Figure 10.1 Total import and export from and to Vietnam by ASEAN countries (1990–2012)
Source: wits.worldbank.org (accessed on 15 October 2013).

accounting for 26 percent of total FDI into Vietnam (13.8 percent of total projects). FDI from Vietnam to ASEAN was USD 4.8 billion (269 projects), mostly to Cambodia, Laos, and Myanmar during the last four years.

Vietnam commits itself to making active contributions to building a strong ASEAN Economic Community (AEC). To achieve the common target of establishing the AEC in 2015, Vietnam has been undertaking a wide range of measures, including in the following areas: trade facilitation, investment promotion and facilitation, and free movement of skilled labor.

As stipulated in the Blueprint for establishing the AEC, trade facilitation is viewed as the key to the development of the AEC and, especially, to the establishment of a single market and production base by allowing the free flow of goods within the region. Trade facilitation is defined as both at-the-border and behind-the-border measures to make trade easier, less costly, and more efficient.

For trade facilitation, Vietnam has implemented various agreements in the ASEAN framework in the last decade. These include the CEPT, ASEAN Trade in Goods Agreement (ATIGA), the ASEAN Strategic Plan of Customs Development for 2005–2010, the adoption of ASEAN Customs Declaration Document, and the implementation of the ASEAN Cargo Processing Model, the ASEAN Single Window (ASW), and the ASEAN roadmap for Integration of Logistics Services.

In order to implement these cooperation agreements, Vietnam has to carry out a number of reforms, both at-the-border and behind-the-border reforms. Customs procedure reform is considered a key activity of the trade facilitation process in Vietnam. The three principles of the customs reform process are: simplification, transparency, and modernization. The objective of the reform is to promote international trade and reduce corruption and smuggling. E-custom implementation is one measure to achieve those objectives. Toward the implementation of the ASEAN Single Window agreement, Vietnam is in the process of developing Vietnam's National Single Window (VNSW). This is also defined as the key facility for economic agents and government agencies to conduct their businesses and duties related to international transportation and trade. There are still many reforms in the field of customs that Vietnam has to fulfill in the coming years. These range from legal framework, customs procedure, to organizational structure and ICT adoption.

Free flow of investment is one core element of a single market and production base in AEC. The main efforts of the Vietnamese government in creating a favorable investment environment are the Investment Law, which came into force in 2006, together with a new Enterprise Law and Intellectual Property Rights Act. The new Investment Law seeks to unify rules relating to investment in Vietnam by making it applicable to both foreign and domestic investors. The Investment Law seeks to create a level playing field for both domestic and foreign investors, and more importantly, to enable free entry into the investment market. According to this Law, investors are allowed to do business without restrictions in a wider range of economic sectors. Results of the Vietnamese government's efforts in attracting FDI were evidenced in FDI inflows into Vietnam recently (Figure 10.2).

Free movement of skilled labor is one of the five core elements to build a single market and production base in AEC. As mapped out by the Blueprint for establishing the AEC, Vietnam and other ASEAN member countries are currently working on:

- To facilitate the issuance of visas and employment passes for ASEAN professionals and skilled labor.
- To facilitate the free flow of services. This entails completing MRAs and developing core competencies for job/occupational skills required in major professional services, including Priority Integration Services (PIS) sectors of e-commerce, healthcare, air travel, tourism, and logistics.
- To enhance cooperation among ASEAN University Network (AUN) members to promote exchange and mobility for both students and staff.
- To strengthen research capability of each ASEAN member country in improving skills, job placements, and developing labor market information networks within ASEAN region.

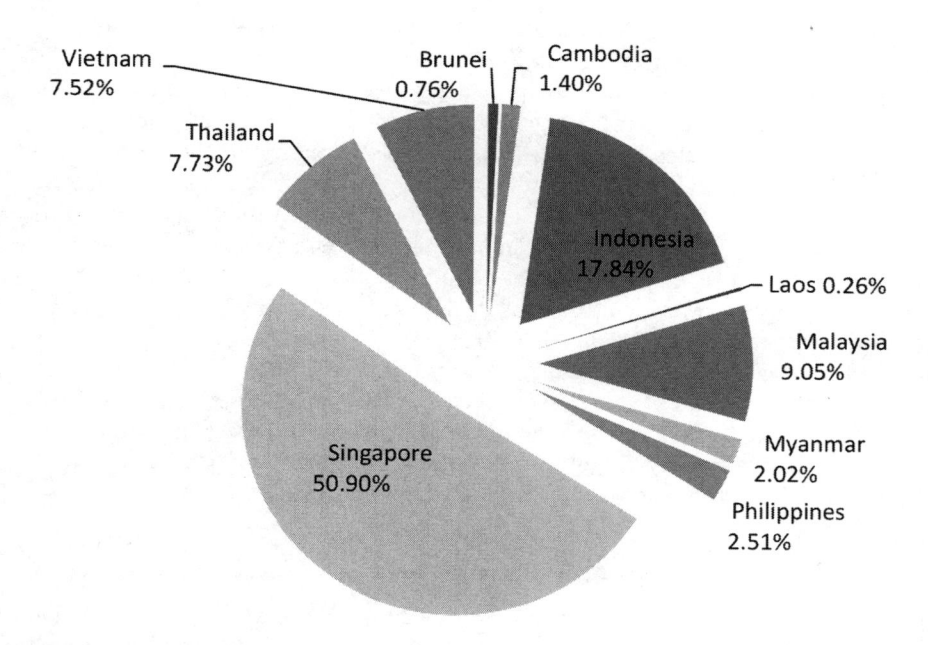

Figure 10.2 FDI inflows into ASEAN countries (2012)
Source: ASEAN Secretariat, ASEAN FDI database (accessed on 8 November 2014).

2.3 Social-cultural perspective

Vietnam shares with other ASEAN countries the traditional "Asian" values, which often refer to individual duties and responsibilities toward the community, greater respect for authority and hierarchy, maintenance of order and stability for the common good. Some scholars and politicians believe that these "Asian" values lay the foundation of the ASEAN norms such as the maintenance of harmony, consensus, informal diplomacy, non-interference, and intramural discussions. From the cultural perspective, this commonness is a prerequisite for the successful integration and effective contribution of Vietnam into ASEAN even though Vietnam is at a different economic development level and has a different political ideology compared to other ASEAN members.

Since the inception of ASEAN in 1967, many of its original values and norms have undergone critical debates. Their legitimacy and efficacy have been seriously challenged since the outbreak of the Asian financial crisis. The enlargement of ASEAN to admit new members with diverse socio-economic and political backgrounds also raises the need for more flexible interpretation and application of those norms and values. Vietnam used to oppose the change in the original ASEAN norms but it now adopts a more flexible view in some cases, including the sensitive ones such as defense, security, and human rights cooperation. This is the evidence of the changes that have gradually taken place inside Vietnamese society with the emergence of civic culture and civil society as a result of international and regional integration.

However, Vietnamese culture is still imbued with the agricultural, non-market characteristics which are the consequence of the agricultural, non-market economy. This creates a cultural gap between Vietnam and the more developed ASEAN countries, which have pursued the market economy for a long time and become more open and more exposed to the Western culture. In this regard, joining ASCC provides Vietnam with more opportunities to increase socio-cultural exchanges with other countries and create an external force to replace the backward cultural institutions that are the barriers to rapid development. ASCC is a valuable instrument to promote cooperation between Vietnam and other ASEAN countries in a number of important fields such as healthcare, education, sport, social security network, gender equality, etc. These contribute to improving the quality of human resources, people's living standards, and poverty reduction in Vietnam and narrowing the development gap and cultural gap between Vietnam and other ASEAN countries.

3 Involvement of Vietnam within East Asia (ASEAN Plus Three)

Since 2010, Vietnam has maintained a policy guideline of "pro-active, active and responsible" for its participation in ASEAN and ASEAN Plus Three (APT) community. In this policy orientation, Vietnam has facilitated ASEAN's agreement on the format of the East Asia Summit (EAS) which would be an outward-looking mechanism admitting and selecting new members on the basis that the admission and selection of new members shall not erode the central role of ASEAN. Vietnam also helped organize successfully the first ASEAN Defense Ministerial Meeting plus 8 (with China, India, Russia, U.S, Japan, Korea, Australia, and New Zealand) or ADMM+8 to kick off a new regional security mechanism. The invention of the ADMM+8 mechanism is a major breakthrough for regional cooperation in the sense that defense cooperation used to be seen as a sensitive issue by some ASEAN countries, including Vietnam. In addition to ADMM+8, Vietnam's idea to organize meetings of police chiefs to address transnational issues such as terrorism, woman trafficking, illegal migration, transnational crime, etc., has been welcomed by ASEAN and its dialogue partners.

Since 1995, Vietnam has undertaken active regional and multilateral economic integration as well as bilateral economic ties. Vietnam's accession to the various ASEAN economic agreements demonstrates its strong commitment to regional economic cooperation. With the aim to realize the ASEAN Economic Community (AEC) in 2015, Vietnam has expedited its economic liberalization in all sectors by implementing key commitments fairly and equally compared to more developed ASEAN members.

Vietnam also considers signing preferential and free trade agreements (PTA/FTAs) with major trading partners in East Asia as part and parcel of its important strategy of international economic integration and diversification. The Vietnam Japan Economic Partnership Agreement (VJEPA) is the first bilateral FTA of Vietnam, which will further enhance Vietnam's economic tie with Japan, its strategic partner. The Vietnam–South Korea FTA is also under negotiation with the objective of promoting trade and investment between the two countries. Recently, the launching of the Regional Comprehensive Economic Partnership (RCEP) Agreement is also strongly supported by the Vietnamese government. This Agreement which involves the participation of ASEAN members and its six FTA partners, will have broader and deeper integration with significant improvements over the existing ASEAN+1 FTAs. Potential gains for Vietnam from PTAs/FTAs are investment capital, technology, knowledge, and best practices for transition to a socialist-oriented market economy. Advanced markets such as Japan, Korea, and other ASEAN economies would be complementary to Vietnam's static comparative advantages and generating dynamic ones. Challenges remain with managing compliance and establishing sound legal and institutional frameworks for PTA/FTA implementation. Vietnam has sought ways and means to closely consult with its economic partners to reduce the adverse trade imbalance, which is mainly caused by the difference of the industrial structure and trade pattern.

Vietnam's contribution to the APT community is thus multidimensional, ranging from deeper economic integration to closer political and security cooperation, especially in Vietnam's major efforts to balance the relationship of ASEAN with China, Japan, and Korea to create a sense of trust and nurture the spirit of community in East Asia.

4 Conclusion

The twentieth century gave birth to a new Vietnamese nation-state, and a political regime with socialist orientation. After 30 years of war and 10 years under the post-war autarkic economic system, the *Doi Moi* launched in 1986 brought about a new phase in Vietnam's development. Despite major successes, the reforms are far from complete. A lot of obstacles still remain and require political resolve to address.

In 1996, Vietnam set out the policy of industrialization and modernization with the objective of becoming a basically industrialized country by 2020. However, there is a heavy pressure from rapid industrialization and modernization on Vietnam's development trajectory. The developed countries in the world had around 300 years to complete their industrialization but Vietnam only has a few decades to fulfill a similar task. In addition to the transition from an agricultural society to industrial society, Vietnam has to conduct the transition from a command economy to market economy.

The current weaknesses of the Vietnamese economy stem from its unsustainable growth model which relies on cheap labor, natural resource exploitation, and capital growth. Although Vietnam has already become a middle-income country at the lower level, it is facing the challenge of falling into the "middle income trap" similar to some other Southeast Asian countries. Vietnam thus needs to change its growth model to obtain higher development achievement. To this aim, the Socio-economic Development Strategy for the Period of 2011–2020, which is the policy bridge for Vietnam to become a modern industrialized country by 2020, sets the focus on sustaining economic growth in harmony with environmental protection to ensure long-term stable economic development.

For more than 25 years of reforms, Vietnam has adapted to as well as resisted the change of values and norms: the economy is moving toward the market direction; the political system is upholding the communist ideology and the party-state; the society is de-atomized and has a more complex structure. The new political, economic, and socio-cultural identity of Vietnam today bears mixed characters, which include the particularities of Vietnam and universalities of the international community.

Regional integration is one of the key words in Vietnam's reform guidelines. In the Cold War era, Vietnam's influence on Southeast Asia and East Asia came from its strategic geo-politic position. The participation of Vietnam in regional mechanisms and alliances was appreciated by its ability to shift the regional balance of power. This realist perception was constructed and exploited by the great powers in their competition for regional influence. At present, the role of Vietnam in the ASEAN and APT community has changed from geo-politic importance to geo-economic importance, and from adopting a divisive line in the past to serving as the bridge at present.

There are three levels of Vietnam's regional integration: at the Mekong subregional level, at the ASEAN level, and at the APT or East Asian level. In the Mekong subregion, Vietnam can help to connect the Mekong countries into the subregional cooperation development program. In ASEAN, Vietnam can help to bridge the development and integration gap between the new ASEAN members with the old ones. In East Asia, Vietnam's deepening international integration, proactive and responsible participation in ASEAN and good relationship with China, Japan, and Korea are important factors contributing to the construction of the APT community.

Regional integration creates pressure for changes in Vietnam's political institution and foreign policy. Vietnam has altered the old concepts of national interest, security, independence, and autonomy. There is a wider agreement that difference in political ideology and political system is not an obstacle for cooperation and for the pursuit of shared interests. In this regard, Vietnam has made consistent efforts to diversify and multilateralize its foreign relations since the early 1990s. At the same time, Vietnam's foreign policy puts the focus on two groups of important countries: neighboring countries and major powers, including advanced economies in the world. Potential members of the APT community are in these two groups.

There are also some differences of interests among the potential members of the APT community hampering the regional integration project. Among the issues that may create tensions are the territorial dispute in the East Sea and the competition for influence among the major powers such as the US and China. Vietnam has insisted on peaceful resolutions to the conflicts and balanced its relationship with major powers thereby contributing to peace, security, stability, and development in the Southeast Asian region. International integration has brought about a common view that Vietnam's peace and prosperity are closely related to the peace and prosperity of ASEAN and East Asia.

Note

1 Doi Moi (Renovation): refers to the economic reforms initiated in Vietnam in 1986 with the objective of creating a "socialist-oriented market economy," which led to the replacement of the centrally planned economy with a more market-based economy, where the private sector plays a significant role in commodity production and the state sector plays a decisive role in the economy.

References

Alagappa, Muthiah (ed.) (2004) *Civil Society and Political Change in Asia: Expanding and Contracting Democratic Space*. Stanford, CA: Stanford University Press.

Chamberlain, Heath (1993) 'On Search for Civil Society in China.' *Modern China* 19(2): 199–215.

Cling, Jean Pierre, Mireille Razafindrakoto and François Roubaud (2011) *The Informal Economy in Vietnam*. Hanoi: International Labor Organization.

Dalton, Russell J. and Ong Nhu-Ngoc (2003) *Civil Society and Social Capital in Vietnam*. Available from: www.democ.uci.edu/resources/virtuallibrary/Vietnam/Vietnam04.pdf (accessed 16 March 2012).

Dalton, Russell J., Pham Minh Hac, Pham Thanh Nghi and Ong Nhu-Ngoc (2003) *Social Relations and Social Capital in Vietnam: The 2001 World Values Survey.* Available from: www.democ.uci.edu/resources/virtuallibrary/Vietnam/Vietnam02. pdf (accessed 10 February 2012).

General Statistical Office (GSO) (2007) *Vietnam - Labor Force Survey – 2007.* Hanoi: GSO.

General Statistical Office (GSO) (2010) *Socio-economic Report 2010.* Hanoi: GSO.

General Statistical Office (GSO) (2011) *Socio-economic Report 2011.* Hanoi: GSO.

General Statistical Office (GSO) (2012) *Socio-economic Report – Quarter I/2012.* Hanoi: GSO.

Gourevitch, Peter (1978) 'The Second Image Reversed: International Sources of Domestic Politics,' *International Organization* 32(4): 881–912.

Ho Chi Minh (1996) *Collected Works.* Book 10, Book 5. Hanoi: National Political Publishing House.

Kim Ngan (2012) *63% Graduated Students are Unemployed – Is There Any Problem in the Quality of the Educational System?* ["63 % sinh viên thất nghiệp, chất lượng giáo dục có vấn đề?"]. Available from: http://giaoduc.net.vn/Giao-duc-24h/63-sinh-vien-tha t-nghiep-chat-luong-giao-duc-co-van-de/227408.gd (accessed 24 November 2012).

Le Bach Duong, Khuat Thu Hong, Bach Tan Sinh and Nguyen Thanh Tung (2003) *Civil Society in Vietnam.* Ha Noi: Center for Social Development Studies.

Milner, Helen and Robert Keohane (ed.) (1996) *Internationalization and Domestic Politics* Cambridge: Cambridge University Press.

Ministry of Agriculture and Rural Development (MARD) (2012) *Agriculture Restructure Scheme to Sustainable and Higher Added Value Development.* Second Draft. May, Hanoi.

Ministry of Planning and Investment (MPI) (2009) *Mid-term Report on Results of the Implementation of the 2006–2010 Socio-economic Development Plan.* Hanoi: MPI.

Moore, Barrington (1966) *Social Origins of Dictatorship and Democracy: Lord and Peasant in the Making of the Modern World.* Boston, MA: Beacon Press.

Pham Ngoc Thach and Ho Khang (2008) *History of the Resistant War against the America (1954–1975)* [Lịch sử kháng chiến chống Mỹ cứu nước (1954–1975)]. Volume VIII. Hanoi: National Political Publishing House.

Putnam, Robert (1993) 'The Prosperous Community: Social Capital and Public Life' *American Prospect* 13(4): 35–42.

Truong Huu Quynh, Dinh Xuan Lam and Le Mau Han (2006) *Introduction to Vietnam's History* [Đại cương lịch sử Việt Nam]. Hanoi: Educational Publishing House.

Truong Tan Sang (2006) *There is no Forbidden Zone in At-corruption* [Không Có Vùng Cấm Trong Chống Tham Nhũng]. Available from: http://Vietnamnet.vn/chinhtri/ 2006/10/620370 (accessed on April 15, 2012).

Tsu, Tang (2002) 'Chinese Politics at the Top: Factionalism or Informal Politics? Balance-of-Power Politics or a Game to Win All.' In *The Nature of Chinese Politics*, edited by Jonathan Unger. Armonk, NY and London: M.E Shape.

United Nation Development Program (UNDP) (2001) *Human Development Report 2001.* New York: UNDP.

United Nation Development Program (UNDP) (2011) *Human Development Report 2011.* New York: UNDP.

Vietnam Communist Party (VCP) (1988) *Resolution XIII of the Politburo on the Tasks and Foreign Policy in the New Context.* Hanoi: National Political Publishing House.

Vietnam Communist Party (VCP) (1991) *Resolution of the Seventh National Congress of the Communist Party of Vietnam.* Hanoi: National Political Publishing House.

Vietnam Communist Party (VCP) (1996) *Resolution of the Eighth National Congress of the Communist Party of Vietnam.* Hanoi: National Political Publishing House.

Vietnam Communist Party (VCP) (2001) *Resolution of the Ninth National Congress of the Communist Party of Vietnam.* Hanoi: National Political Publishing House.

Vietnam Communist Party (VCP) (2006) *Resolution of the Tenth National Congress of the Communist Party of Vietnam.* Hanoi: National Political Publishing House.

Vietnam Communist Party (VCP) (2011a) *Resolution of the Eleventh National Congress of the Communist Party of Vietnam.* Hanoi: National Political Publishing House.

Vietnam Communist Party (VCP) (2011b) 'Political Program on National Development in the Transitioning Period to Socialism (Supplement in 2011)' [Cương lĩnh xây ddy đđy nưư trong thhn kk quá đđ lên chh nghĩa xã hh (b) sung, phát trii năm 2011)], Hanoi: National Political Publishing House.

11 China

An emerging power in the making of the APT community

Wei Min

Both China and ASEAN Plus Three (APT) are undergoing a new historical process, a process that will lead to the formation of a regional community. In the context of the ongoing globalization and continual evolution of the international system, APT integration has gradually become a basic trend in the region. Since the end of the Cold War, international realities have demonstrated that regionalization is not only a key theme of the contemporary era, but also a tool that is able to address problems and challenges that countries face. China, with its growing power as a major actor and the Asian developing region's only UNSC permanent member, will undoubtedly play a key role in the formation of the APT community. Generally speaking, despite the obstacles and disputes that currently exist, APT integration will continue to develop and the interactions of China and other APT members will continue to broaden and become more profound.

1 National perspectives: a historical background

East Asia (APT as its core and principal part) is a unique region, steeped in culture and rich with history. Thus it is not a surprise that throughout history, East Asia has had a significant influence on the world. China has also been and continues to be one of the key actors in the historical development of East Asia.

China is a nation of long history (see Table 11.1) and splendid culture. Archaeological materials show the ancient human "Yuanmou Man," "Lantian Man," and "Peking Man" lived in the land of China 1 million–400 or 500 thousand years ago. After a long primitive society, Xia, the first dynasty in China's history, emerged in about twenty-first century BC. Following Xia, Shang and Western Zhou appeared. After that China entered the Spring and Autumn and Warring States period (i.e. the Eastern Zhou Dynasty). Since Qin unified China in 221 BC, through Han, Wei, Jin, Southern and Northern Dynasties, Sui, Tang, Five Dynasties, Song, Yuan, Ming, Qing dynasty, Republic of China (ROC), and People's Republic of China (PRC), China has experienced a long and continuous history. Throughout history, China has occupied an important position in political, economic, social, and cultural aspects in the world, and made significant contributions to world civilization. It is one of the four ancient civilizations, and a birthplace of papermaking, printing, gunpowder, and the compass.

Before the entry of Westerners in 1511, China and East Asia enjoyed relative stability in the region. Age-old traditions, which had not undergone a revolutionary transition like those in Western Europe, ruled the day and had remained largely unchanged across time. International interactions in the region were done through a traditional nexus in the fields of politics, economics, and culture.

China was then the nominal leader in the region, for it created the "core–periphery" international configuration or "tributary system" that was recognized by its neighbors, and had no intention of actually ruling the surrounding area. This was very different from the Western paradigm based on nation-state and sovereignty. Through history, most Chinese dynasties regarded the maintenance and consolidation of absolute power as the primacy of rule, and from

Table 11.1 Brief chronology of Chinese history

Dynasty	*Period*
Xia	21th century B.C.–16th century B.C.
Shang	The 16th century B.C.–11th century
Western Zhou	The 11th century–770 B.C.
Eastern Zhou (Spring and Autumn and Warring States)	770 B.C.–221 B.C.
Qin	221 B.C.–207 B.C.
Western Han	206 B.C.–24 A.D.
Eastern Han	A.D. 25–220
Three Kingdoms (Wei, Shu and Wu)	A.D. 220–265
Western Jin	A.D. 265–316
Eastern Jin	A.D. 317–420
Northern and Southern Dynasties	A.D. 420–589
Sui	A.D. 581–618
Tang	A.D. 618–907
Five Dynasties	A.D. 907–960
Northern Song	A.D. 960–1127
Southern Song	A.D. 1127–1279
Yuan	A.D. 1271–1368
Ming	A.D. 1368–1644
Qing	A.D. 1644–1911
Republic of China	A.D. 1911–1949
People's Republic of China	A.D. 1949–Present

Source: Compiled from the data of http://www.lishi.net/ Accessed on May 15, 2014.

their view, the key threats to the dynasties were from inside. Therefore, they tended to keep an introverted political thinking, and the neighboring areas were expected to be stable and have good relations with China through a set of arrangements including tributary trade and nominal allegiance to the central kingdom. Basically, it is a defensive, rather than an offensive system, and ensured the relative stability and regulation of the region in most historical periods.

However, with China's rapid decline through a series of events, beginning with the Opium Wars in 1840, continuing through the Japanese invasion of China (since the Sino-Japanese War in 1894) until the end of World War II in 1945, this regional system collapsed. These events had profound impacts on both the region and China. The traditional international system collapsed and almost all nations in East Asia were colonized or semi-colonized by the Western powers and Japan. Besides Japan and Thailand, the other nations were under the control of different Western powers, and East Asia, as a whole, was broken into pieces. For the Chinese, this contentious past has had a profound impact on China's national identity and worldviews today (Gries 2009, 220–232). This was China's one hundred years of humiliation. Under the challenges and invasions from outside, all kinds of crises happened in China, leading to her profound miseries and helplessness. Meanwhile, Chinese ever-lasting national pride and confidence were unprecedentedly hit hard. In sum, the historical process before World War II brought China and East Asia into a new international context. This continues to affect the East Asian nations' international standing and external strategy today.

After World War II, East Asia faced a new international context and a new opportunity for regional development. One after another, East Asian states attained national independence from their colonial masters, albeit at varying paces and in different ways. For China, it completely ended the century-long tumultuous period of domestic unrest and serious external threats. The People's Republic of China was founded in 1949 after a three-year civil war between the Chinese Communist Party (CCP) and Chinese Nationalist Party (CNP).

However, the Cold War re-defined international relations in East Asia by dividing the region into two camps, forcing each country to take sides. The CCP-led New China soon fell into the Cold War, and confronted the US-led camp as a member of the socialist camp.

The Korean War (1950–1953) was a direct result of the competition between the two ideologies and two coalitions. As a result of the Korean War, Sino-US relations were suspended and frozen. At the same time, many neighbors did not establish diplomatic relations with China.

Overall, China had very cold and difficult relations with most of its neighbors in this period. In the context of the Cold War, political ideology dominated the foreign policy-making process of most countries, and China's support of active communists in its regional neighbors contributed to the mistrust in the region.

The normalization of the Sino-US relations in the late 1960s provided countries in the region with the necessary context to come together. One after another in a short period, notably, Japan, Malaysia, the Philippines, and Thailand established formal diplomatic relations with China as an adjustment to the US new policy for China (see Table 11.2). More importantly, on October 1971, the 26th session of the UN General Assembly overwhelmingly adopted Resolution 2758; China's lawful seat in the UN was restored. China's diplomacy subsequently stepped into a new stage as the Asian developing region's only UNSC permanent member. From the late 1970s, dealing with both Soviet Union and Vietnam gradually became the common interest for China and the United States, and both countries thus had a honeymoon period in their relations after World War II.

Almost during the same period, China began to reflect on Mao Zedong's (1893–1976, the founding father of PRC) national policies, and initiated a great policy transformation on the hubris of the 10-year Cultural Revolution; Deng Xiaoping's (1904–1997, the chief architect of China's reform and opening-up) reform and opening-up policy was a historical event for both China and the outside world. China's ideology-based worldview was revolutionarily replaced by realist-based foreign policy paradigm; she began to participate actively and integrate itself into the international system. This had significant implications for East Asia for it led to the betterment of relations

Table 11.2 Time of normalization of foreign relations between China and her neighbors

Country	Time of Normalization
Vietnam	January 18,1950
Myanmar	June 8,1950
Cambodia	July 19,1958
Laos	April 25,1961
Japan	September 29,1972
Malaysia	May 31,1974
The Philippines	June 9,1975
Thailand	July 1,1975
Indonesia	April 13,1950; August 8,1990
Singapore	October 3,1990
Brunei	September 30,1991
Republic of Korea	August 24,1992

Source: Ministry of Foreign Affairs of People's Republic of China website, "Countries and Organizations," available on http://www.fmprc.gov.cn/mfa_chn/gjhdq_603914, accessed May 20, 2014.

Note: On October 30, 1967, Indonesia severed diplomatic relations with China, and resumed formal diplomatic relations on August 8, 1990.

with China's neighbors. This was seen in the region's response to Vietnam's advance in Cambodia, which made China and ASEAN nations come and work together to deal with this regional threat. The close cooperation against Vietnam's actions and China–Vietnam's border military conflict in 1979 pushed China and ASEAN nations together, strengthening their mutual understanding, and promoting the Sino-US cooperation to a new stage during the Cold War.

In the post-Cold War era, China–East Asia relations entered a period of overall development that saw the possibility of integration into a regional community. Indonesia, the biggest nation in Southeast Asia, resumed diplomatic relations with China in August 1990, and it was followed by Singapore and Brunei. The Republic of Korea finally did the same thing on August 1992. This was indicative of the beginning of a new stage in the relations between China and her neighbors.

2 China's role in the APT: an increasingly important regional power

In the new era, almost all nations repositioned economic development rather than political ideology as their priority in foreign policy decision-making. The 1997 Asian Financial Crisis and China's decision not to profit from the crisis marked China's re-emergence as a major player in East Asia. This offered the region a historical opportunity to initiate regional integration. Since then, China's ties with her neighbors have developed greatly; the Southeast Asian perceptions of China in the late 1990s shifted significantly compared with the Cold War; elites and the general public in most countries in the region gradually came to view China as a constructive actor and as a preeminent regional power.

After 2000, and especially in recent years, China's economic rise (see Table 11.3 and 11.4) has become a key factor in the interactions with her neighbors. No one can deny the rise of its influence nationally, regionally, and globally. For China, the rise is both a part and a continuation of the East Asian economic miracle after World War II, following the economic rise of Japan, the NIEs, and ASEAN. Like other neighbors that had experienced economic rise in quick succession, China should also not be looked at as a threat to its neighbors, but an opportunity for East Asia. In China's relations with most of the countries and regions, especially with regards to neighboring countries in East Asia, China's foreign policy priority is to construct and maintain a peaceful and stable international configuration. One of the most important missions for China's foreign policy is to reassure the world that China is rising peacefully, and would not be a threat to the rest of the world.

However, for China's neighbors, China's rise is both an opportunity and a challenge. Further observation is needed to determine whether it is more of an opportunity or a challenge. Some countries in the region are concerned about the security risks generated by China's rise; they are concerned that China might change its existing foreign policy from soft to hard diplomacy.

Table 11.3 China's GDP and economic growth rate (unit: trillion Yuan)

Year	2001	2002	2003	2004	2005	2006	2007
GDP	10.96	12.03	13.58	15.99	18.49	21.63	26.58
Growth Rate	8.3%	9.1%	10.0%	10.1%	9.9%	12.7%	14.2%

Year	2008	2009	2010	2011	2012	2013	2014
GDP	31.40	34.09	40.15	47.31	51.95	56.88	63.65
Growth Rate	9.6%	9.2%	10.4%	9.3%	7.7%	7.7%	7.4%

Source: National Bureau of Statistics of China, Statistical Communique of China on the Economic and Social Development (2001–2014), available on http://www.stats.gov.cn, accessed February 2, 2015.

Under the new regional context, the political and economic cooperation in East Asia seems to contain both opportunities and unpredictable uncertainties.

In any case, China's foreign relations strategy must start from its immediate neighbors: East Asian nations. This is because the region is at the core of China's external relations. Both China's national interests and the region's interests have overlapping areas. China and her neighbors are on their way to reconstructing East Asia. Both China and East Asia should choose the option that history has offered them: the chance to work toward a regional community. A more comprehensive and closer regional community will provide an effective opportunity for the settlement of disputes among nations, a good means to promote economic development for each country, a major contribution to peace and stability in politics and security in the region, and bring about a greater bargaining power when negotiating as a regional bloc with other countries or regions.

3 The three pillars of China–APT interactions: cooperation and challenges

To understand the China–APT relations, it is important to appreciate China's strategic position in both the region and in the world. Since the end of the Cold War, China's key strategic goal has simply been the maintenance and promotion of peace and stability around it. The Chinese government knows rather clearly that only in such an international environment can China's

Table 11.4 Selected yearly China's foreign currency reserves (unit: billion USD)

Year	1996	2001	2006	2011	2012	2013	2014
Volume	105	212.2	1066.3	3181.1	3311.6	3821.3	3843.02

Source: National Bureau of Statistics of China, Statistical Communique of China on the Economic and Social Development (1996–2014), available on http://www.stats.gov.cn, accessed February 2, 2015.

overall national strategy taking economic development as the national policy cornerstone and upholding the reforms and opening-up as the policy approaches – designed by Deng Xiaoping, which was continued by Jiang Zemin, Hu Jintao and Xi Jinping administration – be implemented. Only then can China's economy continue to grow, and its social and political stability be continuously maintained.

Based on this strategic thinking, China's foreign policies changed revolutionarily, and it was inclined to international cooperation by actively participating in, and constructing a number of international cooperation mechanisms, such as ASEAN Regional Forum (ARF), Shanghai Cooperation Organization (SCO), Shangri-La Dialogue (SLD), and many other multilateral cooperation platforms. In the context of globalization, China's change to multilateralism is undoubtedly an essential and beneficial policy option for the promotion of her economic development and national security.

The neighboring region is the focus in China's diplomacy. Close ties in political-security, economic, and cultural affairs between China and other APT members are essential to serve the needs of the Chinese national strategy. Though Chinese leaders often reiterated that China's established policies have remained unchanged at both domestic and international levels, China's strategic intention and external behaviors have been questioned. This is largely because of China's growing economic power and the evolution of international politics.

3.1 Political-security perspectives: common needs and cognitive differences

As is the case for other APT countries, the region's security framework and development trends are related to China's own national security. China believes that a relatively peaceful and stable international environment would be an indispensable prerequisite for its economic transformation; peace is also a common interest for all neighbors in the region. China has taken active efforts to maintain peace in the region and boost its image as a non-threatening emerging power. China's "neighbor strategy" of "Good friends, Good neighbors, and Good partners" is not just a foreign policy slogan, but an actual strategic intention.

However, the East Asian security situation is full of uncertainties. This certainly makes East Asia disappointed with the status quo. In trying to explain the development of the region's international relations, three factors stand out: First, the rise of China and its influences regionally and globally. Second, the US's eastward strategic shift and its strategy toward China. Third is ASEAN's regional role and its possible developments.

First is the factor of China's rise. The China factor seems to be an increasingly important variable in the analysis of regional politics and security. While China is experiencing exciting times with its 30 years of economic growth and rapid increase in comprehensive national power, China realized that the more powerful it was becoming, the more suspicious its neighbors became of her.

China's economic success has had an irrefutable impact politically and economically in East Asia and even in the world. China's main security concern is the possible negative impact of its rise.

As far as China's rise and its possible influences are concerned, there is an obvious difference in perception between the Chinese and the outsiders.

Many Chinese do not think that China has completed the transition into a real strong power in the world, when compared with the developed countries and its once-glorious history. From their perspective, China has a long way ahead before becoming a well-governed state; they believe that China is still undergoing the process of national development, and has accumulated plenty of problems over the course of China's reforms and opening-up. Problems ranging from the uneven development among domestic regions, the gap between urban and rural areas, the huge gap between the poor and the rich, severity of corruption, the social moral degeneration, inadequate social security system, contradictions and conflicts between the officials and the public, unresolved national unification issues, and so on. These problems would produce social instability, as well as obstacles for national progress. Political legitimacy was thus doubted and challenged.

Most Chinese attribute the problems to the stagnant political reforms and the existing power configuration of the regime. The political reality in today's China is that the stability of the regime is first and foremost on the political agenda, and large amounts of social resources are being used on the maintenance of social stability.

Meanwhile, Chinese people tend to argue that China seems too weak, rather than too strong, on the international stage. They also think that China is not a threat to the outside world since its reforms and opening-up. On the contrary, they feel that China has been frequently threatened by the US and even some neighbors in the region. They see the Chinese government as being too weak to protect their and national interests. They feel that self-restraints and excessive tolerance are useless and not conducive for regional harmony. Though this public opinion originates from multiple factors, such as China's unique national attributes and so on, it yearns for a stronger international influence and this yields pressure on China's foreign policy-making on East Asia.

Fortunately, the Chinese government has clearly recognized that China should and must insist on the existing national strategy of economic development as the core, and the peaceful and stable international environment as the precondition. Despite China's economic success, the huge size of its economy and the status as the second largest economic power, China would identify with and accept the international system created and managed by the US, even recognizing US's global leadership and harbor no intentions of replacing it. This low-profile diplomacy is suitable for today's Chinese national identity as the biggest developing country.

Therefore, domestic affairs are most likely to occupy the limelight for the Chinese government in the foreseeable future, and there is no time and no resources for her to attend to international affairs in a high profile manner. Taking into account the Chinese realities, peaceful development is the real and rational option for China.

However, the outside world sees it very differently from China. The outside world tends to think of a nation as a whole and from its own standpoint. To them, China's rise is full of uncertainty, with positive and negative outcomes interwoven together. On the one hand, China's success means a bigger market; more investments from outside would also benefit China's neighbors a lot. It's more of an opportunity than challenge from this regard. On the other hand, China's rise possibly means a stronger competitor in the global economy, and a stronger player in international relations. It is more of a challenge than opportunity for the concerned nations.

Second, we need to consider the US factor. The US is the only superpower in today's world and it is doing its best to maintain its leadership status. It is thus understandable that it tends to regard a rising China as a challenger to the international system. With regards to its "Pivot to the Asia-Pacific" strategy, the United States took the South China Sea dispute as an avenue to realize this policy. An obvious indication is Hillary Clinton, then US Secretary of State, declaring for the first time that the US had its national interests in the South China Sea. This was said at the ASEAN Foreign Ministers' Meeting held in July 2010. It marked Washington's official involvement in the South China Sea issues. This is just one of the measures that the US has taken on China. There are many other evidences, such as the arms sale to China's Taiwan, frequent military reconnaissance activities near the shore, the US President's meeting with the Dalai Lama, large-scale military deployment in East Asia and Western Pacific, the strengthening of the security relations with its Asia-Pacific allies, the US-led joint military excercises around China and so on. From the perspective of many Chinese, these actions reflect the nature of American strategies toward China. The US seems "to see China as the greatest challenge America has ever faced. Demographically, it is much larger than America; economically, it is stronger than America's past rival, the USSR" (White 2011, 81–93).

Some of China's neighbors think that tomorrow's China could bring uncertainties in the region, and they do so either as a US ally or as a party locked in disputes with China over the sovereignty of the East and South China Seas. The latter nations appear to fear the prospect of a rising China using hard power to overpower them in the claims. Thus, they try to abrogate established facts on ownership of the disputed areas, by introducing external powers into the game. Chinese goodwill of maintaining regional peace and stability has thus been ignored and miscalculated as a sign of weakness, and China has been misinterpreted or exaggerated as a proud, assertive, arrogant, aggressive, tough, and ambitious emerging great power. In short, to them, China's rise is not a good thing; it is a disturbing and unpleasant phenomenon. This negative perception is probably the main cause affecting the development of regional security.

If we consider the US factor in the relationship between China and its partners in East Asia, the regional political-security situation would become more perplexed and uncertain. Essentially, the problem of regional security originates from the strategic mistrust or lack of trust between countries, especially between the US and China, between Japan and China, and between some ASEAN nations and China. The mistrusts are undoubtedly a big obstacle in the making of a regional security community, and for China, it's also a huge challenge for its national strategy and foreign policies. Thus, strategic trust must replace a system of strategic threats in international relations in the region. To do so, the Sino-US relationship and ASEAN's strategic role will play a key part.

Lastly, there is the ASEAN factor. It is inevitable that China's rise would bring the world a new player that is much stronger than others. The ensuing competition in many areas makes it understandable for others to worry about China's rise. This is largely because of China's huge size in population and territory. In fact, China has become the focus of regional security since the demise of the Cold War; most disputes over sovereignty in East Asia have continued between China and its neighboring states.

Some of the disputed areas are valuable because of their proximity to international shipping lanes, oil and natural gas, and fishing resources in the waters. Though China has constantly repeated its goodwill to negotiate, compromise, and behave responsibly, considering the regional peace and stability as the foremost and above China's own national interests, and even maintaining a high degree of restraint when these areas were violated and occupied, some countries in this area remain wary and suspicious of how a more powerful China might attempt to resolve the disputes. As China becomes more powerful, other nations in East Asia might be more suspicious of China's strategic intentions, thinking that China will satisfy its own interests first and tending to resort to military means in the relations with its neighbors like any great power despite its repeated promises of peace and non-interference.

Though the international relations in East Asia are filled with mistrust and uncertainties, and differing understanding of China, we still have reasons not to be over-pessimistic about the development of East Asian security:

First, a strong China will not be a security threat, but a stabilizer in the region. Objectively speaking, the view of the "China Threat" is more imaginary rather than real, as it has been said, "China was a magnet for traders when it was peaceful, a rich target for envious and hostile neighbors when it was weak, and a dangerous enemy when it felt threatened and was aroused to defend its place as a civilization" (Wang 2005, 4).

Also, a strong Chinese threat to the world is not necessarily more than what a weak China would have been. The pre-modern history of China and East Asia showed that a united, prosperous and strong China would be a more stabilizing factor for its neighbors and the whole region. Meanwhile, China's economic success is not related whatsoever to threatening its neighbors. Linking economics with politics, it has been said the threat of China does not depend on its economic successes.

Second, Sino-US relations will not enter a strategic collision course. The US factor will not necessarily bring about confrontation between China and the US, and the resulting division of East Asia. China's rise cannot be contained or stopped unless China changes its mind or makes a big mistake. In fact, it is very dangerous to regard China as a threat and even to organize a US-led regional anti-Chinese union politically or militarily.

It goes without saying that that would mean a return of the Cold War, and in the event of such a development, there will be no winners, only losers. Therefore, both China and the US will never want to go face-to-face in a war, and there are many compelling reasons for maintaining relatively stable bilateral relations.

The nature of the Sino-US relations would define East Asian international relations. Since the end of the Cold War, "strategic distrust" has become a central concern in Sino-US relations, and will "inevitably impose very high costs on all concerned if it continues to grow at its current rapid pace" (Wang and Lieberthal 2012). For most rational people, there are real and growing risks if the two nations do not find a way to work together peacefully.

Despite difficulties on many levels and in many fields, the bilateral relations will be too important and influential to fall into a disastrous collision. There will instead be a complex mixture of competition and cooperation. As Henry Kissinger has argued, relations between China and the United States need not – and should not – become a zero-sum game (Kissinger 2011, 523).

The regional approach could be the best way to ensure Sino-US relations remain relatively stable. The realization of a Pacific Community could ease both the fears, and shared purposes would replace strategic uneasiness to some extent. It would also enable other major countries such as Japan, Indonesia, Vietnam, India, and Australia to participate in the construction of a system that will be perceived as a unity rather than polarized between "Chinese" and "American" blocs (Kissinger 2011, 528).

Many nations in the area can look forward to US–China relations that result in the countries balancing each other but not reaching confrontation. Japan's consideration may be representative of some East Asian nations. It is reluctant to see that the United States and China cooperating too well, preferring the United States to compete more than cooperate with China. Japan's fears of China will likely push America toward a strategic contest for primacy with China (White 2011, 81–93). But many others do not wish to see disturbing strategic outcomes: either the United States or China drawn into an intensifying strategic contest, or the United States gradually withdrawing from Asia.

China and her neighbors should take more responsibility to escape from the possible disaster. For China, the big challenge is how to make sure its peaceful goodwill is trusted by outsiders, how to balance this policy and maintain its national interests, how to handle disputes with neighboring countries, and how to ensure Sino-US relations do not become a state of strategic confrontation, as well as how to continue to grow in the context of a much more complex international environment.

Third, the China-ASEAN relation is a strategic pivot in East Asian international relations. To some degree, the current international relations in the region provided ASEAN with a possibility of playing a unique international role, and increasing its international influence. ASEAN, as a neutral regional organization, can play a constructive role in the relationship between China and East Asia, or even between China and the US. On the one hand, ASEAN can balance between US and China, in a strategy that would serve its regional interests; otherwise her transition from neutrality to alliance will lead to regional uncertainty. On the other hand, ASEAN should not be used by some members as a collective platform to rival China; peace and development can be the foundation in the relations between the two.

In short, the political-security in East Asia has been one of the most uncertain and complicated in the world. The situation is the product of reality and history, and can be improved through the regional approach. In the process of regional political and security interaction among nations within and outside the area, we should clearly recognize that China's rise can bring much competition in the region in many regards, but it is not a security threat; Sino–US relations are complicated bilateral ties with both competition and cooperation, but it's unlikely to fall into strategic collision; China's neighbors can look forward to a Sino-US relation where both balance each other, but it is almost definite that they will not see the return of the Cold War to the region; ASEAN, as a mature and neutral sub-regional organization, is given a strategic opportunity in international relations. It can play a constructive role as a balancer and a stabilizer in the areas of politics and security, between China and the US, between China and ASEAN members, and between China and East Asia.

3.2 Economic perspectives: achievements and potential

From an economic perspective, we are more optimistic about the development of economic relations between China and its neighbors. It is worth noting that China's economic development and its economic achievements are integral parts of the East Asian economy after World War II, and to some degree, the Chinese developmental model is a continuation of the Japanese, the NIEs, and the ASEAN model. It is no surprise that the Chinese economy is interwoven with its neighbors. As we can see from Tables 11.5 and 11.6, trade and FDI intra-East Asia is rather significant. With the economic rise of China, there will be closer economic relations among them.

First, as a big nation, whether weak or strong, China has a huge effect on the economic development in the region. When China was excluded from the East Asian and the global markets during the Cold War, the NIEs, and ASEAN countries were able to develop economically in the absence of a

Table 11.5 Proportion of ASEAN nations' trade with partners (2011, billion dollars, %)

Nation	Trade with ASEAN members	Share in ASEAN intra-trade (%)	Trade with China, Japan and Korea	Share in ASEAN trade with CJK (%)	Trade with other world	Share in ASEAN trade with other world (%)
Brunei	2.9	0.49	8.4	1.24	3.3	0.55
Cambodia	3.0	0.50	2.7	0.40	4.58	0.76
Indonesia	99.4	16.6	128.8	19.0	94.3	15.7
Laos	2.5	0.42	0.60	0.0008	0.73	0.12
Malaysia	108.1	18.1	118.6	17.5	112.9	18.8
Myanmar	7.2	1.2	4.6	0.68	1.75	0.29
Philippines	23.7	3.96	35.3	5.20	30.5	5.07
Singapore	205.7	34.4	162.4	23.9	204.6	34.0
Thailand	111.5	18.7	142.6	21.0	103.4	17.2
Vietnam	34.3	5.73	74.2	10.9	45.04	7.49
ASEAN	598.3	100	678.2	100	601.1	100

Sources: ASEAN Community In Figures (ACIF) 2012, The ASEAN Secretariat Public Outreach and Civil Society Division, The ASEAN Official Website; ASEAN Economic Community Chartbook 2012, The ASEAN Secretariat Public Outreach and Civil Society Division, The ASEAN Official Website; The World Factbook: East Asia and Southeast Asia, The CIA Factbook Official Website, accessed March 25, 2014.

Table 11.6 Composition of FDI inflows in ASEAN (2000–2011, %)

	2000	2005	2008	2009	2010	2011
Intra-ASEAN	3.9	9.9	19.7	13.4	15.5	23.0
EU	59.6	27.5	18.0	17.2	18.4	16.0
Japan	2.5	15.5	8.8	8.1	11.7	13.2
China	-0.7	1.4	2.5	4.0	3.0	5.3
US	34.3	7.7	6.6	12.2	13.8	5.1
ROK	-0.2	1.2	3.1	3.8	4.1	1.9
Australia	-1.7	0.6	2.1	2.1	2.8	1.2

Source: ASEAN Secretariat ASEAN Community in Figures ACIF 2012, accessed on March 25, 2014.

strong competitor. After China's entry into the international economic system, especially since China's accession to the World Trade Organization (WTO), China's market is increasingly becoming more important for the neighboring countries' economy.

Over the past half century, China's development strategy has contributed to its transformation from a very poor economy to the second largest and one of the fastest growing economies by GDP in the world. With its reforms and opening-up, as well as increasing interdependence with the world, China sees its economic success as a part of the region's rise, and looks forward to contribution in the regional development. For the future, China will possibly be an economic core in the region, and contribute to the economic development of its neighbors.

Second, the promotion of economic relations between China and her neighbors is due to both its economic needs and strategic needs. Closer trade relations will cause closer regional interdependence. This will eventually benefit the regional political and security situation. This is because economic development is a common interest and political aspiration for most countries in the region. It is also a useful foundation and catalyst for regional peace and stability.

China is now a key member of the East Asia trading bloc, with high intra-bloc trading volumes and strong outward orientation. Today, ASEAN, Japan, and ROK, are individually one of China's key trade partners, and China is the biggest trade partner of her many neighbors. It is important to note that economic issues are higher on the agenda in Sino-East Asian interactions, relative to political-security issues. In the context of today's international relations in East Asia, the development of regional trade is a realistic and efficient approach to constructing a regional community.

Regionally, China's market is fast becoming the anchor of an emerging East Asian Free Trade Area, just as the US market anchors the free trade arrangements of the North American Free Trade Agreement (Ross 2010, 525–545). With economic transformation, China's domestic market means greater markets and more opportunities for other countries, especially for its neighbors. More or less, a bigger Chinese market is good for regional economic cooperation.

Third, China is a diverse and complex economy with multiple sectors, including both labor-intensive and capital-intensive ones. With regards to trade with the rest of the world, China and its neighbors have been exporting increasingly more high-technology products. With regards to trade with its neighbors, China acts as an engine of export growth, with imports outpacing exports. This may change, however, "as China climbs up the value chain and takes over activities that have driven East Asian export growth even within integrated production systems " (Lall and 1 Albaladejo 2004, 1441–1466).

3.3 Socio-cultural perspectives: new impetus and new way

The Chinese government has increasingly emphasized the significance of Chinese culture in the overall domestic development and the promotion of dialogue and understanding between China and its neighbors. In other words, the development and exchange of culture is an indispensable source of China's rise and regional good relations.

With the rapid economic growth, more and more Chinese people go abroad as tourists (see Table 11.7), and neighboring areas, such as Japan, Korea, and Singapore-Malaysia-Thailand, are their preferred destinations (see Table 11.8). This undoubtedly provides APT with much more possibility for the promotion of inter-cultural exchange and inter-understanding among them.

Table 11.7 Selected yearly China's visitors abroad (unit: million visitors)

Year	Outbound Passengers	Private Exit
2001	12.13	6.95
2006	34.52	28.8
2011	70.25	64.12
2013	98.19	91.97

Source: National Bureau of Statistics of China, Statistical Communique of China on the Economic and Social Development (2001–2013), available on www.stats.gov.cn, accessed February 2, 2015.

Table 11.8 Top ten sources of visitors to ASEAN and share to total (unit: ten thousand visitors)

Origin	2009		2010		2013	
ASEAN	3169	48.3%	3482	47.2%	4322.36	44.1%
EU-28	666.8	10.2%	697.1	9.5%	865.26	8.8%
China	420	6.4%	541.6	7.3%	1264.18	12.9%
Japan	321.4	4.9%	335	4.5%	472.11	4.8%
Australia	302.8	4.6%	346.5	4.7%	429.42	4.4%
US	255	3.9%	268	3.6%	317.4	3.2%
ROK	244.8	3.7%	328.6	4.5%	487.1	5%
India	210	3.2%	247.8	3.4%	292.17	3%
China's Taiwan	136.9	2.1%	154.9	2.1%	205.82	2.1%
HK/Russia	85 (HK)	1.3%	90.5 (HK)	1.2%	245.92 (Russia)	2.5%
The rest of the World	754.7	11.5%	882.9	12%	8983.1	9.2%

Source: ASEAN statistics, www.aseansec.org, accessed March 25, 2014.

At the sixth plenary session of the 17th Central Committee of the CPC on October 18, 2011, a pledge was made to boost China's cultural influence internationally by providing the cultural sector with more resources. This move underscored the realization that China is facing an imperative need to boost its "cultural soft power" and enhance its cultural image in the world. This is in line with the trend in which "culture is increasingly acknowledged as an important part of the country's comprehensive competitiveness" (*China Daily* 2011).

With regards to international relations, culture has many roles to play. For one, socio-cultural exchange is a part of international relations; it is a significant ingredient for the formation and construction of a regional identity from the grassroots. Culture is also a source of soft influence, one that is becoming a dominant foreign policy tool in today's world.

For Sino-APT interactions, culture takes on a greater meaning. From China's perspective, its rich culture and heritage continues to have profound impacts on its today. Traditional culture forms the background for policy-making in the Chinese government. Traditional values, customs, norms, cultural paradigms continue to influence the minds and outlook of the Chinese leaders. This does not end here. More importantly, China's rich culture has provided a common rallying point or even a sort of social ideology that guides its people.

In terms of foreign relations, China has emphasized socio-cultural exchanges with its neighbors and other countries around the globe. Chinese culture, much revered by both Chinese and rest of the world alike, for its richness, is a powerful and influential tool for China to promote international understanding and booster its national image as a civilized and cultured nation worthy of much respect. It is little wonder that China has sought to use its culture as a part of its public diplomacy, translating such valuable assets into soft power on the international stage. More importantly, socio-cultural exchange links China up with the rest of the world, influencing how the world perceives China. This will eventually aid the creation of a favorable regional and global environment for China.

In the APT region, China has traditionally been the anchor culture for the region's cultural development. As one of the cradles of civilization, Chinese culture has spread from the Central Plains to the Korean Peninsula, Japan, as well as Southeast Asia. From languages to cultural goods, Chinese culture has permeated into East Asia over the course of history. It is thus no surprise that many East Asian nations have similar cultural traits. In fact, the concept of "Asian values" bears much overlaps with "traditional Chinese values."

However, it must be recognized that the glorious days of Chinese culture were interrupted with China's decline in the nineteenth century. In fact, the geopolitical realities of today no longer allow China to claim hegemony over the region, much less cultural hegemony. Thus, in spite of the similarities in cultures, nations tend to emphasize the originality and independence of their own culture. We cannot expect them to subsume to or pledge allegiance to Chinese culture.

After the end of the Cold War, the Chinese government began to launch more efforts at cultural diplomacy and public diplomacy. We saw increases in China's hosting of overseas scholars, attempts to grow its international media reach, organizing informal business and cultural summits like BOAO Forum for Asia, promoting Chinese culture and language studies, and pushing for several initiatives to increase Chinese instruction, and funding Confucius Institutes overseas, especially in East Asia.

What this means for the region is that while similarities in cultures amongst the East Asian states can help forge a sense of commonality and a regional identity, China is unlikely to be able to command or claim ownership of the identity. Also, attempts by various nations to assert their cultural independence may result in denial or downplaying of the common cultural values that are relics of China's glorious past. Too many of these denials and downplaying may become obstacles for APT regionalism, while an APT community anchored by Chinese culture at its core is extremely unlikely to emerge.

4 China and the process of APT integration

There is a comprehensive consensus among APT politicians and social elites that a regional community is the only realistic and feasible approach to peace and development in the region. They also believe that the formation of a regional community provides possible means for the settlement of numerous disputes among APT nations (the EU is undoubtedly a good example). As such, the future of APT depends on regional integration.

4.1 The impediments

No one is satisfied with the current state of regional cooperation in East Asia. So far, an APT FTA, as the lowest possible form of regional economic integration that would be beneficial to all, has not been realized, let alone more complex political cooperation.

Ultimately, while we acknowledge the possibilities and opportunities for positive interactions between China and other APT members in the region, we must acknowledge and recognize that certain impediments are present to retard the regional integration in East Asia.

For one, the inherent natural differences in geography, climate, population, language, history and culture, history, and the acquired differences in geopolitics, economy, and ideology and so on, together contribute to the region's diversity. Under these unique and diverse conditions, we can expect East Asian integration to be a long and gradual process.

Next is what I call the "Fears of the Chinese Giant" Syndrome. China is emerging as a great power. This will definitely be changing the regional and global power balance. The international status quo will be challenged. While China has repeatedly assured the world that it intends to do so peacefully, it is understandable that others in the APT may be skeptical of it. This is because history is not on China's side of the argument. Historically, the rise of great powers has often led to wars and conflicts as the stability of the status quo becomes challenged. Practically speaking, with China amassing more power, it will definitely have more say and influence in the international relations.

For example, one of the biggest hazards or uncertainties in the development of China's relations with her neighbors could be the island disputes in the East China Sea between China and Japan, and in the South China Sea among China and several ASEAN nations. The disputes have become more and more internationalized and intense and have possibly produced negative impacts on the region. Since states are very often motivated by self-interest rather than altruism for others, it is understandable for the neighbors to fear that they would be powerless should a strong China challenge them for a particular interest. Whether or not these arguments are sound bears little relevance because the fact that these arguments exist already underscores the fact that the region does not trust China. Such mistrust does not go well for regional cooperation and integration.

Third is the lack of regional self-awareness. More often, the countries in APT do not think of themselves as a regional bloc. Frequently, China, Japan, and South Korea would rather act independently in the conduct of international relations, while the Southeast Asian states clamor together as ASEAN only on certain issues. As such, there is a significant lack of an East Asian identity or awareness that East Asian countries belong to the same bloc. This suggests that regionalism is still in its infancy, while it also reminds us that the lack of a regional self-awareness is not conducive for furthering regionalism.

Fourth is the effect of Sino-Japanese relations on regional cooperation. Japan's relations with China continue to be affected by three major factors, namely, historical legacies (war memories), the island dispute, and the United States' role in the region. Also, China and Japan have different interests and hence different strategies for economic integration in APT. As such, China and Japan may find it difficult to work together as equal partners for regional integration in the region. A region-wide East Asian FTA covering ASEAN+3 countries is slow to materialize because China and Japan are seeking bilateral trade agreements rather than multilateral ones (Wang 2004). Japan has been promoting integration among the "ASEAN+6" nations, and Australia, New Zealand, and India became members of the East Asian Summit (EAS). Moreover, the US and Russia joined the EAS in 2011. Obviously, Japan's intention is to deal with a rising China through the introduction of external powers into this region. However, this gives little benefit to the APT regionalization. The process of regional integration seems to move to another APEC, a very loose forum or a "talk shop."

Fifth, political distrust is a big obstacle in regional cooperation. Let's take the regional monetary cooperation as an example. In November 1999, the ASEAN+3 Summit released a "Joint Statement on East Asian Cooperation" that covers a wide range of possible avenues for regional cooperation. Recognizing the need to establish regional financial arrangements to supplement the existing international facilities, the Finance Ministers of ASEAN+3 agreed to strengthen the existing cooperative frameworks in the region through the "Chiang Mai Initiative (CMI)" at their meeting in Chiang Mai, Thailand, in May 2000. Monetary cooperation in East Asia is a long process that requires building collective institutions to start. A major hindrance to a monetary union in East Asia is the region's lack of experience in regionalism. Whatever economic benefits a monetary union may bring, they are "unlikely to be realized in the near future if each country is unwilling to cooperate in the political arena" (Wang 2004).

Lastly are China's concerns about her neighbors acting as or becoming US' strategic partners against it. Some neighbors mistrust China, and China also mistrusts some of its neighbors. As mentioned above, Sino-US relations set the tone for East Asian interactions. China fears that the US is attempting to limit and contain its growth and emergence as a great power. As such, China is vigilant about the fact that the US would use its neighbors in the region to limit its presence, even build a US-led strategic encirclement against China.

Meanwhile, China does not take it easy when some of its neighbors deliberately use China's goodwill of peace and US' strategy toward China, to risk regional confrontation and do whatever they want, so as to give US a strategic bargaining chip. While it is also understandable to have such fears, simply because of numerous economic, military, and political links between China's neighbors and the US, it spells trouble for regional integration. This is simply because mutual trust is a key ingredient for further regional cooperation.

Of course, as a superpower in the world and an active participant in East Asia, the US factor had and has a decisive effect on APT cooperation through its allies, its military presence, and dependence on it by most countries. The abortion of Mahathir's initiative of East Asian Economic Group (EAEG) in 1990 demonstrated American influence on several countries in the area, and American attitude toward APT integration. Recently, the American promotion of the Trans-Pacific Partnership Agreement (TPPA) possibly challenged the development of ASEAN+3 mechanisms and RCEP led by ASEAN. It can be seen that, as a reflection of international relations in the region, the American strategy to APT is an unavoidable factor in the thinking and making of the regional community.

4.2 The driving force

Since the end of the Cold War, China's regional strategy has evolved from one based on a closed bilateral strategy to one that is more open and receptive to multilateralism. Since early 1999, global trade liberalization has been side-lined as regional trade agreements (RTA) have become the preferred choice in APT nations.

In terms of regional economic development and cooperation, China is fast becoming a key pillar and driving force. China tends to support further regional economic cooperation. Its support for free trade and its promotion of the idea that it will be a major source of FDI, foreign aid, and international trade in the future, plays an important role not only in bolstering its national image, but also in strengthening its economic presence and interdependence with its neighbors. China's active participation in East Asian economic integration is a new driving force, one that is more powerful, influential, and active. This provides a stark comparison with the relatively weaker driving force of Japan. The Japanese tend to have more hesitation and are hampered by their domestic limitations and circumstances.

China was the first Asian power to propose the establishment of a free trade area (FTA) with ASEAN. This is because the Southeast Asian region is important to China both geopolitically and economically. The China-ASEAN Free Trade Area (CAFTA) is a clear evidence of China's active role and it should have a demonstrative effect on the region, showing the way for further regional cooperation. The CAFTA and closer bilateral trade ties and economic partnerships with individual ASEAN nations, play very active roles in driving and pushing the process of regional integration. There is strong political will on the part of the Chinese government and the ASEAN leadership to create a CAFTA. The legal framework was signed in November 2002. As part of establishing an FTA, China reached an agreement with the 10 ASEAN countries in October 2003. On January 1, 2010, the CAFTA came into full effect. This will further contribute to China's importance as a regional market. ASEAN enjoys an advantage over China with regards to services. There are also other areas (e.g. agricultural products, timber, automobile parts, biotech, health care, research and development, information and communication technologies, education, tourism) where ASEAN and China can complement each other. Overall, "both qualitative and quantitative analysis provides grounds for cautious optimism about CAFTA's prospects" (Park et al. 2008).

Prompted by the China–ASEAN framework agreement, Japan followed suit. It also pursued the ASEAN-Japan Comprehensive Economic Partnership Agreement (CEPA) (Khairy Tourk 2004). The need to respond to China's growing stature in the region gave Tokyo an incentive to offer ASEAN a concession. This took the form of Japan's signing of a treaty of non-interference in ASEAN's internal affairs. The Southeast Asian nations had long demanded this from Japan. However, it was "only after Beijing had agreed to sign it in early 2003 that Tokyo was ready to follow suit" (Khairy 2004).

In terms of political-security cooperation in the region, China is also a key player whether it is welcome or not. Its massive presence and growing stature has made it an indispensable factor in terms of regional stability and regional security cooperation. The key challenge that lies ahead for China is two-fold: on the one hand, it has to cope with and manage its relations with US, which has always had a significant presence in the Asia-Pacific; on the other hand, it has to reassure its regional neighbors that it is committed to rising peacefully. As mentioned earlier, as much as the region desires regional stability and the various APT countries openly rally for regional peace, mistrust and suspicions are still prevalent. While it is understandable for countries to fear the rise of China, or more accurately, the changing geopolitical landscape in the region, these mistrusts are key obstacles that limit political-security cooperation in the region.

With regard to cultural exchanges, China is also an active participant. Due to historical legacies, Chinese traditional culture shares similarities with APT cultures. While this suggests that there are some commonalities and a common language amongst the APT nations, and that China has actively pushed for the use of its culture in the conduct of its diplomacy, because of the fact that APT countries more often tend to assert their own "unique" cultural identity rather than their commonalities with the Chinese culture, we expect socio-cultural integration to take place less actively. Nevertheless, the inherent commonalities must be recognized as a favorable ingredient that may form the basis for regional understanding and allegiance.

5 Conclusion

The first twenty years of the twenty-first century represented a period of "strategic opportunity" for China's rise, as well as an opportunity for APT's regional development. China will continue to retain the core of its existing domestic and foreign policies, while its style of behavior might change a little over time. For quite a long period of time, China will still need a proper and conducive international environment in the region, and a closer regional community to do so. Regardless of the external environment and perception of China, these Chinese policies will continue unless China's core interests are intolerably violated. This is not a showing of weakness or doing it for others, but its own realistic option based on China's domestic affairs, Chinese tradition, and national conditions.

In the context of China's rise and the adjustment or transformation of the global system, China and its neighbors must increase the strategic trust among them. Despite difficulties and uncertainties, the political-security problems among nations in the region are never unbreakable deadlocks. If we know genuinely that a peaceful and stable region is the common need serving each nation's long-term interests, and regional approach is the realistic and sustainable means to do so, things will be done.

As regards China, it needs to learn how to continue its existing strategies in a harsher international environment. In the case of China, a suspicious perception or even hostility to some degree from neighbors is inevitable, for almost all emerging great powers could face similar situations. Most East Asian countries worried about Japan's great military power and possible domination of East Asia once again after World War II during its economic rise in late 1960s until 1980s.. China, as a strong newcomer of the international system, has much more reason to be questioned and concerned. China should recognize that this is what it has to face in the process of its rise, and much more self-restraint must be needed for both itself and its neighbors.

Also as regards China, it is very important to deal with the Sino–US relations carefully. The US is still the only superpower in the world, and its relative decline (if so) is in fact not beneficial to China's interests. The US may be a troublemaker in China's development, but for many Chinese elites, its presence is understandable in East Asia as a balancer. China and the United States will not necessarily be each other's enemy, nor would this be desired by China's neighbors. In any case, both countries and their complex but crucial relations set the context for relations in the APT region for the foreseeable future.

For China's neighbors, China cannot be easily excluded in their foreign relations for it is a neighbor with a huge size and power. It can be seen that relatively good ties is a win-win option for every country in the region. The preventive measures against China's rise, whichever the form, will probably be irrational and unrealistic because it necessarily takes on unimaginable risk.

Times have changed a lot; confrontation and containment is old-fashioned thinking and behavior not suitable for the new age. Also China cannot be contained. This is because China's rise and its future are chosen and decided mainly by it, rather than by others. China should be encouraged, not discouraged to continue its existing policies. As such, in the changing international politico-economic system, the objective and rational perception of China from its neighbors should be treating China as a friendly competitor rather than an aggressive enemy. All in all, we expect that both China and its neighbors have the ability and political wisdom to cope with the relationships among them. Belief and trust are essential in international relations, and we all should have the belief that the wish of peace and cooperation will come true.

Easier said than done; there is plenty of hard work waiting to be done for all parties in the region for the making of a regional community. On the one hand, all people from APT can do something to speed up bottom-up regionalization. On the other hand, any regional cooperation is fundamentally a political process from the top; intergovernmental interactions are thus the most important driving force in the regional integration. Considering the complicated regional international relations and mistrust rooted in the relations among countries in the area, only ASEAN can play an active role as a leader or driver, and China, Japan, or ROK as supporters or followers, in the making of an APT community.

I strongly suggest that China's regional strategy will be influenced by its neighbors' understanding of China and their policy toward China, and yield an APT community that benefits all. China is for a regional approach as it is a feasible and essential way for China and other APT countries to face and deal with the problems and challenges bilaterally, regionally or globally, and in the long run, even determinate the future of APT, a young but promising international region.

References

ASEAN Community In Figures (ACIF) (2012) 'The ASEAN Secretariat Public Outreach and Civil Society Division', The ASEAN Official Website. Available from: www.asean.org/storage/images/2013/resources/statistics/web_ACIF2012_e-publish.pdf (accessed 25 March 2014).

ASEAN Economic Community Chartbook (2012) 'The ASEAN Secretariat Public Outreach and Civil Society Division', The ASEAN Official Website. Available from: www.asean.org/resources/publications/asean-publications/item/asean-economic-comm unity-chartbook-2012 (accessed 25 March 2014).

China Daily. Available from: www2.chinadaily.com.cn/china/2011–10/19/content_ 13928761.htm (accessed 15 November 2011).

Gries, Peter Hays (2009) *Problems of Misperception in U.S.-China Relations.* Orbis: Published by Elsevier Limited on behalf of Foreign Policy Research Institute, pp. 220–232.

Khairy, Tourk (2004, 'The Political Economy of East Asian Economic Integration,' *Journal of Asian Economics*, 15(5): 843–888.

Kissinger, Henry (2011) *On China*, New York: The Penguin Press.

Lall, Sanjaya and Manuel Albaladejo (2004) 'China's Competitive Performance: A Threat to East Asian Manufactured Exports?' *World Development*, 32(9): 1441–1466.

National Bureau of Statistics of China. *Statistical Communique of China on the Economic and Social Development (1996–2012)*. Available from: www.stats.gov.cn (accessed February 2, 2015).

Park, Donghyun, Innwon Park, Gemma Esther and B. Estrada (2008) "Prospects of an ASEAN–People's Republic of China Free Trade Area: A Qualitative and Quantitative Analysis." October, ADB Economics Working Paper Series, No. 130.

Ross, Robert S. (2010, *The Rise of Chinese Power and the Implications for the Regional Security Order*. Orbis: Published by Elsevier Limited on behalf of Foreign Policy Research Institute, pp. 525–545.

WangGungwu (2005) 'China and Southeast Asia: Changes in Strategic Perceptions'. In *China and Southeast Asia: Global Changes and Regional Challenges*, edited by Ho Khai Leong and Samuel C. Y. Ku. Singapore: Institute of Southeast Asian Studies.

Wang Jisi and Kenneth Lieberthal (2012) *Addressing US-China Strategic distrust*. Beijing: the Center for International and Strategic Studies of Peking University.

White, Hugh (2011) 'Power Shift: Rethinking Australia's Place in the Asian Century.' *Australian Journal of International Affairs*, 65(1): 81–93.

The World Factbook: East Asia and Southeast Asia, The CIA Factbook Official Website. Available from: cia.gov/library/publications/the-world-factbook/wfbExt/region_eas.html (accessed 15 May 2014).

Yunjong Wang (2004) 'Financial Cooperation and Integration in East Asia'. *Journal of Asian Economics*, 15(5): 939–955.

12 Japan

Living in and with Asia

Sachiko Hirakawa

1 Postwar Japan's new identity-formation

In the eighth century, a Japanese commercial envoy to Tang Dynasty drifted to the Indochina peninsula on their voyage. It is believed to be the first Japanese footprint on Southeast Asia soils (Institute of Asian Cultures, Sophia University 2009). Since then, Japan and Southeast Asian have had a long and close relationship until today. From the fifteenth to the seventeenth century, Japan benefited from the prosperous commercial network of Southeast Asia and there were several Japanese communities in Southeast Asia. In the late nineteenth century after breaking its more than bicentennial-long isolation policy from the Westerners,[1] under Japan's modern *Meiji* government Japan was the first non-Western nation to accomplish industrialization. Many Asian students and prospective leaders came to Japan to study the modern nation-building process. On the other hand, many Japanese longed for the unknown region of *Nanyo* (Southward) to stimulate their frontier spirits as well as economic interests (Tarling 2006).

In the 1940s during WWII, Japan's defiant strategy of building the Greater East Asia Co-Prosperity Sphere[2] destroyed the regional order ruled by Western colonialism and stimulated nationalism movements in Southeast Asia. However, the new hierarchical order under Japan's military leadership left huge negative collective memories on Southeast Asian people despite relatively short years. Postwar Japan's relationship with Southeast Asia started with overcoming this remorseful experience with a sense of atonement. As a result this means the process of building up postwar Japan's new identity and searching for alternative regionalism.

Accepting the Potsdam Declaration in August 1945, Japan was put under the control of the Supreme Commander for the Allied Powers (SCAP) led by General Douglas MacArthur. Japan's new Constitution under US auspices was adopted in 1946 and enacted next year. Most notably its Article Nine stipulated that "Aspiring sincerely to an international peace based on justice and order, the Japanese people forever renounce war as a sovereign right of the nation and the threat or use of force as means of settling international disputes. In order to accomplish the aims of the preceding paragraph, land, sea, and air forces, as well as other war potential, will never be maintained. The right of belligerency of the state will not be recognized."[3] Abandoning its military build-up, and with poor indigenous natural resources, postwar Japan had no other means to enhance its national power and international status than becoming a peaceful trading nation.

The quick development of the Cold War situation accelerated Japan's peace process and regaining of her sovereignty. In 1951 in San Francisco, Japan concluded the peace treaty with 48 countries, in which the Soviet Union and the People's Republic of China (PRC) were not included. At the same time, Japan concluded the US-Japan Security Treaty, which allowed US forces to station in its lands. With the loss of diplomatic contacts with Mainland China and the Korean Peninsula,[4] Southeast Asian countries became the only realistic "Asian" partners for Japan. Prime Minister Yoshida Shigeru believed that Japan should devote its efforts primarily to quick economic recovery while minimizing armament with security reliance on the US, which was generally known as the Yoshida Doctrine. Postwar Japan's identity, with a mixture of idealism and pragmatism, was to be found in its three fundamental diplomatic principles in the first diplomatic blue book published in 1956.[5] The first was to adhere to the UN centric position as a member of the global society. Second was to associate with "free countries," which implicitly meant the US camp in the Cold War environment. Third was to maintain its identity as "a member of Asian countries." These three seemed to be uneasy to reconcile, but it reflected the general aspirations of the Japanese people in those days.

Accordingly, Japan's policy toward Southeast Asia, a newly emerging region, was formulated in line with the three principles. Prime Minister Kishi Nobusuke paid special and strategic attention to economic and technical cooperation with Southeast Asia. Visiting twice in 1957, he recognized Southeast Asian newly independent states were in the midst of a struggle of nation-building. Kishi, an anti-communist with a personal inclination of Asianism, believed these nations should accomplish economic development and improve people's living conditions as soon as possible; otherwise they might be easily captivated by communism. From such a viewpoint, he attempted Japan's strong engagement with Southeast Asian industrial development projects, which contributed to both the local and Japanese economy. Conscious of Japan's responsibility in Asia, he even proposed the foundation of the Southeast Asian Development Fund. However, the idea did not materialize due to lack of US and Southeast Asian support (Sudo 1992, Hatano and Sato 2007, Hoshiro 2008). It can be said that Japan was not accepted yet as a trustful member by the regional partners and the attempt was too early.

It was after joining the Organization for Economic Co-Operation and Development (OECD) in 1964 that Japan more confidently conducted regional economic diplomacy. Becoming the first Asian member of the organization whose membership is given only to democratic and developed nations, Japan hosted the Ministerial Conference for Economic Development of Southeast Asia in 1966. It was the first international conference Japan initiated since the end of WWII. The idea of the regional conference was originally floated by the US, which hoped that Japan could take a stronger economic leadership role among Asian free block nations as the Cold War strategy. However, in holding the regional conference, Japan adhered more to the Asian member identity than the free block member identity. Japan persuaded non-aligned and neutral countries in Southeast Asia to equally participate in the conference. As a result, Indonesia and Cambodia participated while Burma declined because of its "strict" neutralist position. Upon its success, the first Ministerial Conference for Agricultural Development of Southeast Asia was additionally coordinated in Tokyo. At the same time, Japan prepared to create independent funds exclusively for Southeast Asian nations within the Asian Development Bank (ADB), which was established in 1966 with US and Japanese sponsorship. When ASEAN was formed in 1967 Japan even showed its interest to join it. Thus Japan institutionally committed itself to Southeast Asian regionalism.

On the other hand, Japan consistently acknowledged its traditional role of a bridge between the East and West. In fact, this sense of responsibility was clear in the Japanese delegation's formal speech upon its accession to the United Nations in 1956: "The substance of Japan's political, economic and cultural life is the product of the fusion within the last century of the civilizations of the Orient and the Occident. In a way, Japan may well be regarded as a bridge between the East and the West. She is fully conscious of the great responsibilities of such a position."[6] Taking after this spirit, in 1967 Foreign Minister Miki Takeo launched his vision of "Asia-Pacific" cooperation. The key idea was that Japan would cooperate more actively with Pacific countries such as the US, Canada, Australia, and New Zealand in order to help the economic development of Asian countries. He asserted it was Japan's moral obligation as the only developed country in Asia to contribute to solving South–North problems on the scale of the Asia-Pacific (Terada 1999b). Commemorating with the centennial *Meiji* restoration, he made a speech that Japan's physical conditions, being a small island nation with poor resources and locating next to huge Asian Continent, essentially determined three diplomatic directions.[7] First, Japan as a maritime nation should not adopt isolationism but stand as a nation in the Asia-Pacific. Second, with no possibility to be autarkic, Japan can secure its survival only by broader trade with outside nations. Third, Japan and the Asian Continent should not become mutual threats but establish mutually good neighborliness. Miki concluded that history clearly showed that whenever Japan strayed from these right paths, the results had been critical failures. Based on such beliefs, Miki helped organize two informal private forums to study the Asia-Pacific regional standpoints; that first was the PBEC (Pacific Basin Economic Council) meeting among regional business elites in 1967 and the other was the PAFTAD (Pacific Trade and Development) meeting among regional academics in 1968. These attempts to form non-governmental epistemic communities helped to later envisage future community building in the Asia-Pacific region (Terada 1999a; Ravenhill 2001).

However, Japan's emergence with its quick economic expansion in overseas markets was not necessarily favorably accepted by the international community. Japanese foreign policy with its overly economic emphasis was blamed as neo-mercantilism or economic imperialism (Constantino 1991). Japanese people were often depicted as "economic animals" which seemingly dismissed decency in human behaviors. Facing such criticism, the Japanese government needed to modify its foreign policies to smooth the relationship with regional partners. As elaborated in later sections, in 1977 Prime Minister Fukuda Takeo announced the Japanese basic Southeast Asian policy emphasising wholehearted relationship and equal partnership. Similarly, in 1978, the succeeding Prime Minister Ohia Masayoshi also proposed the progressive version of his Asia-Pacific regional cooperation. It comprehensively envisioned cultural interchanges and mutual understandings in addition to economic cooperation. His study group interpreted Asia-Pacific nations as a "convergence of civilizations," which aimed to involve more diverse people in the whole region.[8] In 1980, Ohira and Australian Prime Minister Malcolm Fraser jointly took initiatives in organizing the track two framework of the Pacific Economic Cooperation Conference (PECC) among businessmen, scholars, and public servants in their private capacity. This unique tripartite framework provided the foundation of APEC, a governmental framework formed in 1989. Though APEC was publicly proposed by Australian Prime Minister Bob Hawke, the Japanese government fully supported the initiative from behind. To connect Asian developing countries with Pacific developed countries, Japan actively coordinated the reconcilable modality as a mediator between two groupings (Funabashi 1995; Yamakage 1997; Terada 1999b).

Thus, in the late twentieth century, Japan gradually forged its new identity through mainly economic regional cooperation in Asia. Recognizing that Japan was destined to be open and outward-looking to the world for its own survival and prosperity, it cultivated international sensitivity and understanding. Throughout the process, Japan habituated self-checking on others' perceptions of itself. Japan does not support any particular state-centric or hegemonic regionalism any more. Instead, improving the quality of trustful relationship based on an equal footing became Japan's essential policy of regionalism.

1.1 Political-security perspective: US–Japan alliance and human security

In the late twentieth century, Japan's security policy maintained two pillars, namely, purely defensive mandates and the US–Japan alliance. The anti-militarist norm stipulated by Article Nine has constrained the government in deploying the military to serve state objectives. During the Cold War period, the exercise of collective defense right, overseas military expedition, international joint actions accompanying use of force, and possession of weapons of "offensive nature" were strictly self-restrained under a range of interpretations.

As the only nation to be victimized by the atomic bombs in Hiroshima and Nagasaki in 1945, three anti-nuclear principles (not to produce, possess, and import nuclear weapons) have been upheld as important policy guidelines. In addition to its political efforts, Japan attributed its absence of the war to deterrence provided by US–Japan security pact during the Cold War years. After the end of the Cold War, Japan and the US revised their traditional security partnership with broader perspectives for maintaining a stable and prosperous environment in Asia-Pacific (Inoguchi et al. 2011).

At the same time, Japan also developed its independent security role with Japanese characteristics. The turning point was the 1990–1991 Gulf War. Responding to international opinions which requested more security contribution equivalent to Japan's economic power, Japan for the first time decided to dispatch a minesweepers unit of JMSDF (Japan Maritime Self-Defense Force) to the Persian Gulf after the end of the war. While the mission was not appreciated as a major contributor by the international society, the decision was important enough to shake Japanese domestic opinion and governments of neighboring countries. In 1992, after the big national debates, the Peacekeeping Operation Law was passed by the Diet. The so-called PKO Law provided foundation to send the Self Defense Forces (SDF) overseas. Japan's first overseas dispatch of the SDF was to the UN Transitional Authority in the Cambodia (UNTAC) operation. It was a reasonable choice to contribute to a UNPKO in Indochina because the Japanese government had diplomatically committed to the culminating peace process of Cambodia. The Peace Corps consisted of 600 SDF personnel employed as engineers engaged mainly in repairing roads and bridges in areas where the use of force would be unlikely. Through fulfillment of the Cambodian mission, its peacekeeping role gradually gained more public understanding which enabled the government to assign future missions.[9]

In the twenty-first century, Japan engages itself more confidently in international cooperation in non-military security areas. The concept of "human security" is substantially associated with Japan's style of international contribution and alternative security paradigm. Since 1980, Japan has developed such ideas and practice under the name of comprehensive security. This included non-military aspects such as natural disaster, energy, or food as well as traditional hard security. The term "human security" originally referred to the concept issuing from the 1994 United Nations Development Programme report, which pointed out a conceptual shift from an exclusive emphasis on national security to people's security. Prime Minister Obuchi Keizo thoughtfully applied the concept into Japan's own foreign policy. In 1998, in Hanoi, Vietnam, attending the ASEAN summit, he delivered his policy speech in which he stated that the twenty-first century should be a "human centered century," which meant "a century of peace and prosperity built on human dignity."[10] While establishing a Human Security Fund under the auspices of the UN, Japan proactively studied the conceptualization. Based on Japan's proposal, the UN established the Commission on Human Security in 2001, which was co-chaired by Ogata Sadako, and Amartya Sen.[11] The commission's final report of 2003 to the UN Secretary General emphasized that human security concerns not only protect, but also empower people in vulnerable communities. Today the Japanese government interprets that "human security" refers to a comprehensive understanding of all kinds of threats to human beings and consequent reinforcement of means to eliminate them. This is the security area Japan is mainly engaged in in East Asian regional cooperation as later sections describe further.

1.2 Economic perspective: Postwar history of international trade

Postwar Japan's economy started wholly in social devastation and confusion. The economic production facility and network were totally destructed. Poor supply of commodities caused high inflation and a reactive deflation policy impeded economic growth up to 1949. In order to overcome this hardship, the Japanese government under the US occupation adopted a "priority production system" (*Kesisha Seisan Hoshiki*). The method first concentrated limited capital and labor resources on the most fundamental industries such as coal and steel, and then later allocated these productions into secondary important industries. The outbreak of the Korean War of 1950 gave impetus for Japan to reactivate production and business opportunities in systematic ways. Japan was used as the factory and commercial base for the US army moving forward to Korea. Such special procurement increased Japan's revenues and foreign reserves, which enabled more imports of raw materials needed for further production. While investing in the production facilities, Japanese enterprises competed for their productivity and technological innovation. Thus, Japan quickly recovered its industrial ability and experienced a series of economic booms. In 1956, the Japanese Economic White Book stated that it was no longer in the postwar period, which was a phrase well remembered by many Japanese. In 1960, Prime Minister Ikeda Hayato undertook an ambitious "income-doubling plan." The government expanded public investment in hard infrastructure such as highways, subways, and dams while lowering interest rates and taxes to private sectors to motivate spending. Japan's industrial structure was also transformed. Textiles, metals, ships, automobiles, and electric appliances appeared to be major industries.

Consequently, Japan began to return to the world market and international trading system. In 1955, Japan acceded to the General Agreement on Tariffs and Trade (GATT). With growing economic strength, the Japanese government started trade liberalization. An import quota system was mostly eliminated and converted to the tariff system. Japan obtained GATT Article 11 status in 1963 and IMF Article 8 status in 1964, according to which its trade and exchange rate should not be restricted for the reason of balance of payment. Indeed, Japan's trade balance came to record surpluses after 1965. In 1968, replacing West Germany, Japan finally became the world's second largest country in terms of GDP.

From the late 1950s to the early 1970s, the Japanese economy constantly marked high growth rate. The economic miracle was considerable owing to US "reverse course" policy to make Japan a bulwark against communism in Asia. Ironically, however, in the 1970s, the US–Japan relations became troubled due to trade frictions. In 1972 the US demanded a comprehensive quota system to block the inflow of cheaper Japanese textiles into the US market. After that, other sectors such as steel, color TVs, automobiles, VTR, semi-conductors, and super computers were placed in agendas of bilateral nego- tiations. Most problems were solved by Japan's voluntary withdrawal of exporting. Instead, Japanese companies started local production within the US to keep their American market share and in fact increased their interests. In the 1980s, even more friction occurred regarding Japanese imports from the US. Japan accepted US demands by liberalizing its domestic market to import more US products. However, as it did not contribute to the increase of US exports to the Japanese market, the US eventually began to intervene in Japan's economic system itself. In 1989, the Japan–US Structural Impedi- ments Initiatives (SII) was set up and started negotiations. Therefore, when Japan played an active role in forming APEC, Japan hoped to stabilize such Japan–US economic relations within the broader regional framework for free trade.

In the 1990s, Japan's economic growth slowed markedly, resulting in the long recession later called "Lost Decade." Japan suffered from the after- effects of the bubble economy and long recessions. Bankruptcies of major banks with bad debts from the stock and real estate market damaged the whole Japanese economy. The restructuring process of the companies gener- ated unemployment and their production continued to fall downward. Further- more, Japan was not able to catch up with the IT industry in the economy of globalization initiated by the US. In the first decade of the twenty-first cen- tury, Japan still underwent low economic growth and struggled with long spiral of deflation. The phase was even renamed as the "Lost Two Decades." As a means of revitalizing Japanese economy, living with the economic growth of Asia-Pacific region is essential. Therefore, Japan actively pursues bilateral FTA/EPA negotiations and work for Asia-Pacific regional economic integration. In 2012, Japan joined negotiations for the TPP (Trans Pacific Partnership), as well as RCEP (Regional Comprehensive Economic Partner- ship) and China-Japan-Korea FTA projects. Japan's ultimate goal is an accomplishment of FTAAP (Free Trade Area of Asia Pacific), which is APEC's long-term objective.

1.3 Socio-cultural perspective: rethinking the Japan model and the soft power dimension

Japan is a relatively homogenous nation-state, which is unusual in the world. Therefore, it has been often pointed out that modern Japan's outstanding experience of economic development and social advancement is rooted in its intrinsic values or cultural and social uniqueness. The old wartime study by US anthropologists pointed out that Japan has a "shame" culture, whose emphasis is on how one's moral conduct appears to outsiders, while America has basically a Christian "guilt" culture whose emphasis is on the individual's internal conscience (Benedict 1946). From the insider's perception, a Japanese sociologist described Japanese unique national characteristics as "*amae*," dependency on others. He explained Japanese society as one based on the Japanese psychological tendency to depend upon another's benevolence. It can also be defined as "to wish to be loved," a request for indulgence of one's perceived needs (Doi 1971).

In the 1980s, other countries often learned from Japan's economic success. Ezra Vogel (1979), in his book *Japan as Number One*, highlighted developed Japanese as one of the world's most effective industrial powers. This is attributed to not only economic productivity but also other social abilities, such as to govern efficiently, to educate its citizens, to control crime, to alleviate energy shortages, and to lessen pollution. Some Southeast Asian leaders modeled after Japan's working culture and values.. In 1978, Singapore launched the "Learn from Japan" campaign. Seeing Singapore as a similar nation with regards to lack of natural resources, and dependent on human capital, Prime Minster Lee Kuan Yew openly admired the Japanese style of management, attributing the success of its productivity improvement to the loyalty of its workers. Similarly, Malaysian Prime Minister Mahathir bin Mohamad launched the "Look East" (basically "Look Japan") policy in 1981. Mahathir's central concept of "Look East" essentially referred to the Japanese work ethic.[12] In opposition, some Westerners such as Karel van Wolferen provided more critical accounts of the business, social, and political structure of Japan (Wolferen 1989). He criticized the inefficiency in the system caused by a complicated political-corporate relationship, an unaccountable enigma which has its origin in the culture and history of the nation. The criticism sounds prophetic especially when the Japanese economy experienced long recessions in the 1990s. During the "Lost Decades," Japanese business models and social traditions were fundamentally questioned, which led to a lot of reforms.

Despite its domestic political and economic problems, in the beginning of the twenty-first century Japan was marked with a different image as a culturally and socially matured nation. Though historically Japan had good reputation to import other cultures and adapt them to its own, Japan's hybrid culture receives world attention today (Bestor et al. 2011). For example, the concept of Cool Japan was coined as an expression of Japan's emergent status as a cultural soft power especially in the Asian market. The survey of youth culture and the role of J-pop, *manga*, anime, fashion, film, consumer electronics, architecture, cuisine, and phenomena of cuteness such as Hello Kitty, showed that Japan's cultural influence has expanded internationally (McGray 2002). More recently, the boom outreached the Japanese people's close lifestyle. The TV program, *Cool Japan*, aired by Japan's National Broadcast (NHK) since 2006, has presented Japan's unique aspects selected from the perspectives of foreign visitors. Most popular topics aired included; toilet seat with automatic washing bidet, *ohanami* (cherry blossom watching and drinking party), 100 Yen (one coin) shop, meticulous wax-works of food samples, *izakaya* (Japanese style drinking bar), "super" public baths or *onsen* (hot spring) amusement parks.[13] They illustrate much broader perspectives such as high quality of basic commodities, service hospitality, habits of treating goods carefully, wisdom of living a simple and reasonable life. Taking an opportunity from the 2020 Tokyo Olympic Game, now the Japanese government is more self-consciously promoting such Japanese culture to enhance its soft power.

2 Involvement of Japan within the region (ASEAN)

2.1 Political-security perspective: fostering Japan–ASEAN partnership

The Japan–ASEAN bilateral dialogue dates back to 1973, when the two sides established a Forum on Synthetic Rubber. It primarily aimed to settle trade frictions between Malaysia and Japan. However, ASEAN as a unitary actor became Japan's counterpart because other members shared similar concerns. The rapidly growing presence of Japanese businesses in Southeast Asian cities caused not only economic but social and cultural frictions with local communities. Japanese Prime Minister Tanaka Kakuei's 1974 visit to Indonesia and Thailand caused serious anti-Japan movements and boycotts of Japanese products by the local people. This shocked the Japanese government enough to rethink its Southeast Asian policy to make the relationship more amicable and sustainable. As a new approach, the Japan-ASEAN Forum was launched in March 1977 to promote broader and closer cooperation in areas of industrial development, trade, food, and agriculture. In August 1977, Prime Minister Fukuda Takeo was invited to the second ASEAN Summit in Kuala Lumpur, and at the last stop of his ASEAN tour in Manila, he unveiled Japan's basic Southeast Asian policy.

The so-called "Fukuda Doctrine" addressed three pillars for the future course of Japan–ASEAN relations and Japan's role in the region.[14] First, Japan will not become a military power. Second, Japan is willing to expand cultural and social ties with ASEAN based on a "heart to heart" understanding in addition to the political and economic ones. Third, Japan wishes to co-operate with ASEAN as "equal partners," and will work for Southeast Asian regional stability especially through contacts with the Indochina states.

In the speech, Fukuda appreciated that Japan was called "an especially close friend of ASEAN" during the meeting and declared Japan's goal was to become the "true friend" of ASEAN, whose relationship should not be based merely on material or economic motivations. In 1978, the Japan and ASEAN foreign ministerial meeting was held as a follow up of the summit agreement. The conference discussed not only Japan–ASEAN relations but also broadly world political and economic issues. The Japanese Foreign Minister promised to reflect ASEAN's voice in the G7 summit. He also asked the US to meet with ASEAN foreign ministers and show joint support for ASEAN. Thus, Japan showed its willingness to solidify ASEAN's unity and improve its status in the international society.

In 1987, Prime Minister Takeshita Noboru attended the third ASEAN summit in Manila and made a speech entitled "Japan and ASEAN: A New Partnership toward Peace and Prosperity." Reiterating "heart to heart" understanding of the 1977 Fukuda Doctrine, Takeshita enumerated three basic policies toward ASEAN: First is to strengthen the economic resilience of ASEAN, second is to promote political coordination between Japan and ASEAN, and third is to promote cultural exchanges. Accordingly, Takeshita announced the foundation of the Japan-ASEAN Development Fund of more than US$2 billion to stimulate ASEAN economies. On the other hand, Japan constantly worked to bridge ASEAN with Asia-Pacific cooperation. In April 1989, Takeshita visited Southeast Asia again and made a speech in Jakarta entitled "Japan and ASEAN: Thinking together and advancing together,"[15] in which he explained how the Japan–ASEAN relationship is placed in Asia-Pacific cooperation. He clearly stated that the ASEAN's example of achieving diversity-tolerant cooperation must be most respected as a model for Asia-Pacific cooperation. Based on such multi-faceted and steady cooperation, the Asia-Pacific should promote a free and open trading system in accordance with global rules. Takeshita emphasized that the true value of Japan–ASEAN cooperative relations would be tested in the Asia-Pacific.

Complying with the Fukuda doctrine which promised to bridge ASEAN and other Indochina states, Japan consistently supported ASEAN's member-ship expansion and institutional evolution process throughout the 1990s. For example, Japan actively supported the establishment of the ASEAN Regional Forum (ARF) (Yuzawa, 2010). In January 1997, Prime Minister Hashimoto Ryutaro made a Southeast Asian trip and showed his vision of Japan–ASEAN relations in the globalization age. Succeeding main ideas of Fukuda and Takeshita, Hashimoto proposed Japan–ASEAN joint endeavors focusing on three areas: First, to promote broader and deeper exchanges between Japan and ASEAN at the top and all other levels. Second, to deepen mutual understanding and to expand multilateral cultural cooperation for the pre-servation and harmony of unique traditions and culture. Third, to tackle universal concerns such as terrorism and the environment. Japan's commit-ment was soon tested by the Asian financial crisis in 1999. For ASEAN nations' recovery, Japan created the Japan-ASEAN Solidarity Fund in 1999 and the Japan-ASEAN General Exchange Fund (JAGEF) in 2000.

In January 2002, in Singapore, Prime Minister Koizumi Junichiro made a speech on Japan's Southeast Asian policy in which he stated that the goal was "the creation of a community that acts together and advances together."[16] He added the community should be achieved through expanding East Asia cooperation founded upon the Japan–ASEAN relationship. At the December

2003 ASEAN-Japan Commemorative Summit in Tokyo, the two sides agreed on the "Tokyo Declaration for the Dynamic and Enduring ASEAN Japan Partnership in the New Millennium" and launched the Japan-ASEAN Plan of Action, a comprehensive framework to address future relations in the fields of economics and finance, politics and security, as well as cultural cooperation. In 2004, Japan signed the Treaty of Amity and Cooperation in Southeast Asia (TAC), which marked a milestone in Japan–ASEAN security relations. In 2006, Japan established the ASEAN Integration Fund. Also, Japan continues its cooperation to support the ASEAN Connectivity Coordinating Committee for the implementation of the Master Plan by setting up a Japan Task Force. In 2011, Japan and ASEAN signed the significant document entitled "Joint Declaration for Enhancing ASEAN-Japan Strategic Partnership for Prospering Together," which noted with "deep satisfaction the progress achieved through our long-standing friendship and strategic partnership based on the Tokyo Declaration."[17] Thus, Japan has consistently associated with ASEAN's evolutionary history as a close friend.

2.2 Economic perspectives: aid, trade, investment

After WWII, Japan's immediate issue in Southeast Asian policy was the reparation settlement. Because of its own financial difficulties, the bulk of the reparation payment was usually exercised by means of commodity and service grants. Meanwhile, Japan started its ODA in 1954 when joining the Colombo Plan, a British proposed aid program for South and Southeast Asia. Reparations and aids initially took the form of the export of technology and industrial plants, which allows Japanese companies to enter Southeast Asian markets. It also created the production linkages between these countries and Japan. Furthermore, Japan's economic interests were expanded by the tying of the ODA to the purchase of Japanese goods and services, especially large infrastructure projects. These initiatives were often interpreted as an aggressive economic drive or "economic animal" by many trading partners.

Acknowledging such criticisms and its elevating international status, Japan modified its ODA policy. The nature of the ODA changed from self-oriented purpose to a non-egoistic and recipients-oriented one. While adapting the "untying" system, Japan increased the amount of the ODA toward ASEAN. After concluding the last reparations to the Philippines in 1976, Japan announced the double increase of ODA within five years, later on rescheduled within three years because of the appreciation of the yen. Through a series of mid-term plans, Japanese ODA expanded rapidly from US$1.42 billion in 1977 to a historic high of US$ 13.8 billion in 1995 (Hook et al. 2012). In 1989 and from 1991 to 2000, Japan was the world largest donor and occupied over 20 percent of the total amount of world ODA. The recipients were traditionally dominated by Asian countries. Figure 12.1 shows the recent scale of Japan's ODA to East Asia. Currently, Japanese ODA for East Asia manifested that its goals are to deepen open regional cooperation and integration based on sharing universal norms, and to secure regional stability through promoting mutual understanding.[18]

Japanese Foreign Direct Investment (FDI) also contributed to make the linkages between Japan and Southeast Asian economies. In the 1950s and 1960s, Japan's FDI essentially attempted to secure supplies of natural resources with major investments in resource extraction in Southeast Asia. The Nixon statement in 1971 terminated a fixed exchange rate system and led to the appreciation of the yen against the dollar. The oil shock in 1973 increased energy and production costs for companies inside Japan, and forced them to restructure from reliance on heavy industry. The rise of domestic labor cost generated an upsurge of Japanese FDI in East Asia. The main site was the Newly Industrialized Economies (NIEs), namely South Korea, Taiwan, Hong Kong, Singapore. Decisively in 1985, the Plaza Accord which appreciated the value of the yen against the US dollar by up to 70 percent, led to a threefold increase of Japanese FDI worldwide. In the late 1980s, the geographical concentration of Japanese FDI began to shift from the NIEs to the ASEAN 4 (Thailand, Indonesia, Malaysia, the Philippines), reflecting rising wage and currency costs of NIEs. In the early 1990s, with the further appreciation of the yen against the US dollar, Japanese investments in ASEAN nations significantly increased. Such a shifting process, which can be seen as a development pattern of the Flying Geese Model,[19] deepened regional economic interdependence. In other words, the Japanese companies' overseas production network contributed to the de-facto regionalization of East Asia (Katzenstein and Shiraishi, 1997, 2006). Furthermore, the concentration of Japanese ODA and FDI in East Asia produced a distinctive pattern of trade relations between Japan and the region. Japan's total trade values with East Asia came to exceed that with the US in the early 1980s. Since then, trade relations between Japan and ASEAN have grown (Figure 12.2). As of 2010, Japan's trade values with ASEAN exceeded US$213,870 million (US$112,868 million for exports, US$101,002 million for imports). It occupied 14.6 percent of Japan's total trade values, which is second to China (20.7 percent) and surpassed that to the US (12.9 percent) (Figure 12.3).

The Japan-ASEAN Center, established in 1981 based on the Agreement Establishing the ASEAN Promotion Center on Trade, Investment, and Sightseeing, recently put more emphasis on increasing investments and tourists from ASEAN to Japan, reversing the past tendency from Japan to ASEAN.

2.3 Socio-cultural perspectives: solidifying people-to people relations

Japan's basic ODA principle is to cultivate "ownership" of the recipients, thus contributing to a lasting relationship. In 1962, the Japanese government established the Overseas Technical Cooperation Agency (OTCA), which started a number of educational exchange programs with ASEAN states. Malaysian, Thai, and Filipino scholars began studying in Japan under

(Net disbursements, US$ million)

Rank	Country or region	Grants				Loan aid			Total
		Grant aid	Grants provided through multilateral institutions	Technical cooperation	Total	Amount disbursed	Amount recovered	Total	
1	Viet Nam	20.38	—	148.27	168.65	1,866.99	388.94	1,478.05	1,646.71
2	Cambodia	83.14	8.95	55.95	139.09	45.67	2.32	43.36	182.44
3	Mongolia	45.20	—	29.67	74.88	56.55	20.78	35.77	110.65
4	Myanmar	54.82	13.27	37.96	92.78	—	0.00	0.00	92.78
5	Laos	42.10	—	51.06	93.16	0.01	4.75	-4.73	88.43
6	Timor-Leste	7.48	—	11.35	18.82	0.01	—	0.01	18.84
7	Malaysia	0.36	—	23.57	23.93	184.49	213.63	-29.14	-5.21
8	Thailand	13.86	1.29	71.48	85.34	203.69	531.53	-327.85	-242.51
9	Philippines	55.49	2.44	85.49	140.97	295.63	855.41	-559.78	-418.81
10	China	9.99	—	131.68	141.67	390.76	1,370.79	-980.04	-838.37
11	Indonesia	18.86	0.34	131.61	150.47	672.01	1,702.02	-1,030.01	-879.53
	ODA for multiple countries in East Asia	0.42	0.40	8.55	8.97	—	—	—	8.97
	East Asia region total	352.10	26.69	788.78	1,140.88	3,715.83	5,150.02	-1,434.19	-293.31
	(ASEAN total)	289.01	26.29	607.47	896.48	3,268.50	3,758.44	-489.94	406.54

Figure 12.1 Japan's assistance in the East Asia region (2012)
Source: Japan's ODA White Paper 2013, Ministry of Foreign Affairs, Japan, http://www.mofa.go.jp/policy/oda/page_000044.html, accessed July 30, 2015.

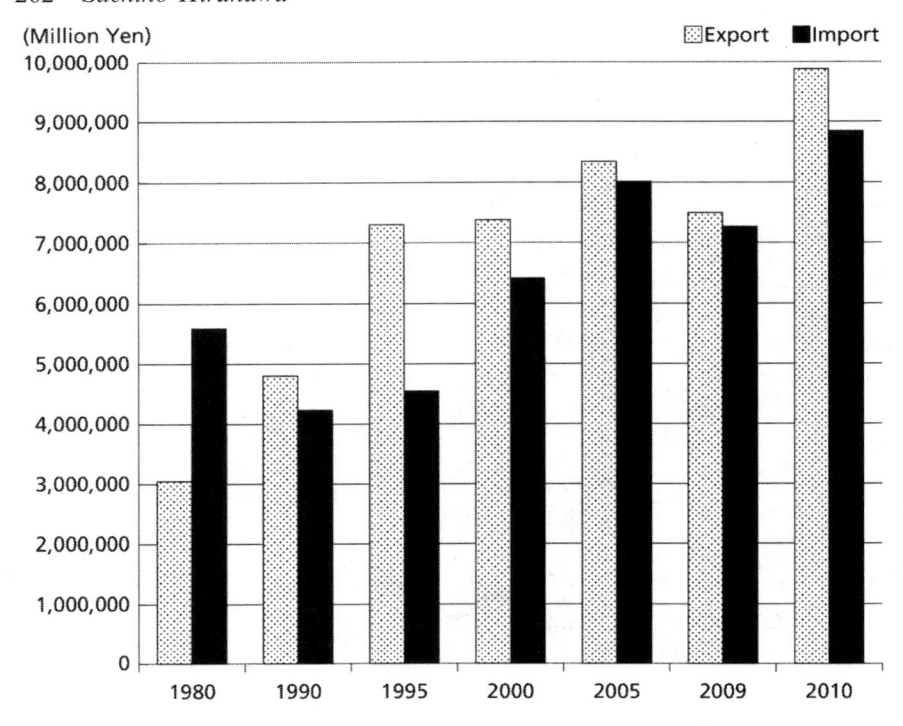

Figure 12.2 Japan's trade value with ASEAN, 1980–2010 (in million yen)
Note: Data of Vietnam is not included in 1980 and 1990.
Source: ASEAN-JAPAN CENTER, http://www.asean.or.jp/en/asean/know/statistics/Latest_Statistics.html. The Summary Report on Trade of Japan Dec.1980, Dec.1990, Dec.1997, Dec. 2002, Dec. 2007 and Dec. 2010 (Japan Tariff Association), accessed July 30, 2015.

Japanese government scholarships. OTCA was later in 1974 reorganized into the Japan International Cooperation Agency (JICA). ASEAN countries had been the main participants of these personnel and educational projects. Meanwhile, Japan's cultural diplomacy started in 1972 when the Ministry of Foreign Affairs founded the Japan Foundation, which was the first organization specializing in international cultural exchanges. It opened branches in Jakarta and Bangkok. After the 1977 Fukuda Doctrine, Japan set up programs for ASEAN to initiate people-to people relations and cultural exchanges, particularly among youth and intellectuals. In 1978 under the Fukuda aid program, 5 billion yen was specifically designated for an ASEAN Cultural Fund.

Throughout the 1980s, Japanese prime ministers continued to create projects of people and cultural exchanges with ASEAN. In 1980 Ohira Masayoshi introduced the ASEAN Youth Scholarship Program. In 1981 Suzuki Zenko proposed the establishment of a local ASEAN training center in each nation

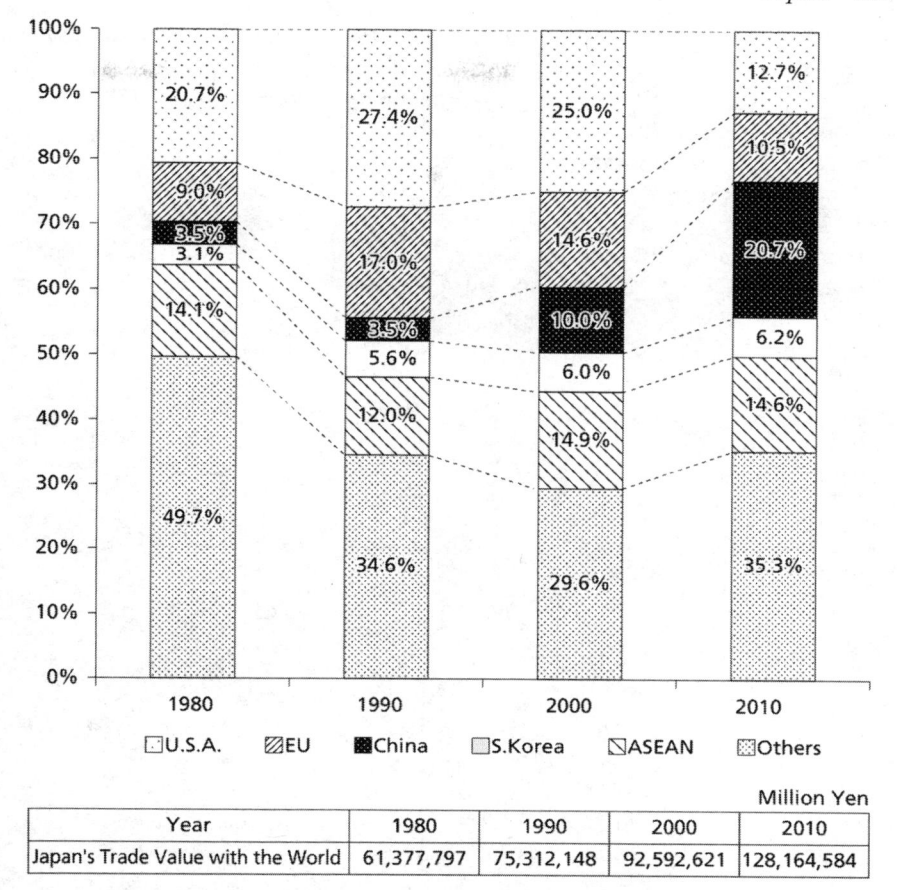

Million Yen

Year	1980	1990	2000	2010
Japan's Trade Value with the World	61,377,797	75,312,148	92,592,621	128,164,584

Figure 12.3 Trend of Japan's trade value with its major trading partners
Note: * EU indicates EC (1980, 1990), EU15 (2000), EU27 (2010).
Source: ASEAN-JAPAN CENTER, http://www.asean.or.jp/en/asean/know/statistics/Latest_Statistics.html. The Summary Report on Trade of Japan Dec.1980, Dec.1990, Dec. 2002 and Dec. 2010 (Japan Tariff Association), accessed July 30, 2015.

and expressed Japan's readiness to offer US$100 million for the projects. In 1984 Nakasone Yasuhiro announced the 21st Century Friendship Program to boost personnel exchange in the cultural and education areas. Then in 1987 Takeshita Noboru announced the Japan-ASEAN Comprehensive Exchange Program to expand technical, academic, research, athletic, and cultural exchanges. Takeshita also offered greater financial assistance for foreign students as well as promotion of inter-ASEAN technical exchange and the creation of the Center for Promotion of Cultural Exchange between Japan and ASEAN. Nakasone's program was extended for five years and an additional 4,000 ASEAN youths came to Japan. Furthermore, Japan set up a US

$7billion scholarship in the ADB to meet ASEAN needs for management education in their rapidly growing economies. The number of ASEAN students in Japan has been increasing constantly (Figure 12.4).

Both Japan and ASEAN are vulnerable to natural disasters. Japan was among the first to rush aid and assistance to victims of the tsunami in Aceh in 2004 and Cyclone Nargis in Myanmar in 2008. ASEAN returned the favor in 2011 at the time of the Great East Japan Earthquake in March 2011. Japan appreciated that after a special ASEAN-Japan Ministerial Meeting in April, the Secretary-General of ASEAN led a team of volunteers, the "Caravan of

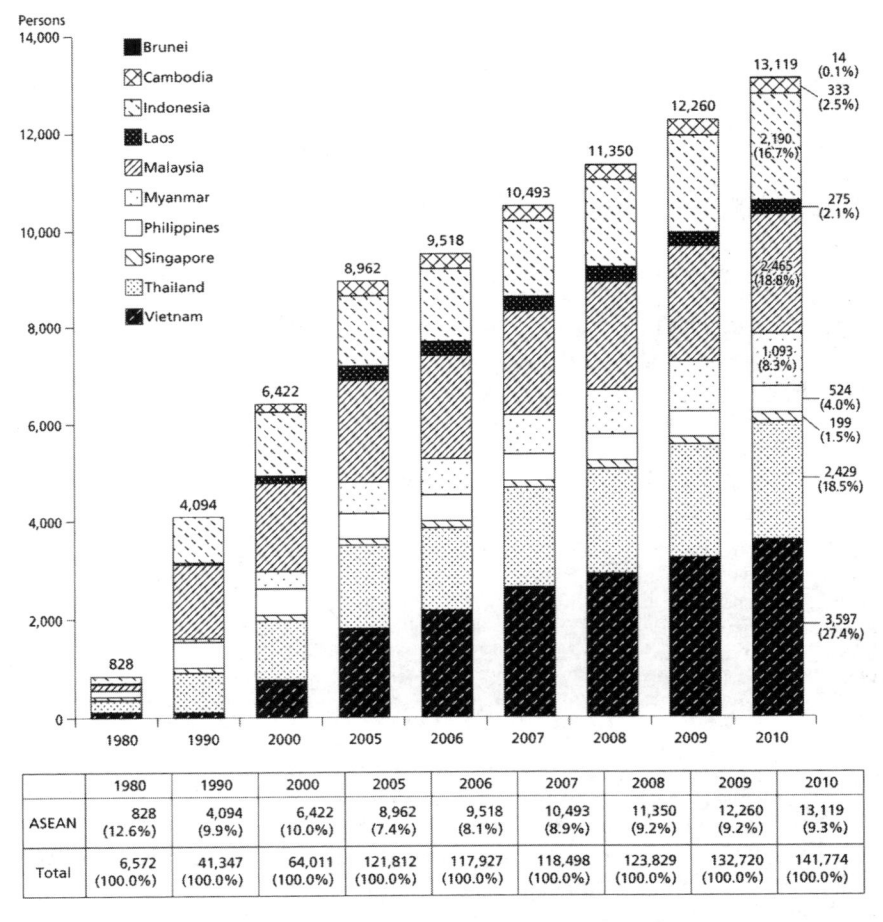

	1980	1990	2000	2005	2006	2007	2008	2009	2010
ASEAN	828 (12.6%)	4,094 (9.9%)	6,422 (10.0%)	8,962 (7.4%)	9,518 (8.1%)	10,493 (8.9%)	11,350 (9.2%)	12,260 (9.2%)	13,119 (9.3%)
Total	6,572 (100.0%)	41,347 (100.0%)	64,011 (100.0%)	121,812 (100.0%)	117,927 (100.0%)	118,498 (100.0%)	123,829 (100.0%)	132,720 (100.0%)	141,774 (100.0%)

Figure 12.4 Trend in the number of students from ASEAN in Japan
Source: ASEAN-JAPAN CENTER, http://www.asean.or.jp/en/asean/know/statistics/Latest_Statistics.html. Ministry of Education, Culture, Sports Science and Technology, Japan. International Students in Japan (Website of the Japan Student Services Organization, accessed in December 2011), accessed 30 July 2015.

Goodwill," to Japan. ASEAN–Japan cooperation in disaster management continues after the disasters. In 2012, Japan started a new youth exchange project which is named the "Kizuna" (which means "Bond") project. It aims to share Japan's lessons in revival efforts in response to the earthquake. They are projected to benefit approximately 18,000 youths of ASEAN and Japan. Furthermore, Japan provided funds for ASEAN's Task Force for the establishment of the ASEAN Coordinating Center for Humanitarian Assistance on disaster management (AHA Center), equipping it with state-of-the-art technology and information system. Japan also assisted the development of the ASEAN Regional Emergency Stockpile System in Subang, Malaysia. In addition, Japan is committed to continue to work with ASEAN to establish the Disaster Management Network for ASEAN. These humanitarian projects are based on the political principle of people-to people, or heart to heart relationships with Southeast Asia.

3 Involvement of Japan within APT

When Japan was invited to the first ASEAN Plus Three meeting in 1997, Japan perceived it as a useful framework especially to immediately cope with the ongoing Asian Financial Crisis (AFC). Starting with Thailand in July, Indonesia, South Korea, the Philippines, and Malaysia successively suffered from their plunged currencies in the market. Despite its own financial woe under economic recessions, Japan quickly took responsibility to pledge assistance to neighbors facing economic hardship in order to stabilize the regional economy. In August, Tokyo hosted the international conference to rescue Thailand's currency crisis. In September, Japan proposed the creation of the Asian Monetary Fund (AMF), which would coope with the financial difficulties and provide a regional safety net with the Japanese initiative. The Ministry of Finance designed the institution as a regional version of the IMF, with a more nuanced understanding of the Asian politico-economic background. However, the proposal did not materialize because of strong opposition from the U.S. Alternatively, in February 1998, the Japanese government announced the New Miyazawa Initiative with US$30 billion. The initiative offered financial assistance packages to revitalize Asian domestic economies on bilateral bases. Unlike the IMF rescue package, this bilateral scheme did not demand any significant restructuring conditionality. A number of East Asian states such as Thailand, Malaysia, Indonesia, the Philippines, and South Korea took advantage of the initiative. Based on the exercise of New Miyazawa Initiative, Japan signed currency bilateral swap agreements with individual recipients.

The above situation further served the foundation of establishing the Chiang Mai Initiative (CMI) under the APT framework in 2000. In fact, ASEAN had already established the intramural system of bilateral currency swap agreements for the crisis, which had not worked so well by then. Japan with its founding funds effectively reactivated the existing ASEAN system by extending the function to the APT countries. As a result, the process of CMI did not only substitute for the Japan's unsuccessful multilateral AMF proposal, but also marked the effectuation of the APT framework itself and gave confidence for future East Asian cooperation. In 2011, the APT countries further institutionalized the development of the CMI initiative into the CMIM (Chiang Mai Initiative Multilateralization.) The new mechanism was accompanied with the establishment of a permanent regional office of the AMRO (Asian Macroeconomic Research Office) to investigate the regional economic situation. Thus, the CMIM is one of the best examples which show the fruits of APT cooperation.

The ASEAN Plus Three Emergency Rice Reserve (APTERR), which was signed in 2011, is regarded as another successful initiative. Japan played a critical role in supporting the agricultural and food security cooperation. Similar to the case of the CMI, the process toward APTERR is basically a revitalization of ASEAN's original cooperation scheme by expanding it to the APT with Japan's effective initiative. ASEAN had established the cooperation framework of rice reserve system since the agreement of the ASEAN Emergency Rice Reserve (AERR) in 1979. However, the AERR was not fully functioning and actually it was not practiced even in the serious food crisis created by abnormal weather in Indonesia in 1998. The same year's announcement of ASEAN Vision 2020 did include the agenda of the reinforcement of food security system. Responsively, the 1999 joint statement of APT addressed promotion of agricultural cooperation as one of the areas which should be strengthened.[20] At that time, Japan coincidentally advocated international cooperation on food security and had just started an international proposal on a food reserve system in the WTO agricultural negotiations. The proposed food assistance schemes and systems were primarily aimed at helping developing countries. Thus, Japan was quite ready for the establishment of the food security system in East Asia (Morikawa 2012).

The Japanese government, through JICA, financially and technically supported the whole process at every step. In 1998, the Meeting of ASEAN Ministers on Agriculture and Forestry (AMAF) decided to revitalize AERR and started special workshops under Thai initiative. In October 2001, the Thai government reported the result of a comprehensive research on the issues of the regional rice situation and feasibility of the food security system to the SOM-AMAF Plus Three meeting. After three stages of investigation, the second meeting of SOM-AMAF Plus Three in 2002 formally agreed on the establishment of the regional emergency rice reserve system and its action programs. In 2003, the three-year pilot program started. The ASEAN Food Security Information System (AFSIS) project was established in order to continuously collect and organize data necessary for the analysis of supply and demand of rice reserves. In the 2011 APT summit, Prime Minister Noda Yoshihiko announced Japan's assistance for the procurement of rice and other food in response to the flood disasters in the Mekong River basin as a preparatory project prior to the effectuation of the APTERR agreement. Thus Japan consistently committed to extensive agricultural assistance and reinforcement of food security mechanism in East Asia.

Lastly, Japan believes education for the young generation is essential and decisive to enhance regional community building. The Second Joint Statement of East Asia Cooperation of 2007 addressed the importance of "forging a sense of an East Asian identity and consciousness, people-to-people exchanges."[21] Accordingly in 2009, Japan and Thailand proposed setting up conferences focusing on this aspect and held the first meeting in Thailand next year. Meanwhile, in 2009, the second China–Japan–Korea trilateral summit, based on the proposal by Japanese Prime Minister Hatoyama Yukio, agreed on launching the Campus Asia program which would promote educational changes with the assurance of quality. In practicing this academic scheme, the Japanese government additionally prepared an independent category which extended to ASEAN, which as a result could cover ASEAN Plus Three countries. In 2011, Tokyo hosted an International Symposium on quality assurance in higher education in East Asia. Although Northeast Asia and Southeast Asia now respectively promote their own educational cooperation framework, they eventually might be integrated in the future (Kuroda 2013).

4 Conclusion

This chapter has reviewed how postwar Japan has molded its new identity and re-established its position in the context of Asian regionalism. For Japan, Southeast Asia has been a place for self-checking if it is going on the right track, which is far different from the war-time regionalism. In the early two decades, Japan's policy tended to be still self-centered because its strategic goal of economic recovery preoccupied the policymakers despite their awareness of Japan's identity as a member of Asia. When Japan regained its international status in the late 1960s to early 1970s, Japan's behavior with too much economic emphasis was again seriously questioned, which set up a new diplomatic orientation and its identity in Asia.

For postwar Japan, a pacifist trading country, living in a peaceful and prosperous region and forging good relationships with others directly means its own security. Therefore its overwhelming economic advantages should be shared with other partners and be used to solidify mutual connectedness in the region. Such trustful partnerships cannot be made instantly. Mutual understanding of culture or history, which is non-economic and non-material, among the peoples of the region would guarantee the sustainability of regional bonds. This is the area on which Japan should persistently concentrate its economic power most. In addition to Japan's own past, ASEAN's sincere and steady efforts toward unity or community building also gave valuable lessons to Japan. Closely associated with ASEAN's challenge toward region making, Japan was able to crystalize its regionalism policy in Asia first into the 1977 Fukuda Doctrine, which remains as the fundamental guideline until today.

Japan's broader regional policy such as that on East Asia and Asia-Pacific has always walked with ASEAN step by step, while cultivating trusting partnerships.

After the Fukuda Doctrine, the Japanese Ministry of Foreign Affairs began to survey opinion polls in the ASEAN region almost every five years.[22] Most recent result indicates that the ASEAN countries had a positive image about their relations with Japan. Notably, on how they viewed their country's relations with Japan, more than 90 percent of the respondents answered "friendly" or "somewhat friendly." In addition, more than 90 percent answered that they considered Japan to be "a trustworthy friend" or "trustworthy, but with some reservations." Japan was ranked first as "the most reliable country" with 33 percent of the respondents who selected Japan among 11 countries. The data seems to justify postwar Japan's practice to wish to be a close friend to ASEAN.

Japan's basic stance in the APT is to support ASEAN centrality. This is because Japan firmly believes that establishing a caring and people-centered ASEAN Community based on the rule of law is consistent with Japan's regional vision. In this sense, Japan promotes ASEAN's role as a strategic partner in the changing dynamics of the region. Japan believes that the unity of ASEAN can function as a hub for regional cooperation and this provides stability and prosperity not only in Japan–ASEAN relations but also in the whole East Asian region.

Notes

1 The Dutch East India Company was exceptionally permitted to enter at Dejima, an artificial island for a trading spot at Nagasaki.
2 It was assumed to consist of Southeast Asia, India, a part of Oceania, in addition to Japan, Manchuria, and the China bloc.
3 Translation is excerpted from Hook et al. (2012: Appendix 1.1).
4 Japan normalized relations with the Republic of Korea (ROK) in 1965 and the PRC in 1972.
5 www.mofa.go.jp/mofaj/gaiko/bluebook/1957/s32-contents.htm (accessed July 30, 2015).
6 Address of Mamoru Shigemitsu, Deputy Prime Minister and Foreign Minister of Japan, before the UN General Assembly, December 18, 1956. www.mofa.go.jp/policy/un/address5612.html (accessed July 30, 2015).
7 www.mofa.go.jp/mofaj/gaiko/bluebook/1968/s43-shiryou.htm#1-4 (accessed July 30, 2015).
8 A study group on Pacific Basin, "The official report of Pacific Basin Cooperation Plan (for Prime Minister Ohira's policy study group)," submitted in May 1980.
9 Japan dispatched the SDF to the UN missions of Mozambique (1993–1995), Rwanda (1994), the Golan Heights (1996–2013), East Timor (2002–2004), Haiti (2010–2013), Nepal (2007–2011), Sudan (2008–2011) and South Sudan (2011 to present).
10 Toward the Creation of A Bright Future for Asia, December 16, 1998 www.mofa.go.jp/region/asia-paci/asean/pmv9812/policyspeech.html (accessed July 30, 2015).
11 Ogata served Head of United Nations High Commissioner for Refugees (UNHCR) from 1991 to 2001. Sen is an Indian economist. His work in welfare economics was awarded the Nobel Memorial Prize in Economic Science in 1998.

12 Miyado Daigo, Responding to Southeast Asia, *Japan Quarterly* 30(2), April/June 1983, 118–121. The article is reproduced in Mendl (2001).
13 Cool Japan Web site, www.nhk.or.jp/cooljapan/en (accessed July 30, 2015).
14 The whole speech text is printed in Sudo (1992, 2002), Lam Peng Er ed. (2013).
15 The text of Takeshita speech is printed in Sudo (2002).
16 Japan and ASEAN in East Asia: A Sincere and Open Partnership, Speech by Prime Minister of Japan Junichiro Koizumi (January 14, 2002, Singapore) www.mofa.go.jp/region/asia-paci/pmv0201/speech.html (accessed on July 30, 2015).
17 Joint Declaration for Enhancing ASEAN-Japan Strategic Partnership for Prospering together (Bali Declaration) November 18, 2011. www.mofa.go.jp/region/asia-paci/asean/conference/pdfs/bali_declaration_en_1111.pdf (accessed July 30, 2015).
18 For Japan's current ODA policy, see www.mofa.go.jp/policy/oda/index.html (accessed July 30, 2015).
19 The term was first proposed as Asian development model by Akamatsu Kaname in 1962. The model suggests the process of developing countries catching up with developed ones, with Japan at the head.
20 Joint statement on East Asia Cooperation, 28 November, 1999. www.mofa.go.jp/region/asia-paci/asean/pmv9911/joint.html (accessed July 30, 2015).
21 Second Joint Statement on East Asia Cooperation: Building on the Foundation of ASEAN Plus Three Cooperation. www.mofa.go.jp/region/asia-paci/asean/conference/asean3/joint0711.pdf (accessed July 30, 2015).
22 The Ministry of Foreign Affairs commissioned IPSOS Hong Kong Limited to conduct an opinion poll on Japan in the seven ASEAN countries (Indonesia, Malaysia, the Philippines, Singapore, Thailand, Vietnam, and Myanmar) in March 2014. (The poll was conducted online with about 300 literate respondents aged 18 years or older in each country.) The Ministry has commissioned opinion polls for the ASEAN region seven times in the past (1978, 1983, 1987, 1992, 1997, 2002, and 2008).

References

Benedict, Ruth (1946) *The Chrysanthemum and the Sword: Patterns of Japanese Culture*, Boston, MA: Houghton Mifflin Company.

Bestor, Victoria Lyon, Theodore C., Bestor and Akiko Yamagata (eds) (2011) *Routledge Handbook of Japanese Society and Culture*. New York: Routledge.

Constantino, Renato (ed.) (1991) *Southeast Asian Perceptions of Japan*, Quezon City: Karrel, Inc.

Doi Takeo (1971) *The Structure of Amae [Amae no Kozo]*, Tokyo: Kobundo.

Flath David (2014) *The Japanese Economy*, 3rd edition, New York: Oxford University Press.

Funabashi, Yoichi (1995) *Asia Pacific Fusion: Japan's Role in APEC*. Washington, DC: Institute for International Economics.

Hatano, Sumio and Susumu Sato (2007) *Gendai Nihon no Tonan Ajia seisaku [Modern Japan's Southeast Asian Policy]: 1950–2005*, Tokyo: Waseda University Press.

Hook, Glen, Julie Gilson, Christopher W. Hughes, Hugo Dobson (eds) (2012) *Japan's International Relations: Politics, Economics and Security*, 3rd edition, London and New York: Routledge, .

Hoshiro, Hiroyuki (2008) *Ajia Chiiki Syugi no Yukue [The Rise and Fall of Japan's Regional Diplomacy: 1952–1966]*, Tokyo: Bokutakusha.

Inoguchi Takashi, G. John Ikenberry and Yoichiro Sato (2011) *The US-Japan Security Alliance: Regional Multilateralism*, New York: Palgrave Macmillan.

Institute of Asian Cultures, Sophia University (2009) *New edition Introduction to Southeast Asian Studies* [*Shinban Nyumon Tonan Ajia Kenkyu*], Tokyo: Mekong.

Iokibe, Makoto (ed.) translated and annotated by Robert D. Eldridge (2011) *The Diplomatic History of Postwar Japan*, London and New York: Routledge.

Katzenstein, Peter J. and Takashi Shiraishi (eds) (2006) *Beyond Japan: The Dynamics of East Asian Regionalism*, Ithaca, NY: Cornell University Press.

Katzenstein, Peter J. and Takashi Shiraishi (eds) (1997) *Network Power: Japan and Asia*, Ithaca, NY: Cornell University Press.

Kojima, Takaaki (2006) *Japan and ASEAN Partnership for a Stable and Prosperous Future*, Singapore: Institute of Southeast Asian Studies.

Kuroda Kazuo (2013) "Regional Integration and Cooperation in Higher Education," in *Regional Integration in East Asia: Theoretical and Historical Perspectives*, edited by Amako Satoshi et al. Tokyo: United Nations University Press.

Lam Peng Er (ed.) (2013) *Japan's Relations with Southeast Asia: The Fukuda Doctrine and Beyond*, Abingdon: Routledge.

McGray, Douglas (2002) 'Japan's Gross National Cool', *Foreign Policy*, 1 May.

Mendl, Wolf (ed.) (2001) *Japan and South East Asia*, London and New York: Routledge.

Morikawa, Yuji (2012) *New Political Dynamics in Forming East Asian Region* [*Higashi Ajia Chiiki Keisei no Aratana Seijirikigaku*], Tokyo: Kokusaishoin.

Oba, Mie (2014) *Asia as a Multi-layered Region: In Search for Co-existence in Conflicts* [*Jusoteki chiiki toshiteno Ajia-Tairitsu to kyozon no kouzu*], Tokyo: Yuhikaku.

Pempel, T. J. (2005) *Remapping East Asia: The Construction of a Region*. Ithaca, NY: Cornell University Press.

Ravenhill, John (2001) *APEC and the Construction of Pacific Rim Regionalism*, Cambridge: Cambridge University Press.

Sudo, Sueo (1992) *The Fukuda Doctrine and ASEAN: New Dimensions in Japanese Foreign Policy*, Singapore: Institute of Southeast Asian Studies.

Sudo, Sueo (2002) *The International Relations of Japan and South East Asia: Forging a New Regionalism*, London and New York: Routledge.

Tarling, Nicholas (2006) *Regionalism in Southeast Asia: To Foster the Political Will*, London and New York: Routledge.

Terada, Takashi (1999a) 'The Japanese Origins of PAFTAD: The Beginning of Asia Pacific Economic Community', *Pacific Economic Papers*, 292, Australia-Japan Research Center.

Terada, Takashi (1999b) 'The Genesis of APEC: The Australia-Japan Political Initiatives', *Pacific Economic Papers*, 298, Australia-Japan Research Center.

Terada, Takashi (2013) *East Asia and Asia-Pacific: Contending Regional Integration* [*Higashi Ajia to Ajia Taiheiyo: Kyogo Suru Chiiki Togo*], Tokyo: Tokyo University Press

Wolferen, Karel Van (1989) *The Enigma of Japanese Power: People and Politics in a Stateless Nation*. New York: A.A. Knopf.

Yamakage, Susumu (1997) *Changing ASEAN: Self-transformation and Regime-Formation* [*ASEAN power: Ajia Taiheiyo no Chukaku e*], Tokyo: Tokyo University Press.

Yuzawa, Takeshi (2010) *Japan's Security Policy and the ASEAN Regional Forum: The Search for Multilateral Security in the Asia-Pacific*, London and New York: Routledge.

Vogel, Ezra (1979) *Japan as Number One: Lessons for America*, Cambridge, MA: Harvard University Press.

13 Major Perspectives of South Korea and ASEAN Cooperation

Pan Suk Kim

South Korea (hereafter Korea) has emerged from the Korean War as a major player in the global economic market as well as in the development of the Asian region. Along with Korea's growth over the last few decades, the relationship between Korea and the Association of Southeast Asian Nations (ASEAN) has also grown at a rapid pace. From bilateral trade and investment to assistance during natural disasters, the history behind this successful relationship is significant in order to analyze the future path of the ASEAN cooperation as well as the disparities and challenges faced by both as a consequence of global economic fluctuations and growth in the Asian and Southeast Asian regions.

1 National perspectives

Often eclipsed by its two powerhouse neighbors Japan and China, Korea has proven to be a powerhouse in its own right in recent decades. Growing at a tremendous rate from a developing nation into a democratic country and full member of the OECD's Development Assistance Committee (DAC), Korea is an important case study for those in international development looking to recreate the Korean miracle of rapid industrialization. It is important to analyze the evolution that took place during the period of Japanese colonization and the aftermath of the Korean War when Korea, a recipient of foreign aid, began the implementation of programs such as the *Saemaul Undong* (New Village Movement) to develop rural areas of the country beginning in 1970 (Choi, 2011). The *Saemaul Undong* is a movement seeking community development and modernization.[1] The lessons of Korea's development are important in understanding its current state of affairs in regional cooperation in the ASEAN.

Korea was one of the poorest countries in the world in the mid-twentieth century. Approximately a half century ago, Korea was poorer than two-thirds of the countries in sub-Saharan Africa, Malaysia, the Philippines, and Mexico. After more than five hundred years as a Hermit Kingdom, it remained an insular region under the *Joseon* dynasty (1392–1897) and the Korean Empire (1897–1910), followed by Japanese colonization (1910–1945) and the United States Army Military Government in Korea (1945–1948), and was left devastated by the Korean War (1950–1953).

The Korean War took place on the Korean peninsula from June 25, 1950 to July 27, 1953. The Korean War broke out when North Korea invaded South Korea. During the Korean War, a significant number of casualties occurred including South Koreans and the UN forces. (Sixteen member countries of the United Nations, including the United States, the Philippines and Thailand, came to the defense of South Korea.) According to the data from the U.S. Department of Defense (2000), the United States suffered 33,686 battle deaths, along with 2,830 non-battle deaths, during the Korean War and 8,176 missing in action. The Korean Ministry of National Defense (2013) reported some 373,599 civilian and 137,899 military deaths. Furthermore, many people were wounded and major buildings and infrastructure in Korea were destroyed nation-wide. In terms of postwar recovery, Korea and the United States agreed to a military alliance under the name of the Mutual Defense Treaty, which was an agreement between Korea and the United States enacted on October 1, 1953. It was a military alliance between Korea and the United States, establishing the basis of military cooperation between the two countries on North Korean policy. In addition, tens of thousands of United States Forces have been stationed in Korea although the number has somewhat decreased over the years. After the Korean War, the United States provided a substantial volume of foreign aid for rehabilitation and it really helped the recovery of the Korean economy and infrastructure. Korea and the United States are now important economic partners. Nearly 60 billion dollars of trade volume between the two countries displays the significant economic interdependence between the two states.

Although much of the focus on Korea's development begins in the late 1960s at the beginning of the country's accelerated growth, the foundations and characteristics which affected and continue to affect Korea's long-term success became rooted in its culture much earlier. One example is the importance of education in the Korean culture, and how it has contributed to an efficient labor force with a strong work ethic. In the first decade of the twentieth century, "modern" schools had already been established, some by Christian missionaries (Tsurumi 1984; Booth 1998) and many Korean youths were able to enroll in primary school. After 1945, both primary and secondary enrollments increased at a rapid pace. In the 1960s, only 26 percent of the male labor force and 48 percent of the female labor force had less than five years of education (McGinn et al. 1980). This gave Korea a large advantage to take the lead in furthering education reforms as well as providing a labor force equipped to lead rapid industrial growth when compared with other developing countries (Rodrik 1995).

That being said, the reforms made in education and infrastructure did not come without other transformations that were made in both rural and urban areas in the 1950s and 1960s after the Japanese colonial period and the Korean War. In terms of rural development, there was radical land-to-the-tiller agrarian reform – one of the few peaceful agrarian reforms of its type to have been accomplished in the post-colonial world – which gave subsistence incomes to the vast majority of the Korean population while income inequalities were instantly leveled (Douglass 2000). Therefore, a strong rural foundation was set for the majority of the populace and the Korean government was allowed great autonomy to construct a "developmental state" in an environment that was still unaffected by urbanization (Kim and Kim 1999; Kim 2012). A developmental state is often characterized by having strong state intervention or state-led macroeconomic planning in Asia including Korea, Taiwan, and Singapore.

The story of the remarkable post-war growth of the Korean economy revolved around the growth of its *chaebols* (Michael et al. 1998; Choi et al. 2008). A *chaebol* (conglomerate) can be defined as a business group consisting of large companies which are owned and managed by family members or relatives in many diversified business areas (Yoo and Lee 1987), or a gigantic business group which is controlled by a family or closely related members, and growth aided by government support (Cho 1997; Choi et al. 2008). In sum, the term *"chaebol"* (conglomerate) literally means a wealthy financial clan and it generally refers to a large, family-owned business group in Korea. There are several dozen large Korean family-controlled corporate groups which fall under this definition including Samsung, Hyundai, LG, SK, GS, Lotte, Hanjin, Hanwha, Kumho, Doosan, etc. In comparison, *zaibatsu* is a Japanese term referring to a large industrial and/or financial business group during the Meiji era. The *chaebol*'s organizational form has benefits and shortcomings. The benefits of *chaebols* include easy diversification in businesses with established reputation, and recognition of *chaebols'* brand name, scope economies by synergy effects, scale economies by large size, improvements in decision making by having cumulated knowledge and experiences of many companies in a *chaebol*, and improvements in capturing new business opportunities with vast knowledge in many fields of business (Park and Shin 2008). However, the negative aspects of *chaebols* need to be examined carefully. Shortcomings of *chaebols* are: lack of business transparency, high risks of businesses due to the CEO's autocratic decision-making, increase in exit costs by losing timely exit of unprofitable businesses, increase in management costs due to the bureaucratic organization, inefficient resource allocation, lack of timely decision-making and adaptation, and delay of development in core capabilities (Park and Shin 2008).

A growing, well-educated middle class in Korea contributed to an export-led industrialization as well as the desire for a democratic government. The April Student Revolution in 1960 resulted in the resignation of then-President Rhee Syng-man, the first President of Korea in 1948–1960. After a transitional government led by Yun Bo-seon and Chang Myon, Park Chung-hee became the de facto leader of the country since leading the coup d'état of May Sixteenth in 1961 and became the chairman of the Supreme Council for National Reconstruction. He ruled Korea for 18 years and he is credited with the industrialization and rapid economic growth of Korea through export-oriented industrialization.[2]

Shortly after the assassination of President Park Chung-hee in 1979, Major General Chun Doo-hwan seized power in a coup d'état against Park's successor Choi Kyu-hah. Escalating student protests in Seoul and Gwangju resulted in the Gwangju Democratization Movement. The event is sometimes called the 518 (May 18) Democratic Uprising, in reference to the date the uprising began in 1980. Chun Doo-hwan took several suppressive measures and the June Democracy Movement in 1987 brought hundreds of thousands of citizens to the streets in Seoul and major local cities that forced Chun to surrender to demands for a direct presidential election. Chun's rule ended in 1988 when Roh Tae-woo won the first direct election in 30 years.

During these political upheavals, Korea's industrial development policy also underwent major changes. The policy can be divided broadly into four phases: export drive and development of skilled human resources in the 1960s, heavy and chemical industry (HCI) promotion and building of local technological capacity in the 1970s, trade liberalization and technology-oriented industrial policy in the 1980s, and globalization and information technology industry promotion in the 1990s (Kim 2008).

During the 1980s, Korea looked to Southeast Asia as it expanded globally along with the rest of East Asia in increasing its direct foreign investment and intraregional trades. On September 22, 1985, finance ministers from Britain, France, West Germany, Japan, and the United States signed the Plaza Accords. As a result, the Japanese yen began to appreciate against the U.S. dollar and Japan began to reallocate their firms to ASEAN countries where there was an abundance of natural resources and relatively cheaper labor (Chua et al. 1999). Korea has a similar trade structure as Japan and also expanded trading in ASEAN during the 1980s, increasing the share of its manufactured goods from 46 percent in 1963 to 92 percent in 1988 (Chua et al. 1999).

As Korea became fully democratic, it became more interested in the concept of Asian regionalism. Part of this increasing interest was due to a search for a way to bring about greater peace and stability in the area. This manifested itself through the creation of the East Asian Study Group (EASG) and the East Asia Vision Group (EAVG), brought about under Kim Dae-jung's administration in 1998–2003 and its cooperation with NGOs and interest groups. They formed in 2000 and 1999, respectively, and produced academic guidance for the creation of the best possible regional cooperation. Areas of research included how far to extend Asian regionalism (for example, including places such as India or Australia which are technically outside of East Asia) and the speed at which the process should occur. Their findings supported the expansion of Asian regionalism beyond North East Asia and were enthusiastic about moving toward Southeast Asian countries. While this occurred as planned, their timeline did not. The data suggested that since some countries were reluctant about expanding regionalism, it would be best to go through the process gradually and step by step. However, quickly after the research was released, the decision was made in 2004 (the 8th annual APT meeting) to hold an East Asia Summit as well as the annual ASEAN Plus Three (APT) meeting in 2005. While Korea's endeavors led to a greater inclusion of the Plus Three countries, their guidelines on how to do so were largely pushed aside.

In the twenty-first century, Korea has broadened its scope of cooperation to include other nations who have taken an interest in ASEAN, namely India, Australia, and New Zealand. As an emerging market economy with the forecast of becoming one of the three largest global economies by 2030, India has cooperated with both ASEAN and Korea in the areas of information and communication technologies, health and pharmaceuticals, agriculture, security, tourism, and culture. It should be noted that Korea and ASEAN must also work together in addressing the new regime of Kim Jung-un in North Korea and increasing security threats made by the rogue nation that threaten peace in Asia. In July 2013 at the 20th ASEAN Regional Forum (ARF) in Brunei, there was "uniform agreement" that Pyongyang needs to denuclearize (Miller 2013). The chairman of ARF, in his statement of the ARF meeting, singled out the North by urging peace, security, and stability in the Korean Peninsula. The statement explained that most minsters encouraged North Korea to comply fully with its obligations to all UNSC (United Nations Security Council) Resolutions and reaffirmed their commitments to fully implement all the relevant UNSC Resolutions (ASEAN Regional Forum 2013). To this end, ASEAN is fully committed in continuing the efforts to stabilize and denuclearize the Korean Peninsula.

2 Role in the ASEAN Plus Three community

Attempts for regional integration did not occur in Asia until the mid-1990s in a re-emergence of regionalism throughout the world. ASEAN began to deepen regional cooperation among member countries at that time. Meanwhile, there had been many suggestions for regional cooperation among Northeast Asian countries (Kim et al. 2010). However, Korea has had one of the longest investment relationships with the ASEAN compared with other East Asian countries. The first Korean overseas direct investment to the ASEAN was established by the Korea South Development Corporation in 1968 to develop forests in Indonesia (Yul 2004).

Since the 1980s, Korean firms have been looking to Southeast Asia as a source of inexpensive labor. Korea also began exporting manufactured goods produced in Southeast Asia to developed countries. Korean investments in ASEAN began to increase in the late 1980s, concentrating in labor-intensive industries such as footwear, textiles, and electronics (Yul 2004). ASEAN and Korea initiated sectoral dialogue relations in November 1989. Korea was accorded a full Dialogue Partner status by ASEAN at the 24th ASEAN Ministerial Meeting in July 1991 in Kuala Lumpur. Since the ASEAN–ROK (Republic of Korea) partnership was elevated to a summit level in 1997 in

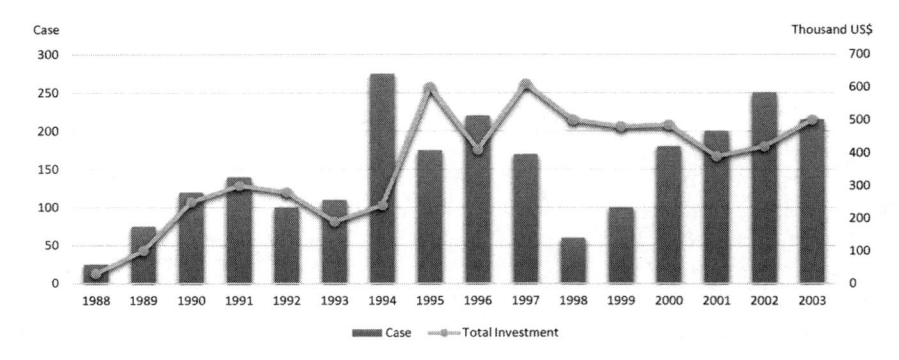

Figure 13.1 Trend of Korean Total Investment to ASEAN
Source: Yul (2004) from the Export-Import Bank of Korea Database.

Kuala Lumpur, relations between ASEAN and Korea have broadened and deepened (ASEAN 2012).

Korean investments in Southeast Asia have declined since the East Asian financial crisis and the banking collapse of Indonesia (1997–1998). Although relations between Korea and ASEAN have recovered, the rate of investment remains below the level of 1997. Among Korea, China, and Japan, Korea's intra-regional trade with the APT is among the lowest of the group. The APT economies accounted for only 38.8 percent of Korea's total foreign trade during the 2001–2003 period, though its bilateral trade relations with China and ASEAN rose remarkably during that time. Key trading partners of Korea are still the US (17.5 percent), Japan (14 percent), China (13 percent), and the EU (12 percent) (Bui 2008). Despite economic setbacks in the shadow of China's economic boom, new regional economic initiatives have been proposed within the APT communities. The Chiang Mai Initiative, created in May 2000 at a meeting of the APT finance ministers as a set of bilateral swap agreements, was an agreement among the APT to promote regional monetary and financial cooperation. Long-term visions that have stemmed from the Chiang Mai Initiative include exchange rate cooperation and monetary integration in the region as well as an Asian Monetary Fund (Henning 2009).

Korea and the ASEAN have continued a positive relationship and dialogue in the new millennium. A Joint Declaration on Comprehensive Cooperation Partnership was signed at the 8th ASEAN-ROK Summit on November 30, 2004 in Vientiane, Laos. The ASEAN-ROK Plan of Action (POA) was adopted to implement the Joint Declaration at the 9th ASEAN-ROK Summit on December 13, 2005 in Kuala Lumpur. The 13th ASEAN-ROK Summit on October 29, 2010 in Hanoi agreed to elevate the ASEAN–ROK dialogue relations from comprehensive cooperation to strategic partnership. In order to concretize the elevation, the Leaders adopted the Joint Declaration on ASEAN-ROK Strategic Partnership for Peace and Prosperity and its Action Plan, which covers the period of 2011–2015 (ASEAN 2012).

In November 2011, the ASEAN–ROK Summit was held in Bali, Indonesia. At the Summit, Korea announced the intention to send a resident Ambassador to ASEAN and the establishment of the Korean Mission to the ASEAN in Jakarta in 2012. Beyond economic and trade talks, the Summit was an opportunity for both parties to discuss a wide range of issues of growing importance. These included green growth, forestry, post-harvest technology, disaster management, information and communication technology (ICT), tourism, education, and human resources development. Also noted was the establishment and operation of the ASEAN-Korea Centre in Seoul inaugurated in 2009.[3]

3 Three pillars

Member countries of ASEAN and the Republic of Korea have forged several declarations to work together on common challenges facing Southeast Asia and East Asia in the twenty-first century. The Joint Declaration on Comprehensive Cooperation Partnership was adopted on November 30, 2004 at the 8th ASEAN-ROK Summit to focus on future cooperation covering political, economic, environmental, social, cultural fields and international affairs. An ASEAN-ROK Plan of Action[4] was adopted at the 9th ASEAN-ROK Summit on December 13, 2005 that covers more concrete initiatives reflected in the Joint Declaration. The major pillars of the treaties and declarations include political-security cooperation, economic cooperation, and cooperation through social and cultural exchange.

3.1 Political-security perspectives

Issues concerning security in Asia have risen in the past three decades along with its growing political influence and military capabilities on a global scale (Jones and Smith, 2007; Lee, 2010). Both Southeast and Northeast Asia share some of the same challenges concerning security. The strained relationship between China and Taiwan, a failed state such as North Korea, energy and food security, transnational terrorism, separatist violence, religious extremism, and ethno-religious tension are among some of the main issues that have affected Asia in recent years. To deal with these challenges, ASEAN-ROK has attempted to cooperate on combating terrorism (the ASEAN-ROK Joint Declaration for Cooperation to Combat International Terrorism), ASEAN support for a nuclear weapons-free Korean Peninsula, and the Treaty of Amity and Cooperation in Southeast Asia (TAC) to resolve disputes and conflicts peacefully by following these fundamental principles: (1) mutual respect for the independence, sovereignty, equality, territorial integrity, and national identity of all nations; (2) the right of every state to lead its national existence free from external interference, subversion or coercion; (3) non-interference in the internal affairs of one another; (4) settlement of differences or disputes by peaceful means; (5) renunciation of the threat or use of force; and (6) effective cooperation among themselves.[5]

The ASEAN-ROK Plan of Action also reaffirms TAC principles of "sovereign equality, territorial integrity and non-interference in the domestic affairs of other States" and "to accede to the Treaty to further promote regional peace, security, stability, prosperity, mutual confidence and trust" under the section on Political and Security Cooperation. The world has had to grapple with the threat of transnational terrorism since the September 11 Al-Qaeda attacks on the United States. ASEAN has also played a new role in combating terrorism in the new century, most notably after the Bali bombings of 2002 (Lee 2010).

Eight priority areas for ASEAN and APT in the area of transnational crimes are terrorism, human trafficking, arms smuggling, sea piracy, money laundering, illicit drug trafficking, international economic crime, and cyber-crime. The establishment of the Senior Officials Meeting on Transnational Crime (SOMTC) Plus ROK Consultation has worked in fighting drugs and working with law enforcement on immigration, transport security, and prevention of financing of terrorists (ASEAN Secretariat 2005).

In non-traditional security areas such as environmental security, especially in the industrial and mining areas, Korea is ahead of Southeast Asia in constructing a civil society to lead in policing and providing feedback on the dangers to the environment of certain investments and policies (Koh 2010). In such non-traditional areas, Korea is in a position to share its experiences with networking between its civil society and those in Southeast Asia. Because of this, ASEAN+ROK have agreed to work together in the areas of food, agriculture, and forestry to launch cooperation projects to: "exchange information and technology, and to develop joint-research projects in the fields of food production, poverty alleviation, agricultural and livestock industry, agricultural machinery, agricultural products marketing, improvement of agricultural infrastructure and development of rural areas; enhancing human resources development in the agriculture, livestock and fisheries sectors through programs such as organizing workshops in ASEAN countries, the dispatch of experts (e.g. in agriculture technologies, food sanitary laws and post-harvest handling) to ASEAN Member Countries, agricultural extension, etc.; and encourage the progress of agriculture-related industries such as agricultural technologies and crop varieties development and breeding technologies through the conduct of exhibitions, expositions and seminars" (ASEAN Secretariat 2005). ASEAN and Korea have also agreed to share information and technology in the areas of food safety, animal and plant quarantine, and disease control.

Additional areas of security in ASEAN-ROK cooperation are energy, environment, security, combating infectious diseases, and cooperation for reducing regional natural disasters. In these matters of security, ASEAN and Korea have pledged to enhance capacity building in energy security and renewable energy to reduce fossil energy use; increase training programs and degree courses in Korea for ASEAN students in the field of the environment; cooperate in preventing forest destruction; promote the development and transfer of clean technology; cooperate in establishing effective monitoring and surveillance systems for newly emerging infectious diseases; provide Korean technical assistance to ASEAN for establishing and improving local hospitals; joint efforts to prevent the spread of HIV/AIDS; and expand scientific and technological cooperation and information exchange to establish an early-warning system to reduce the risks of natural disasters (ASEAN Secretariat 2005).

Although expanding exchanges between diplomats and government officials and strengthening cooperation through conferences and training is necessary to build a stronger coalition against terrorism and maintain stability in Asia, there has been criticism from some scholars who have argued that although ASEAN has been successful in consensus building, there remain differences on how to approach security cooperation and efficacy (Lee 2010). Despite some roadblocks, Korea and Southeast Asia have mutual interests and competitive advantages in creating strategic management to make East Asia and Southeast and Northeast Asia secure from natural and man-made disasters.

3.2 Economic perspectives

In 2003, ASEAN became Korea's fifth largest trading partner, taking 10.4 percent of Korea's total volume and its third largest investment destination in cumulative terms (Yul, 2004). ASEAN is now Korea's second largest trading partner. ASEAN–Korea trade currently occurs primarily between Korea and ASEAN's relatively richer inner core – Indonesia, Malaysia, the Philippines, Singapore, Thailand, and Brunei Darussalam. But Korea's trade with its relatively poorer periphery – Cambodia, the Lao People's Democratic Republic (Lao PDR), Myanmar, and Vietnam – is also growing rapidly (Park 2012). By June 2007, Korea owned 40,137 registered HIV/AIDS projects with a registered capital of $116.5 billion (USD) (Thien 2009). There are also lessons from the Korean economic experience which experienced a GNP growth average of 7.8 percent per annum between 1961 and 2000. Korea's experience has become a part of ASEAN's industrial development strategy. Through FDI, Korea brings to the table their experience and knowledge of high technology as well as capital sources (Thien 2009).

Common features of the ASEAN countries that have experienced rapid growth are appropriate macroeconomic policies, high savings and investment rates, and high investment on education. On the other hand, some ASEAN countries kept their economy relatively closed and self-supplied for much longer. This means that ASEAN countries and Korea are still at various stages of development. Notably, according to the World Bank criteria, Korea, Brunei, and Singapore are high-income countries, Malaysia is above average, Thailand, Indonesia, and the Philippines are average income countries, and Cambodia, Laos, Myanmar, and Vietnam (CLMV) are low income. Vietnam is catching up rapidly and has the highest economic growth in the region over the last few years, 8.2 percent in 2006 and 6.8 percent during the whole *Doi Moi* period between 1986 and 2005.

ASEAN countries have changed from import substitution industrialization to being more export-oriented. Some countries have changed their policies at varying times while some have barely changed at all, like Laos. Overall, the openness of ASEAN economics ranges from relatively low to extremely high (such as Singapore), even more so than China, Japan, and Korea. Trading remains focused on machinery and electronic products. ASEAN also exports a lot of mineral products such as crude oil to Korea. Both Korea and ASEAN have rapidly increased their trade with China since the 1990s. Their trade with each other (ASEAN-ROK) has also been increasing, but at a smaller rate than with China. Korea hopes to sell more automobiles, plastic, chemicals, and steel to ASEAN countries and gain a higher market share than Japanese and Chinese companies. In addition, ASEAN and Korea remain highly dependent on the US market and consider the US market an important export market.

There are many opportunities for every state or company involved due to high economic growth rates and a large market. Free trade agreements (FTAs) will accelerate trade development and increase competitiveness. However, the gap in socioeconomic development among countries in the region, the large dependence on the US market, and the dramatic economic growth of China have negative effects on the trade development of member countries in the region. Despite this, it is still a win-win cooperation (Park et al. 2012).

The ASEAN-ROK Plan of Action to Implement the Joint Declaration on Comprehensive Cooperation Partnership provides concrete initiatives for further economic cooperation. This includes enhanced interactions to establish comprehensive economic cooperative relations through the existing ASEAN Economic Ministers-ROK (AEM-ROK) Consultations, the Senior Economic Officials' Meeting (SEOM)-ROK Consultations and between respective ASEAN sectoral and other bodies and the ROK in areas such as finance, construction and transportation, agriculture and commodities, labor, tourism, energy, Information and Communications Technology (ICT), forestry, mining and fisheries; promote cooperation and exchanges between business organizations of ASEAN and the ROK to pursue closer private sector collaboration; and to strengthen cooperation of private sector within the context of East Asia Business Council (EABC) with the view to promoting greater linkages between firms in ASEAN, Republic of Korea, Japan, and China. Other areas include mutual efforts for trade expansion, an ASEAN-ROK Free Trade Agreement, and investment expansion.

3.3 Socio-cultural perspectives

Korea and ASEAN countries have had large cultural influences on each other since the globalization of the 1990s. Interracial relationships in Korea have become commonplace in much of the countryside with the increase of migrant workers and mail-order brides, mostly from China and Southeast Asia. As a result, there is an estimated 150,000 migrant wives currently in Korea, with a third of those marriages taking place in rural areas; as many as half of all rural school children are now of mixed race (Lim, 2011).

Southeast Asian youth have also come to Korea for education in record numbers while Korean Studies has grown in popularity in ASEAN countries. One example is in Indonesia where at Gadjah Mada University (UGM), one of the oldest and largest universities in the nation, a three-year Korean language program called Program Studi Bahasa Korea was established in 2003. In Korea, the Korea International Cooperation Agency (KOICA) has worked with leading Korean universities such as KDI School and Yonsei University to create full scholarships for Southeast Asian scholars for short-term and long-term degree programs in Korea.

In Southeast Asia, Korean pop culture and music, also known as the Korean Wave, has swept the region by storm since the late 1990s and early 2000s. Also known as *hallyu*, the Korean Wave has been used as part of the Korean foreign policy to strengthen political and economic relations with neighboring countries (Chachavalpongpun 2010). The Korean Wave has specifically influenced the Vietnamese with the popularity of Korean dramas, in part because of similar Confucian values and ideals espoused in these shows (Kim 1999, 2010; De Vries and Kim, 2011).

Chachavalpongpun (2010) argues that the popularity of the Korean Wave has in many ways changed the views of Koreans in parts of Southeast Asia using several pieces of evidence including the increase in the number of tourists from Southeast Asia to Korea and vice versa. For example, the Ministry of Foreign Affairs of Thailand reported that Korean tourists to Thailand continue to rise, totaling over 710,000 in 2002, while Thai tourists visiting Korea similarly surged to 74,000 in the same year.

In the 1980s, Japan had the largest number of visitors to ASEAN member countries from East Asia (see Figure 13.2). In the 2000s, the overall situation has been changed. Japanese visitors to ASEAN member counties are stagnant over the years and their number is now similar to the number of Korean visitors to ASEAN member countries. As of 2010, however, China has the largest number of visitors to ASEAN member countries from East Asia. According to the Korea Tourism Organization (2010), the top 10 destinations for Korean tourists in 2010 are: China (32.6 percent), Japan (19.5 percent), USA (8.9 percent), Hong Kong (7.1 percent), Thailand (6.5 percent), Philippines (5.9 percent), Vietnam (4.0 percent), Singapore (2.9 percent), Macau (2.7 percent), and Indonesia (2.4 percent). Five ASEAN member countries are among the top 10 countries Koreans visited in 2010.

Also, a study conducted by Shim Doo-bo, a Korean professor who taught at the National University of Singapore (NUS), found that after the immense popularity of Korean televised dramas, Korean housewives living in Singapore felt that they were better treated by local Singaporeans (Chachavalpongpun

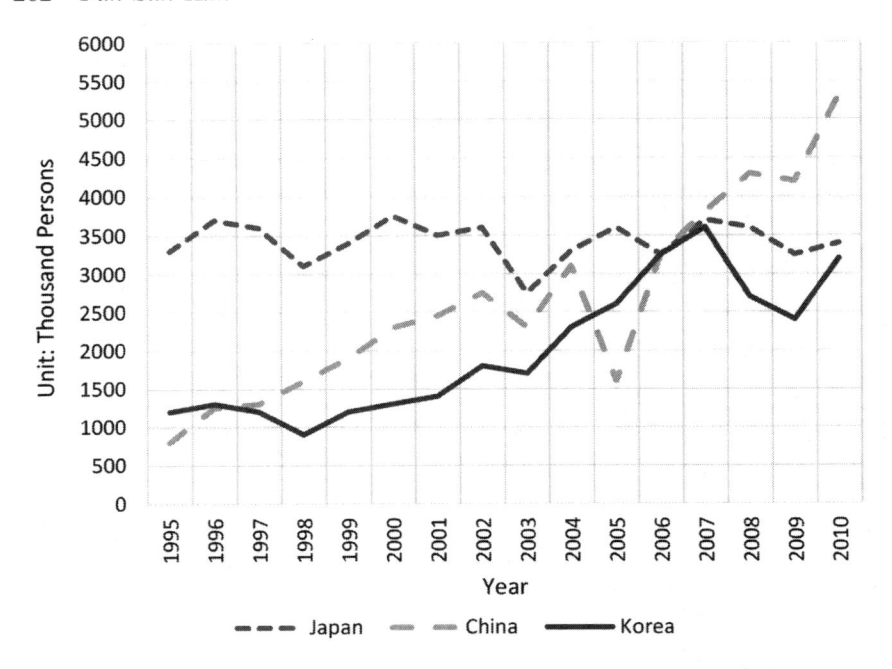

Figure 13.2 Number of visitors to ASEAN member countries from Japan, China, and Korea
Source: ASEAN Secretariat (2011).

2010). However, there have been problems in both ASEAN countries and Korea damaging Korea's reputation. For example, some Korean tourists in Southeast Asia created a negative image for themselves due to reports of their cultural misunderstandings and behavioral mistakes (Chachavalpongpun 2010).

To work through these differences and strengthen the ties between ASEAN and Korea, APT has recognized the need to build partnerships to promote and strengthen exchanges in the fields of culture, tourism, education, and media. The ASEAN-ROK Future-Oriented Cooperation Project Fund (FOCPF) does that by offering exchange programs for government officials and educational programs for junior and mid-level diplomats to encourage mutual understanding. There are also plans for Korea to establish a Korea Foundation Centre in two or three ASEAN Member Countries to introduce Korean culture and the Korean language. Programs for Koreans and people of ASEAN countries have been established at the "Korea Foundation Cultural Centre" in Seoul which was established in 2005. There is also the ASEAN-Korea Centre in Seoul that was established in March 2009 to promote economic and socio-cultural cooperation between ASEAN and Korea.

To build on the popularity of Korean pop culture, ASEAN-ROK agreed in its plan of action to have a mass culture exchange that would: (1) encourage mutual participation in International Film Festivals that are held in ASEAN and the ROK and increase exchange of popular culture through instruments such as films, TV programmes, and print media; and (2) extend Korean training programmes for ASEAN experts and students in the fields of TV, film, theatre, dance, and music production to develop human resources of ASEAN popular culture. Along the lines of pop culture's appeal on Southeast Asian youth, ASEAN has also sought to expand youth exchanges and promote ASEAN and Korean studies, scholarships for ASEAN teachers to study the Korean language, and fellowships for ASEAN students majoring in Korean Studies. Sports exchange and education cooperation in the form of student exchange, workshops, and joint research and training are a few more examples of how ASEAN and Korea are committed to educating students and educators both in practical and cultural matters.

Confucian principles of family loyalty and respect for elders are appreciated throughout the region. They serve as the basis of programs such as the project entitled "Home Care for the Older People in the ASEAN Countries" inspired by the Korean experience, and developed and replicated volunteer based home care models by adapting key features of the Korean model to suit local socio-cultural and economic contexts. The Korean government has extended technical assistance to the project, whose detailed work plans have been reviewed by participating agencies selected. Also, a Regional Workshop on Rehabilitation and Community-Based Rehabilitation was organized in 2001 with the objective of (1) assessing the extent and magnitude of various types of disabilities in the ASEAN countries; and (2) selecting certain types of disability prevention and rehabilitation practices for ASEAN collaboration.[6] Future plans include implementing the ROK-ASEAN Home Care Service nationwide across ASEAN and raising awareness of care for the elderly in communities.

The human rights of migrant workers and providing support for foreign wives and their children have also been brought to the forefront. In Korea, migrant wives from Southeast Asia and their mixed children have faced a variety of problems including poverty, domestic violence, and the inability to communicate in Korean. The baby boom seen among foreign wives in Korea is unprecedented in the country's history. While the birth rate has fallen among Korean women, the number of biracial children born to foreign women married to rural Korean farmers is steadily increasing and has brought with it dilemmas concerning language, poverty, and discrimination that the Korean government has never dealt with before. The Korean government has taken greater action in finding solutions to better integrate multicultural families. Several initiatives in the last several years have included establishing a high school for mixed race students in Seoul, interracial marriage courses with the incentive of receiving 1 million Korean won for completing the course for Korean men marrying foreign women offered by the Ministry of Gender Equality and Family (MOGEF) in co-operation with local governments,[7] and accepting mixed race men into the Korean military since January 1, 2011. The abuse of migrant workers, women, and children is a problem faced in all APT countries. Therefore, ASEAN has developed initiatives to protect these vulnerable groups. In 2007, the ASEAN Leaders signed a Declaration on the Protection and Promotion of the Rights of Migrant Workers. At the 15th ASEAN Summit in October 2009, the Leaders endorsed the Terms of Reference for an ASEAN Commission for the Promotion and Protection of the Rights of Women and Children, and called for its establishment by the 16th ASEAN Summit in 2010.

3.4 *The Korean Wave or* hallyu

While it is difficult to calculate how much the "Korean Wave" (or *hallyu*) has contributed to Korea–ASEAN relations, one cannot deny its impact, especially at the general public level. The Korean Wave (*hallyu*) refers to the increase in the popularity of Korean entertainment and culture in Asia and other parts of the world. Ever since Korean dramas hit the shores of its nearest neighbors, the exchange of tourism and culture between Korea and other Asian countries has grown exponentially (especially those coming into Korea). One example (out of many) of this is the 2007 Rain (popular Korean entertainer "Bi") concert in Singapore at which all tickets (including $345 USD seats) were all sold out; in fact, Rain made $20 million USD alone in 2006 (Kim 2010). Another earlier example is the large amount of *Winter Sonata* tours that occurred, especially for Japanese tourists. During this same time, the amount of investments, including FDI, increased as well. Korea is in a unique place out of the "plus three" countries to ASEAN in that it has the least bitter history with Southeast Asian countries. This provides Korea an opportunity to interact with Southeast Asia on a cultural level without the past cultural imperialism memories whispering to every citizen who engages with Korean media.

It is interesting, and even necessary, to note that *hallyu* as a whole was accidental. The dramas, such as *Winter Sonata* and *Dae-Jang-Geum* (*Jewel in the Palace*), were created for domestic consumption. They were initially imported by neighboring countries largely due to their cheap price, which in 2001 was around US$840 (Kim 2010). However, despite bad time slots and being a new, foreign product, the dramas did surprisingly well, so well that fans petitioned to have TV networks reshow them, and thus the Korean Wave began. There has been much thought given to why Korean media has been able to be so successful. This is mirrored in the interpretations different countries have for the underlying story behind *Jewel in the Palace*. Each country gave a different interpretation and a different reason for its success. For example, the success was attributed to the lesson about the triumph of morality in China while in India it was seen as a woman's success story. Overall, Korea has a lot of cultural commonalities with countries throughout Asia and even beyond. Given its fast changes in the past three generations, recent Korean history has a lot to draw from when making media production and that is bound to resonate with audiences from countries going through the same thing (i.e. modernization, the changing role of women in society, etc.).

Due to *hallyu's* accidental success, there were many gaps among the government, the private sector, and the general public regarding Korea's place in the world. The idea of using *hallyu* to promote Korea's culture did not begin to be talked about by politicians until around 2006–2007, when then-mayor of Seoul and then-Presidential Candidate Lee Myung-bak introduced his "Seven Point Plan" (a way to renew the country's foreign policy) which included "Cultural Korea" as its last point. This has been changing, however, in recent years. One example of this is the Korean Tourism Organization (KTO) working with SM Entertainment in 2011 to stage a concert in France with the intention to promote Korean travel and K-Pop (KTO 2010). In 2012, the Ministry of Culture, Sports and Tourism also put in a plan to bolster the popularity of Korean media by setting up an advisory committee made up of 19 leading people in Korea's cultural scene (including various CEOs, a fashion designer, an English literature scholar, a theater director, and others) to meet monthly and discuss how to keep *hallyu* strong and how to introduce more aspects of Korean culture.

While the Korean Wave has helped to improve the relations between the Korean people and their Southeast Asian neighbors, these gaps, especially between the general public and those in charge of spreading *hallyu*, have led to some damage to relations that must be repaired. The increase in tourism has brought all sorts of Koreans to Southeast Asia and not all of them are welcome. There have been an increasing number of cases of misconduct (Chachavalpongpun 2010; Kim 2010). In order to fix this, it would be helpful for the Korean government to remind citizens of their role as representatives of Korea when they are abroad and also for Korea to support two-way exchanges of culture. Perhaps if Koreans knew more about the culture of various Southeast Asian countries, there would be less problems and everyone would benefit.

Of course, there have been positive changes as well in relations due to the Korean Wave. *Winter Sonata* helped to improve the image of Korea and Koreans in Japan, which had previously seen Korea as its closest geographical neighbor, but also one of its farthest nations psychologically. Reportedly, Korean women living in Singapore are being treated better by locals. Thais are also reported to have a softening image of Korea and better understanding of Korean culture. Despite unaddressed wounds regarding Korea's participation in the Vietnam War, Korean dramas constituted about 40 percent of airing dramas in Vietnam before the government stepped in to balance it (Kim, 2010). This means that Korea is in a great position to improve its relations with ASEAN countries.

4 Korea's contribution toward ASEAN Plus Three integration

The economic identity of ASEAN remains fragile while dealing with the inevitable economic integration of the region. In December 2005 during a summit of Asian Heads of State and Government in Kuala Lumpur, the identity of Southeast Asia as a sub-region was barely noticeable when a tentative East Asia Economic Community was announced for the year 2020 that would not only include Northeast and Southeast Asian economies, but also the ones from India and Australia/New Zealand (Régnier 2006). Despite challenges to integration, narrowing the development gap has been an important task of the ASEAN Heads of State in the last decade. In April 2012, Southeast Asia agreed to work collectively to form a single economic community in the region by the year 2015 and build up its five sub-regional growth areas, which includes the resurging Brunei, Indonesia, Malaysia, and Philippines-East ASEAN Growth Area (BIMP-EAGA) using funds from the ASEAN Infrastructure Fund (AIF) (Estabillo 2012).

The initiative for integration was launched in 2000 with the Initiative for ASEAN Integration (IAI) to narrow the development divide and enhance ASEAN's competitiveness as a region.[8] Korea contributed US$5 million to support five IAI projects between 2003 and 2007. Furthering its commitment to ASEAN, Korea increased its contribution to the ASEAN-ROK Special Cooperation Fund (SCF) by US $1,000,000.00 in the fiscal year of 2005 to support the effective implementation of various actions and measures proposed in the ASEAN Plan of Action.

At the 12th ASEAN-ROK Summit, Korea committed its support to the IAI and decided to contribute its second and third tranche of US $5 million each, for IAI for the year 2008–2012 and 2013–2017, and also to double Official Development Assistance (ODA) to the ASEAN by 2015, and to share its experiences in economic and social development by dispatching volunteers under its World Friends Korea initiative. For the second tranche of US $5 million to IAI for the year 2008–2012, two projects have been identified, namely: (1) strengthening CLMV (Cambodia, Laos, Myanmar and Vietnam) Capacity for the ASEAN-ROK Cyber University; and (2) supporting the multi-purpose Rainwater Management Project for the four ASEAN Countries Sharing the Mekong River (ASEAN, 2012).

Korea continues to develop and promote cooperation projects in ASEAN in a variety of areas including human resources and social development, water and flood management, and programs for the elderly and disabled. Many of these projects have been implemented through KOICA under the auspices of the Ministry of Foreign Affairs. In the period from 1991 to 2008, Official Development Assistance to ASEAN was in excess of US $348 million. Funding from the ASEAN-ROK Cooperation Fund from 1990 to 2007 totaled US $36 million; this includes the yearly Special Cooperation Fund (SCF) of US $2 million and the yearly Future Oriented Cooperation Fund (FOCPF) of US $1 million.[9] Efforts to promote sustainable growth and accelerate regional economic integration will be an important long-term goal of the APT as multilateral efforts increase to ensure regional security, prosperity, integration, and cooperation. East Asian regional integration with ASEAN is important to Korea for a variety of reasons. East Asia has remained resilient in the face of the global recession and ASEAN is well-positioned to drive East Asia's growth as one of the fastest growing economies in the region.

5 Conclusions

Korea and ASEAN have increasingly expanded collaboration over the decades to meet critical political, economic, and environmental issues in a rapidly growing continent. Political-security, economic, and socio-cultural partnerships will be a requirement to tackle the challenges of urbanization, globalization, climate change, and an aging population. There remain opportunities for growth in the ASEAN–Korea agenda as both East Asia and Southeast Asian countries face similar stresses in trade, health, the budget, and education. Under the leadership of Korean President Park Geun-hye (2013–2018), it is predicted that business will remain the same between Korea and ASEAN. For example, between Thailand and Korea, there still remains the commitment to more than double bilateral trade to $30 billion USD by 2016 which was agreed upon several weeks before the December 2012 presidential election (Sutanthavibul, 2013). President Park has met with ambassadors of ASEAN countries since the beginning of her presidency and has reiterated the importance of ASEAN and ROK cooperation. Also, due to the Regional Comprehensive Economic Partnership negotiations, launched between ASEAN's Free Trade Agreements partners and ASEAN+6 countries in November 2012, the relationship between ASEAN and Korea is predicted to grow significantly within the next five years (Lee, 2013).

In this current worldwide economic downturn, investors are looking toward emerging markets such as Vietnam to replicate the success that East Asia has displayed in recent decades. In addition, it is predicted that Asia's share in the world gross domestic product (GDP) could grow to 52 percent by 2050 (ADB 2011). Further estimates conclude that Asia will be led by seven countries in ASEAN and East Asia in the next 40 years. There will be China, India, Indonesia, Japan, Korea, Thailand, and Malaysia. Under the Asian Development Bank's Asian Century scenario, these seven countries' share of population by 2050 would be 75 percent of Asia and their GDP would be 90 percent of Asia. That alone will account for 45 percent of global GDP with the average per capita income of $45,000 (in PPP) compared with $37,300 for the world as a whole (ADB 2011).

It is clear that the promise held in the ASEAN–Korea relations has yet to fully reach its full potential as both parties will likely drive the global economy for the next half century. To achieve this opportunity of growth and success, Asia's leaders must manage the challenges that ASEAN has outlined in its goals including the need for integration, striving for good governance, tackling global warming and climate change that will affect the health and livelihoods of millions if unchecked, and dealing with income disparities that could destabilize the region (Kim and Argyriades 2015).

However, in order to effectively meet the challenges of our time, Korea and ASEAN need to reflect upon what has been achieved in the past, and come up with a new framework for the future. Part of this framework should include strengthening economic ties as well as people-to-people communication to prevent localism. Through its own history and struggle to achieve democracy and self-sufficiency, Korea is an important ally for rural development and poverty eradication in Southeast Asian nations. ASEAN plays an important role in East Asia Cooperation even though the conversation is usually about what East Asia can do for it. Without the active participation and the positive effort of ASEAN, East Asia Cooperation will lose the most basic and stable axis (Kim and Argyriades 2015).

In terms of a geo-political dimension, there are several Asian regional organizations including ASEAN, SAARC (South Asian Association for Regional Cooperation), and others. Based on ASEAN, APT including China, Japan, and Korea was developed and now there is also discussion to expand it to ASEAN+4 (including China, Japan, Korea, and India), or more. Over the years, these regional entities are expected to grow larger, although its development pace might be slower than expected. In the area of economic integration, there are various stages of economic integration around the world: economic and monetary union, economic union, customs and monetary union, common market, customs union, and multilateral free trade area through a free trade agreement (FTA). The increase of such regional organizations or regimes would promote Asian regionalization (Asianization) and the possible development of the Asian Union in the future (Kim 2011b). However, the public administration network in Asia was not well developed in the past. Comparative studies on Asian public administration have also not been well developed (Kim and Kim 1999; Kim 2009, 2010, 2011a, 2011b). In recent years, the Asian Association for Public Administration (AAPA) and the Asian Group for Public Administration (AGPA) have been developed in addition to the Eastern Regional Organization of Public Administration (EROPA). These entities could develop over the years in promoting further development of public administration in Asia.

Along the lines of the ASEAN community playing a leading role in East Asian relations, Korea will also need to play a crucial role in the ASEAN Socio-Cultural community to combat human rights abuses against migrant workers and their families in East Asia. This includes promoting gender equality and implementing national laws that protect both migrant workers and those who are smuggled across borders. The security of foreign workers in both ASEAN and East Asian countries is a significant problem that threatens further integration, immigration, and human rights in Asia.

Lastly, the Korean experience in the last 50 years in developing and strengthening its trade and industrial sectors can be shared with ASEAN in the latter's promotion of human resource and technology development. Several significant lessons that can be taken from the Korean industrial development experience include an emphasis on private sector development, an outward-looking industrial development strategy, an adaptation to changes in the economic environment, and a consistent and harmonized policy approach. Using these lessons of Korea's development strategy, the ASEAN states can adjust and adapt their policies to make sure they work for emerging economies in the twenty-first century and beyond.

Notes

1 More detailed information can be found at www.saemaul.net. (Accessed on October 10, 2015).
2 Current South Korean President Park Geun-hye is the first child of Park Chung-hee.
3 Chairman Statement of the 14th ASEAN-ROK Summit, 18 November 2011. Available at www.aseankorea.org/files/upload/board/64/11/ROK-CS.pdf (accessed 15 October 2015).
4 www.aseankorea.org/files/upload/pdf/ASEAN-ROK_Action_Plan_Final.pdf (accessed 10 October 2015).
5 http://law.go.kr/trtyInfoPWah.do?trtySeq=2151&chrClsCd=010203 (accessed 20 October 2015).
6 www.aseansec.org/AADCP/repsf/docs/03-006b-FinalMainReportOnly_Appendx_not_included.pdf (accessed 20 October 2015).
7 Kwon, Mee-yoo. Korean Men With Foreign Brides to Get W1 Mil. In Subsidy. 8 August 2009. www.koreatimes.co.kr/www/news/nation/2009/08/117_49722.html (accessed 25 October 2015).
8 Initiative for ASEAN Integration (IAI) Strategic Framework and IAI Work Plan 2 (2009–2015). Available at www.aseansec.org/22325.pdf (accessed 23 October 2015).
9 Source: The ASEAN-Korea Centre website. Available at www.aseankorea.org/main/publish/view.jsp?menuID=002001007003 (accessed 20 October 2015).

References

ASEAN Regional Forum (2013) Chairman's Statement of the Twentieth ASEAN Regional Forum, Bandar Seri Begawan, Brunei Darussalam, 2 July.

ASEAN Secretariat (2005) ASEAN-ROK Plan of Action to Implement the Joint Declaration on Comprehensive Cooperation Partnership. Adopted by the Heads of State/Government at the 9th ASEAN-Republic of Korea Summit in Kuala Lumpur, Malaysia on 13 December.

ASEAN Secretariat (2011) *ASEAN Statistical Yearbook*. Jakarta: ASEAN Secretariat.

Asian Development Bank (ADB) (2011) *Asia 2050: Realizing the Asian Century.* Manila: Asian Development Bank.

Association of Southeast Asian Nations (ASEAN) (2005) 2005 ASEAN-Republic of Korea Plan of Action to Implement the Joint Declaration on Comprehensive Cooperation Partnership adopted on 13 December 2005 in Kuala Lumpur, Malaysia by the Heads of State/Government.

Association of Southeast Asian Nations (ASEAN) (2012) *ASEAN Republic of Korea Dialogue Relations.* Jakarta: ASEAN Secretariat.

Booth, Anne (1998) *Initial Conditions and Miraculous Growth: Why is South East Asia Different from Taiwan and South Korea.* London: SOAS, University of London.

290 *Pan Suk Kim*

Bui, Truong Giang (2008) *Intra-regional Trade of ASEAN Plus Three: Trends and Implications for East Asian Economic Integration*. Seoul: Korea Institute for International Economic Policy (KIEP).

Chachavalpongpun, Pavin (2010) 'A Fading Wave, Sinking Tide? A Southeast Asian Perspective on the Korean Wave,' in *Korea's Changing Roles in Southeast Asia*, edited by David I. Steinberg, Singapore: ISEAS Publishing, pp. 244–282.

Cho, Dong Sung (1997) *Hankook Chaebols*. Seoul: Maeil Business News Korea (in Korean).

Choi, Du Sig, Mitchell, Paul and Palilhawadana, Dayananda (2008) 'Exploring the Components of Success for the Korean Chaebols', *Journal of Business and Industrial Marketing* 23(5): 311–322.

Choi, Jin-Wook (2011) 'From a Recipient to a Donor State: Achievements and Challenges of Korea's ODA.' *International Review of Public Administration* 15(3): 36–51.

Chua, Soo Y., Dibooglu, Selahattin and Sharma, Subhash C. (1999) 'The Impact of the US and Japanese Economies on Korea and Malaysia after the Plaza Accords.' *Asian Economic Journal*, 13(1): 19–37.

De Vries, Michiel and Kim, Pan Suk (eds) (2011) *Value and Virtue in Public Administration: A Comparative Perspective*. Basingstoke: Palgrave Macmillan.

Douglass, Mike (2000) 'Turning Points in the Korean Space-Economy: From the Developmental State to Intercity Competition, 1953–2000. *Working Paper Series*, Stanford University: The Freeman Spogli Institute for International Studies.

Estabillo, Allen V. (2012) 'ASEAN Vows to Accelerate Economic Integration Efforts.' *Minda News*, 5 April. Available from: www.mindanews.com/top-stories/2012/04/05/asean-vows-to-accelerate-economic-integration-efforts (accessed 1 October 2014).

Henning, Randall C. (2009) 'The Future of the Chiang Mai Initiative: An Asian Monetary Fund? Policy Brief, Peterson Institute for International Economics, February.

Jones, David Martin and Smith, M.L.R. (2007) 'Making Process, Not Progress: ASEAN and the Evolving East Asian Regional Order.' *International Security* 32(1): 165–169.

Kim, Bun W. and Kim, Pan Suk (1999) *Korean Public Administration: Managing the Uneven Development*. Elizabeth, NJ: Hollym.

Kim, Chuk-Kyo (2008) *Korea's Development Policy Experience and Implications for Developing Countries*. Seoul: Korea Institute for International Economic Policy.

Kim, Joong-Keun (2010) 'The Korean Wave: Korea's Soft Power in Southeast Asia,' in *Korea's Changing Roles in Southeast Asia*, edited by David I. Steinberg, Singapore: ISEAS Publishing, pp. 283–303.

Kim, Pan Suk (ed.) (2009) *Public Administration and Public Governance in ASEAN Member Countries and Korea*. Seoul: Daeyoung Moonhwasa Publishing Company.

Kim, Pan Suk (ed.) (2010) *Civil Service System and Civil Service Reform in ASEAN Member Countries and Korea*. Seoul: Daeyoung Moonhwasa Publishing Company.

Kim, Pan Suk (ed.) (2011a) *Public Sector Reform in ASEAN Member Countries and Korea*. Seoul: Daeyoung Moonhwasa Publishing Company.

Kim, Pan Suk (2011b) 'Integrating Asian Administrative Space through Asianization toward the Asian Union', *Asian Review of Public Administration* 22(2): 4–17.

Kim, Pan Suk (2012) 'A Historical Overview of Korean Public Administration: Discipline, Education, Association, International Cooperation and beyond Indigenization.' *International Review of Administrative Sciences* 78(2): 217–238.

Kim, Pan Suk and Argyriades, Demetrios (eds) (2015) *Democratic Governance, Public Administration and Poverty Alleviation*. Brussels: Bruylant Publishing Company.

. Koh, David (2010) 'South Korea and Southeast Asia: Ideas for Deepening the Partnership,' in *Korea's Changing Roles in Southeast Asia*, edited byDavid I. Steinberg, Singapore: ISEAS Publishing, pp. 31–47.

Korea Tourism Organization (2010) Statistics of Tourism. Unpublished internal document. Seoul: Korea Tourism Organization.

Lee, Chung-Min (2010) Divergence Amidst Convergence: Assessing Southeast and Northeast Asian Security Dynamics, in *Korea's Changing Roles in Southeast Asia*, edited byDavid I. Steinberg, Singapore: ISEAS Publishing, pp. 48–74.

Lee, You-kyung (2013) 'New South Korean President to Build Fences with Asia'. *New Straits Times*. Published on February 5, 2013.

Leong, Ho Khai (2007) *ASEAN-Korea Relations: Security, Trade and Community Building*. Singapore: ISEAS Publishing.

Lim, Faustino John (2011) 'Korea's Multicultural Future?' *The Diplomat*, 20 July.

McGinn, Noel F., Snodgrass, Donald R., Kim, Yong B., Kim, Shin B., Kim, Quee Y. (1980) *Education and Development in Korea*. Cambridge, MA: Harvard University Press.

Michael, P. G., Bernstein, J., Searls, D. and Peckerar, M. (1998) 'Korea's Focus on Market Dominance', *Semiconductor International* 21(1): 118–122.

Miller, Jonathan B. (2013) 'Leveraging ASEAN's Role on North Korean Denuclearization.' *Forbes*. 23 July.

Ministry of National Defense [Korea] (2013) 'Casualties of the Korean War' (in Korean). Archived by the [Korean] Institute for Military History Compilation (IMHC) on 20 January.

Park, D., Park, I. and Estrada, G.E.B. (2012) 'The Prospects of an ASEAN-Korea Free Trade Area (AKFTA): A Qualitative and Quantitative Analysis.' *ASEAN Economic Bulletin*, 29(1): 29–45.

Park, Hong Y. and Shin, Geon-Cheol (2008) 'Advantages and Shortcomings of Korean Chaebols', *International Business and Economics Research Journal* 7(1): 57–66.

Régnier, Phillipe (2006) 'Perspectives from Development Economics: The Case of Southeast Asia.' *Journal of Current Southeast Asian Affairs*, 25(3): 73–82.

Rodrik, D. (1995) 'Getting Interventions Right: How South Korea and Taiwan Grew Rich.' *Economic Policy*, 10(20): 53–107.

Sutanthavibul, Virasak (2013) 'The Impact of Asian Leadership Changes.' *The Bangkok Post*. Published onFebruary 11, 2013.

Thien, Tran Chi (2009) *Properties and Motives of Korean FDI into ASEAN*. Seoul: Korea Development Institute.

Tsurumi, Patricia (1984) 'Colonial Education in Korea and Taiwan,' in Ramon Myers and Mark Peattie, *The Japanese Colonial Empire*, Princeton, NJ: Princeton University Press.

US Department of Defense (2000) 'Korean War Death Stats Highlight Modern DoD Safety Record. US Department of Defense News Articles written by Kathleen T. Rhem (American Forces Press Service) on 8 June.

Yoo, S.J. and Lee, S.M. (1987) 'Management Style and Practice of Korean Chaebols', *California Management Review* 29(4): 95–110.

Yul, Kwon (2004) 'Toward a Comprehensive Partnership: ASEAN-Korea Economic Cooperation.' *East Asian Review* 16(4): 81–98.

Appendix 1
Regional map

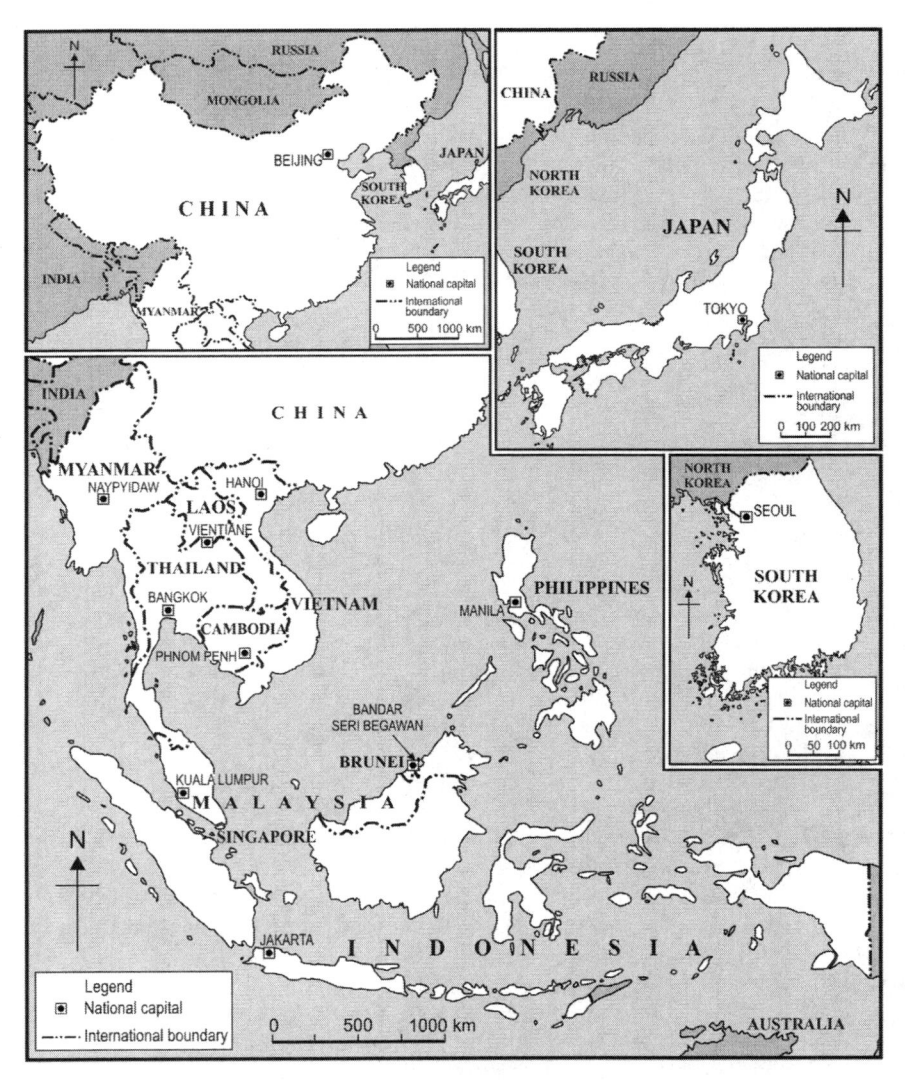

Figure A.1 Map of Southeast Asia, including China, Japan and South Korea

Appendix 2
Country surveys

BRUNEI DARUSSALAM

CAPITAL	**BANDAR SERI BEGAWAN**
CURRENCY	**BRUNEI DOLLAR (BDN)**

SURFACE AREA [1]	**5,770 SQ KM**
OFFICIAL LANGUAGE	**MALAY**

LIFE EXPECTANCY AT BIRTH [2] (YEARS)

	1990	2000	2011
BOTH SEXES	73.7	76.2	78.1
FEMALE	75.8	78.6	80.5
MALE	71.6	74.0	75.8

POPULATION

TOTAL IN 2012 (millions) [3]	**0.4**
ANNUAL GROWTH RATE 2012 [4]	**1.6%**

ETHNIC GROUPS [5] (2011) — PERCENTAGE

- MALAY 65.7%
- CHINESE 10.3%
- OTHER 20.6%
- OTHER (indigenous) 3.4%

RELIGIOUS AFFILIATIONS [6] (2011) — PERCENTAGE

- MUSLIM (official) 78.8%
- CHRISTIAN 8.7%
- BUDDHIST 7.8%
- OTHER (incl. indigenous beliefs) 4.7%

NET INTERNATIONAL MIGRATION RATE [7] — PER 1,000 POPULATION

1990 to	1995 to	2000 to	2005 to	2010 to	2015
2.2	3.1	3.5	2.0	1.8	

AGE STRUCTURE [8] (2012) — PER AGE GROUP

- 0 – 14 | 15: 25.7%
- 15 – 64: 70.3%
- 65+: 4.0%

LABOUR FORCE [9] (1995) — BY OCCUPATION

- AGRICULTURE 2.5%
- INDUSTRY 8.9%
- SERVICES 88.6%

GROSS DOMESTIC PRODUCT (GDP) AT PURCHASING POWER PARITY (PPP) — CURRENT US$

	1980	1985	1990	1995	2000	2005	2010	2012
MILLIONS [10]	7,367	7,888	9,232	12,164	14,113	17,567	19,973	21,635
PER CAPITA [11]	38,163	35,366	35,934	41,235	42,536	47,760	49,861	52,482

KEY IMPORTS [12] iron & steel, motor vehicles, machinery & transport equipment, manufactured goods, food, chemicals

KEY EXPORTS [13] crude oil, natural gas, garments

FOOTNOTES
1. *World Bank Open Data*, s.v "Surface area," accessed March 1, 2014, http://data.worldbank.org .
2. Asian Development Bank, *Key Indicators for Asia and the Pacific 2013*, accessed March 1, 2014, http://www.adb.org/ .
3&4. Ibid.
5. *The World Factbook*, s.v. "Brunei," accessed March 1, 2014, https://www.cia.gov/library/publications/the-world-factbook/ .
6. *The World Factbook*, s.v. "Brunei," accessed March 1, 2014, https://www.cia.gov/library/publications/the-world-factbook/ .
7. Asian Development Bank, *Key Indicators for Asia and the Pacific 2013*, accessed March 1, 2014, http://www.adb.org/ .
8&9. Ibid.
10. *World Bank Open Data*, s.v "GDP, PPP," accessed March 1, 2014, http://data.worldbank.org .
11. *World Bank Open Data*, s.v "GDP per capita, PPP," accessed March 1, 2014, http://data.worldbank.org .
12. *The World Factbook*, s.v. "Brunei," accessed March 1, 2014, https://www.cia.gov/library/publications/the-world-factbook/ .
13. Ibid.

CAMBODIA

CAPITAL	**PHNOM PENH**
CURRENCY	**CAMBODIAN RIEL (KHR)**

SURFACE AREA [1]	**181,040 SQ KM**
OFFICIAL LANGUAGE	**KHMER**

LIFE EXPECTANCY AT BIRTH [2] (YEARS)

	1990	2000	2011
BOTH SEXES	55.4	57.5	63.0
FEMALE	57.1	58.4	64.4
MALE	53.8	56.5	61.6

POPULATION

TOTAL IN 2012 (millions) [3]	**14.8**
ANNUAL GROWTH RATE 2012 [4]	**1.7%**

ETHNIC GROUPS [5] — PERCENTAGE

KHMER 90% — VIETNAMESE 5% — CHINESE 1% — OTHER 4%

RELIGIOUS AFFILIATIONS [6] (2008 est.) — PERCENTAGE

BUDDHIST (official) 96.9% — MUSLIM 1.9% — CHRISTIAN 0.4% — OTHER 0.8%

NET INTERNATIONAL MIGRATION RATE [7] — PER 1,000 POPULATION

1990 to	**1995** to	**2000** to	**2005** to	**2010** to	**2015**
3.4	3.0	1.6	-1.8	-3.7	

AGE STRUCTURE [8] (2012) — PER AGE GROUP

| 0 | 14 | 15 | 64 | 65+ |

31.0% — 64.0% — 5.0%

LABOUR FORCE [9] (2012) — BY OCCUPATION

AGRICULTURE 71% — INDUSTRY 10% — SERVICES 19%

GROSS DOMESTIC PRODUCT (GDP) AT PURCHASING POWER PARITY (PPP) — CURRENT US$

MILLIONS [10]

1980	1985	1990	1995	2000	2005	2010	2012
			7,424	11,474	20,143	30,615	36,477

PER CAPITA [11]

1995	2000	2005	2010	2012
689	939	1,508	2,131	2,454

KEY IMPORTS [12]
petroleum products, cigarettes, gold, construction materials, machinery, motor vehicles, pharmaceutical products

KEY EXPORTS [13]
clothing, timber, rubber, rice, fish, tobacco, footwear

FOOTNOTES

1. *World Bank Open Data*, s.v "Surface area," accessed March 1, 2014, http://data.worldbank.org .
2. Asian Development Bank, *Key Indicators for Asia and the Pacific 2013*, accessed March 1, 2014, http://www.adb.org/ .
3 & 4. Ibid.
5. *The World Factbook*, s.v. "Cambodia," accessed March 1, 2014, https://www.cia.gov/library/publications/the-world-factbook/
6. Ibid.
7. Asian Development Bank, *Key Indicators for Asia and the Pacific 2013*, accessed March 1, 2014, http://www.adb.org/ .
8. Ibid. Age structure of Cambodia is adapted from raw data (2012) which is not equal to 100%: 1) Population aged 0-14 years (%): 31.1%; 2) Population aged 15-65 years (%): 63.6%; 3) Population aged 65 years (%): 5.2%
9. Asian Development Bank, *Key Indicators for Asia and the Pacific 2013*, accessed March 1, 2014, http://www.adb.org/ . Labor force by occupation of Cambodia is adapted from raw data (2012) which is not equal to 100%: 1. Agriculture: 71.1%; 2. Industry: 9.7%; 3. Services: 19.3%
10. *World Bank Open Data*, s.v "GDP, PPP," accessed March 1, 2014, http://data.worldbank.org .
11. *World Bank Open Data*, s.v "GDP per capita, PPP," accessed March 1, 2014, http://data.worldbank.org .
12. *The World Factbook*, s.v. "Cambodia," accessed March 1, 2014, https://www.cia.gov/library/publications/the-world-factbook/ .
13. Ibid.

INDONESIA

CAPITAL **JAKARTA**

SURFACE AREA [1] **1,904,570 SQ KM**

CURRENCY **INDONESIAN RUPIAH (IDR)**

OFFICIAL LANGUAGE **BAHASA INDONESIA**

LIFE EXPECTANCY AT BIRTH [2] (YEARS)	1990	2000	2011
BOTH SEXES	62.1	65.6	69.3
FEMALE	63.8	67.3	71.1
MALE	60.5	64.1	67.7

POPULATION
TOTAL IN 2012 (millions) [3] **247.2**
ANNUAL GROWTH RATE 2012 [4] **2.3%**

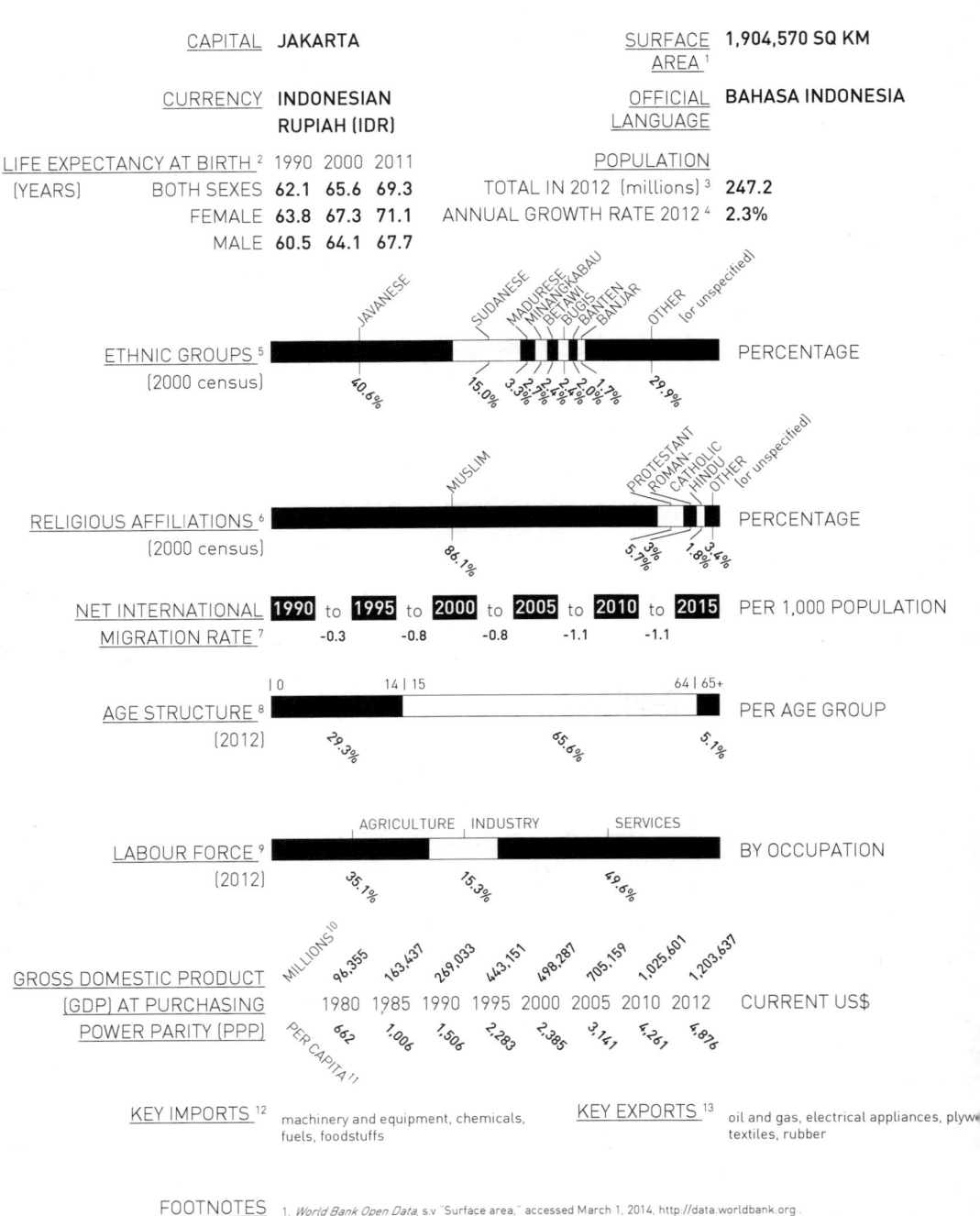

ETHNIC GROUPS [5] (2000 census) — PERCENTAGE
JAVANESE 40.6%, SUDANESE 15.0%, MADURESE 3.3%, MINANGKABAU 2.7%, BETAWI 2.4%, BUGIS 2.0%, BANTEN 1.7%, BANJAR, OTHER (or unspecified) 29.9%

RELIGIOUS AFFILIATIONS [6] (2000 census) — PERCENTAGE
MUSLIM 86.1%, PROTESTANT 5.7%, ROMAN-CATHOLIC 3%, HINDU 1.8%, OTHER (or unspecified) 3.4%

NET INTERNATIONAL MIGRATION RATE [7] — PER 1,000 POPULATION
1990 to 1995 to 2000 to 2005 to 2010 to 2015
-0.3 -0.8 -0.8 -1.1 -1.1

AGE STRUCTURE [8] (2012) — PER AGE GROUP
| 0 — 14 | 15 — 64 | 65+
29.3% 65.6% 5.1%

LABOUR FORCE [9] (2012) — BY OCCUPATION
AGRICULTURE 35.1%, INDUSTRY 15.3%, SERVICES 49.6%

GROSS DOMESTIC PRODUCT (GDP) AT PURCHASING POWER PARITY (PPP) — CURRENT US$
MILLIONS [10]: 96,355 (1980), 163,437 (1985), 269,033 (1990), 443,151 (1995), 498,287 (2000), 705,159 (2005), 1,025,601 (2010), 1,203,637 (2012)
PER CAPITA [11]: 662, 1,006, 1,506, 2,283, 2,385, 3,141, 4,261, 4,876

KEY IMPORTS [12] machinery and equipment, chemicals, fuels, foodstuffs

KEY EXPORTS [13] oil and gas, electrical appliances, plywood, textiles, rubber

FOOTNOTES
1. *World Bank Open Data*, s.v "Surface area," accessed March 1, 2014, http://data.worldbank.org .
2. Asian Development Bank, *Key Indicators for Asia and the Pacific 2013*, accessed March 1, 2014, http://www.adb.org/ .
3&4. Ibid.
5. *The World Factbook*, s.v. "Indonesia," accessed March 1, 2014, https://www.cia.gov/library/publications/the-world-factbook/ .
6. Ibid.
7. Asian Development Bank, *Key Indicators for Asia and the Pacific 2013*, accessed March 1, 2014, http://www.adb.org/ .
8&9. Ibid.
10. *World Bank Open Data*, s.v "GDP, PPP," accessed March 1, 2014, http://data.worldbank.org .
11. *World Bank Open Data*, s.v "GDP per capita, PPP," accessed March 1, 2014, http://data.worldbank.org .
12. *The World Factbook*, s.v. "Indonesia," accessed March 1, 2014, https://www.cia.gov/library/publications/the-world-factbook/ .
13. Ibid.

LAO PDR

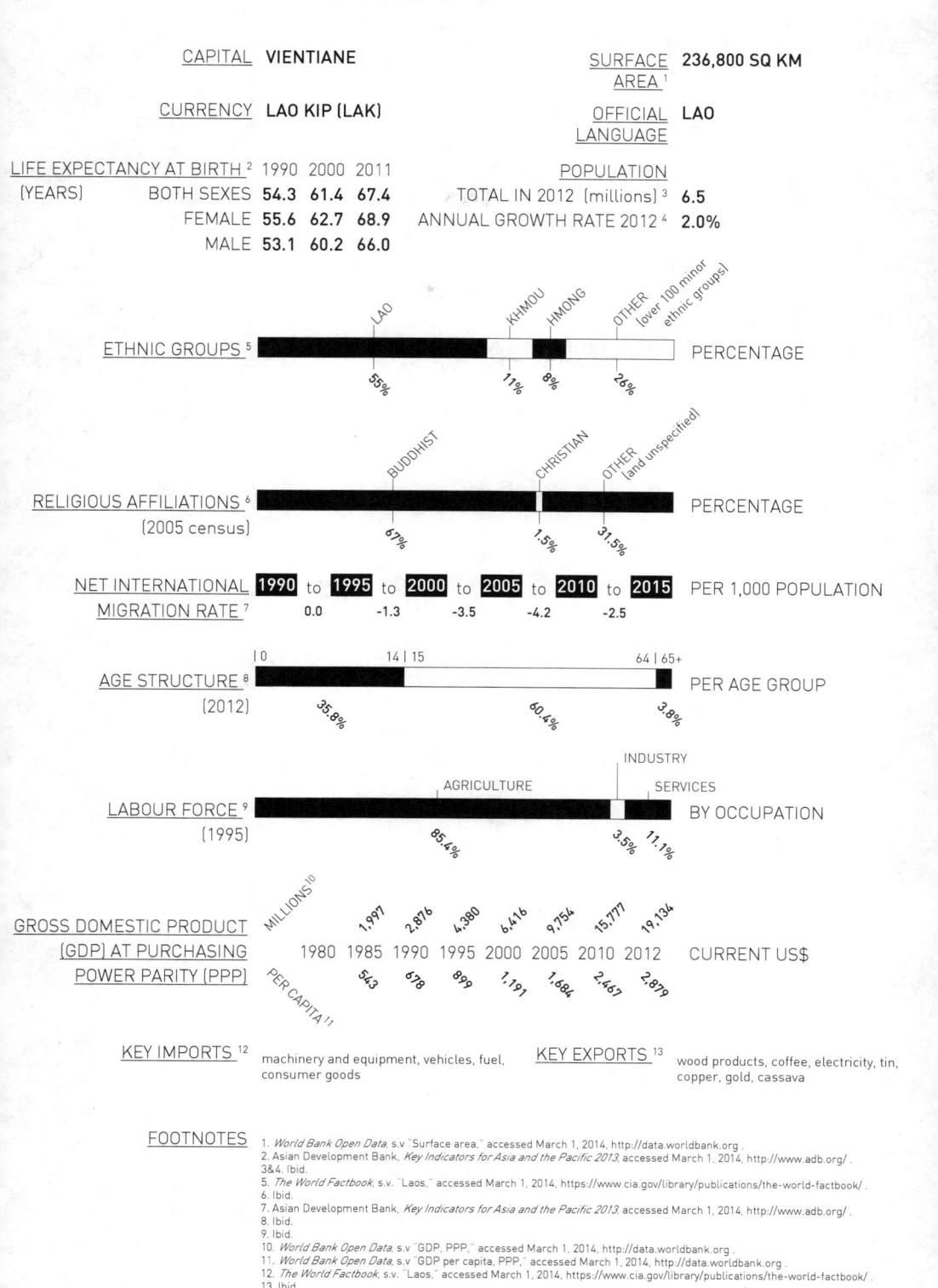

CAPITAL **VIENTIANE**

SURFACE AREA [1] **236,800 SQ KM**

CURRENCY **LAO KIP (LAK)**

OFFICIAL LANGUAGE **LAO**

LIFE EXPECTANCY AT BIRTH [2] (YEARS)

	1990	2000	2011
BOTH SEXES	54.3	61.4	67.4
FEMALE	55.6	62.7	68.9
MALE	53.1	60.2	66.0

POPULATION

TOTAL IN 2012 (millions) [3] **6.5**

ANNUAL GROWTH RATE 2012 [4] **2.0%**

ETHNIC GROUPS [5] — PERCENTAGE

LAO 55% KHMOU 11% HMONG 8% OTHER (over 100 minor ethnic groups) 26%

RELIGIOUS AFFILIATIONS [6] (2005 census) — PERCENTAGE

BUDDHIST 67% CHRISTIAN 1.5% OTHER (and unspecified) 31.5%

NET INTERNATIONAL MIGRATION RATE [7] — PER 1,000 POPULATION

1990 to	1995 to	2000 to	2005 to	2010 to	2015
0.0	-1.3	-3.5	-4.2	-2.5	

AGE STRUCTURE [8] (2012) — PER AGE GROUP

| 0 | 14 | 15 | 64 | 65+ |

35.8% 60.4% 3.8%

LABOUR FORCE [9] (1995) — BY OCCUPATION

AGRICULTURE 85.4% INDUSTRY 3.5% SERVICES 11.1%

GROSS DOMESTIC PRODUCT (GDP) AT PURCHASING POWER PARITY (PPP) — CURRENT US$

MILLIONS [10]

	1980	1985	1990	1995	2000	2005	2010	2012
MILLIONS [10]			1,997	2,876	4,380	6,416	9,754	15,777	19,134
PER CAPITA [11]			543	678	899	1,191	1,684	2,467	2,879

KEY IMPORTS [12] machinery and equipment, vehicles, fuel, consumer goods

KEY EXPORTS [13] wood products, coffee, electricity, tin, copper, gold, cassava

FOOTNOTES

1. *World Bank Open Data*, s.v "Surface area," accessed March 1, 2014, http://data.worldbank.org .
2. Asian Development Bank, *Key Indicators for Asia and the Pacific 2013*, accessed March 1, 2014, http://www.adb.org/ .
3 & 4. Ibid.
5. *The World Factbook*, s.v. "Laos," accessed March 1, 2014, https://www.cia.gov/library/publications/the-world-factbook/ .
6. Ibid.
7. Asian Development Bank, *Key Indicators for Asia and the Pacific 2013*, accessed March 1, 2014, http://www.adb.org/ .
8. Ibid.
9. Ibid.
10. *World Bank Open Data*, s.v "GDP, PPP," accessed March 1, 2014, http://data.worldbank.org .
11. *World Bank Open Data*, s.v "GDP per capita, PPP," accessed March 1, 2014, http://data.worldbank.org .
12. *The World Factbook*, s.v. "Laos," accessed March 1, 2014, https://www.cia.gov/library/publications/the-world-factbook/ .
13. Ibid.

MALAYSIA

CAPITAL	**KUALA LUMPUR**
CURRENCY	**MALAYSIAN RINGGIT (MYR)**

SURFACE AREA [1]	**330,800 SQ KM**
OFFICIAL LANGUAGE	**BAHASA MALAYSIA**

LIFE EXPECTANCY AT BIRTH [2] (YEARS)

	1990	2000	2011
BOTH SEXES	**70.1**	**72.1**	**74.3**
FEMALE	**72.1**	**74.3**	**76.5**
MALE	**68.1**	**70.0**	**72.1**

POPULATION
TOTAL IN 2012 (millions) [3] **29.3**
ANNUAL GROWTH RATE 2012 [4] **1.3%**

ETHNIC GROUPS [5] (2004 est.)
PERCENTAGE

MALAY 50.4% · CHINESE 23.7% · INDIGENOUS 11% · INDIAN 7.1% · OTHERS 7.8%

RELIGIOUS AFFILIATIONS [6]
PERCENTAGE

MUSLIM 60.4% · BUDDHIST 19.2% · CHRISTIAN 9.1% · HINDU 6.3% · CONFUCIANISM, TAOISM & OTHER (traditional chinese) 2.6% · OTHER (or unknown) 1.5% · NONE 0.8%

NET INTERNATIONAL MIGRATION RATE [7]
PER 1,000 POPULATION

1990 to 1995	to 2000	to 2005	to 2010	to 2015
5.4	3.3	3.8	3.2	0.6

AGE STRUCTURE [8] (2012)
PER AGE GROUP

0 — 14	15 — 64	65+
26.5%	68.3%	5.2%

LABOUR FORCE [9] (2012)
BY OCCUPATION

AGRICULTURE 12.6% · INDUSTRY 18.1% · SERVICES 69.3%

GROSS DOMESTIC PRODUCT (GDP) AT PURCHASING POWER PARITY (PPP)
CURRENT US$

MILLIONS [10]	1980	1985	1990	1995	2000	2005	2010	2012
	33,827	55,963	90,961	161,330	221,398	313,496	429,358	494,696
PER CAPITA [11]	2,445	3,550	4,995	7,784	9,453	12,131	15,185	16,919

KEY IMPORTS [12]
electronics, machinery, petroleum products, plastics, vehicles, iron and steel products, chemicals

KEY EXPORTS [13]
semiconductors and electronic equipm palm oil, petroleum and liquefied natu gas, wood and wood products, palm oi rubber, textiles, chemicals, solar pane

FOOTNOTES
1. *World Bank Open Data,* s.v "Surface area," accessed March 1, 2014, http://data.worldbank.org .
2. Asian Development Bank, *Key Indicators for Asia and the Pacific 2013,* accessed March 1, 2014, http://www.adb.org/ .
3&4. Ibid.
5. *The World Factbook,* s.v. "Malaysia," accessed March 1, 2014, https://www.cia.gov/library/publications/the-world-factbook/.
6. Ibid.
7. Asian Development Bank, *Key Indicators for Asia and the Pacific 2013,* accessed March 1, 2014, http://www.adb.org/ .
8. Ibid.
9. Ibid.
10. *World Bank Open Data,* s.v "GDP, PPP," accessed March 1, 2014, http://data.worldbank.org .
11. *World Bank Open Data,* s.v "GDP per capita, PPP," accessed March 1, 2014, http://data.worldbank.org .
12. *The World Factbook,* s.v. "Malaysia," accessed March 1, 2014, https://www.cia.gov/library/publications/the-world-factbook/ .
13. Ibid.

MYANMAR

CAPITAL **NAYPYIDAW**

SURFACE AREA [1] **676,590 SQ KM**

CURRENCY **MYANMAR KYAT (MMK)**

OFFICIAL LANGUAGE **BURMESE**

LIFE EXPECTANCY AT BIRTH [2] (YEARS)

	1990	2000	2011
BOTH SEXES	57.3	61.9	65.2
FEMALE	58.7	63.3	66.9
MALE	55.9	60.5	63.5

POPULATION

TOTAL IN 2012 (millions) [3] **61.0**

ANNUAL GROWTH RATE 2012 [4] **1.0%**

ETHNIC GROUPS [5] — PERCENTAGE

BURMAN 68%, SHAN 9%, KAREN 7%, RAKHINE 4%, CHINESE 3%, INDIAN 2%, MON 2%, OTHER 5%

RELIGIOUS AFFILIATIONS [6] — PERCENTAGE

BUDDHIST 89%, CHRISTIAN (Baptist) 3%, CHRISTIAN (Roman Catholic) 1%, MUSLIM 4%, OTHER 2%, ANIMIST 1%

NET INTERNATIONAL MIGRATION RATE [7] — PER 1,000 POPULATION

1990 to	1995 to	2000 to	2005 to	2010 to	2015
-0.7	-0.6	0.0	-4.4	-2.1	

AGE STRUCTURE [8] (2012) — PER AGE GROUP

| 0 | 14 | 15 | 64 | 65+ |

25.3%, 69.5%, 5.2%

LABOUR FORCE [9] (1995) — BY OCCUPATION

AGRICULTURE 64.1%, INDUSTRY 9.1%, SERVICES 26.8%

GROSS DOMESTIC PRODUCT (GDP) AT PURCHASING POWER PARITY (PPP) [10] — CURRENT US$

MILLIONS

1980	1985	1990	1995	2000	2005	2010	2012
					49,207	92,419	109,813

PER CAPITA

2005	2010	2012
888	1,546	1,801

KEY IMPORTS [11] fabric, petroleum products, fertilizer, plastics, machinery, transport equipment, cement, construction materials, crude oil, food products, edible oil

KEY EXPORTS [12] natural gas, wood products, pulses, beans, fish, rice, clothing, jade and gems

FOOTNOTES

1. *World Bank Open Data*, s.v "Surface area," accessed March 1, 2014, http://data.worldbank.org .
2. Asian Development Bank, *Key Indicators for Asia and the Pacific 2013*, accessed March 1, 2014, http://www.adb.org/ .
3&4. Ibid.
5. *The World Factbook*, s.v. "Burma," accessed March 1, 2014, https://www.cia.gov/library/publications/the-world-factbook/ .
6. Ibid.
7. Asian Development Bank, *Key Indicators for Asia and the Pacific 2013*, accessed March 1, 2014, http://www.adb.org/ .
8&9. Ibid.
10. Ibid
11. *The World Factbook*, s.v. "Burma," accessed March 1, 2014, https://www.cia.gov/library/publications/the-world-factbook/ .
12. Ibid.

PHILIPPINES

CAPITAL	**MANILA**	SURFACE AREA [1]	**300,000 SQ KM**
CURRENCY	**PHILIPPINE PESO (PHP)**	OFFICIAL LANGUAGE	**FILIPINO, ENGLISH**

LIFE EXPECTANCY AT BIRTH [2]
(YEARS)

	1990	2000	2011
BOTH SEXES	65.2	66.8	68.8
FEMALE	68.0	70.0	72.2
MALE	62.5	63.7	65.5

POPULATION

TOTAL IN 2012 (millions) [3]	95.8
ANNUAL GROWTH RATE 2012 [4]	1.7%

ETHNIC GROUPS [5]
(2000 census)

TAGALOG 28.1%, CEBUANO 13.1%, ILOCANO 9%, BISAYA/BINISAYA HILIGAYNON/ILONGGO 7.6%, 2.5%, BIKOL 6%, WARAY 3.4%, OTHER 25.3% — PERCENTAGE

RELIGIOUS AFFILIATIONS [6]
(2000 census)

CATHOLIC (Roman Catholic) 80.9%, CATHOLIC (Aglipayan) 2%, MUSLIM 5%, EVANGELICAL 2.8%, IGLESIA NI KRISTO 2.3%, OTHER (Christian) 4.5%, OTHER 1.8%, UNSPECIFIED 0.6%, NONE 0.1% — PERCENTAGE

NET INTERNATIONAL MIGRATION RATE [7]

1990 to 1995	to 2000	to 2005	to 2010	to 2015	PER 1,000 POPULATION
-1.0	-2.1	-2.1	-2.8	-2.8	

AGE STRUCTURE [8]
(2012)

0	14	15	64	65+	PER AGE GROUP
34.5%		61.7%		3.8%	

LABOUR FORCE [9]
(2012)

AGRICULTURE 32.1%, INDUSTRY 9%, SERVICES 58.9% — BY OCCUPATION

GROSS DOMESTIC PRODUCT (GDP) AT PURCHASING POWER PARITY (PPP) — CURRENT US$

MILLIONS [10]	64,253	77,727	114,267	143,483	185,642	260,987	365,336	419,583
	1980	1985	1990	1995	2000	2005	2010	2012
PER CAPITA [11]	1,356	1,431	1,845	2,061	2,391	3,041	3,910	4,339

KEY IMPORTS [12]
electronic products, mineral fuels, machinery and transport equipment, iron and steel, textile fabrics, grains, chemicals, plastic

KEY EXPORTS [13]
semiconductors and electronic products, transport equipment, garments, copper products, petroleum products, coconut oil, fruits

FOOTNOTES

1. *World Bank Open Data*, s.v. "Surface area," accessed March 1, 2014, http://data.worldbank.org .
2. Asian Development Bank, *Key Indicators for Asia and the Pacific 2013*, accessed March 1, 2014, http://www.adb.org/ .
3&4. Ibid.
5. *The World Factbook*, s.v. "Philippines," accessed March 1, 2014, https://www.cia.gov/library/publications/the-world-factbook/ .
6. Ibid.
7. Asian Development Bank, *Key Indicators for Asia and the Pacific 2013*, accessed March 1, 2014, http://www.adb.org/ .
8. Ibid.
9. Ibid.
10. *World Bank Open Data*, s.v. "GDP, PPP," accessed March 1, 2014, http://data.worldbank.org .
11. *World Bank Open Data*, s.v. "GDP per capita, PPP," accessed March 1, 2014, http://data.worldbank.org .
12. *The World Factbook*, s.v. "Philippines," accessed March 1, 2014, https://www.cia.gov/library/publications/the-world-factbook/ .
13. Ibid.

SINGAPORE

CAPITAL	**SINGAPORE**
CURRENCY	**SINGAPORE DOLLAR (SGD)**
SURFACE AREA [1]	**710 SQ KM**
OFFICIAL LANGUAGE	**MANDARIN, ENGLISH, TAMIL, MALAY**

LIFE EXPECTANCY AT BIRTH [2] (YEARS)

	1990	2000	2011
BOTH SEXES	**75.6**	**78.1**	**81.9**
FEMALE	**78.0**	**80.1**	**84.3**
MALE	**73.3**	**76.1**	**79.6**

POPULATION

TOTAL IN 2012 (millions) [3] **5.3**
ANNUAL GROWTH RATE 2012 [4] **2.5%**

ETHNIC GROUPS [5] (2012 est.) — PERCENTAGE

- CHINESE 74.2%
- MALAY 13.3%
- INDIAN 9.2%
- OTHER 3.3%

RELIGIOUS AFFILIATIONS [6] (2010 est.) — PERCENTAGE

- BUDDHIST 33.9%
- MUSLIM 14.3%
- TAOIST 11.3%
- CATHOLIC 7.1%
- HINDU 5.2%
- OTHER (Christian) 11%
- OTHER 0.7%
- NONE 16.4%

NET INTERNATIONAL MIGRATION RATE [7] — PER 1,000 POPULATION

1990 to	1995 to	2000 to	2005 to	2010 to	2015
8.5	14.3	13.7	11.4	30.9	

AGE STRUCTURE [8] (2012) — PER AGE GROUP

0–14	15–64	65+
16.5%	73.8%	9.7%

LABOUR FORCE [9] (2012) — BY OCCUPATION

- AGRICULTURE 0.1%
- INDUSTRY 14.3%
- SERVICES 85.5%

GROSS DOMESTIC PRODUCT (GDP) AT PURCHASING POWER PARITY (PPP) — CURRENT US$

	1980	1985	1990	1995	2000	2005	2010	2012
MILLIONS [10]		17,622	31,665	55,871	94,991	136,481	193,557	292,201 / 322,996
PER CAPITA [11]	7,300	11,573	18,336	26,952	33,884	45,374	57,557	60,800

KEY IMPORTS [12] machinery and equipment, mineral fuels, chemicals, foodstuffs, consumer goods

KEY EXPORTS [13] machinery and equipment (including electronics and telecommunications), pharmaceuticals and other chemicals, refined petroleum products

FOOTNOTES

1. *World Bank Open Data*, s.v "Surface area," accessed March 1, 2014, http://data.worldbank.org .
2. Asian Development Bank, *Key Indicators for Asia and the Pacific 2013*, accessed March 1, 2014, http://www.adb.org/ .
3&4. Ibid.
5. *The World Factbook*, s.v. "Singapore," accessed March 1, 2014, https://www.cia.gov/library/publications/the-world-factbook/ .
6. Ibid.
7. Asian Development Bank, *Key Indicators for Asia and the Pacific 2013*, accessed March 1, 2014, http://www.adb.org/ .
8. Ibid.
9. Ibid.
10. *World Bank Open Data*, s.v "GDP, PPP," accessed March 1, 2014, http://data.worldbank.org .
11. *World Bank Open Data*, s.v "GDP per capita, PPP," accessed March 1, 2014, http://data.worldbank.org .
12. *The World Factbook*, s.v. "Singapore," accessed March 1, 2014, https://www.cia.gov/library/publications/the-world-factbook/ .
13. Ibid.

THAILAND

CAPITAL **BANGKOK**

CURRENCY **THAI BAHT (THB)**

SURFACE AREA [1] **513,120 SQ KM**

OFFICIAL LANGUAGE **THAI**

LIFE EXPECTANCY AT BIRTH [2] (YEARS)

	1990	2000	2011
BOTH SEXES	**72.5**	**72.5**	**74.1**
FEMALE	**75.8**	**76.5**	**77.5**
MALE	**69.3**	**68.8**	**70.8**

POPULATION

TOTAL IN 2012 (millions) [3] **64.4**

ANNUAL GROWTH RATE 2012 [4] **0.4%**

ETHNIC GROUPS [5] (2010 est.) — PERCENTAGE

- THAI 95.9%
- BURMESE 2%
- OTHER 1.3%
- UNSPECIFIED 0.9%

RELIGIOUS AFFILIATIONS [6] (2010 est.) — PERCENTAGE

- BUDDHIST 93.6%
- MUSLIM 4.9%
- CHRISTIAN 1.2%
- OTHER 0.2%
- NONE 0.1%

NET INTERNATIONAL MIGRATION RATE [7] — PER 1,000 POPULATION

1990 to	1995 to	2000 to	2005 to	2010 to	2015
1.8	-3.8	1.9	3.4	1.5	

AGE STRUCTURE [8] (2012) — PER AGE GROUP

0 – 14	15 – 64	65+
18.5%	72.1%	9.4%

LABOUR FORCE [9] (2012) — BY OCCUPATION

- AGRICULTURE 38.9%
- INDUSTRY 14.9%
- SERVICES 46.2%

GROSS DOMESTIC PRODUCT (GDP) AT PURCHASING POWER PARITY (PPP) — CURRENT US$

	1980	1985	1990	1995	2000	2005	2010	2012
MILLIONS [10]	50,921	85,627	163,124	278,260	309,038	445,195	583,524	645,175
PER CAPITA [11]	1,075	1,646	2,883	4,718	4,957	6,791	8,788	9,660

KEY IMPORTS [12] capital goods, intermediate goods and raw materials, consumer goods, fuels

KEY EXPORTS [13] electronics, computer parts, automobiles and parts, electrical appliances, machinery and equipment, textiles and footwear, fishery products, rice, rubber

FOOTNOTES

1. *World Bank Open Data*, s.v "Surface area," accessed March 1, 2014, http://data.worldbank.org .
2. Asian Development Bank, *Key Indicators for Asia and the Pacific 2013*, accessed March 1, 2014, http://www.adb.org/ .
3&4. Ibid.
5. *The World Factbook*, s.v. "Thailand," accessed March 1, 2014, https://www.cia.gov/library/publications/the-world-factbook/ .
6. Ibid.
7. Asian Development Bank, *Key Indicators for Asia and the Pacific 2013*, accessed March 1, 2014, http://www.adb.org/ .
8. Ibid.
9. Ibid.
10. *World Bank Open Data*, s.v "GDP, PPP," accessed March 1, 2014, http://data.worldbank.org .
11. *World Bank Open Data*, s.v "GDP per capita, PPP," accessed March 1, 2014, http://data.worldbank.org .
12. *The World Factbook*, s.v. "Thailand," accessed March 1, 2014, https://www.cia.gov/library/publications/the-world-factbook/ .
13. Ibid.

VIET NAM

CAPITAL	HANOI	SURFACE AREA [1]	330,957 SQ KM
CURRENCY	VIETNAMESE DONG (VND)	OFFICIAL LANGUAGE	VIETNAMESE

LIFE EXPECTANCY AT BIRTH [2] (YEARS)

	1990	2000	2011
BOTH SEXES	65.5	71.9	75.1
FEMALE	67.4	73.8	77.1
MALE	63.7	70.2	73.1

POPULATION

TOTAL IN 2012 (millions) [3] 88.8

ANNUAL GROWTH RATE 2012 [4] 1.1%

ETHNIC GROUPS [5] (1999 census) — PERCENTAGE

KINH (VIET) 85.7%, TAY 1.9%, THAI 1.8%, MUONG 1.5%, KHMER 1.5%, HMONG 1.2%, NUNG 1.1%, OTHERS 5.3%

RELIGIOUS AFFILIATIONS [6] (1999 census) — PERCENTAGE

BUDDHIST 9.3%, CATHOLIC 6.7%, HOA HAO 1.5%, CAO DAI 1.1%, PROTESTANT 0.5%, MUSLIM 0.1%, NONE 80.8%

NET INTERNATIONAL MIGRATION RATE [7] — PER 1,000 POPULATION

1990 to	1995 to	2000 to	2005 to	2010 to	2015
-1.0	-0.9	-0.8	-1.1	-1.0	

AGE STRUCTURE [8] (2012) — PER AGE GROUP

0 – 14	15 – 64	65+
22.9%	70.6%	6.5%

LABOUR FORCE [9] (2012) — BY OCCUPATION

AGRICULTURE	INDUSTRY	SERVICES
47%	15%	38%

GROSS DOMESTIC PRODUCT (GDP) AT PURCHASING POWER PARITY (PPP) — CURRENT US$

	1980	1985	1990	1995	2000	2005	2010	2012
MILLIONS [10]		33,010	48,641	81,390	123,687	193,945	289,835	336,221
PER CAPITA [11]		561	737	1,130	1,593	2,354	3,334	3,787

KEY IMPORTS [12] machinery and equipment, petroleum products, steel products, raw materials for the clothing and shoe industries, electronics, plastics, automobiles

KEY EXPORTS [13] clothes, shoes, electronics, seafood, crude oil, rice, coffee, wooden products, machinery

FOOTNOTES

1. *World Bank Open Data*, s.v "Surface area," accessed March 1, 2014, http://data.worldbank.org .
2. Asian Development Bank, *Key Indicators for Asia and the Pacific 2013*, accessed March 1, 2014, http://www.adb.org/ .
3 & 4. Ibid.
5. *The World Factbook*, s.v. "Vietnam," accessed March 1, 2014, https://www.cia.gov/library/publications/the-world-factbook/ .
6. Ibid.
7. Asian Development Bank, *Key Indicators for Asia and the Pacific 2013*, accessed March 1, 2014, http://www.adb.org/ .
8. Ibid.
9. Ibid. Labor force by occupation is aggregated from raw data which is not equal to 100%:1) Agriculture: 47.4%; 2) Industry: 14.4%; 3) Services: 38.3%
10. *World Bank Open Data*, s.v "GDP, PPP," accessed March 1, 2014, http://data.worldbank.org .
11. *World Bank Open Data*, s.v "GDP per capita, PPP," accessed March 1, 2014, http://data.worldbank.org .
12. *The World Factbook*, s.v. "Vietnam," accessed March 1, 2014, https://www.cia.gov/library/publications/the-world-factbook/ .
13. Ibid.

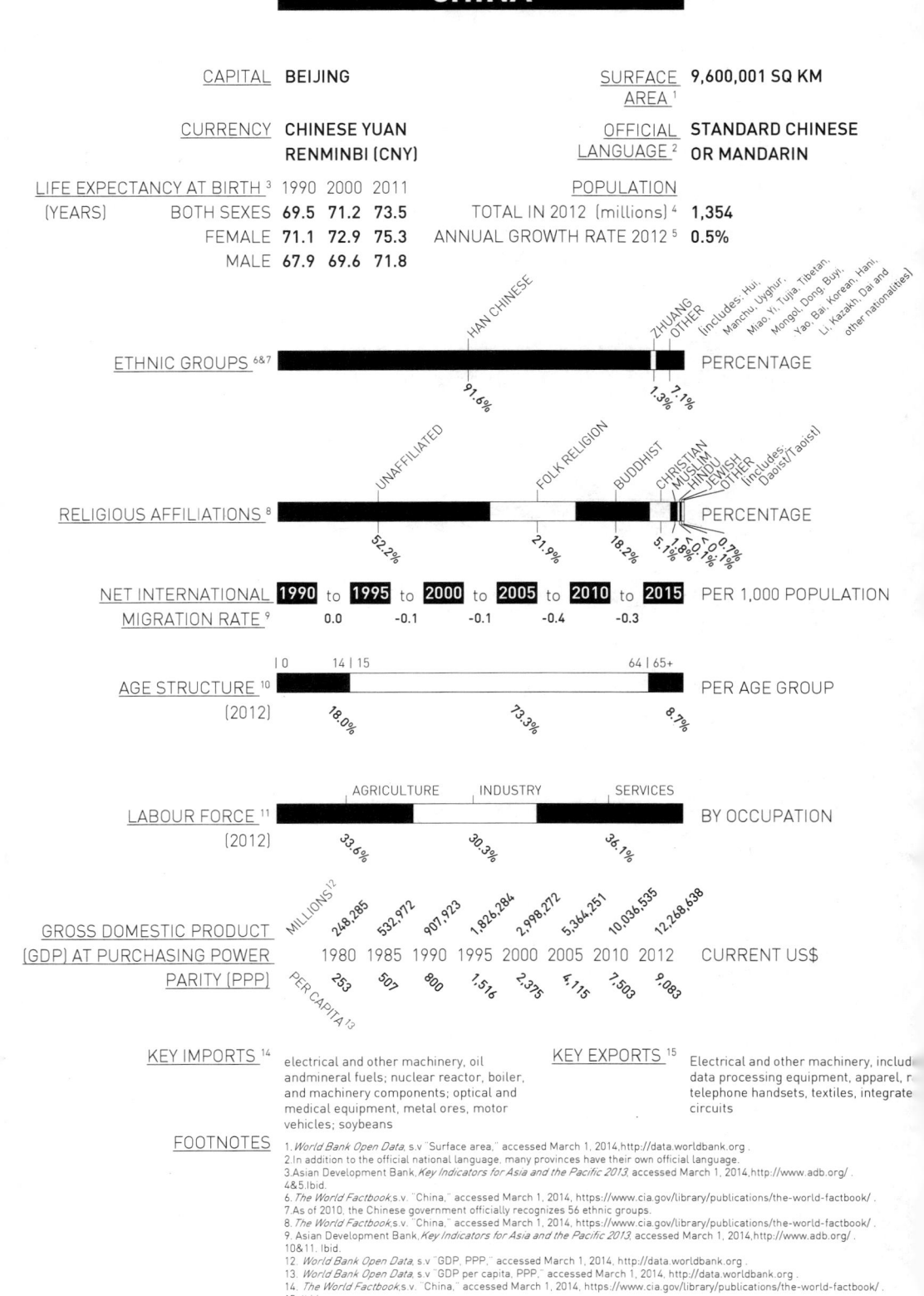

CHINA

CAPITAL **BEIJING**

SURFACE AREA [1] **9,600,001 SQ KM**

CURRENCY **CHINESE YUAN RENMINBI (CNY)**

OFFICIAL LANGUAGE [2] **STANDARD CHINESE OR MANDARIN**

LIFE EXPECTANCY AT BIRTH [3] (YEARS)

	1990	2000	2011
BOTH SEXES	69.5	71.2	73.5
FEMALE	71.1	72.9	75.3
MALE	67.9	69.6	71.8

POPULATION

TOTAL IN 2012 (millions) [4] **1,354**

ANNUAL GROWTH RATE 2012 [5] **0.5%**

ETHNIC GROUPS [6&7] PERCENTAGE

HAN CHINESE 91.6% ZHUANG 1.3% OTHER 7.1% (includes: Hui, Manchu, Uyghur, Tibetan, Miao, Yi, Tujia, Dong, Buyi, Mongol, Dong, Buyi, Hani, Yao, Bai, Korean, Hani, Li, Kazakh, Dai and other nationalities)

RELIGIOUS AFFILIATIONS [8] PERCENTAGE

UNAFFILIATED 52.2% FOLK RELIGION 21.9% BUDDHIST 18.2% CHRISTIAN 5.1% MUSLIM 1.8% HINDU <0.1% JEWISH <0.1% OTHER 0.7% (includes: Daoist/Taoist)

NET INTERNATIONAL MIGRATION RATE [9] PER 1,000 POPULATION

1990 to	1995 to	2000 to	2005 to	2010 to	2015
0.0	-0.1	-0.1	-0.4	-0.3	

AGE STRUCTURE [10] (2012) PER AGE GROUP

| 0 | 14 | 15 | 64 | 65+ |
| 18.0% | | 73.3% | | 8.7% |

LABOUR FORCE [11] (2012) BY OCCUPATION

AGRICULTURE 33.6% INDUSTRY 30.3% SERVICES 36.1%

GROSS DOMESTIC PRODUCT (GDP) AT PURCHASING POWER PARITY (PPP) CURRENT US$

	1980	1985	1990	1995	2000	2005	2010	2012
MILLIONS [12]	248,285	532,972	907,923	1,826,284	2,998,272	5,364,251	10,036,535	12,268,638
PER CAPITA [13]	253	507	800	1,516	2,375	4,115	7,503	9,083

KEY IMPORTS [14] electrical and other machinery, oil and mineral fuels; nuclear reactor, boiler, and machinery components; optical and medical equipment, metal ores, motor vehicles; soybeans

KEY EXPORTS [15] Electrical and other machinery, includ[...] data processing equipment, apparel, r[...] telephone handsets, textiles, integrate[...] circuits

FOOTNOTES

1. *World Bank Open Data*, s.v. "Surface area," accessed March 1, 2014, http://data.worldbank.org .
2. In addition to the official national language, many provinces have their own official language.
3. Asian Development Bank, *Key Indicators for Asia and the Pacific 2013*, accessed March 1, 2014, http://www.adb.org/ .
4 & 5. Ibid.
6. *The World Factbook*, s.v. "China," accessed March 1, 2014, https://www.cia.gov/library/publications/the-world-factbook/ .
7. As of 2010, the Chinese government officially recognizes 56 ethnic groups.
8. *The World Factbook*, s.v. "China," accessed March 1, 2014, https://www.cia.gov/library/publications/the-world-factbook/ .
9. Asian Development Bank, *Key Indicators for Asia and the Pacific 2013*, accessed March 1, 2014, http://www.adb.org/ .
10 & 11. Ibid.
12. *World Bank Open Data*, s.v. "GDP, PPP," accessed March 1, 2014, http://data.worldbank.org .
13. *World Bank Open Data*, s.v. "GDP per capita, PPP," accessed March 1, 2014, http://data.worldbank.org .
14. *The World Factbook*, s.v. "China," accessed March 1, 2014, https://www.cia.gov/library/publications/the-world-factbook/ .
15. Ibid.

JAPAN

CAPITAL **TOKYO**

SURFACE AREA [1] **377,955 SQ KM**

CURRENCY **JAPANESE YEN (JPY)**

OFFICIAL LANGUAGE **JAPANESE**

LIFE EXPECTANCY AT BIRTH [2] (YEARS)

	1990	2000	2011
BOTH SEXES	78.8	81.1	82.6
FEMALE	81.9	84.6	85.9
MALE	75.9	77.7	79.4

POPULATION
TOTAL IN 2012 (millions) [3] **127.6**
ANNUAL GROWTH RATE 2012 [4] **-0.2%**

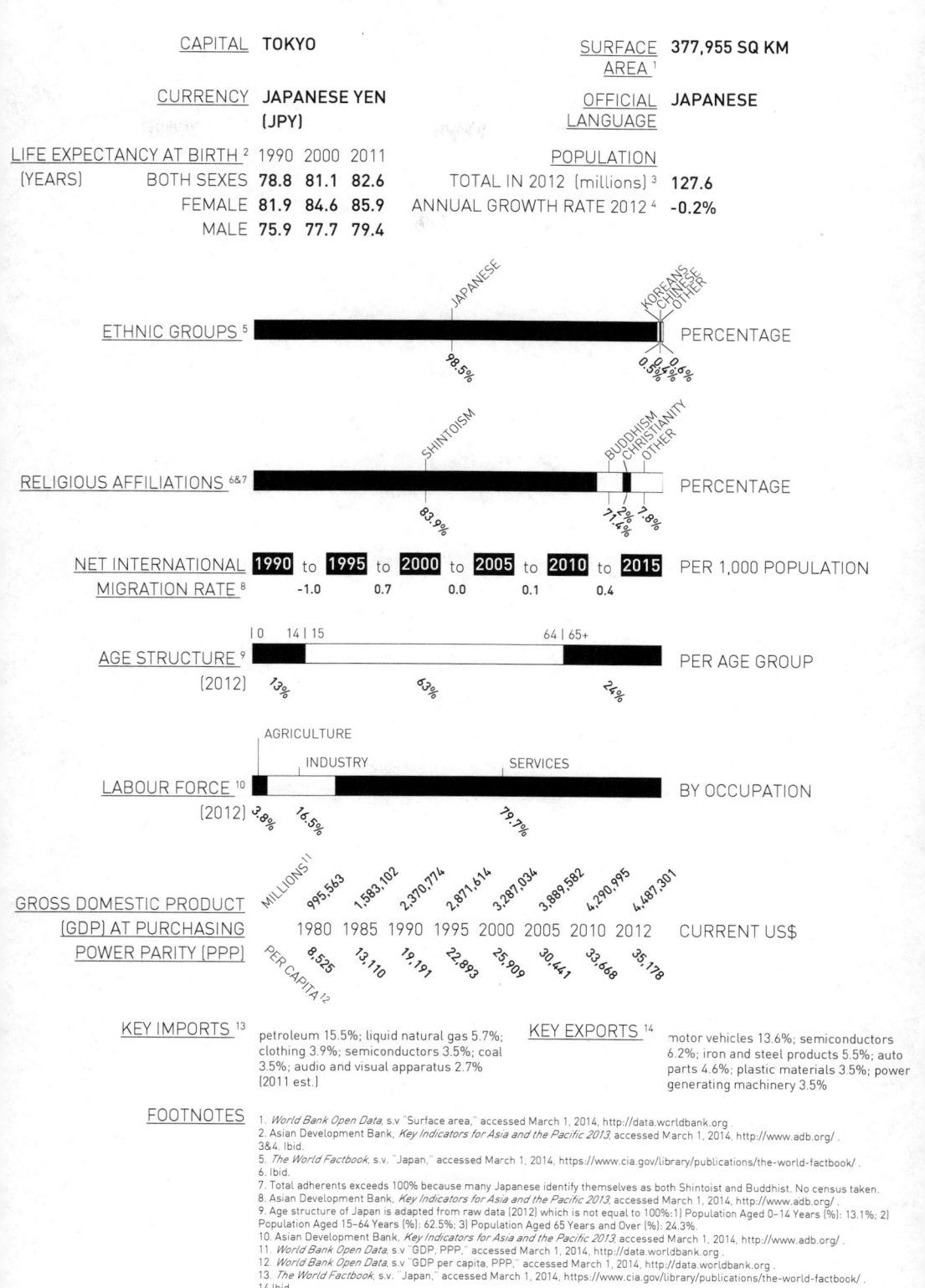

ETHNIC GROUPS [5] — PERCENTAGE
JAPANESE 98.5%; KOREANS 0.5%; CHINESE 0.4%; OTHER 0.6%

RELIGIOUS AFFILIATIONS [6&7] — PERCENTAGE
SHINTOISM 83.9%; BUDDHISM 71.4%; CHRISTIANITY 2%; OTHER 7.8%

NET INTERNATIONAL MIGRATION RATE [8] — PER 1,000 POPULATION

1990 to	1995 to	2000 to	2005 to	2010 to	2015
-1.0	0.7	0.0	0.1	0.4	

AGE STRUCTURE [9] (2012) — PER AGE GROUP
0 | 14 | 15 ... 64 | 65+
13%; 63%; 24%

LABOUR FORCE [10] (2012) — BY OCCUPATION
AGRICULTURE 3.8%; INDUSTRY 16.5%; SERVICES 79.7%

GROSS DOMESTIC PRODUCT (GDP) AT PURCHASING POWER PARITY (PPP) — CURRENT US$

MILLIONS [11]	PER CAPITA [12]

	1980	1985	1990	1995	2000	2005	2010	2012
MILLIONS [11]	995,563	1,583,102	2,370,774	2,871,614	3,287,034	3,889,582	4,290,995	4,487,301
PER CAPITA [12]	8,525	13,110	19,191	22,893	25,909	30,441	33,668	35,178

KEY IMPORTS [13]
petroleum 15.5%; liquid natural gas 5.7%; clothing 3.9%; semiconductors 3.5%; coal 3.5%; audio and visual apparatus 2.7% (2011 est.)

KEY EXPORTS [14]
motor vehicles 13.6%; semiconductors 6.2%; iron and steel products 5.5%; auto parts 4.6%; plastic materials 3.5%; power generating machinery 3.5%

FOOTNOTES

1. *World Bank Open Data*, s.v "Surface area," accessed March 1, 2014, http://data.worldbank.org .
2. Asian Development Bank, *Key Indicators for Asia and the Pacific 2013*, accessed March 1, 2014, http://www.adb.org/ .
3&4. Ibid.
5. *The World Factbook*, s.v. "Japan," accessed March 1, 2014, https://www.cia.gov/library/publications/the-world-factbook/ .
6. Ibid.
7. Total adherents exceeds 100% because many Japanese identify themselves as both Shintoist and Buddhist. No census taken.
8. Asian Development Bank, *Key Indicators for Asia and the Pacific 2013*, accessed March 1, 2014, http://www.adb.org/ .
9. Age structure of Japan is adapted from raw data (2012) which is not equal to 100%:1) Population Aged 0–14 Years (%): 13.1%; 2) Population Aged 15–64 Years (%): 62.5%; 3) Population Aged 65 Years and Over (%): 24.3%.
10. Asian Development Bank, *Key Indicators for Asia and the Pacific 2013*, accessed March 1, 2014, http://www.adb.org/ .
11. *World Bank Open Data*, s.v "GDP, PPP," accessed March 1, 2014, http://data.worldbank.org .
12. *World Bank Open Data*, s.v "GDP per capita, PPP," accessed March 1, 2014, http://data.worldbank.org .
13. *The World Factbook*, s.v. "Japan," accessed March 1, 2014, https://www.cia.gov/library/publications/the-world-factbook/ .
14 Ibid.

SOUTH KOREA

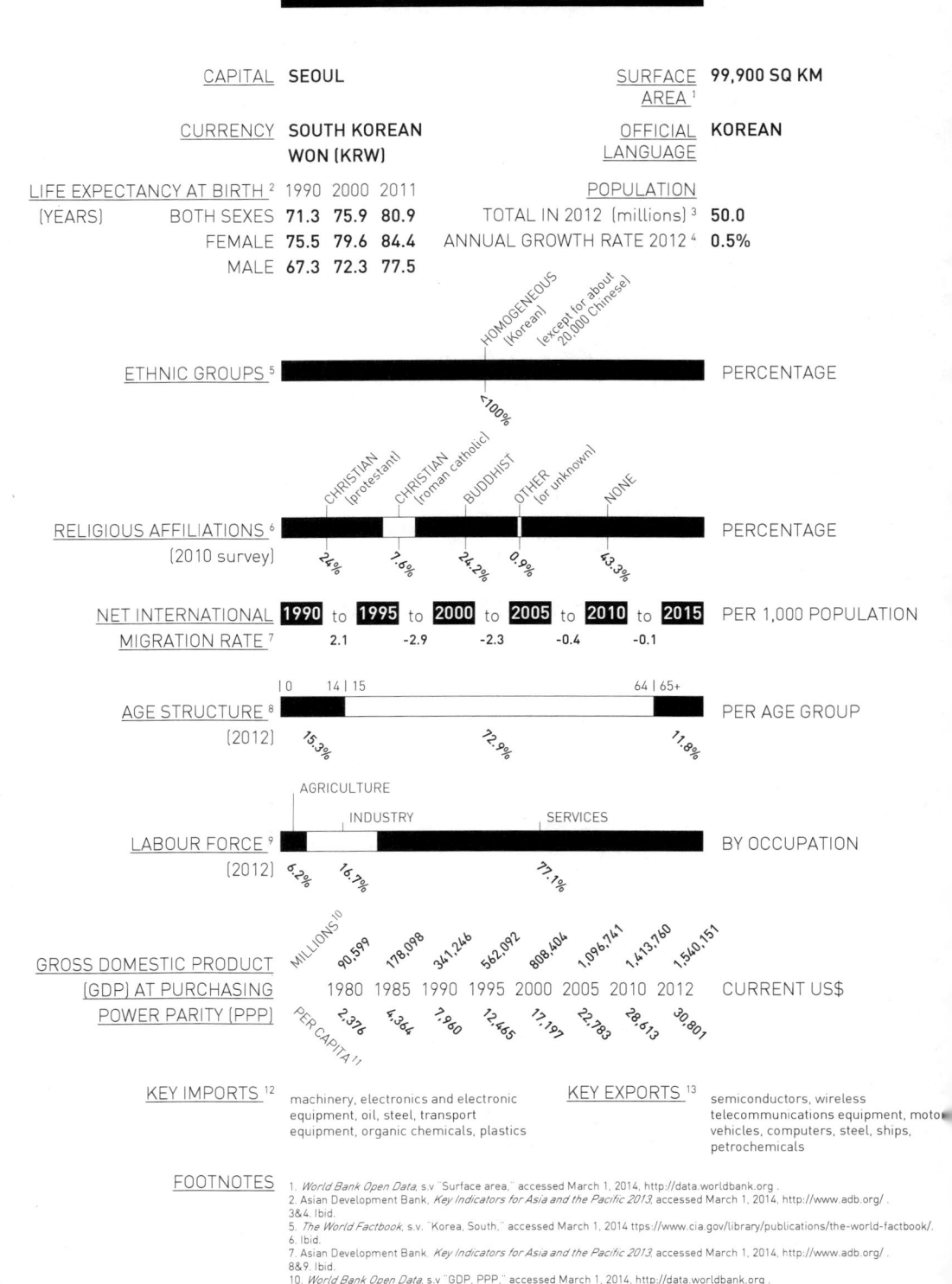

CAPITAL **SEOUL**

CURRENCY **SOUTH KOREAN WON (KRW)**

LIFE EXPECTANCY AT BIRTH [2] (YEARS)

	1990	2000	2011
BOTH SEXES	71.3	75.9	80.9
FEMALE	75.5	79.6	84.4
MALE	67.3	72.3	77.5

SURFACE AREA [1] **99,900 SQ KM**

OFFICIAL LANGUAGE **KOREAN**

POPULATION
TOTAL IN 2012 (millions) [3] **50.0**
ANNUAL GROWTH RATE 2012 [4] **0.5%**

ETHNIC GROUPS [5] — PERCENTAGE
HOMOGENEOUS (Korean) (except for about 20,000 Chinese) <100%

RELIGIOUS AFFILIATIONS [6] (2010 survey) — PERCENTAGE
CHRISTIAN (protestant) 24% | CHRISTIAN (roman catholic) 7.6% | BUDDHIST 24.2% | OTHER (or unknown) 0.9% | NONE 43.3%

NET INTERNATIONAL MIGRATION RATE [7] — PER 1,000 POPULATION

1990 to	**1995** to	**2000** to	**2005** to	**2010** to	**2015**
2.1	-2.9	-2.3	-0.4	-0.1	

AGE STRUCTURE [8] (2012) — PER AGE GROUP
|0   14 | 15 ... 64 | 65+
15.3% | 72.9% | 11.8%

LABOUR FORCE [9] (2012) — BY OCCUPATION
AGRICULTURE 6.2% | INDUSTRY 16.7% | SERVICES 77.1%

GROSS DOMESTIC PRODUCT (GDP) AT PURCHASING POWER PARITY (PPP) — CURRENT US$

MILLIONS [10]

	1980	1985	1990	1995	2000	2005	2010	2012
	90,599	178,098	341,246	562,092	808,404	1,096,741	1,413,760	1,540,151
PER CAPITA [11]	2,376	4,364	7,960	12,465	17,197	22,783	28,613	30,801

KEY IMPORTS [12] machinery, electronics and electronic equipment, oil, steel, transport equipment, organic chemicals, plastics

KEY EXPORTS [13] semiconductors, wireless telecommunications equipment, motor vehicles, computers, steel, ships, petrochemicals

FOOTNOTES
1. *World Bank Open Data*, s.v. "Surface area," accessed March 1, 2014, http://data.worldbank.org .
2. Asian Development Bank, *Key Indicators for Asia and the Pacific 2013*, accessed March 1, 2014, http://www.adb.org/ .
3&4. Ibid.
5. *The World Factbook*, s.v. "Korea, South," accessed March 1, 2014 ttps://www.cia.gov/library/publications/the-world-factbook/.
6. Ibid.
7. Asian Development Bank, *Key Indicators for Asia and the Pacific 2013*, accessed March 1, 2014, http://www.adb.org/ .
8&9. Ibid.
10. *World Bank Open Data*, s.v. "GDP, PPP," accessed March 1, 2014, http://data.worldbank.org .
11. *World Bank Open Data*, s.v. "GDP per capita, PPP," accessed March 1, 2014, http://data.worldbank.org .
12. *The World Factbook*, s.v. "Korea, South," accessed March 1, 2014, https://www.cia.gov/library/publications/the-world-factbook
13. Ibid.

Appendix 3

Timeline of key ASEAN milestones
Azmi Mat Akhir and Alice D. Ba

1967	Birth of ASEAN
1969	Establishment of a Fund for ASEAN
1971	Declaration on Zone of Peace, Freedom and Neutrality (ZOPEAN)
1975	First ASEAN Labour Ministers Meeting
	First ASEAN Economic Ministers Meeting
1976	Treaty of Amity and Cooperation in Southeast Asia (TAC)
	First Leaders ASEAN summit
	ASEAN/Bali Concord 1
	Agreement on the Establishment of the ASEAN Secretariat
1977	ASEAN Preferential Trading Arrangements
	ASEAN Swap Arrangements
	First Meeting of the ASEAN Education Ministers
1978	First Meeting of ASEAN Inter-Parliamentary Organization (became ASEAN Inter-Parliamentary Assembly (AIPA) in 2007)
	Establishment of the ASEAN Cultural Fund
1979	Agreement on ASEAN Food Security Reserve (AFSR)
	First Meeting of the ASEAN Agriculture and Forestry Ministers
1980	First ASEAN Energy Ministers Meeting
	First ASEAN Health Ministers Meeting
1981	First ASEAN Environment Ministers Meeting
	Basic Agreement on ASEAN Industrial Complementation (AIC)
1983	Basic Agreement on ASEAN Industrial Joint Ventures (AIJV)
1984	Brunei Darussalam joined ASEAN
1986	First ASEAN Law Ministers Meeting (regularized in 1993)
	Agreement on ASEAN Energy Cooperation
	ASEAN Petroleum Security Agreement
1987	Declaration on Political, Economic and Functional Cooperation
	Protocol on Amending Treaty of Amity and Cooperation
1989	Basic Agreement on ASEAN Industrial Projects (AIP)

1992	Agreement on the Common Effective Preferential Tariff (CEPT) Scheme for ASEAN Free Trade Area (AFTA)
	Framework Agreement on Enhancing ASEAN Economic Cooperation
1994	Establishment of Fund for ASEAN
	First ASEAN Regional Forum (ARF)
1995	Treaty on the Southeast Asia Nuclear Weapons-Free Zone (SEANWFZ)
	ASEAN Framework Agreement on Services (AFAS)
	Socialist Republic of Vietnam joined ASEAN
	First ASEAN Ministerial Meeting on Youth
1996	First ASEAN Transport Ministers Meeting
	Basic Agreement on ASEAN Industrial Cooperation (AICO)
1997	Laos and Myanmar joined ASEAN
	Memorandum of Understanding on the Establishment of the ASEAN Foundation
	First ASEAN Finance Ministers Meeting
	Declaration on Transnational Crime
	First ASEAN Ministerial Meeting on Transnational Crime
	ASEAN Vision 2020
1998	Second Protocol on Amending Treaty of Amity and Cooperation
	First Meeting of ASEAN Tourism Ministers
	First Informal Meeting of ASEAN Ministers on Rural Development and poverty eradication
	Agreement on ASEAN Investment Area (AIA)
	Hanoi Plan of Action (HPA)
1999	Cambodia joined ASEAN
	ASEAN Surveillance Process
2000	First meeting of High Level Task Force on the AFTA-CER Free Trade Area (AFTA-CER-FTA)
	ASEAN Troika
	Declaration on Cultural Heritage
	Political Declaration in Pursuit of a Drug Free ASEAN 2015
	e-ASEAN Framework Agreement
2001	First ASEAN meeting of Telecommunications and IT Ministers
	Rules of Procedure of the High Council of TAC
2002	ASEAN Agreement on Transboundary Haze Pollution
2003	Conference of the Parties to the ASEAN Agreement on Transboundary Haze Pollution
	Declaration on Strengthening Participation in Sustainable Youth Employment
	Bali Concord II
	First ASEAN Ministerial Meeting on Disaster Management
2004	Declaration on the Elimination of Violence Against Women in the ASEAN Region

Vientiane Action Programme (VAP) 2004–2010

ASEAN Security Community (ASC) Plan of Action

ASEAN Economic Community (AEC) Plan of Action

ASEAN Socio-Cultural Community (ASCC) Plan of Action

ASEAN Plan of Action on Narrowing the Development Gap (NDG)

ASEAN Framework Agreement for the Integration of Priority Sectors

ASEAN Declaration against Trafficking in Persons Particularly Women and Children

2005	Statement on "One Vision, One Identity, One Community"

Kuala Lumpur Declaration on Establishment of ASEAN Charter

Agreement to Establish and Implement the ASEAN Single Window

Establishment of the ASEAN Development Fund

Coordination Agreement on Technical Assistance and Training to Combat Money Laundering and Terrorist Financing

Memorandum of Understanding on the ASEAN SWAP arrangement (by all 10 central banks)

ASEAN Agreement on Disaster Management and Emergency Response

2006	Inaugural ASEAN Defence Ministers Meeting (ADMM)

Framework Agreement on Visa Exemption

2007	Singapore Declaration on Climate Change, Energy and the Environment

Declaration towards One Caring and Sharing Community

ASEAN Committee of Permanent Representatives created

AEC Blueprint

Declaration on Protection and Promotion of Rights of Migrant Workers

Declaration on Acceleration of the Establishment of the ASEAN Community by 2015

ASEAN Charter

2008	Statement on the ASEAN Charter
2009	Declaration on [ASEAN] Intergovernmental Commission on Human Rights (AICHR)

APSC Blueprint

ASCC Blueprint

Roadmap for an ASEAN Community (2009–2015)

2010	Third Protocol on Amending Treaty of Amity and Cooperation

ASEAN Commission on the Promotion and Protection of the Rights of Women and Children created

2011	Bali Concord III (RCEP/AFEED)

Agreement on the Establishment of the ASEAN Coordinating

	Centre for Humanitarian Assistance on Disaster Management
	Ha Noi Declaration on the Adoption of the Master Plan on ASEAN Connectivity
2012	ASEAN Comprehensive Investment Agreement enacted
	Joint Declaration of the ASEAN Defense Ministers on Enhancing ASEAN Unity for a Harmonized and Secure Community
	First ASEAN Ministerial Meeting on Women
	ASEAN Human Rights Declaration
2015	First Dateline for Achieving the ASEAN Community

Appendix 4

Timeline of key ASEAN+3 milestones
Azmi Mat Akhir and Alice D. Ba

1997	First ASEAN–Japan Summit
	First ASEAN–Republic of Korea Summit
	First ASEAN–China Summit
	First (Informal) Meeting of ASEAN+3
1999	First East Asia Cooperation/ASEAN+3 Summit (Joint Statement on East Asia Cooperation)
	First APT Finance Ministers and Central Bank Governors Meeting
2000	First Meeting of ASEAN Economic Ministers+3
	First ASEAN+3 Foreign Ministers Meeting
	Chiang Mai Initiative
2001	First ASEAN Agriculture and Forestry Ministers+3 Meeting
	First ASEAN+3 Labour Ministers Meeting
	East Asian Vision Group (EAVG) Report: "Towards an East Asian Community: Region of Peace, Prosperity and Progress"
2002	First ASEAN+3 Tourism Ministers Meeting
	First ASEAN+3 Environment Ministers Meeting
	Final report of East Asian Study Group (EASG)
	Asian Bond Market Initiative (ABMI)
2003	Establishment of ASEAN+3 Finance Cooperation
	Declaration on Revitalising Tourism for ASEAN+3
	APT meeting of Ministers of Cultures and Arts
	APT meeting of Ministers of Social Welfare and Development
	Track 1.5 East Asia Forum (EAF)
	Track 2 Network of East Asian Think Tanks (NEAT)
2004	First ASEAN+3 Ministerial Meeting on Transnational Crime (AMMTC+3)
	First ASEAN+3 Health Ministers Meeting
	First ASEAN+3 Ministerial Meeting for Social Welfare and Development
	First ASEAN+3 Telecommunications and IT Ministers Meeting (TELMIN)

	APT Ministerial Meeting on Transnational Crime
	APT Energy Ministers Meeting
2005	First East Asia summit
2007	Declaration on East Asian Energy Community
	East Asia Cooperation and the APT Cooperation Work Plan (2007–2017)
	APT Ministers Meeting on Youth
2008	Economic Research Institute for ASEAN and East Asia
	Asian Bond Market Initiative (ABMI) Roadmap
2009	Guidelines to implement the Second Joint Statement on East Asia Cooperation and the APT Cooperation Work Plan (2007–2017)
2010	Joint Declaration on APT Civil Service Cooperation
	ASEAN+3 Comprehensive Strategy on Food Security and Bioenergy Development (APTCS-FSBD) Framework and Strategic Plan of Action on Food and Energy Security (SAP-FES) 2010–2013
	Chiang Mai Initiative on Multilateralization (CMIM)
	Inclusion of United States and Russia into EAS
2011	Agreement on the ASEAN+3 Emergency Rice Reserve (APTERR)
	ASEAN+3 Macroeconomic Research Office (AMRO)
2012	Chiang Mai Initiative Multilateralisation (CMIM) Fund increased from US$120 billion to US$240 billion
	APT Plan of Action on Education: 2010–2017
	ASEAN+3 Conference on Civil Service Matters Work Plan (2012–2015)
	Work Plan on Enhancing APT Cooperation in Culture
	Work Plan on Enhancing APT Cooperation through Information and Media 2012–2017
	Work Plan to Implement the Asian Bond Market Initiative (ABMI) New Roadmap
	APT Emergency Rice Reserve Agreement
	Report of East Asia Vision Group
2013	Strengthening efforts to prevent and combat transnational crimes
	Revised East Asia Cooperation and the APT Cooperation Work Plan 2013–2017
	Asian Bond Market Initiative New Roadmap

Index